Pre-Restoration Stage Studies

LONDON : HUMPHREY MILFORD

OXFORD UNIVERSITY PRESS

NEW INN, GLOUCESTER

Drawn by Walter H. Godfrey; based on Britten's engraving

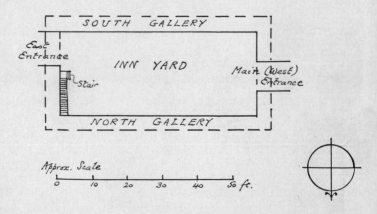

PRE-RESTORATION STAGE STUDIES

BY

WILLIAM J. LAWRENCE

CAMBRIDGE

HARVARD UNIVERSITY PRESS

MCMXXVII

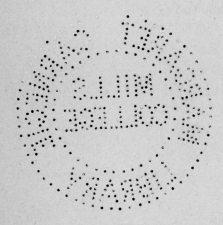

PRINTED AT THE HARVARD UNIVERSITY PRESS

CAMBRIDGE, MASS., U.S.A.

TO

ERNEST LAW

A SLIGHT ACKNOWLEDGEMENT
OF A DEEP INDEBTEDNESS

Preface

MY aim in this book is to enlarge the Elizabethan scholar's horizon by helping him to climb certain craggy peaks of knowledge, all of which are trackless and most of them untrodden. The studies it comprises have been selected for the purpose from two courses of lectures I had the honour of giving concurrently, by gracious invitation, at Harvard University and Radcliffe College in the first half of the academic year 1925–26. In the majority of these new ground is broken, not, I hope, without the bringing to light of some treasure-trove. All have been carefully revised and minutely documented, and one or two have been amplified. I have not deemed it advisable to eliminate each and every token of the basic lecture form, since the lecture form, though not without its blemishes when solidified in cold print, permits at difficult moments a simplicity and clarity and directness of statement for whose absence no added literary grace can compensate.

Though private acts of friendship do not call for public acknowledgement, I should deem myself churlish and ungrateful were I to remain silent regarding the generosity of my old collaborator, Mr. Walter H. Godfrey, in supplying me with a pen-and-ink sketch and a ground plan of the yard of the venerable New Inn at Gloucester, both of which are essential for a proper understanding of the long-miscomprehended physical characteristics of the primitive sixteenth-century playing places. Without the duly attested plan, my lecture on the subject would, I fear, have proved nugatory; and my thankfulness, therefore, to the donor is commensurate with the knowledge of my escape.

W. J. L.

MONKSTOWN, Co. DUBLIN
May, 1927

Contents

I. The Inn-Yard Playing Places: Their Up-
   rise and Characteristics   3
II. The Inn-Yard Play   28
III. The Practice of Doubling and its Influ-
   ence on Early Dramaturgy   43
IV. The Elizabethan Stage Jig   79
V. "Hamlet" as Shakespeare Staged It . .   102
VI. The Elizabethan Nocturnal   122
VII. Stage Traps in the Early English Theatre   145
VIII. Early Composite Plays   176
IX. Illusion of Sounds in the Elizabethan
   Theatre   199
X. Elizabethan Stage Realism   221
XI. Characteristics of Platform Stage Spec-
   tacle   251
XII. The Rise and Progress of the Complex-
   Disguise Play   277
XIII. Elizabethan Stage Properties   299
XIV. The Origin of the Substantive Theatre
   Masque   325
XV. Early Dramatic Collaboration: A Theory   340
XVI. Early Prompt-Books and What They
   Reveal   373

Index   415

Pre-Restoration Stage Studies

I

THE INN-YARD PLAYING PLACES : THEIR UPRISE AND CHARACTERISTICS

WRITING in the first number of *The Review of English Studies*, that conspicuous man of the theatre, Mr. Harley Granville Barker, gives expression to some pungent reflections upon Sir Edmund Chambers's monumental work on *The Elizabethan Stage*, maintaining *inter alia* that the distinguished historian makes a false start in underestimating the influence on the trend of acting and play writing — and he might very well have added on theatrical architecture and playhouse economy — exercised by the early inn-yard playing places. He is certain that in them

it was that the vitality which carried Elizabethan drama to its heights was generated, not at Court, in the Universities or at Paul's. What was done in the inns, then, must be far more significant, will have had a far stronger influence, than any tradition which may have been carried across from the semi-scholastic, more ceremonial stage. . . . On the inn-stages, emotional acting began to come by its own. This, I suggest, was the making of the drama's popularity; it was upon this that the dramatists now built up their art.[1]

I quote this because my lecture to-day is designed to fortify Mr. Granville Barker's position, to clarify the befogged atmosphere, and uproot a baneful fallacy. Curiously enough, when I set about preparing it, from notes on the subject made at various intervals during

[1] *The Review of English Studies*, i, 61, "A Note upon Chapters XX and XXI of *The Elizabethan Stage*."

the past twelve years, I had no idea that the ordering of the data would lead to an important discovery, a discovery revolutionising existing concepts of the old inn-yard playing places. But, while this brought with it a certain thrill, it proved on second thought disconcerting, since it involved public recantation of opinions long held and put years ago into cold print. To shift the point of view in one's historical perspective is as irksome a task as the starting life all over again at middle age; none the less, the interests of truth are paramount.

Hitherto, scholars have believed that the story of the inn-yards is negligible, the trivial prologue to a very engrossing play, but I hope to show you that it was in sooth the play's foundation-laying first act. In other words, my time and yours will have been wasted, if I fail in this lecture to convince you that the old inn-yard playing places were something better than temporary makeshifts, and that they have a right to be considered the first English theatres. But before proceeding on our quest, it is necessary to recall that public acting had taken place in the inn-yards of the city and suburbs of London for at least a score of years before the erection of the first building to be called a theatre.[1] It would have been remarkable if in that time blemishes had not been eliminated and enduring conventions established. Moreover, if from first to last these inn-yard playing places were the ramshackle contraptions of popular (and scholarly) imagining, it is difficult to account for the fact that they continued to be regularly frequented in the winter months by gentle and simple for fully a quarter of a century after the suburban theatres began to be

[1] For inn-yard acting in 1557, see Chambers, *The Mediaeval Stage*, ii, 190; for 1559, *Calendar of State Papers, Venetian, 1558-80*, p. 27, letter of February 6, 1558-59.

built, and were not wholly abandoned by the players even in later Jacobean days.

One finds some difficulty in arriving at the exact characteristics of the Elizabethan inn-yards. Views of them abound, but they are not contemporary views.[1] In London nearly all the old inn-yards have disappeared, and the few that remain have been transmogrified out of all resemblance. Structural alteration began somewhere about the early Caroline period with the introduction of the stagecoach. Happily, however, a few inn-yards in remote country places still retain many of their pristine characteristics, sufficient, mayhap, to permit of the exercise of cautious conjecture. My friend, Mr. Walter H. Godfrey, architect by profession and theatrical antiquary by choice, has obligingly drawn for me a view and ground plan of the well-preserved old yard of the New Inn at Gloucester, and from these I hope presently to make some important deductions. The ground plan, I may say, is from an original survey of a few years ago; but the view is old, a simplification of an engraving in Briton's *Antiquities of England and Wales*.[2]

What we particularly require to bear in mind is that the chief and larger of the London inns were carriers' inns, and that it was in their yards, because of their better accommodation, that the players acted.[3] But a serious drawback was allied with their choice. It restricted

[1] See Thornbury's *Old and New London*, i, 378, and vi, 79 and 85; Charles G. Harper, *The Holyhead Road*, i, 12; *The English Illustrated Magazine*, viii (1890), 194, view of the old Bell Inn, Holborn, in Philip Norman's article on "Inns and Taverns of old London."

[2] Reproduced in Green's *Short History of the English People* (illustrated edition, 1893), ii, 567. Built *circa* 1450, the New Inn is now converted into a hotel.

[3] See J. Q. Adams, *Shakespearean Playhouses*, p. 9, for a useful map showing the location of the principal inn-yard playing places.

their days of playing and caused them to give offence to
the puritans by their anxiety to play on Sundays. In a
sermon preached at Paul's Cross on August 24, 1578,
and duly published, John Stockwood argued that

if playing in the Theater or any other place in London, as there are
by sixe that I know too many, be any of the Lordes wayes (which
I suppose there is none so voide of knowledge in the world wil
graunt) then only it may, but ought to be vsed, but if it be any of
the wayes of man, it is no work for ye Lords Sabaoth, and therefore
in no respecte tollerable on that day.[1]

From this and a subsequent passage now to be quoted
it is apparent that the six playing places spoken of as
superfluous were inn-yards. Later on, we find Stockwood saying:

For reckening with the leaste, the gaine that is reaped of eighte
ordinarie places in the Citie whiche I knowe, by playing but once a
weeke (whereas many times they play twice and somtimes thrice) it
amounteth to 2000 pounds by the year.[2]

This limitation of the playing days to a maximum of
three per week was due to the fact that the players shared
the use of the inn-yards with the carriers. It is this
divided occupation, the serving of a double purpose,
that has given rise to what I am forced by weight of evidence to stigmatise as the fallacy of the removable stage
and the improvised auditorium. But, first of all, let us
try and see what use the carriers made of the yards.
Unfortunately we have no direct evidence showing in
what manner or how often the yards were utilised by
them in the last quarter of the sixteenth century, but we
have sound evidence for a later period, and from this it
might possibly be safe to make a few deductions. In
The Carriers' Cosmography of John Taylor, the Water-

[1] Chambers, *The Elizabethan Stage*, iv.
[2] *Ibid.*, 199, 200.

Poet, published in 1637, details are given of three notable inns whose yards were formerly playing places, though of a fourth, the Bell in Gracious Street, no mention is made. In considering these, we must bear in mind that in the course of half a century the traffic had probably increased, and, with the abandonment of the inn-yards by the players, had doubtless been concentrated. Otherwise, by taking the evidence as wholly applicable to the end of the sixteenth century, we should be forced to the conclusion that acting at the Black Bull in Bishopsgate Street was possible only on Sundays: a conclusion not alone against the evidence, but running counter to the elementary principles of playhouse economy, since no body of players could subsist on the profits of one performance a week. But the truth is that conditions had never been stable. According to Taylor, no carriers following any particular route remained loyal for long to any particular inn. But we find that in his day the yard of that quondam playing place, the Cross Keys in Gracious Street, was occupied on Thursdays and Fridays by the carrier of Colchester, the carrier of Witham, the Post of Ipswich, and the carrier of Malden. They all arrived on the one day and left on the next. On the other hand, the yard of the Black Bull in Bishopsgate Street was much less at liberty. The carrier of Hadham was there on Mondays and Tuesdays and again on Fridays and Saturdays; there also, on Tuesdays and Wednesdays, was the waggon from Saffron Walden; and on Thursdays and Fridays the yard was held possession of by waggons and coaches from Cambridge. The third notable old playing place, the Belle Sauvage without Ludgate, was occupied only from Friday to Monday in each week, and the sojourners there were the carriers of York and Doncaster.

In the absence of data it is rarely wise to speculate, but, looking back half a century, is it not rational to conclude that, since the players brought him indirectly a good deal of money, the innkeeper would hardly enter into agreements with such a plurality of carriers as would seriously incommode them? At least two hindrances could have been occasioned by his lack of forethought: a grave limitation of the days of acting, and an equally grave limitation of permanent seating accommodation. Let us not forget that in the inn-yard, as in the regular public theatre, the seated parts were the most profitable parts. If, after due consideration, we concede the possibility that in any one yard as many as three large waggons could have been loaded or unloaded at the one time, then the probability of that yard possessing a permanent stage and a built-up grandstand for spectators becomes very remote. It was by some such process of reasoning that the idea of the removable stage sprang into existence, though in reality, with such a congestion, a permanent stage would have proved less objectionable than any scaffolding for spectators. When one comes to think of it, a stage, being about the height of a waggon, would have answered very well for the loading and unloading of heavy goods. Once deposited there for the carriers, weighty boxes or barrels could readily have been pushed, rolled, or lifted on to the waggons. Up to the present, however, the few arguments that have been advanced in favour of a permanent inn-yard stage base on untenable premises. Graves, in his interesting section on "The Inn-yards and the early Theatres" in his thesis on *The Court and the London Theatres during the reign of Elizabeth* [1] maintains that because all stages then had traps, no inn-yard stage could have been removable. But the stage of the Hope Theatre

[1] Pages 40, 41.

in 1614, as the building contract shows,[1] was removable,
and a greater number of traps was employed then than
was employed a score of years previously. It is a little-
known fact that before 1600 only two traps were provided, though one of them was a device of some complexity. Later on we learn of five.

One has to summon up all one's moral courage before
venturing to pontify on this vexed question of the removable stage. The scholar who should maintain that
the removable stage of the Hope, so far from being an
innovation, was simply a reversion to type would be difficult to confute, though he would find himself nonplussed
on being asked for his proofs. The chances are, however,
that Elizabethan investigators will not always remain at
loggerheads on this point. To prove that other permanent obstructions were erected at an early period in the
inn-yards to turn them the more completely into playhouses is to make some headway towards establishing the
principle of the permanent stage. Such proofs are in my
possession: they constitute the discovery I have already
spoken of; but before I advance them it is requisite that
we should first visualise the salient characteristics of an
old inn-yard.

On this subject I can speak with unwonted decision,
for the very good reason that, whereas no normal published illustration of an old inn-yard shows (or could
show) more than three sides of the yard, Mr. Godfrey's
ground plan of the yard of the New Inn at Gloucester
shows four, and by its unexampled completeness makes
surprising revelation. Oblong in shape, these old yards
were essentially of the nature of courtyards, since the inn-
buildings ran round the four sides. In their general structure, as well as their spaciousness, they were well adapted

[1] Chambers, *The Elizabethan Stage*, ii, 466.

for transformation into playing places, and that without losing any of their initial efficacy. When so transformed — reckoning that many stood in the yard — I think they were capable of accommodating from five to six hundred spectators. It must be borne in mind that every inn had at least two rows of projecting galleries ranged along the two longer sides. A few of the old London inns had as many as three,[1] but I am inclined to believe that most of the inns resorted to by the players had only two. It was customary for the lowermost row to be extended around the whole four sides, but I cannot speak with any certainty regarding the disposition of the other rows. At Gloucester, where there were two galleries, there was only one completely circulating gallery, and the chances are that that was the rule. On examining Mr. Godfrey's plan one sees that in the left-hand corner near the front gateway a straight staircase led up to the gallery, but access to the other gallery could be gained only from the inn. It may be that originally there was another staircase at the back on the opposite side, leading up to the same gallery, but, if so, no trace of it now remains.[2] On this point I shall have something of importance to say later. It is imperative that we should first consider the one great surprise afforded by Mr. Godfrey's plan. It establishes, what has not hitherto been suspected, that besides the deeply arched gateway at the front there was another at the back. Probably this arrangement was rather common: we have traces of it in Elizabethan London.

[1] Cf. Charles G. Harper, *The Holyhead Road*, i, 12, for view of the yard of the Bull and Mouth, St. Martin's Le Grand. This shows three galleries around two sides.

[2] This second staircase, if provided at all, is more likely to have been a feature of the larger yards frequented in London by carriers than of the normal-sized yards. But a single staircase could have been placed at either end of the yard, according to the structure of the inn and the requirements.

Ordish quotes from Meymott's privately printed book on old Paris Garden Manor, to show that the Falcon Inn in Southwark had two large gateways, but he is at a loss to know, what we can now determine, exactly where the second gate stood.[1] Malone, who conceived only of a front gateway, has some discussion of inn-yard performances, in which he says: "We may suppose the stage to have been raised in this area, on the fourth side, with its back to the gateway of the inn, at which the admission was taken." [2]

On first thought this conjecture seems feasible, since, with the stage so positioned, the gateway, if bisected by a curtain or screen, could have been made to serve the double purpose of a rear stage and a dressing-room or property store; but to arrange that the public should gain admittance through a gateway and then block up the gateway with a stage does not, on maturer reflection, strike one as very sensible. Acceptance of Malone's theory would certainly entail belief in a removable stage, since no permanent obstruction could have been allowed there. Under normal conditions there was probably more vehicular traffic through the front gate than the back one, viewing the fact that the front entrance was on a main and more commodious thoroughfare. On the other hand, the grave inconvenience of having to keep putting the stage into position and removing it again could have been obviated by building it in front of and into the back gateway, thus leaving the front entrance free at all times for the use of either carriers or playgoers. The entrance-way to the early Shoreditch and Bankside theatres was undoubtedly opposite the stage, and in that probably

[1] T. F. Ordish, *Early London Theatres*, pp. 277, 278.
[2] Malone, *Variorum Shakespeare* (1821), iii, 72.

followed the inn-yard precedent.[1] It seems likely also that there was a wicket in the inn-yard gate, otherwise it would surely have been difficult to collect the money from any considerable body of inrushing people.

Though the yard itself, the overhanging galleries, and the available inn-rooms would have afforded accommodation for a goodly number of spectators, there is some reason to believe that special seating was also provided. Among the several documents published for the first time in Sir Edmund Chambers's monumental work, not the least valuable is the memorandum of a dispute which took place in July, 1567, between John Brayne, of the Red Lion Inn at Stepney, and William Sylvester, a carpenter, concerning the stability of certain "scaffolds" erected by Sylvester at the said inn for the accommodation of the public, and for which Brayne had contracted to pay him £8. 10. 0, equal to about £50 of the present currency.[2] Such a sum we may rest assured — the dispute bearing witness — was not spent on any trivial contrivance. That such scaffolds, as distinguished from stages, were regularly provided in the inn-yard playing places there is evidence to show. To begin with, in the Act of Common Council of December 6, 1574, for the better regularising of inn-yard performances, certain grievances and evils were enumerated in the preamble in justification of civic interference, and among them a complaint that "sundry slaughters and maimings of the Queen's subjects have happened by ruins of skaffoldes, frames and stagies, and by engynes, weapons and powder used in plaies." [3] The phrasing here serves a useful purpose because it shows

[1] For Appleton Morgan's blunder on this score (*Titus Andronicus*, Introd., p. 28, Bankside Series), see Graves, *The Court and the London Theatres during the reign of Elizabeth*, pp. 39, 40.

[2] *The Elizabethan Stage*, ii, 379.

[3] Adams, *Shakespearean Playhouses*, p. 23.

that a scaffold was something different from a stage, synonymous as the terms are usually taken to be.[1] Confirmation of this inference is to be found in Higgins's *Nomenclator*, as published in London in 1584, wherein "fori" is defined as "the galleries or standings for the beholders of plaies: the scaffolds."

The second item of evidence is provided by a passage in the 1596 edition of Lambarde's *Perambulation of Kent*, in which the author gives some details of the pilgrimage to Boxley and points out that those who made it escaped from disbursing fees:

no more than such as goe to Parisgarden, the Bell Sauage, or Theater, to beholde Beare baiting, Enterludes, or Fence play, can account of any pleasant spectacle, unlesse they first pay one pennie at the gate, another at the entrie of the Scaffolde, and the thirde for a quiet standing.[2]

We have here indication that in and about 1596 the same system of admission was pursued at all places of amusement, and that the scaffold was the next division in succession to the inn- or theatre-yard. If we seek further evidence of the permanency of the inn-yard scaffolds, we shall find it in a statement made by Richard Flecknoe a full quarter of a century after the yards had ceased to be used for acting. Writing in 1664, in his *Short Discourse of the English Stage*, Flecknoe says that the old players were

without any certain Theatres or set Companies till about the beginning of Queen Elizabeth's reign they began to assemble into Companies, and set up Theatres, first in the City (as in the Innyards of the Cross-Keyes and Bull in Grace and Bishopsgate Street

---

[1] Cf. *Shakespeare's England*, ii, 285, note 2. This was an editorial addition unapproved of by the writers.

[2] Edition of 1596, p. 233; not to be found in the first edition of 1576. Adams (*Shakespearean Playhouses*, p. 15, note) is probably correct in surmising that it was written some years before publication.

at this date to be seen) till that fanatic spirit which then began with the stage and after ended with the throne, banished them thence into the suburbs.[1]

One can interpret Flecknoe's statement regarding what still remained to be seen only as referring to some relics of the old scaffolds and possibly stages: it signifies permanency or it signifies nothing.

There was, I think, another name for these inn-yard scaffolds. In Act I, scene 4, of *Lady Alimony*, that mysterious old play of uncertain date, we find the Boy saying of the assembled audience:

Sir, all our boxes are already stored and seated with the choicest and eminentest damosellas that all Seville can afford. Besides, Sir, all our galleries and ground-stands are long ago furnished. The groundlings within the yard grow infinitely unruly.

Remark here the reference to ground-stands, or what in the race-course parlance of to-day we should call grand-stands. The inn-yard scaffolds were undoubtedly ground-stands, and they may be presumed to have occupied some portion of the two long sides of the yard. Conceive of this, and bear in mind simultaneously the two rows of galleries immediately above, and at once you place the inn-yard playing places directly in the main line of architectural evolution. It would be idle to look further afield for the chief source of inspiration on which the builders of the first outlying theatres drew. Durand and Graves have gone sadly out of their way to deduce the primitive theatre auditorium from special court contrivances of a much earlier period and a purely temporary order.[2] At best, these could only have afforded a

[1] Spingarn, *Seventeenth Century Critical Essays*, ii, 92.
[2] Durand, in *Publications of the Modern Language Association*, xiii, 505 ff.; Graves, *The Court and the London Theatres during the reign of Elizabeth*, pp. 43–47.

precedent by way of the inn-yards, and their influence on the inn-yards may be postulated but cannot be proved. This much we know for certain. The Dutch sketch of the Swan indicates the adoption at an early period of the principle of the ground-stand with two circulating galleries, the principle which was maintained in English theatre-building for more than a couple of centuries. That principle, I firmly believe on the evidence, was first tried out publicly in the inn-yard playing places. No doubt the circular or polygonal shape of the regular theatres, when it came, was derived from the bull- and bear-baiting circuses; and it seems highly probable that the custom of hoisting the flag and blowing the three trumpet-blasts came from the same source. But everything else in the early theatres was the result of inn-yard experience: even the place where the groundlings stood was still styled the yard. Since entertainments at court were gratuitous affairs, it will not be pretended that the banqueting hall, when specially fitted up, had private boxes, such as the theatres first had, so private that some of them were provided with lattices. Here, too, the inn-yard exerted its influence. It was complained in the Act of Common Council of 1574, already referred to, that the great inns used by players had "chambers and secret places adjoining to their open stagies and gallyries," where acts of immorality had taken place.

One may also claim without much fear of contravention that, if only in a rudimentary way, the principle of the rear stage and the upper stage had its inception in the inn-yards. Though it must be conceded that the early academic drama, in basing on Italian drama and adopting its neo-Plautine conventions, had introduced window scenes, still it was the presence of permanent ⮐ casements in the inn-yards and their proved theatrical gratefulness that led to the firm establishment of the window-scene convention in popular drama, and made the provision of practicable windows in the tiring-house front of the theatre an early essential.

It may be, too, that in one other structural respect the inn-yard playhouse proved a source of inspiration. Recall to mind now the emphasis I laid a little while back on the provision in the yard of a corner staircase leading up to the first gallery. My firm belief is that, wherever the stage was placed, it had to be close to this staircase. Once the action began, the staircase formed the only means of ready access to the first gallery, and the first gallery had on occasion — especially in siege scenes — to serve as an upper stage. I draw attention to this point because there are some grounds for thinking that this visible staircase afforded a model for a possible characteristic of the regular theatre stages whose existence is not commonly suspected, despite the fact that a noted scholar has advanced some evidence in support of its provision. Writes Professor George Pierce Baker in his *Development of Shakespeare as a Dramatist:*[1]

> Perhaps the direction in Brome's *Covent Garden Weeded* that Dorcas, who has just appeared above "upon a bellconie" shall "run down stairs" means only that she shall be heard running down them behind the scenes, but one is not so sure in *Two Murders in One* (Bullen's Old Plays, IV, 19–22) that some construction connecting the lower and the upper stage was not used. Merry, the murderous innkeeper, states his plan to lure his neighbour, Beech, to the garret, and there kill him. He says:
>
> > "And therefore I place the hammer here
> > And take it as I follow Beach up staires,
> > That suddenly, before he is aware,
> > I may with blowes dash out his hatefull brains."

---

[1] Page 82.

Later he bids Beech "Goe up these staires, your friends do stay above," picking up the concealed hammer as his victim precedes him. Later when Rachel, the sister, goes to see who is above, the direction is not, as elsewhere, *Exit*, but *Exit up*.

Baker's suspicions receive ample confirmation from a great variety of evidence that escaped him, evidence so abundant that I cannot pretend in the limited time at my disposal to discuss more than the half of it. On this, as on other points, it is advisable to proceed chronologically, so as to avoid the risk of applying late data to an early period. In the first part of the *Contention of the Two Famous Houses of Yorke and Lancaster*, Elinor, at the beginning of the incantation scene, says:

> Here, Sir John, take this scrole of paper here,
> Wherein is writ the questions you shall aske.
> And I will stand upon this Tower here,
> And hear the spirit what it cries to you,
> And to my questions, write the answers downe.

Then the direction is, not "Exit," but "She goes up to the Tower." Again, in *Julius Caesar*, V, 3, Cassius and Pindarus are supposed to be standing on a hill. Cassius bids the man go higher up and tell him what he sees. No "exit" is marked, but five lines later Pindarus utters an exclamation, showing that he had been watching, and proceeds to describe the capture of Titinius. Cassius orders him to come down, and two lines later he is evidently again on the lower stage, since Cassius bids him "come hither" and stab him. Here a ready means of access to the upper stage seems imperative.[1]

---

[1] Note the direction in *The Wonder of Women, or Sophonisba*, V, 2: "Cornets sound a march. Scipio leads his train up to the mount." This surely implies an outer staircase. Why phrase it thus, if an ordinary departure through the stage doors was intended?

In *Look About You*, scene 23 represents the interior of an inn. John asks, "Where is he?" and Skink replies, "Up them stairs." Then John says:

> Follow me brother; come, old Fauconbridge;
> Keep the stairs, sheriff.

It has been inferred from these references to visible staircases that the rear stage stood at a slight elevation and was approached by steps,[1] but as solid beds and good-sized scaffolds were often thrust out from the rear stage the assumption is, I think, unwarranted.

In another Rose play, *Englishmen For My Money*, III, 1,[2] the scene is a room in Pisaro's house, and the action evidently passes above. A knock is heard, and Pisaro says, "Some looke downe below, and see who knocks." Nearly forty lines later Moore, when about to depart, is warned to

> Take heede how you go downe, the staires are bad.
> Bring here a light.

In a subsequent scene the three daughters are on the upper stage and their three English lovers below. At line 1859 Mathea says, "Prepare your armes, for thus we flie to you." Evidently the girls all rush down the stairs, for we have at once the direction, "They embrace." I hardly think they jumped over the balcony into their lovers' arms. Mention of this, the only alternative, brings to mind the many scenes in chronicle histories

---

[1] See Wegener, *Bühneneinrichtung des Shakespearischen Theaters*, pp. 56, 57; Creizenach, *Geschichte*, iv, 420, note; Neuendorff, *Die englische Volksbühne im Zeitalter Shakespeares*, p. 125; Reynolds, *Some Principles of Elizabethan Staging*, i, 24, 25; *Studies in Philology*, xiii, 117, 118, T. S. Graves on "Notes on Elizabethan Theatres." Graves scouts the evidence advanced by the others, but thinks the elevated rear stage was not wholly unknown.

[2] In Baugh's recension of the play, to which all my references apply. The original is undivided.

and other kinds of plays where the characters leap down
to the stage from above,[1] and, despite the fact that the
Elizabethan players were nothing if not acrobats, one is
somewhat puzzled to know how the feat was performed
without incurring broken bones. Could it have been that
the player took a step or two down the visible staircase
and then jumped? Since the scenes in which these
gymnastic feats were performed were mostly siege scenes,
that is to say, scenes in which the storming of walls was
generally effected by means of scaling ladders, one antici-
pates the objection that with the presence of a connecting
staircase the use of ladders would have been superfluous;
but it must always be clearly borne in mind that no
feature of the tiring-house background had existence for
the spectators until it was pressed into the service of the
scene. In practice there was no actual permanent background, everything unused being suppressed by convention. Here we encounter a relic of the mediaeval principle
of multiple or simultaneous staging.

In Middleton's *The Family of Love*, I, 3, is to be found
a curious allusion to Rowley and Juby's lost play of *Samson*, a play originally produced at the Fortune in or about
July, 1602. Note the following speeches:

Glister.	And from what good exercise came you three?
Gerardius.	From a play where we saw most excellent Sampson excel the whole world in gate-carrying.
Dryfat.	Was it performed by the youths?
Lipsalve.	By youths? Why I tell thee we saw Sampson, and I hope 'tis not for youths to play Sampson. Believe it I saw Sampson bear the town-gates on his neck from the lower to the upper stage, with that life and admirable accord, that it shall never be equalled, unless the whole new livery of porters set to their shoulders.

[1] Examples will readily be found in *King John I, Henry VI, Fortune by Sea and Land*, and *The Turke*.

Creizenach, in discussing this scene, is compelled, by his belief that all means of communication between the lower and upper stage were hidden from the audience, to assume that Samson in the Fortune play simply went up a ladder.[1] In that case, the impersonator of the character deserved all Middleton's commendation, for he performed a very considerable feat. No doubt the property gates were of no great weight, but they were certainly extensive, and to carry them up a ladder on one's neck required some doing. Rather would it seem that a staircase was employed. By a curious coincidence *The Family of Love* presents us with some direct evidence concerning the existence of this outer and visible staircase. In the opening scene, after the departure of Glister and his wife, Maria speaks two lines, and the scene closes with the direction, "Maria ascends." "To the upper stage," says Bullen in a footnote, and I agree. There is no reason why it should have been put thus, unless she were to be seen ascending.

Occasionally the evidence is contradictory and of doubtful value. At a certain juncture in the undivided play, *Tu Quoque*,[2] Gertrude, without any "exit" being marked, passes from the upper stage to the lower, making her way to Geraldine, and as she goes Joyce, standing above, keeps commenting on her progress. At first this looks like further proof, but immediately afterwards Joyce disappears above and soon reënters below. There may have been a reason, of course, why Joyce came down another way, but all the same the situation is puzzling. Even if we concede this outer visible staircase to the early public theatres, it by no means follows that all passing from the upper stage to the lower or *vice versa* would be performed by its means. Sometimes the ac-

---

[1] *English Drama in the Age of Shakespeare*, p. 375.
[2] See Hazlitt's *Dodsley*, vi, 203.

tion would require the journey to be made out of sight, through the tiring-house. But concerning the provision of a visible staircase in the private theatres, one halts between two opinions. It is conceivable that, where the stage was small and the tiring-house front narrow, there would have been little room for the staircase; yet, strange to say, evidence of its seeming existence can readily be found in private-theatre plays. Let us look, to begin with, at one or two Blackfriars plays of different periods. In *Philaster*, II, 4, Pharamond transfers himself very rapidly from the upper stage to the lower, though there is no indication of his temporary disappearance. A little later, when Megra and her attendants make a like journey, the first quarto of the play has a marginal note, "They come down to the King." In Act II, scene 4, of *The Devil is an Ass*, a slightly later Blackfriars play, we find Fitzdottrell saying:

> This way, wife. Up to thy gallery; do, Chuck,
> Leave us to talke of it, who understand it.

Here, it would appear, he pointed to a staircase. Mrs. Fitzdottrell is not seen again until two scenes later, when she shows herself at an upper window. Then, we jump a decade and come in 1628 to another Blackfriars play, *The Lover's Melancholy* of Ford. In Act III, scene 2, — a room in Thamasto's house, — Kala, the waiting maid, anxious that Menaphon should behold the interview between Thamasta and Parthenophill, says to him:

> O, speak little
> Walk up these stairs; and take this key, it opens
> A chamber door, where, at that window yonder,
> You may see all their courtship.

Then again, in Act III, scene 4, of Suckling's *Brennoralt*, a still later Blackfriars play, Brennoralt, pointing, says, "This was the entry, these the stairs."

For the Whitefriars *circa* 1606 we have the evidence of *The Dumb Knight*, V, 1, where the Jailor says:

Madam, those stairs direct you to his lodging.

Concerning the Cockpit, a later private theatre, the evidence is curiously contradictory. In Heywood's *The Captives*, employment of the outer staircase, presuming that it existed, was (possibly for realism's sake) clearly shirked. In Act IV, scene 3, we get, "Enter Dennis with the Fryar from above upon his backe." Dennis evidently comes down a ladder carrying a dummy body. Later on Fryar Richard says, "Here's a ladder left," and lifts up the body. Then comes the direction, "Exit, Carry him up." Yet, as we have seen, it was another Cockpit play that first gave Professor Baker an inkling of the existence of the outer staircase; and, curiously enough, there is further evidence on the point in that play besides the evidence he has cited. In Act II, scene 2, a tavern scene, the Vintner, after he has given instructions to his servants, is himself bidden in an imperative direction to "run down the staires." Here the puzzle is to know what stairs.

The possibility of the existence of an outer tiring-house staircase seems to me a matter of so much importance that I make no apology for citing some further instances from later public-theatre plays which seem to support the theory. They are all taken from Globe plays. In the first place, note the following dialogue from the second act of *The Second Maiden's Tragedy:*

Anselmo.   Which way took the villain,
That marriage felon — one that robs the mind,
Twenty times worse than any highway-striker,
Speak, which way took he?
Votarius. Marry, my lord, I think —
Let me see, which way was't now? — up yon stairs.

Again, in *Bonduca*, IV, 3, the use of the staircase is implied by the action of Nennius and Caratach in ascending a hill to mark the Roman army's advance. They do not disappear from sight, and, lacking a staircase, one fails to see how the journey was accomplished. So, too, in *The Sea Voyage*, I, 3, a desert island, we get further visions of the staircase (though the thing may be a mirage). After Aminta, from her elevated post, has warned the captain as to his vessel, we have the direction, "Lamure and Franville go up to see the ship." In Act II, scene 2, the vision recurs with intenser vividness where Albert and Aminta ascend "a near rising hill" to see who has blown the hunting-horns, more especially as Albert begins a speech on the lower level and finishes it on the upper.

I have already advanced fairly sound reasons for believing that the inn-yard playing places, structurally considered, had a marked influence on the physical characteristics of both the stage and the auditorium of the first outlying public theatres. Even if we take this as proved, it was not the only influence they exercised. It cannot for a moment be doubted that the scheme of early theatrical economics, and the peculiarities of monetary allocation, were a mere continuance of inn-yard routine. For half a century before the erection of the first theatre in the fields, systematisation of methods of money-gathering had gradually being going on. A modern analogy will serve to show its nature. Some forty years ago, when buskers first began to perform on the sands at the popular seaside resorts, they were utterly dependent on the good will of the spectators for what pecuniary reward came to them. They sent round the hat and gathered what they could. Gradually, as the pierrot troupe developed, improvements set in: a rudimentary stage and tiring-house was erected about high-water mark, and an adjoining space railed in, so that a modest charge for admission might be levied. In this, history had once more repeated itself. If we go back to the last quarter of the fifteenth century, to the period when strollers acted moralities in country inns and other places, we find that no system of a regular charge had then been instituted. Like the primitive busker, the morality player always appealed to his audience midway in the performance, before it had time or inclination to melt away. On this point, the testimony of the old morality of *Mankind* is as amusing as it is informative. Just as the simple-minded audience has been aroused to a high pitch of expectation by the announcement that Titivillus, the chief of the devils, is about to appear, intimation is made that money is about to be gathered from one and all, "else there shall no man him see." It was probably in keeping with the scriptural aphorism, that money is the root of all evil, that the onus for its gathering was thrown upon the Devil. Says Nowadays:

> He is a worshipful man, sirs, saving your presence,
> He loveth no groats, nor pence, or twopence,
> Give us red royals, if ye will see his abominable presence.

But second thoughts are best, and New Guise, fearing that this exorbitant demand will defeat its purpose, interrupts the speaker, and tells the audience to do the best they can.

Thus originated the term "gathering" applied to players' dues, a term so loosely employed a century later, when payment was regularly exacted beforehand at the theatre doors, that much confusion has been created in the minds of Elizabethan investigators (I myself being among the blunderers) [1] regarding the methods pursued.

[1] *The Elizabethan Playhouse and Other Studies*, 2d series, p. 99. The statement here made that gatherers went round during the performance is inaccurate.

By what gradations the inn-yard players of London city advanced from dependence on voluntary contributions to a scale of fixed charges one is powerless to determine. The perfected system had doubtless been in vogue for more than a decade before the Act of Common Council of 1574 regularised inn-yard performances and made the innkeeper the responsible party.[1] He was then compelled to take out a license for acting and to enter into bonds for "the keeping of good order" during the performances. It was likewise enacted that a proportion of the admission money was to be paid to the municipality towards the maintenance of the poor, mine host to be responsible for its payment. Thus early was the principle of the amusement tax instituted. Since all the responsibility fell on the innkeeper, the inference is that he was known to derive considerable profit from the performances given in his yard. Some, but undoubtedly not all, of his pecuniary returns accrued from the eatables and drinkables consumed by the spectators while at the play: habits of this kind were then acquired by the English playgoer, from which he has never been able to shake himself free. When the first outlying public theatres came to be built the old system was still followed. The theatre, instead of being provided with refreshment rooms, had an adjacent taphouse from which eatables and drinkables were brought, as required. The taphouse was the property of the theatre owners and was generally leased to a victualler. Shakespeare's Globe had a convenience of this kind, and its contiguity may be surmised from the old ballad describing the destruction of the historic theatre by fire, wherein it was lamented that:

[1] For the Act, see W. C. Hazlitt, *The English Drama and Stage*, p. 27. A summary is given by Adams, *Shakespearean Playhouses*, pp. 22–25.

Noe shower his raine did there down souse,
In all that sunshine weather,
To save that great renownéd howse,
Nor thou, O alehouse, neither.[1]

But the private theatre at once broke away from the old practice. There, though no refreshment room was provided and wine and beer had still to be sent for by boys, the storing was done on the premises.

Viewing the responsibilities thrust upon him, there is reason, as I have already hinted, to believe that the inn-keeper had other sources of profit from inn-yard playing besides the sale of food and drink. The dispute in 1567 between Brayne the grocer — who was afterwards part-owner of Burbage's Theater — and his carpenter goes to indicate that whatever ground-stands were put up in inn-yards for the accommodation of spectators were not put up at the players' expense. And we may be sure that the profits derived from stands erected by the innkeeper went to the innkeeper. It is reasonable even to assume that the players would have had no claim upon him for the spectators he accommodated in the private rooms overlooking the yard. Apart from that, the chances are that they allowed him the profits of certain portions of the yard, some of which he had specially fitted up for playgoers and some not, in lieu of rent. We must re-member that that was precisely the manner in which rent was paid in the public theatres. The owners of the theatres were known as housekeepers, and they bore the same relation to the players as the innkeeper bore to the inn-yard players.

To my mind, the methods of inn-yard gathering and allocation were very much as follows. With the excep-tion of those who occupied private rooms and, possibly,

[1] Collier, *Annals of the Stage* (1831), i, 387, 388.

the upper gallery, all the spectators would enter by the yard gate and pay there a preliminary fee of admission. That fee was the players' perquisite. It amounted to a penny or twopence at most, and carried with it the right to stand in the yard. Inside, there were opposite entrances to the ground-stands (much as we see in the Dutch sketch of the Swan) and a staircase leading to the first gallery. Those who elected to go to one of these divisions paid a further fee on reaching the approach to it. It may be that the players shared half of the receipts of all the places in the yard but the yard with the innkeeper, or it may be that the innkeeper had all the profits of the ground-stands and the players half the profits of the galleries. On this score, we can do no more than make *a posteriori* deductions, arguing back from public-theatre procedure. It is true that in the early days of Burbage's Theater the players received nothing beyond the preliminary admission money, but we must bear in mind that everybody then paid the preliminary fee, and that the house probably accommodated twice as many spectators as the average inn-yard.[1] Hence, the inn-yard players must necessarily have enjoyed some further concession. But I see no reason to doubt that, notwithstanding variations due to differences of size and accommodation, the principle pursued in the inn-yards was fundamentally identical with the principle pursued in the first public theatres.[2]

[1] Lawrence, *The Elizabethan Playhouse and Other Studies*, 2d series, p. 96.
[2] Cf. Chambers, *The Elizabethan Stage*, iv, 229, 230.

II

THE INN-YARD PLAY

THERE are two possible methods of classifying Elizabethan plays, both legitimate and both illuminating. You may adopt Polonius's plan — without accepting all his weird compounds — and divide them into tragedies, comedies, histories, pastorals, and whatnot; or you may pursue the equally profitable course of sorting them out according to their place of origin and the particular kind of audience for which they were intended. The complexity and distinctiveness of Elizabethan drama becomes evident once it is grasped that in no other period does the English drama admit of this dual classification. In later days the dominance of professionalism obliterated all landmarks. When, however, we review the dramatic output of the last forty years of the sixteenth century and the first lustrum of the century succeeding, so marked are the distinctions that, basing on internal evidence only, we can say with some confidence, this was a University or Inns-of-Court play, this a public-theatre play and this a private-theatre play. The lines between each type are sharply drawn, and, to the clearsighted, not difficult to distinguish.

The University or Inns-of-Court play, when of a serious order, generally discussed a classic theme in a semi-classic, wholly pedantic way, or, when the theme was otherwise than classic, disfigured it with symbolic inter-act dumb shows and dreary choruses. That the academic dramatist was not always oblivious of the defects of his genus is amusingly demonstrated by the words put, at Cambridge in *The Return from Parnassus*, into Will Kemp's mouth: "Few of the university pen play well; they smell too much of that writer Ovid, and that writer Metamorphosis, and talk too much of Proserpina and Jupiter."[1]

When, for a change, lighter fare was demanded at the Universities or Inns of Court, it generally took the form of a neo-Terentian comedy freely translated from the Italian. But, in either case, the aim apparently was not so much to recreate the audience as to conciliate the critic. The appeal was aridly intellectual.

The public-theatre dramatist, on the other hand, was primarily a vendor of emotions. Classic or romantic, all themes were discussed by him in familiar terms. The ancient Roman was made a man and a brother by adroitly associating him with helpful anachronisms. Of artistic shaping or restraint there was little: noble thoughts were jostled by idle conceits and coarse buffoonery.

Midway between the drama of the scholars and the drama of the people came the drama of the classes, or what might at a pinch be styled the courtier drama, the prerogative of the private theatre. Long the monopoly of the boy player, and therefore fortuitously passionless, the private-theatre play of our restricted period was remarkable for its verbal rapier play, the nice conduct of euphuistic dialectics, and the chasing to death of the wire-drawn conceit. Nor is this all. The private-theatre play deserves to rank as the *fons et origo* of modern musical comedy, inasmuch as it was distinguished by its profusion of interspersed song, sometimes relevant, sometimes not.

[1] Act IV, scene 2, line 15.

Strange to say, while these types, the University or Inns-of-Court play, the public-theatre play and the private-theatre play, have all been fully recognised and amply discussed, scholars have unaccountably ignored the existence of an intermediary and, so far as the public drama is concerned, initiatory type. I refer to the inn-yard play. The fact that this type has been confused with the public-theatre type is simply another proof that the first inn-yard playing places were at the head of the main stream of theatrical evolution, and not in its backwaters. I hope to be able to demonstrate that specific inn-yard plays have come down to us, and that they possess denotements which distinguish them from plays of the public-theatre order.

There is good reason to suppose that the establishment of the first inn-yard playhouse, or of a yard with specially erected ground-stands, which afforded accommodation for all sorts and conditions of people, had taken place at least a decade before the building of the first public theatre, and probably as early as 1560.[1] The event, let the precise date be what it may, was epoch-marking. It distinguishes the period when the professional dramatist emerged and the popular drama became fuller-bodied and received rudimentary shaping. Kickshaws of the old morality type no longer sufficed to allay the public appetite. One glimpses the first rude beginnings of the popular five-act drama, and especially of that type of drama with the ready-made plot, the chronicle history, so stirring in its action, so appealing to the combative

[1] There was acting at the Boar's Head without Aldgate in 1557, but we know not under what conditions. A play performed there in September of that year, *A Sackfull of News*, gave such offence to the Privy Council as to occasion the arrest of the players and seizure of the prompt-book. (Dasent, *Acts of the Privy Council*, vi, 168.)

and bloodthirsty instincts of the mob. Here, too, that idol of the folk, the happy-go-lucky, irresponsible Clown, with his faculty of saying a good deal more than was set down for him, gained firm foothold.

But when all is said there is, unfortunately, an ugly gap in the history of dramaturgic evolution. It can readily be shown that certain specific inn-yard plays have come down to us, but we have no reason to believe that any of them were written before 1576, and belong to the pre-theatrical period. Nevertheless, it will prove far from profitless to inquire how many of the old printed plays were written for inn-yard performance.

Confronted by the corpus of the later sixteenth-century drama, we have to ask ourselves by what means the inn-yard play can be distinguished. Does text or title-page yield us differentia? My reply to that would be in the affirmative, but I should take care to add that they tell us most when they tell us nothing. I think that when one comes across a sixteenth-century play whose title-page fails to convey by what company it was acted or where, one has reasonable grounds for believing that it was an inn-yard play. With theatre plays it was customary to give that information, but no title-page has ever definitely conveyed that a play was acted in an inn-yard. The truth is that, once the public theatre was established, the inn-yard playing place acquired an inferior status, and, despite its convenience for winter acting, came to be looked upon by the players simply as a necessary evil. Hence there was no boasting on title-pages of a company's association with an inn-yard, notwithstanding that certain companies, as I shall show, acted almost wholly in inn-yards for lengthened periods. For such companies at such periods new plays must have been occasionally written, and they would have to conform to inn-yard convenience. Variety was demanded, and as yet the players had no great stock. On this score, I take leave to quote a relevant passage from Schelling's useful book, *Elizabethan Drama:* [1]

The middle point numerically falls, curiously enough, just short of the date of Elizabeth's death, so that we may affirm that just about as many plays were staged during the forty-five years of the queen's reign as were performed in the thirty-nine that followed to the closing of the theatres. But if we turn to the two periods of eleven years each (from 1589 to 1600 and from 1601 to 1611) which constitute Shakespeare's active career, we find a preponderance of nearly four to three in favour of the earlier period. (The figures of my rough list are 377 plays in the earlier period against 279 in the latter.) Indeed, no decade of the drama can vie with the last of Queen Elizabeth in dramatic or, for that matter, in other literary activities. Certainly, no less than four hundred plays were written and acted within those ten years, an average per year more than double that which appertains to the whole period.

Creative activity would depend on the number of the companies in existence, but, taking the notable year of 1576 as a *terminus a quo*, the further we go back the smaller will be the individual repertory and the greater the need for creative activity.

Much as there was in common between the inn-yard stage and the public-theatre stage, the former had certain innate and unamendable structural deficiencies which one would naturally expect to find reflected in the plays written for it, assuming that such have come down to us. We know from a superabundance of stage directions that the public theatre had two or more solid doors of entrance, but, for very good reason, we have no trace of their prototypes in the inn-yards. Since the inn-yard stage had no specially built tiring-house, and depended for its background on the yard wall, it must have been

[1] Vol. ii, p. 373.

wholly devoid of entering doors. No inn door could have
been utilised on an elevated stage — if one may indulge
in a pleonasm to emphasise a point. Hence, when we
come across a late sixteenth- or very early seventeenth-
century play which makes no mention of doors, indicating other modes of entrance or none at all, we are entitled
to assume that we have discovered an inn-yard play.
Take, for example, the anonymous comedy entitled *The
Weakest Goeth to the Wall*, which, on its publication in
1600, was described, without any mention of the place of
performance, as having "bene sundry times plaide by the
right honourable Earl of Oxenford, Lord Great Chamberlain of England his seruants." Since it is not on record
that Oxford's Men ever occupied a theatre, it is reasonable to suppose that when they came to London they
acted in an inn-yard. When, in the spring of 1602, they
were amalgamated with Worcester's Men, their place of
acting was at the Boar's Head, and we have also some
slight trace of them at the same inn previously.[1] When
we come to examine *The Weakest Goeth to the Wall* by the
light of these facts, we find that the stage direction for
the opening dumb show indicates the entrance of the
characters, not through doors, but at the corners of the
stage. Afterwards, we simply get the notification, "Enter So-and-So," without any clue to the whence or how.
   Just here I find it necessary to say that the investigation we have in hand must be pursued with extreme
caution. It is highly probable that not all sixteenth-
century plays unallotted to any company or to any
theatre and devoid of all reference to entering doors were
London inn-yard plays. Apart from this, of the kind
already identified some may have been pirated versions
of London plays prepared for performance by coun-

[1] Adams, *Shakespearean Playhouses*, p. 16.

try strollers. But even if I should make the mistake of reckoning one or two plays of this type in the inn-yard category, no serious harm would be done, seeing that the conditions of acting in the country closely approximated to the methods of the inn-yards. Luckily, however, there is a sufficiency of undoubted inn-yard plays to warrant us in arriving at a conclusion.

Besides the lack of all reference to stage doors, there is one other denotement of the inn-yard play, equally due to the peculiar physical conditions. The sheer inability to provide a curtain-shrouded upper stage necessitated the avoidance of certain situations, common enough in public-theatre and private-theatre plays, calling for the exposure of an upper room wherein passed considerable action. For this deficiency, however, the presence of a ready-made balcony and an elevated window in some degree compensated. Characters could speak realistically from above, and city walls could be vigorously stormed.

It will be profitable, I think, at this stage of our investigation, to determine what London companies between, say, 1583 and 1602, acted for whole seasons, and sometimes for several years on end, in the inn-yards: the idea being to establish which of their plays were written for performance in the yards. Undoubtedly, the chief of these were the Queen's Men and the Admiral's Men. It was apparently the custom of the Queen's Men to act in the summer in one of the theatres in Finsbury Fields, and, for the convenience of the public, to repair in the winter to a city inn-yard. From November, 1583, to February, 1584, we find them holding forth alternately at two neighbouring inns, the Bull in Bishopsgate Street and the Bell in Gracious Street. Early in 1587 we get traces of them again in a city inn, apparently the Belle

Sauvage on Ludgate Hill. Somewhat fuller, and perhaps more significant, is the record of the Admiral's Men. From 1589 to 1591 they were playing in some unidentifiable inn-yard. Immediately afterwards the company was dissolved, but only to be reorganised in 1594.

Among the Queen's Men's plays bearing indication of having been written for inn-yard performance are some by Peele and Greene, notably *The Troublesome Raigne of King John, David and Bethsabe, Jack Straw, Friar Bacon and Friar Bungay, Alphonsus, King of Arragon,* and *James IV,* together with some of doubtful attribution, such as *The True Tragedy of Richard III, The Famous Victories of Henry V,* and *The Cobler's Prophesie.*

It is to be noted that the two parts of *The Troublesome Raigne of King John* were published in 1591 with the full notification "as it was (sundry times) publikely acted by the Queens Maiesties Players, in the honourable Citie of London." Neither the Theater nor the Curtain was in that honourable city, and, if the play had been acted in any theatre, the fact would surely have been stated. Hence, before we proceed beyond the title-page, a case is established for inn-yard performance; and, on examination, nothing in the two parts runs counter to the primary indication. The characters simply "enter": no mention is made of doors either on their coming in or going out. Equally significant is the silence concerning gates. Whereas in Shakespeare's *King John* the Herald enters "to the Gates," in this play we have merely, "Enter the King's heralds with Trumpets to the wals of Angiers: they summon the toune." The inference is that, while in the theatre proper there was a practicable city gate, in the inn-yard there was none. Satisfactorily enough, this is in accord with the deducible limitations of the inn-yard stage.

Though entered on the Stationers' Register five years previously, *The Love of King David and Fair Bethsabe, With the Tragedie of Absalom* was apparently first published in 1599, and then without attribution to any company or any theatre. The text of the play is corrupt, and it is hardly safe to take it as affording scientific evidence, but one or two points may be noted. What has long proved a puzzling situation occurs at the opening of the piece, where the Prologue "draws a curtain and discovers Bethsabe, with her maid, bathing over a spring," while "David sits above viewing her." The difficulties of staging this have exercised the intelligence of several expert investigators, but none has been able to advance a sensible solution.[1] It seems to me, however, that once you realise, what never yet has been realised, that *David and Bethsabe* was originally an inn-yard play, you have practically cleared up the mystery. You cannot picture the scene on any such stage as the one represented in the Dutch sketch of the Swan or the one in Kirkman's so-called Red Bull view, but you can picture it on the inn-yard stage, once you are familiar with its characteristics. All you have to do is to recall that the lower gallery ran round at least three sides of the yard. Put the stage in a corner not far from the outer staircase, place David on the nearest side gallery about level with the front stage, and the problem is solved. This, no doubt, was a special arrangement, due to the necessity of following the Biblical narrative, but it would have answered very well also for the staging of the siege scenes. There is surely some significance in the fact that the situation is unique in sixteenth-century drama. Nothing similar is to

[1] Cf. Chambers, *The Elizabethan Stage*, iii, 48. The references given here are not full; see *Shakespeare's England*, ii, 305, Schelling, *Elizabethan Drama*, i, 171, etc.

be traced until we come to *The Second Maiden's Tragedy*,[1]
a Globe play of 1611; and for a sound analogue we have
to proceed until we come to Ford's *Love's Sacrifice*.[2] The
assumption would be that the physical conditions of the
first theatres did not permit of the staging of any such
situation.

Old stage directions had a curious trick of disappearing
on occasion in the printing, with the result that silence on
a point is often delusive. Hence the necessity for the
exercise of caution. In the first act of *David and Bethsabe* there is a siege scene in which a tower is stormed and
taken, though there is no slightest hint in text or direction of the use of scaling-ladders. If to me it seems not
improbable that the assault was made by means of the
staircase leading to the gallery, it is because there is some
indication, later in the scene, of the use of the staircase.
Cusay makes his appearance below and is requested by
Joab, the victorious, to "come up." The direction which
follows simply says, "He comes."

The Life and Death of Jack Straw, printed in 1594 without any details of the company to which it belonged or
the place where it was acted, is of somewhat doubtful
authority on the point of inn-yard procedure. It is in
the uncommon four-act form and has undoubtedly been
abbreviated. One notes that no reference is made to
entering doors and that the play is singularly devoid of
properties. The chances are that the original was an inn-
yard play, but there is little room to doubt that the
text as we have it was arranged for the use of country
strollers.

In a somewhat tortuous way, I have arrived at the
conclusion that Greene's *Friar Bacon and Friar Bungay*
and *Alphonsus, King of Arragon*, were both inn-yard

[1] Act V, scene 1.   [2] Act V, scene 1.

plays and closely associated. The brazen head which proved so effective a property in *Friar Bacon* doubtless originated with it, as the head figures in the romance on which the play was founded. It was utilised again in the fourth act of *Alphonsus, King of Arragon*, a play which bears indications of having been written for inn-yard performance. At its close we find the direction, "Exit Venus; or, if you can conveniently, let a chair come down from the top of the stage, and draw her up." Now, a dramatist writing for a regular theatre would not have had any doubts about this matter. He would have known exactly what could be, and what could not be, done. The uncertainty expressed here shows that Greene was writing for an inn-yard, where the equipment was not so complete. It is highly probable that most of the carriers' yards had a crane for the hoisting of heavy goods, but it may not always have been convenient to place the stage below the crane. Other and more important necessities may have compelled the use of another position.

The True Tragedie of Richard III was printed in 1594, "as it was playd by the Queenes Maiesties Players." In examining the text one notes, in the first case, that there is no mention of entering doors, and secondly, that there are no divisions between acts. Nothing being half so infectious as fallacious belief, it is the fashion now among scholars to concede (on the strength of the great number of undivided old plays) that public-theatre plays were acted without breaks. The subject is much too vast a one to enter upon here,[1] but I may say that, so far as inn-yard performances are concerned, I doubt very much

[1] Cf. *The Review of English Studies*, ii, 295, Sir Mark Hunter on "Act and Scene-Divisions in the Plays of Shakespeare"; also *The New Statesman* for September 20, 1924, my article on "The Shakespearean Fallacy of the Hour."

whether the innkeeper or the audience would have relished the lack of opportunity to give undivided attention to the consumption of eatables and drinkables.

We cannot be sure that *The Famous Victories of Henry V* (which dates from before 1588) was originally an inn-yard production, but it was certainly acted in an inn-yard. An anecdote told in *Tarlton's Jests* [1] of Knell and Tarlton in the play reveals that it had been given at the Bull in Bishopsgate Street. If, as I have said, we cannot be sure that it was written for inn-yard performance, there is nothing, on the other hand, in the text which runs counter to such a supposition. Perhaps, indeed, in my anxiety to hold the scales even, I have made here too mild a statement. The truth is that the nature both of the play's construction and of the stage directions tends to support that hypothesis. Not only is there no trace of the use of entering doors, but back-stage action is largely avoided. Certainly, the balcony was pressed into service, but we have absolutely no clue to the use of the curtained rear stage. This does not argue that the curtained annex had no place in the general scheme of inn-yard provision, but it permits of the conclusion that, in the inn-yards, rear-stage action was not clearly visible from all parts, and for this reason was, as far as possible, shunned. The possibilities are, indeed, that the optical difficulties arising from the oblong shape of the yard ranked among the considerations which induced the early theatre builders to adopt a circular or octagonal form.

Let us take a glance now at the Admiral's Men's early repertory. Among plays belonging to them that I feel disposed to place in the inn-yard class are the two parts of *Tamburlaine*, *The Battle of Alcazar*, and *The Wounds of Civil War*. Before turning to *Tamburlaine*, it is impor-

[1] Ed. Halliwell, pp. 13, 24.

tant to note that all Marlowe's plays, save those belatedly
printed and bearing signs of sophistication, preserve a
rigorous silence regarding the presence of entering doors.
Marlowe's dramatis personae simply "enter" or come on
at "the one side" or "the other side." Here it is a question of examining, as far as possible, "the true and perfect copies," to use the old phrase, since in the *Faustus*
quarto of 1616, otherwise an enlarged and revised text
made for use in a theatre, we find mention of doors.
What I most fear, however, is that most investigators,
when they come to consider the two parts of *Tamburlaine*
from our present standpoint, will boggle, as I myself
momentarily boggled, over Bajazeth's cage and Tamburlaine's chariot, and murmur to themselves that such massive and unwieldy properties could ill be accommodated
within the restricted space of an inn-yard stage. Well,
all I can say is that, if this should prove to them an in-
surmountable difficulty, they will be forced to the conclusion, by sheer dint of Marlowe's silence, that solid
entering doors had no place in the Theater and the Curtain. And the exasperating thing is that, if they chose to
take that stand, nobody could advance a single item of evidence to show the untenability of their position. All that
we know for certain is that the Swan, in 1595, had massive double doors, though I think it might be safely
postulated, on the strength of sundry stage directions in
Rose plays, that Henslowe's theatre had some sort of
doors at least a lustrum earlier.

Before we part from *Tamburlaine* it is as well for us to
note that the title-page of the first quarto, as published
in 1590, describes the play as "deuided into two Tragicall
Discourses, as they were sundrie times shewed upon
Stages in the Citie of London, By the right honorable
the Lord Admyrall, his seruantes."

Perchance my hearing may be defective, but this speaks to me of exclusive inn-yard performance. From time to time the Admiral's Men may have shifted from inn to inn, much as the carriers shifted — a circumstance which would account for the curious use of the word "stages." To take an alternative reading and assume that the two parts saw the light on different stages would be to ignore the evidence presented by the prologue to the second part.

Happily, we do not require to seek for internal evidence to prove that *The Battle of Alcazar* and *The Wounds of Civil War* are inn-yard plays, since one of them, at least, is in a sophisticated state. External evidence establishes the point beyond yea or nay. In the late sixteenth century, publication never took place within a few months of production, and both these plays were issued in that fecund publishing year of 1594, the year in which the Admiral's Men abandoned inn-yard playing for good and first took up occupation of a regular theatre. They began acting at the Rose in May, precisely at the time *The Wounds of Civil War* was entered on the Stationers' Register as a publicly performed play.

Research on our present subject must not be too restricted. One or two inn-yard plays fell from the press in the early seventeenth century. No doubt by that time efforts had been made to bring the inn-yard stage up to the level of efficiency attained by the public-theatre stage, but there were fundamental defects incapable of amendment. Consequently, no great risk is run in continuing to apply the old tests, especially as one particular play, printed in 1602 as acted by Worcester's Men, gives to them favourable reaction. This is the anonymous *How a Man may Choose a Good Wife from a Bad*. That it was an inn-yard play, both internal and external evidence

testifies. In dealing with it, as with the many plays published in 1594 and 1607, we must bear in mind that publication often indicates either the collapse or the reor-
ganisation of the producing company. There was a strict
rule among the players, generally laid down under penal-
ties in their articles of association, that no play was to
be printed while the company held together. Now, the
period of the publication of *How a Man may Choose a
Good Wife from a Bad* was the period when Worcester's
Men and Oxford's Men united. Early in 1602 Worcester's Men had been acting at the Boar's Head,[1] and it
was not until the following August that they made their
first appearance in a public theatre. It cannot be pretended that *How a Man*, etc., was a Rose play of August,
1602 to February, 1602–03, since publication was not at
all likely to have followed so quickly on production. If
sold to a printer at the time of the Worcester Men's re-
organisation, the play can hardly have been otherwise
than an inn-yard play, and an examination of its text
goes to fortify that conclusion. It was well adapted for
both inn-yard and general country performance, since it
demands no use of entering doors or of an upper stage,
and requires only such properties as tables, stools, and
cushions — nothing beyond what the average inn in town
or country could readily provide.

[1] Chambers, *The Elizabethan Stage*, iv, 334, 335.

III

THE PRACTICE OF DOUBLING AND ITS INFLUENCE ON EARLY DRAMATURGY

IN that highly mysterious, much-discussed old play, *Sir Thomas More*, there is a pleasant scene in the conjectured fourth act [1] where some vagrant players, having learned that More is entertaining the Lord Mayor and Aldermen of London at his house at Chelsea, wait upon him to offer their services. They have no fewer than seven interludes in their repertory, and More decides that they shall present *The Marriage of Wit and Wisdom* before his guests. That point being settled, he asks the Chief Player casually, "How many are ye?" and gets as reply, "Four men and a boy, Sir." This evokes the comment that, in the circumstances, since boys then played all the female characters, there must be few women in the play, but Sir Thomas is quickly undeceived, the Player assuring him that there were three. "And one boy play them all!" ejaculates the mildly astonished Chancellor, "By'r lady, he's loaden!"

Here we have, what we seldom find in Elizabethan drama, a deft splash of historical colour. Whatever the reason, — whether it was that trained players were scarce or that a good-sized troupe could not look for a pecuniary return in keeping with its numbers, — the fact remains that professional companies in More's time, say, from 1480 to 1535, his inclusive dates, invariably consisted of four players. One would probably not be very far astray

[1] C. F. Tucker Brooke, *The Shakespeare Apocrypha*, p. 403.

in assuming that in the beginning this limitation was imposed by sheer economic necessity, but, admitting the postulate, the number became so far the rule that it was not even exceeded in those rare cases where questions of ways and means had no longer to be considered. From Henry VII's reign to Elizabeth's no court troupe of professional interlude players ever numbered more than four. This fact requires emphasising because it has been seriously obscured by the misapprehensions of several noted investigators.[1] In and about 1485, Henry VII had two distinct sets of players, each four in number, the one a company known as "The Players of the King's Interludes," and the other a seasonal association called "The Players of the King's Chapell," made up of adult choristers of the Chapel Royal, which, so far from being an organisation, varied in its components, and only came into being for a month or two in the year. Socially disparate, the two never coalesced. The professionals were paid half-yearly wages, or what would be better styled retaining fees, and the amateurs received a douceur for each of their few — mostly Christmas — performances. The regular royal interlude players, it is to be noted, were appointed for life. Except at periods of festivity, their constant attendance at court was not indispensable, and in the intervals they were allowed to travel.[2] Henry VIII maintained his father's household, but in 1514, for some reason not apparent, he decided to supplement the old company of interlude players by an extra company of

[1] Collier, *Annals of the Stage* (1831), i, 36, 48; for repetitions of the blunder see *infra*, p. 45, note 1.

At an earlier period four was the norm in France. In 1392 the Duke of Orleans's court troupe consisted of four players. See Petit de Julleville, *Les Mystères*, i, 358.

[2] C. W. Wallace, *Evolution of the English Drama up to Shakespeare*, pp. 58, 59, 66, 119.

four. Probably this was done that one company might always be in attendance, each being allowed to travel in turn. Unfortunately, what was in reality a simple duplication has come to be looked upon by three such eminent scholars as Wallace, Adams, and Chambers [1] as an individual accretion, with the result that the court interluders from that time onwards have been considered as consisting of one company of eight men, instead of two companies of four. If Henry VIII merely increased the number of players in his father's old company, we should expect to find the members of the enlarged organisation all playing together, and to find payments being made to them under the one heading. That is precisely what we do not find. The elder set was distinguished as "the King's old players," and the new set as "the King's players"; and from the fifth year of Henry's reign we have records of separate payments (or rather Christmas "rewards") to each. Thus on 8 Henry VIII, January 4, £3.6.8 was paid to "the King's players" and £4.0.0 to "the King's olde players." [2] And in later years the same distinction was maintained.

Possibly to some of you this may not seem a matter of sufficient importance to warrant the attention I have given to it, but the truth is always worth striving for, and in this case it affords me the necessary springboard. From the beginning, professional interlude players were not habituated to acting together otherwise than in troupes of four, and the old morality writers had to fashion and follow a scheme of dramatic construction thoroughly in keeping with that limitation. It is noteworthy, however, that authors who wrote specially for the royal choir

[1] Wallace, *op. cit.*, p. 119; J. Q. Adams, *Life of Shakespeare*, p. 103; Chambers, *The Mediaeval Stage*, ii, 187, *The Elizabethan Stage*, ii, 79.

[2] Collier, *op. cit.*, i, 75.

boys were not so hampered, since as many as ten or twelve boys were available for court acting. But the more vigorous native drama has always been dependent upon professionalism; and this strict, long-persisting limitation of the numbers of an adult company, eloquent as it is of economic pressure, shows that the interlude and the morality, though nurtured at court, owed their growth and full-bloodedness to popular support.

The problem, then, that confronted the early morality writer was: given a company of four players, how to introduce a plenitude of characterisation? Remarkably far-reaching was the issue, since a solution was achieved by the fashioning of a constructive formula which not only had potent influence for nearly a century on methods of acting by its constant fostering of versatility in the player, but firmly established the broad technical principles upon which the maturer sixteenth-century drama came to be based. A ready clue to this solution is afforded us by the title-page of several early morals, where it is intimated that "foure men may well and easely play this enterlude." The reason for notifications of this order becomes apparent when we examine the title-page of *The Conflict of Conscience*, printed in 1581, on which a table is given showing how the eighteen characters in the play could be acted by six persons, "most convenient," we are told, "for such as be disposed either to show this Comedie in private houses or otherwise." Other tables of a similar nature are to be found in several earlier plays of a purer morality type, and all, when examined conjunctively, admit of certain important inferences.

Since it is not to be supposed that moralities were written with an eye to the subsequent convenience of amateurs, there is no reason to doubt that what was stated as practicable on these tables had already been done: that where, for example, a play was said to be readily actable by four people, it had originally been thus acted. Internal evidence of this essential doubling is yielded us in George Wapfull's *Tyde Taryeth for No Man*, a moral for four players, printed in 1576. This piece entailed hard work on its representatives, viewing the fact that two men had each to play as many as six characters, not to speak of a third man playing four. At line 1214 in the Farmer facsimile there is a direction intimating that the character of Courage "fighteth to prolong the time while Wantonnesse maketh ready," which apparently shows that it had been found in the performance of the play that more time was necessary for the actor's change from male to female attire than the mere delivery of the dialogue provided. At line 1220 Courtier (or, to speak by the card, the exponent of Courtier) returns as Wastefulness, and at line 1246 Greediness, who went off at line 1198, returns as Wantonness, Wastefulness's wife. Note, these were all changes of characterisation, not incidental assumptions of disguise. Technically speaking, the actor who doubles, plays two or more of the dramatis personae: to personate a character which assumes several disguises is not to double. In this connection it is noteworthy that the title-page of *Lusty Juventus* (1561) has no table of allotment, merely acquainting the reader that "Foure may play it easily, taking such partes as they thinke best, so that any one take of those partes that be not in place at once." Here we have a crude formulation of the fundamental principle of doubling, a principle, it is to be observed, not bowed down to on the title-page of *The Interlude of Welth and Helth*, which tells us that four may play it easily, though at one particular juncture Health, Wealth, Liberty, Ill Will, and

Shrewd Wit, five characters in all, occupy the stage at
once. My impression is that this statement was de-
signedly mendacious, made with the idea of attracting
and deluding the large body of amateurs, in town and
country, looking for plays adapted for four players.
Originally, the interlude would appear to have been
acted by five. It belongs to the period of about 1556, a
period when some slight extension of the conventional
number of interlude players in a company was being
made, although the primal rule of four (to judge by later
printed plays) was not wholly abrogated. *The Triall of
Treasure* and *Like Will to Like*, published respectively
in 1567 and 1568, were both written for five players.

Sir Edmund Chambers's first trace of doubling is in
the Croxton *Play of the Sacrament*, conjecturally assigned
to the period of 1480. The text of this piece, from the
original manuscript in Trinity College, Dublin, has been
twice printed, the last time in Manly's *Specimens of the
Pre-Shakespearean Drama*.[1] A list of the characters,
twelve in number, is given at the end of the play, together with the intimation, "ix may play it at ease."
Here we have clearly a play designed for amateur performance. It would be idle, I think, to deduce from it
that doubling was regularly practised in the old miracle
plays. Where plays were performed by coöperative guilds
there was no serious check on the supply of actors (of a
kind), and no pressing economic necessity for limitation
of number. Hence, doubling as a basic element of dramatic construction cannot be said to have had any existence before the uprise of the morality.[2]

In the absence of a table of character allotment or of a
definite statement on the subject, there is one sound

[1] Vol. i, p. 276.
[2] For doubling in the court masques in the Cornish period, see Reyher,
Les Masques Anglais, p. 83.

method whereby we can arrive at the precise number of players originally required by an old morality or comedy. (In the case of tragedy it has less application.) Many early allusions show that it had long been customary to bring all the characters on at the end of the play, that is to say, such as subsisted throughout: there were no absurd resurrections such as we sometimes see at curtain-fall in the theatre to-day. Thus on December 11, 1603, we find Carleton writing to Chamberlain:

"Now, all the actors being together on the stage, as use is at the end of the play, the sheriff made a short speech," etc., etc. [1]

Old stage directions substantiate this similitude. In *The Valiant Scot*, an anonymous Caroline play, we get, about thirty lines from the close, "Enter all in state."

The test is serviceable. When one applies it to Heywood's *Interlude of the Wether* (1533), one finds that the play has ten characters, all of whom are on the stage in the last scene. Since no professional troupe of that period had more than half that number of players, the inference is that the piece was written for court performance by ten choir boys; and the soundness of that inference is demonstrated by the fact that Heywood was synchronously training, and writing for, boy players. [2] Armed with this knowledge, and given the number of actors in a play of specific, or approximately accurate, date, the student should have no difficulty in determining for what kind of actors and what kind of audience the play was written. In a word, there are possibilities of early scientific classification hitherto undreamt of, the division, as it were, of the atoms into electrons.

If we assemble in chronological order all the sixteenth-

[1] Ellis, *Original Letters*, 3d series, i, 31. The practice long obtained. There is a neat allusion to it in the last scene of Congreve's *The Way of the World*.   [2] Wallace, *Evolution*, p. 84.

century plays which bear indications, either on tables or otherwise, of the number of players required for their performance, preserving in mind that dates of publication are but varying approximations to dates of production, we shall be able by careful analysis to trace the progress towards dramaturgy, to see how the science of construction was delayed by the persistence of the four-man principle, and how in its turn, when it began to get momentum, it was instrumental in institutionalising acting and in creating a demand for greater histrionic supply. In the following representative but incomplete list of such plays the date or approximate date of publication comes first, and the title is followed by the number of characters and the number of players:

1533	Heywood's *Interlude of the Wether*....	{ 10 by 10 (boy players).
ca. 1556	*The Interlude of Welth and Helth*	5 players.
1560	*Impacient Poverty*...................	8 by 4.
1560	*Lusty Juventus*	10 by 4.
1560–1577	*Misogonus*.........................	15 by 8.
1565	*King Daryus*.......................	21 by 6.
1565	W. Wager's *Enough is as Good as a Feast*	18 by 7.
1566	Phillips's *Pacient Grissel*.............	23 by 8.
1567	Pickering's *Horestes*.................	25 by 6.
1567	*The Triall of Treasure*...............	16 by 5.
1567	Lewis Wager's *Life & Repentance of Marie Magdalene*................	{ 14 by 4 (professionals).
1570	*Cambyses, King of Persia*............	38 by 8.
ca. 1570	*The Longer Thou Livest, the More Foole Thou Art*	16 by 4.
1573	*Newe Custom*.......................	11 by 4.
1576	*Tyde Taryeth for No Man*	18 by 4.
1576	*Common Conditions*.................	6 players.
1579	*The Marriage of Wit and Wisdom*	19 by 6.
1581	*The Conflict of Conscience*	18 by 6.
1598	*Mucedorus*	originally 15 by 8; Q. 3 (1610) calls for 17 by 10.

In this list, to preserve consistency, the prologue (save in the case of *Mucedorus*, where the table maker very properly departs from the old custom) has in every instance been reckoned as a character, in accord with the method adopted in the old tables. In scanning it, what one first remarks is the persistence amidst variability, to so late a date as 1576, of the four-man system; and, but for one restraining circumstance, one would be inclined to say that the approximate dates for *The Longer Thou Livest*, *Newe Custom*, and *Tyde Taryeth for No Man* are either widely astray or misleading. But the evidence yielded us shows that, whereas in and about 1560, partly due to his own deficiencies and partly to those of the player, the dramatist was unable so to juggle with more than ten characters that they could be sustained by four players, by 1576 both histrionic versatility and the science of construction had so progressed that an increase of eighty per cent had taken place in the number of characters that could be undertaken by four players. Nor must one make the mistake of considering all the moralities in a mass. A further scrutiny of the table shows that with the advent of the transitional type, the type that mingled historical personages or familiar characterisations with the old abstractions and indulged the public with a greater wealth of portraiture, there came an immediate tendency to increase the number of players. It cannot be readily assumed that plays written for six or eight players were designed for and performed by choir boys, because choir-boy organisations generally numbered ten or twelve constituents, and it is reasonable to suppose that dramatists in writing for them would take the line of least resistance, and avoid the constructive worries inseparable from prearranged doubling by availing of the greatest possible number of players. The distinguishing note of the amateur play in the second and third quarters of the sixteenth century was the comparatively greater number of players it demanded, or, if that statement is a little too sweeping, the greater number by which it was performed. For example, it may be taken as certain that the twelve players who, in or about 1539, acted the nineteen characters in Bale's transitional morality of *Kynge Johan* were not professionals.

Mention of Bale reminds me that Chambers states that Bale's *Three Laws* required only five players, a deduction probably made from the divisions in the prefixed table of unallotted characters, though this cannot be taken to be anything more than a mere list of the dramatis personae.[1] I doubt the accuracy of this statement, because when I tried to work out the table on the allotment principle I found it was impossible to double some of the characters grouped together in one or two of the divisions.

The wise morality writer was sensible enough to confine himself to a small cast of characters, a number little in excess of the number of his exponents; by this means he attained group acting and fuller play for the cut and thrust and parry of his dialogue. To this small band the authors of *Hickscorner* and *The Interlude of Youth* belonged. But the great majority disdained to cut their suit according to their cloth, and, heedless of the fact that unrestraint condemned them to a constructive system which meant a series of duologues, diversified only by an occasional soliloquy, aimed simply at profuse characterisation. Had it not been for the essential brevity of the morality, which generally took about an hour to perform, the strain upon the players would have been beyond human endurance. One can surmise its severity from the

[1] Chambers, *The Mediaeval Stage*, ii, 188.

distribution of *The Longer Thou Livest, the More Foole Thou Art*, in which the burden of fifteen characters fell upon a four-man company, one man being compelled to play five characters (reckoning the prologue as one), two others four each, and the fourth man two. Added to this, the work was initially rendered the more trying by the fact that the early morality writer was slow in evolving a scheme of construction which obviated the necessity of alternation of character. Could the player have completed one character before assuming another, his task would have been less onerous, but often after appearing successively as A and B he had to come on again as A before proceeding to personate C. Every alternation was equivalent in point of labour to the assumption of a new character. However much earlier an improvement may have taken place, alternation does not wholly disappear from the plays on my list until we come to *The Conflict of Conscience*, a transitional morality, printed in 1581 and notable for being divided into acts and scenes. In this no player assumed a second character until the first had entirely said his say. Thenceforward, in the theatre play, alternation was generally avoided, though circumstances occasionally caused a return to the practice, and it failed wholly to disappear before the Caroline period.

It requires to be borne in mind that, besides the labour of multiple character acting, there was always a possibility of a further burden being imposed on the unfortunate morality player. In *Impacient Poverty* the exponent of Envy had not only to double other parts, but in his identity as Envy to come on in the disguise of Charity; just as Misrule in the same play had to assume the disguise of Mirth. Complicated construction of this order, unless we can conceive that the players had wonderful versatility and no revealing mannerisms, must have been excellently calculated to create profound confusion in the minds of an average audience. Recall that no programmes were provided in those days to help out matters. Shakespeare's public was equally thrown on its own resources. I shall have something to say later on as to how this difficulty was surmounted on the regular stage in the early seventeenth century. Meanwhile, it is requisite to point out that the disadvantages under which the morality players laboured in adopting the doubling system were clearly recognised at an early period by those who wrote for them. The main result of their forethought was that certain important characters, such as the Vice, were allowed to enjoy a monopoly of their representatives. In other words, they were not doubled. But we must bear in mind that this principle had serious limitations, for the more characters there were of this order, the more doubling was entailed on the other players. Thus it was that the handicap under which the players laboured reacted on nascent dramaturgy and effectively stayed its progress. The necessity to afford time for the frequent changes of dress occasioned the painful recurrence of long and tedious harangues. Truth to tell, the morality writer was striving to dance his hornpipe in fetters, and that too before he had learned his hornpipe.

The technical difficulties which regularly confronted the early professional players were so abundant that one is forced to the conclusion either that they possessed wondrous personative powers, a rich gift of mimicry, and an uncommon knack of disguise, or — what seems more likely — that the public of their time had the child's imagination and illimitable capacity for make-believe. It is true that the types and characters in morals were largely differentiated by dress, mostly symbolic and often fantastic, but there were occasions when the player had to make such rapid changes that there was hardly time for an elaborate alteration of attire. In *The Marriage of Wit and Wisdom*, Snatch at one juncture has to transform himself to Honest Recreation while a poor ten lines are being uttered, and, worse still, when Honest Recreation departs to return as Irksomeness the change has to be made within the short space of time represented by the delivery of three lines. When we seek to know how the thing was done, we find a clue to the *modus operandi* in *Mind, Will, and Understanding*, where Lucifer comes on "in a devil's array without, and within as a proud gallant." This means, according to Collier's convincing interpretation,[1] that the actor had a gallant's dress under his devil's array. After soliloquising, Lucifer goes out, "devoideth and cometh in again as a goodly gallant," so as to prove the better tempter. One finds a curious improvement of this effect in that much later theatre play, *The Birth of Merlin*,[2] in the scene where the Devil changes to a gallant, with hat and feather, sword and hangers, in full sight of the amazed Clown. The fact that the old stage devil wore a flaming vizard with horns draws attention to the extreme gratefulness of the vizard as a factor in character differentiation. Even if the morality player had face-paint at his service (which I doubt), he had little time, once the play began, to apply it. Happily for him, the creative property-man had already begun to emerge. Vizards were fashioned to symbolise vices and indicate traits: all unconsciously there was renewal of one of the fundamental conventions of the ancient Greek theatre.

[1] *Annals of the Stage* (1831), ii, 288.
[2] Act III, scene 4 (Tucker Brooke's division, *The Shakespeare Apocrypha*, p. 368).

In *The Marriage of Wit and Wisdom* Irksomeness, represented as a monster with a club, wore a vizard, and Wit at long last came in with it on his sword, in demonstration of the fact that he had killed him. After 1572, when mask-wearing in public by women first became fashionable, a great impetus was given to stage use of vizards, an abuse which culminated in the clumsy convention of the masked marriage. Another grateful method of quick changing was by means of "the reversible cloak," a stage device to whose serviceableness in disguising, reference is made in Jonson's *The Devil is an Ass.*

We have seen that with the loosening of the allegorical bonds by the transitional-morality writers, and the interfusion of historical and tragic elements in the dramaturgic scheme, there came a disruption, though not an abandonment, of the four-man system. Little by little the man-power increased. *The Triall of Treasure* and *Like Will to Like* demanded five players,[1] *King Daryus* six, W. Wager's *Enough is as Good as a Feast* and Phillips's *Pacient Grissel* (in 1566) eight. But it is to be noted that with the gradual increase in the size of companies came an equivalent increase in the number of dramatis personae, with the result that the players found no release from their old galley slavery. In Pickering's *Horestes* twenty-five characters had to be sustained by six players, and in Preston's *Cambyses, King of Persia,*

[1] The period when the five-man company began may be approximated by the following extract from the record of the Privy Council Meeting of May 6, 1546 (*Letters & Papers Foreign & Domestic, Henry VIII*, vol. xxi, [1546], part 1, no. 748):

"Five persons naming themselves the Earl of Bath's servants, who four days ago were committed to the Counter for playing lewd plays in the suburbs of London, to be released upon bond not to play without the Council's license; a letter herein to the Lord Mayor."

THE PRACTICE OF DOUBLING

1
thirty-eight by eight. By 1581 the maximum number of
doubled characters for a single player had increased. In
The Conflict of Conscience, one unlucky man was bur-
dened with no fewer than six characters, and three played
fourteen between them.

We have now reached the era of the specific theatre
play, a type to which the transition may be said to have
been insensible, not only because the full-blown morality
contained the germs of comedy, tragedy, and chronicle
history, but because it had come at last to be written —
probably for inn-yard service — in acts and scenes.
Doubling still remained a dual principle, but its laws
underwent modification and became more sharply defined. In the old moralities it was seldom that more than
one character permeated the play, and was given a
monopoly of the services of its exponent. In the theatre
play, not only were the hero and heroine never doubled,
but the interpreters of the main characters rarely played
more than one part. These restrictions were due to some
extent to the longevous custom of bringing on all the
surviving characters of importance at the end of the
play, but a question of professional status seems also to
have had bearing. There were two distinct grades of
common players, the sharers, so called from the fact that
a certain portion of the daily takings was divided un-
equally among them, and the hirelings, who were paid
weekly wages out of the sharers' receipts. The hirelings
were in reality the sharers' articled servants, and, though
it was from their ranks that the sharers were recruited,
the two, as might be surmised, were not upon the same
professional plane. Their relationship was very much
that of officer and private. In the traffic of the scene
most, practically all, of the drudgery devolved upon the
hirelings, and it is among them we must look for the suc-

cessors of the old doubling interluders. Work of this sort made or marred, killed or cured: those who survived became, by dint of their experience, technically accomplished, good all-round players. Of the labour that fell to the hireling's lot at the close of the century we find evidence in those working synopses of stage action, mainly dealing with exits and entrances, commonly known as *platts*, though the term should be, more properly, *plots*.[1] For example, the plot of *Frederick and Basilea* shows that in that play sixteen players undertook twenty-seven parts, two playing as many as five each. In *The Battle of Alcazar* the formidable number of forty-two characters was sustained by twenty-five players (a remarkably large company, it must be said, for the period), but in this instance no player wrestled with more than three parts, and most of the doublers were allotted only two. High-water mark was reached in the First Part of *Tamar Cam*, in which Dick Juby personated seven characters, Tho. Marbeck and Thos. Parsons six each, Will Parr five, and George Somersett five, besides dressing to come on as silent figures in processions. Contrasted with such herculean labour, the doubling indicated on the title-page of Q. 3 of *Mucedorus*, printed in 1610 and giving the text of the augmented version of the play, is of a very mild order. Eighteen parts were played by ten players, six characters enjoying each a monopoly of its exponent. The six comprised all the principals, including Mouse, the Clown, fairly sound proof that in Jacobean days doubling was confined to the hirelings. Two players sustained four parts each, and one of them was apparently a youth of some skill, considering that

[1] Chambers, *The Elizabethan Stage*, iv, 404; Greg, *The Henslowe Papers*, p. 127; *The Review of English Studies*, i, 257 ff., Greg on "The Evidence of Theatrical Plots for the History of the Elizabethan Stage."

he had to play three women of varying ages and a boy. Some little alternation of character is to be noted, but none of it onerous. Comedy and Envy, after appearing in the induction, both sustain three characters in the play, and both come on again in their emblematic rôles in the epilogue. Save at one juncture, deft construction obviates any necessity for rapid changing, but Tremolio is required to transform himself into the Wild Man within a minute or two, or while Mucedorus declaims but eight lines.

One difficulty shirked, as we have seen, by the old morality writers had to be faced and overcome by the Elizabethan theatre dramatist. Its nature has been indicated in the report of an interview with Mr. A. E. Filmer, formerly producer of the Birmingham Repertory Theatre, given in *The Shakespeare Journal* for January, 1923. In discussing the recent Birmingham revival of Dekker's *The Shoemaker's Holiday*, Mr. Filmer pointed out that one of the disadvantages of doubling parts in a stock company, necessary as the expedient often was, was "that when a character is supposed to disguise himself in a play, the audience, accustomed to see an actor play more than one part and recognising the actor through the disguise of the character, jumps to the conclusion that he is simulating a different character." And then he added, "This, I gather, happened when Rowland Lacy came on as Hans in *The Shoemaker's Holiday*."

The same liability to blunder existed in Shakespeare's day, but it was minimised by the establishment of a new dramaturgic principle. No character that was written to be doubled was allowed to assume disguise. In other words, the doublers and the disguisers represented two separate grades of players. Disguise was permissible only to the chief characters, and was therefore limited to the actor sharers and to one or two boy players of women. And just here it must be said that, if the sharers disdained doubling, it was not wholly because of the drudgery it entailed; associated with it there must have been some implication of inferior status, seeing that they were capable on occasion of undergoing equal drudgery in matters of disguise. One's mind reverts in this connection to that curious type of piece, the complex-disguise play, a type which sprang into vogue at the Rose Theatre early in the last decade of the sixteenth century, and in which, as in Chapman's *The Blind Beggar of Alexandria*, the whole action and interest arose out of the variety of disguises assumed with celerity by one or more of the leading characters.

A few seeming exceptions are to be found to the rule that players of principal parts were not to double, but these can be readily explained away. Thus in composite plays, where each act was a separate play, the chief players were forced to sustain a variety of parts. But this was no infringement of the rule, since doubling meant playing two or more parts in the one play. Again, as the induction was not an integrant of the play, as most plays with inductions could be, and many have been, played without them, it was permissible, though not often done, for a chief actor to take part in the induction as well as in the play. In a measure, there was precedent for this, as it had long been customary for one of the principals to speak the prologue and epilogue, and an induction is little more than a prologue in dialogue. We have here, I think, an explanation of the circumstance that in Munday's two Robin Hood plays — notable as the first "rehearsal" plays on record—Skelton and Sir John Eltham, after coming forward as the organisers of the performance, figure most unillusively in the action as Friar Tuck and Little John.

In the country, small bands of strollers were often forced through sheer limitation of numbers to take all sorts of unimaginable liberties with their audiences, but, the excuse being lacking, a like latitude was not allowed in the city. Yet even among the chief London companies we find evidence of occasional, though doubtless rare, resort to the crudest and most illusion-marring of expedients. There is trace, for example, of clumsy substitution, and we have to ask ourselves why such an abomination should have been evér practised. By substitution I mean the acting of one part by two players. Mr. C. J. Sisson has recently reminded us of what Crofton Croker, the play's original editor, told us long before, that, according to the extant prompt manuscript of Massinger's *Believe as You List*, two of the characters, Calistus and Demetrius, were played each by two different actors at a short interval.[1] Several explanations of this anomaly suggest themselves. A clumsy, unscientific distribution of the characters at rehearsal might have led to difficulties that could be surmounted only by substitution. Or we might take it that the prompter simply blundered in marking his book, and in the second instance put down the wrong names opposite the characters. Greg has shown that mistakes of this kind were certainly committed by the maker of the extant "plot" of *The Battle of Alcazar*. But I hardly think that this explanation applies here, and I fear that, repugnant and reprehensible as was the expedient, there were occasions when it had to be resorted to. It is a nice question, however, whether there was ever substitution in the acting of principal characters. With the minor fry the offence would not be nearly so great. A messenger

[1] *The Review of English Studies*, i, 428, 429, "Bibliographical Aspects of Some Stuart Manuscripts."

might be acted at one time by one man and at another by another without creating any puzzlement. It was the message, not the man, that mattered. But the leading characters would be more closely followed, and tricks could not have been played with them with impunity. The question demands some discussion — more, unfortunately, than I can give it here, because it has been more than once surmised that on one occasion Shakespeare availed of substitution.[1] Purely on account of the remarkable emphasis laid in *The Winter's Tale* on the striking resemblance between Hermione and Perdita, it has been suggested that the characters of the mother and daughter were doubled. To admit that would be to provide a substitute for Perdita in the scene where the two finally meet. At a pinch that might have been done, despite the fact that on their meeting Perdita has to speak five lines. The very brevity of the speech gives colour to the suspicion. It may be that I put the poet on too high a pinnacle, but the subterfuge seems to me unworthy of Shakespeare. There was no shortage of capable boy players of women in the King's company; and, to my mind, it would have been better to assign the mother and daughter to two boys of a size and leave it to the audience to imagine the resemblance than, in this final emotional moment, to "depart from life and the likeness of truth."

Though the companies of choir-boy players were never severely restricted in the number of their components, acting being neither their sole nor their main occupation and economic conditions having no particular sway, yet we have evidence that doubling was practised to some slight extent in the early private theatres.

---

[1] Most recently voiced by A. H. Tolman, *Falstaff and Other Shakespearean Topics*, pp. 159, 160.

The curious thing is that the expedient cannot have been so rarely resorted to at Paul's or the Blackfriars at the dawn of the seventeenth century as to necessitate any explanation or apology to the audience when practised, the only grounds on which Marston could have been justified in drawing attention, in the induction to his Paul's play, *Antonio and Mellida*, to the fact that "the necessitie of the play" required that the parts of Alberto and Andrugio should be doubled. The doubling evidently did not apply to the Second Part, in the fifth act of which the two characters are seen together in a dumb show; and in Part I there was no great liability to confusion, seeing that the two never appeared in the same act until the fifth act was reached. I do not pretend to know why Marston made this oblique apology, unless perchance it were that some exigency had compelled him to run counter to a recognised taboo and make the actor of so important a character as Andrugio double it with another.

Distinctively a private-theatre dramatist, Marston, it is to be noted, generally framed his plays for eighteen characters. That is the precise number in each of the two parts of *Antonio and Mellida*, though the dramatis personae in both are not identical; and it is likewise the precise number in his two Blackfriars plays, *The Dutch Courtezan* and *The Wonder of Women, or Sophonisba*. It is furthermore to be observed that, although Jonson's *Poetaster* had twenty-six characters, no more than eighteen were seen on the stage together—precisely the maximum out of a possible twenty-three assembled at any one time in Chapman's *The Widdowes Tears*. I am inclined to believe on the strength of this evidence that, irrespective of a few supernumeraries, the regulation number in a children's company at the beginning of the seventeenth century was eighteen. My impression is that the private-theatre play in the days of Farrant's Blackfriars was not constructed for doubling, and that Marston, bowing to the old system, avoided doubling as far as possible. But Jonson and Chapman, in writing primarily for the public theatre, had become habituated to different methods, and, in indulging in a wealth of characterisation, were inconsiderate enough to give the boys a good deal of extra work.

This particular opulence is a distinguishing quality of Elizabethan drama. Inherited from the transitional moralities, the rich mine showed no signs of exhaustion before Caroline days. Possibly its working was maintained by public taste, and the appetite grew by what it fed on. Streaked as it was with historical elements, the transitional morality gave birth to the chronicle play, and the vogue of the chronicle play, with its stupendous cast of characters, expanded liberty into license and established a convention under which the hirelings groaned, a despotic convention from which it was difficult to gain release. In the circumstances, the problem which confronted the pioneer public-theatre dramatists was not so much how to reconcile large casts with comparatively small companies (since that had already been solved by the morality writers) as, while availing of the escape that abundant minor doubling afforded, to lighten the burden of those on whom it fell. It was not doubling that was the player's bugbear, but the irksomeness and fatigue of the character alternation with which it had for so long been necessarily accompanied. That was the problem the first public-theatre dramatists had to solve, and, so far as it was scientifically and humanly possible, they solved it. Accidental circumstances, however, occasionally upset all their calculations. There were times when the particular composition of a company, some sudden shuffling of the cards through the death or secession of a player, made imperative a return to that primitive system of doubling of which character alternation was a concomitant. In spite of all precautions, the old Jack-in-the-box kept springing up again and again; yet, when all is said, the prime trouble had been seriously abated.

Briefly, then, the method whereby the early public-theatre dramatists obviated the existing necessity for character alternation was as follows: once the machinery of the play had been properly started, no new character was introduced until an old one was extinguished. Obviously it was only the minor characters who could be got rid of in this more or less arbitrary fashion—a restriction which undoubtedly played a part in reserving doubling for the minor players. It is distinctly unfortunate that the determination of this law should have been so long delayed, since ignorance of its ruling has led more than one fine Shakespearean scholar into quagmires of doubt and perplexity. I need cite only one instance. In that golden monograph of his on the greatest of poets, Sir Walter Raleigh laments how, "when Shakespeare has no further use for a character, he sometimes disposes of him in the most unprincipled and reckless fashion." In proof of this, he goes on to consider the harsh fate meted out to poor Antigonus in *The Winter's Tale*, and says: "Up to the time of his sudden death Antigonus has served his maker well; he has played an important part in the action, and by his devotion and courage has won the affection of all the spectators." [1]

[1] *Shakespeare*, p. 137. Cf. A. H. Tolman, *Falstaff and Other Shakespearean Topics*, p. 60, on Adam's mysterious disappearance in *As You Like It*. Here it cannot be argued that the character was suddenly eliminated

This is considering too curiously. Shakespeare had to
get rid of Antigonus at all costs, much as he may have
loved him, simply because his exponent was wanted to
play another part. It was a sheer matter of economic
necessity. Harsh as was Antigonus' fate, it is more
satisfactory from an artistic standpoint than the unex-
plained disappearance of the Fool from *King Lear*. Once
a character was visually or narratively annihilated, the
Elizabethan audience dismissed it from their minds, and,
on the subsequent appearance of its exponent, assuming
that he had any recognisable mannerisms, was not per-
plexed to know whether he was masquerading in purposeful disguise or representing an entirely new character. We
need not hug the flattering delusion to our souls that
Shakespeare ever gave any thoughts to posterity. As
dramatist, he was purely a time server, but a time server
of so rare and radiant a quality that in writing for the
hour he wrote for eternity.

Prime among the misconceptions that have arisen
through woeful ignorance of the principles of doubling is
the idea that Elizabethan dramatic construction was
loose and shambling. Though it enjoyed a freedom that
progress subsequently abrogated, it was a freedom within
the law. To dub it amorphous is to write oneself an ass.
Despite the fact that it gave no allegiance to the unities,
and was precluded from all necessity to reckon with the

because the actor was wanted to play another part. The cast of the play was
so small that all necessity for doubling was precluded. Moreover, since Adam
was not, and could not be, killed off, he should, in accord with the principle
of "all on in the last scene," have at least appeared at the end. My belief is
that the play as we have it represents a belated revision of the text, with
elimination of a scene or two in which Adam subsequently figured. Professor
Tolman comments (pp. 74, 75) upon certain inconsistencies existing between
the earlier and the later Touchstone, practically making the Clown two persons. This, too, points to clumsy revision by a second hand.

scene-painter and the scene-shifter, nevertheless it had its own rigid mechanical restraints. The influence of doubling on Elizabethan dramaturgy is best to be observed in the chronicle history, the one particular kind of derivative drama in which the pleader evinced most anxiety to stick to his brief, but in which the truth had often to be distorted because of the imperiousness of prevailing constructive methods. If, for example, we take 2 *Henry VI*, and bear in mind that its forty-seven characters had to be sustained by something like eighteen people, more than half of whom were constrained to play only one part, it is easy to see how the necessary moving of the pieces on the board so that there might be abundant doubling of the pawns, as it were, without resort to alternation, led to departure from prescript in matters both of fact and of chronology.

I purpose now analysing one or two typical old plays, not only with the view of demonstrating the accuracy of the conclusions I have just been propounding, but also to show you that Shakespeare's constructive methods were almost the same as Marlowe's. Let us begin with the First Part of *Tamburlaine*. My study of this play has convinced me that it was written for a company of about eighteen players, reckoning four boys for the female parts. The two virgins were doubtless doubled by the representatives of the two maids, Anippe and Ebea. No trace of alternation can be discovered throughout the play. In Act I we become acquainted with thirteen characters, twelve men and one woman, but with its finish Magnetes disappears. After the second act we see no more of Cosroe, Menophon, Ortygius, Ceneus, Mycetes, or Meander. In other words, by the beginning of the third act seven players have been released to play other parts. In the third act the number is further extended by the death of Agydos, but, on the other hand, eight new characters appear, of whom a possible four may have had exponents previously seen. By this time all the un-doubled characters have appeared, but new characters continue to stream on. In Act IV we make the acquaintance for the first time of the Soldan of Egypt, Capolin, and the King of Arabia; and in Act V, of the Governor of Damascus, Philemus, and the two virgins.

In the Second Part of *Tamburlaine* there are about twenty-six characters, and of these sixteen (equivalent to twelve adult players and four boys) come on in the first act. In Act II, Sigismund and Zenocrate die, and Frederick, Baldwin, Gazellus, and Uribassa say their last say, leaving five men and possibly a boy available for future service. Six new characters come on in Act III, the kings of Jerusalem, Trebizond, and Soria, the captain of Balsera, his wife Olympia and their son — all, to my mind, doubled parts. The supply, however, is slightly renewed by the deaths of the captain and his son. In Act IV, Perdicas is new, — and fleeting, — Calyphas and Olympia are killed. In the last act five fresh characters emerge, all of them borne by players who had previously been seen, some in more than one character.

Marlowe's *Edward II*, if I mistake not, must have been designed for a larger body of players than the body for which the Tamburlaine plays were written. It called for a company of about twenty-two in number — say, ten sharers, eight hirelings, and four boys. Consequently, though there are thirty characters in the play, the doubling would have been more distributed and less severe. Like others of its class, it is a sort of historical pageant or human panorama, since only three of its dramatis personae are fundamental enough to permeate the entire action; the rest are episodic. Unfortunately, to speak

of the various acts of this play is to beg the question;
the text is undivided, and the accepted divisions are at
best hypothetical. Moreover, I am not unmindful that
there exists to-day a growing school of deadly confident
investigators which stubbornly maintains that Shakespeare — and, by a parity of reasoning, most other public-theatre dramatists — avoided writing plays in acts and
scenes. All I have at present to say on that score, however, is that, if the public-theatre drama of Elizabethan
and Jacobean times was based so far on principles opposed to those of the private-theatre drama as neither
to recognise act divisions nor to admit of act intervals,
then it is difficult to see how any scheme of doubling
having for its main aim the avoidance of character
alternation can have been carried out.

In Act I of *Edward II*, following the divisions in the
Mermaid *Marlowe*, we are introduced to fifteen characters, fourteen males and one female. By the disappearance of the Bishop of Coventry, Beaumont, old
Mortimer, and the three poor men, six adult actors are
at once freed for future service. It is not improbable
that the six came on again in the second act as Young
Spencer, Baldock, Arundel, James, the messenger, and
the guard, characters which all then first appear. Other
newcomers in this act are the King's niece and two female
attendants, the latter of whom, being mutes, hardly
come into the reckoning. At its close, the King's niece,
the messenger, and the guard, having fretted and strutted
their hour, are heard no more; and we carry over two
adults and a boy for purposes of later casting. In all,
seventeen players have been seen in this act, a fair indication of the size of the company. In Act III the fresh
faces comprise Prince Edward, Old Spencer, Levune, and
the Herald, but the first two disappear with the act, thus

leaving two adult players for future use. And "the cry is 'still they come,'" for in Act IV we make the acquaintance of five new and mostly short-lived characters, Sir John of Hainault, Rice ap Howell, the Abbot, Mower, Leicester, and a messenger. Not only do the whole of these, excepting Leicester, depart for good with the close of the act, but with them go Arundel, Baldock, and the two Spencers. By dint of this wholesale slaughter, nine adult players are freed to serve the dramatist in the last act, and it takes it all to do, for in the last act ten new characters appear. Such was the method of construction pursued that all necessity for character alternation on the part of the doublers was apparently precluded. Only one possibility of the sort suggests itself. Since the Archbishop of Canterbury appears only in the first and last acts, it is not improbable that his representative sustained some episodic character in the interim.

So much water had raced and roared through old London Bridge in the days between Marlowe's tragic taking-off and Shakespeare's rise to supremacy, that one naturally looks for a broad divergence between the individual dramaturgic schemes of the two. And that one does not find. How faithfully Shakespeare followed the old fundamental principles becomes apparent once one has analysed perhaps not his greatest, but certainly his most famous, play. That there was a considerable amount of doubling in *Hamlet*, and that the action was so arranged that it might be effected in the easiest possible way no one, I think, on taking thought, will feel disposed to deny. No Elizabethan company rejoiced in the possession of as many as twenty-nine players, and there are twenty-nine characters in the play. I feel assured that, as in the plays already analysed, the sequences of disappearances indicate the method of doubling and throw some light on the technical restraints occasioned by the recurring mechanical difficulty.

Act I introduces us to thirteen of the dramatis personae. Of these, Francisco, Bernardo, and Marcellus are not seen later. The Players, two men and a boy, come on in Act II, scene 2, and disappear after Act III, scene 2. The second act writes *finis* to the careers of Voltimand, Cornelius, and Reynaldo. Rosencrantz and Guildenstern emerge in Act II, scene 2, and are last seen in Act IV, scene 3. Polonius is killed in the third act, just before the Ghost walks for the last time; and Ophelia is drowned in the fourth, the act in which Fortinbras and the Captain appear for the first time. New characters in Elizabethan fifth acts were almost invariably doubled characters, and seven come on in *Hamlet*, though only five indulge in speech. It is noteworthy also that out of the thirteen dramatis personae seen in Act I only five — Hamlet, Horatio, Laertes, Claudius, and Gertrude — permeate the play. And of these five only one remains alive at the close.

In accord with Lord Beaconsfield's dictum that it is the unexpected that always happens, I take leave to think that the perfectly obvious "doubles" in *Hamlet* were precisely those which were carefully avoided. Latterday barnstormers have frequently demonstrated with what ease Polonius and the First Gravedigger, the Ghost and the Priest, and Ophelia and Osric, can be doubled, but I have good reasons for doubting whether these concatenations had any remote precedent. Though the necessary intermediate annihilation of a character might suggest to the dramatist how the services of the released actor might be further utilised, he would, I think, occasionally be given pause by the status of the actor. Polonius and the Ghost were important rôles and must have been sustained by two sharers; there is a tradition, indeed, that Shakespeare himself originally played the Ghost. Personally, I cannot see sharers trenching on the pitiful prerogative of the hirelings. Nor can I picture the fair Ophelia tied neck and crop to Osric. If there is one thing more than another of which I am reasonably certain, it is that the responsibilities of heroship and heroineship were considered all-sufficing, that Hyperion was not linked with a satyr.

Time permits only of a hasty reference to others of Shakespeare's plays, but I think if you analyse *Julius Caesar* you will find that the constructive method is very much as in *Hamlet*, with this distinction, of course, that as the dramatis personae number more, there must have been more doubling. Not that I wish to imbue your minds with the idea that the one broad dramaturgic scheme had strict application to all genres. In the writing of comedy the dramatist was less beset with difficulties, since its trend was towards economy of characterisation. *As You Like It*, for example, having no more than twenty characters — sixteen males and four females — could have been given by a company so well equipped as the Chamberlain's without any doubling. It is true that Charles the Wrestler disappears after Act I, scene 2, and Le Beau after Act II, scene 2, but, as I have already pointed out, characters were not always relegated to the puppet-box simply to obtain a further histrionic supply. Much depended on circumstances. In an essay contributed to *The Stratford Town Shakespeare*, Mr. Henry Davey echoes Brandl's old theory that the sudden disappearance of the Fool in *King Lear* is best accounted for by the assumption that a boy player doubled the part with Cordelia. This hypothesis, however, is somewhat difficult to swallow. Proof that leading female characters were ever doubled is wholly lacking; and to me the postulate is incredible. It involves a very troublesome case of character alternation. Beyond doubt, minor female characters were — in fact (from the scarcity of boys) had to be — doubled, a boy playing a female attendant at one juncture playing another at another; but the doubling of a male and a female character was an irksome task, viewing the difference in attire and the difficulties of female make-up — all the more so if alternation were demanded. The evidence for mixed doubling of this order is very slight and admits only of the deduction that none but adult players ever resorted to it, and that the female characters so doubled were of an elderly type.[1] The two casts preserved in the belated quarto of *The Duchess of Malfi* show that originally Underwood doubled Delio and a Madman, Nick Tooley doubled Forobosco and another Madman, and R. Pallant doubled a Doctor, a Court Official, and Cariola, a female attendant, this last a not unimportant rôle.[2] Slight alternation was demanded of Underwood, but not, I think, of any of the rest. As it happens, the only other item of evidence bearing on the subject is of dubious authenticity. It is to be found in a pseudonymous contribution to the old *Shakespeare Society Papers*[3] in which one "Dramaticus" gives the alleged original cast of *The Shoemaker's Holiday*, assembled, we are told, from certain marginalia in an early printed copy of

[1] One item of Caroline evidence is, however, opposed in part to this conclusion. In the revival of *The Wild Goose Chase*, given at the Blackfriars in 1631, John Honeyman doubled the parts of Mariana, the courtesan, and the Young Factor (*The Review of English Studies*, iii, 222). But alternation was not called for, and there was plenty of time for the change. Obviously, however, players competent at once to sustain youthful female characters and manly rôles must always have been scarce.

[2] Chambers, *The Elizabethan Stage*, iii, 510.

[3] Vol. iv, p. 111.

the play. We are not told, however, of the whereabouts of this copy, and it has never come to light since. I am not surprised that Dr. Greg should have unhesitatingly condemned this cast as a forgery on the grounds that three out of the four female parts are assigned to grown men,[1] because I myself have found other pretty valid reasons for suspecting its genuineness. Humphrey Jeffes is represented as doubling the parts of Jane and the Nobleman, but Jane is on at the end of Act V, scene 2, and the Nobleman enters with the King at the beginning of the next scene and immediately begins to speak. Of all quick changes, this must have been about the quickest on record.

After the morality period, tables of character distribution in printed plays become scarce. Personally, I know of only three, the two in the original and the expanded versions of *Mucedorus*, and the table in *The Fair Maid of the Exchange* in 1607. In the last mentioned, the list of characters is preluded by the mendacious statement that "Eleauen may easily acte this Comedie," mendacious, that is, if we are expected to carry out the instructions given. There are in all twenty-one characters in the play, not a severe number for an average early seventeenth-century company, yet only seven of them (including, it is to be noted, the heroine) monopolise their representatives. Three players were expected to play four parts each, and one player two. My belief is that this was an arbitrary distribution made on behalf of strollers or amateurs, and not to be taken as indicative of the original method of presentation. At any rate, whatever decision is justifiable, the table is inoperative. In Act I, as in most first acts in most plays, there is no doubling. In Act II, scene 1, Scarlet comes on as Flower, and Bobbington re-

<hr />

[1] *The Review of English Studies*, i, 101.

turns as Berry only three short lines after his departure, to make two brief speeches before the close of the scene. Here the change is not only of an astonishing, almost incredible rapidity, but of a nature hardly permissible to any but the lowest class of incompetents. In Act III, scene 1, Bernard comes on as Boy, Berry as Richard Gardiner, and Scarlet as William Bennet; and alternation shows itself when Boy returns as Bernard. In Act IV, scene 1, Bennet reverts to Flower, and Bernard comes on as Mrs. Flower. In the next scene Flower appears as Ralph, and Gardiner as the First Sergeant. In Act V, scene 1, Ralph returns as Flower, and the First Sergeant as Berry—and then the table collapses! Bernard actually comes on while Mrs. Flower, one of his doubles, is on the stage, and, such is the force of bad example, the Sergeant is afterwards found confronting his stage *alter ego*, Berry. Not since the heyday of the moralities had so much alternation on the regular London stage been practised; and it is impossible to believe that any professional playwright would have written the play for performance in this clumsy way. According to the table, we even find that one of the four-part players was expected to accomplish the herculean feat of impersonating two elderly women, a man, and a boy. Surely he, and not the great Edward Alleyn, deserved Heywood's praises as

> . . . being a man
> Whom we may rank with (doing no wrong),
> Proteus for shapes.

Some years ago, when I first began to investigate this subject, I was inclined to believe that a good deal might be learned from the few early seventeenth-century printed plays which contain casts, but I have been bitterly disillusioned on that score. We have, all told, thirteen plays of this order, and the primary misfortune in connexion with them is that, with the exception of *The Duchess of Malfi*, which dates from 1613, all are of the Caroline period, the period when doubling was in its decline. Added to this, few afford sound evidence, even for their period. In most cases sundry trivial characters, together with the names of their exponents, have been omitted from the casts, a provoking circumstance, seeing that it was the trivial characters that were mostly doubled. In the conditions, a rigidly scientific examination is out of the question, but the possibilities are that little detail of moment has been lost to us. In Suckling's unacted tragedy, *The Sad One*, which was written before 1641, we get in Act IV, scene 4, a talk between a poet and two players, in which some equivoke is indulged in concerning doubling; and the impression to be gained from this is that, although yet followed to a mild extent, the time-honoured expedient was falling into decay. The truth of the matter is that a change had set in in Jacobean times. In the dying years of the sixteenth century no London company but would have cheerfully faced the task of presenting a play with the formidable number of thirty-two characters; yet in 1612 we find two companies temporarily uniting forces to act Heywood's *The Silver Age*, a play of exactly that number.[1] If this does indicate a growing distaste for excessive doubling, one despairs of ever being able to interpret historical omens.

Let us look, however, at the evidence afforded by the casts of these Caroline plays, imperfect and misleading as it may be. In Massinger's *The Roman Actor* fourteen players are shown taking sixteen characters, but curiously enough, though several hirelings played parts, the only doubling revealed fell to the lot of a sharer,

[1] Cf. *Modern Language Notes*, xxxiv (1919), 337, J. Q. Adams on "Shakespeare, Heywood and the Classics"; Chambers, *The Elizabethan Stage*, iii, 345.

T. Pollard, whose name stands opposite the characters of Aelius, Lamia, and Stephanos. This remarkable reversal of custom somewhat mystifies, but we have still another puzzle. Of the sixteen characters, four were sustained by boy players of women, though the adult players, sharers and hirelings, of the King's company certainly numbered more then than twelve. Since the full man-power had not been drawn upon, what was the necessity for resort to doubling? It was not as if anything was gained by economising in players: a sharer got his share even on days he did not act.[1]

Contrast with this the evidence — the much sounder evidence — of the prompt-book of *Believe as You List*, a King's Men's play of a couple of years later. Here we have no clue to any doubling by the sharers, though Pollard was in the cast, but we note that the non-sharers were kept very busy, Rowland Dowle and Richard Baxter playing three parts each, and W. Penn and William Patrick, two. One uses the term "parts" here in a very broad sense, since some of the doubling merely involved walking on, a duty that in later days would have fallen to the lot of a super.

Let us see, now, what sort of system, if any, was being followed at other theatres in the Caroline period. What we have been discussing applies to the Globe and Black-friars. Marmion's *Holland's Leaguer*, a Salisbury Court play of 1631, presents us with a cast of sixteen undoubled characters, but, as mention is made below of "two whores, panders, officers," the evidence is incomplete and there-

---

[1] Note Compass's speech (relative to his wife's bastard) in *A Cure for a Cuckold*, II, 3:

"Because I was out o' th' way, when 't was gotten, shall I lose my share? There's better law amongst the players yet, for a fellow shall have his share, though he do not play that day."

fore untrustworthy. For the Queen's Men at the Cockpit the evidence is abundant, but not wholly satisfying. Shirley's comedy, *The Wedding*, shows a cast of fourteen without any doubling, a blissful state of affairs from the old player's standpoint, almost too good to be true. But we must bear in mind that in one particular way Shirley was an innovative dramatist. Chase claims for the heroic play a reduction in the number of dramatis personae as a distinguishing characteristic, but one agrees with Schelling that Shirley pioneered the way. Other Caroline Cockpit plays by other authors are, I think, more revealing with regard to the Queen's Men's methods. Heywood's *The Fair Maid of the West*, Part I, has a cast accounting for eleven of the dramatis personae, but eighteen small parts remain undistributed, and many of these must have been doubled. Even in the tabulated list two characters (whose portrayal necessitated slight alternation) fell to the lot of Christopher Goad. In the first and second acts he played Forset, but in Act III, scene 1, came on as the Spanish Captain, only to return as Forset later in the act. Simple alternation such as this gave very little trouble. Finally we come to Nabbes's *Hannibal and Scipio*, a Cockpit play of two or three years later. In this, sixteen characters are distributed and seven not, the latter including Crates, Lucius, four ladies, and a messenger. Eight enjoyed a monopoly of their representatives, but, on the other hand, four of rhe specified players sustained two parts each.

Once Shirley began pioneering the way as economiser of characterisation and the vogue of the heroic play set in, doubling ceased to operate as a dramaturgic principle. But, purely as an histrionic expedient, despite some hibernation, it has survived to our own times.

IV

THE ELIZABETHAN STAGE JIG

FOR those who have failed fully to recognise how plastic and adaptable the English language remained in the late sixteenth century, there exists much puzzlement in the fact that the term "jig" had then three distinct meanings — that, though primarily applied to a hot and hasty dance or an equivalent dance tune, it also came to signify a short lyrical farce and a particular kind of street ballad. Yet by keen exercise of the historical sense one can arrive satisfactorily at the conclusion that the three meanings were closely interlinked. The thing was simply a matter of gradual telescopic extension, the second implication having been educed from the primary one, and the third from the second. Song and dance have always been closely associated, and if we assume, as seems highly probable on the strength of certain evidence,[1] that it was customary for the players in the theatres and inn-yards early in the last quarter of the sixteenth century to conclude the day's entertainment with

---

[1] In 1582 Stephen Gosson, in expatiating on the influence of the Devil in his *Playes Confuted in Five Actions*, gives him a trifle more than his due in saying:

"For the eye, besides the beauties of the houses and the stages, he sendeth in garish apparell, masques, vaulting, tumbling, dauncing of gigges, galiardes, moriscoes, hobby-horses, shewing of juggling castes, — nothing forgot, that might serve to set out the matter with pomp, or ravish the beholders with variety of pleasure."

It is obvious that not all these features were dramatic incidentals.

a lively dance, it is quite comprehensible that, through the initiative of some bright comedian, the dance developed into a brief lyrical farce retaining characteristics which revealed its source of origin. But the ways of art are not the ways of nature, and the primitive jig was no queen bee's aerial mate, to lose its life with its act of procreation. Long after our assumed secondary development we find evidence that these two, the dance and the farce, existed side by side. When Thomas Platter, the Swiss traveller, visited the Globe Theatre on September 21, 1599, and saw a performance of Shakespeare's *Julius Caesar*, he noted in his diary that "at the end of the comedy they danced according to their custom with extreme elegance. Two in men's clothes and two in women's gave this performance, in wonderful combination with each other." Afterwards he repaired to the Curtain, where, according to his note, "at the end they danced very elegantly both in English and in Irish fashion." With the limited time at the players' disposal, one can readily understand that it was not always possible to give a lyrical farce lasting for close on half an hour, after the play; and that on divers restricted occasions the spectators, recognising that half a loaf was better than no bread, remained content with a simple dance.

Of the early lyrical farce in action no vivid account has come down to us, but that it was fundamentally a thing of dance can be sensibly deduced from an opinion of Bacon's, expressed in his essay, "On Masques and Triumphs": "Acting in song, especially in dialogues, hath an extreme good grace; I say acting, not dancing (for that is a mean and vulgar thing)." He might have added, "and delighted in only by the Great Unwashed," for his stricture was certainly directed against the dramatic jig.

The transition from a simple dance to a song and dance with dramatic action could have been easily effected, for the way had long been paved. For half a century before the erection of the first London theatre most of the songs in the Court (and perhaps other) farces and moralities were set to dance tunes, and sung by the players while dancing. We get clear evidence of this in the interlude of *The Four Elements*, which belongs to the year 1520 or thereabouts.

But the suggestion for the dramatic jig could not have come from this source. If there were outer inspiration at all, it came from the May games of the folk. In the beginning, according to my concepts, the dramatic jig was a lyric farce for not more than two or three characters, written in rhyme, and sung and danced to a single popular tune. It was distinguished from all preceding farce by the fact that it was wholly devoid of spoken dialogue. Because of the lack of musical variety, this formula would have made for monotony, unless the jig were of an unsatisfying brevity, a defect which the comedians would soon cudgel their brains to amend. The solution was found in setting the jig to a series of well-diversified tunes, as well as in increasing the number of characters, so that a merry story of intrigue might be fully told. We have not very many old jigs to base upon, but assuming that it is safe to proceed upon the *ex pede Herculem* principle, it would appear that in the perfected system not more than four or five tunes were pressed into service in the one piece; and that a tune, once it was introduced and sung to by the various characters, held possession until some new development of the action took place.

Here we arrive at a new art form, virtually the genesis of English opera. One looks in vain for a Continental prototype. What was in essence the first Italian opera buffa, Orazio Vecchi's *L'Amfiparnaso*,[1] dates only from 1594, a year or two after the dramatic jig had been perfected. Apart from that, the two moulds had absolutely no resemblance. In its dependence on popular tunes, the jig was the precursor of eighteenth-century ballad opera, with this distinction, that whereas *The Beggar's Opera* and its class were hybridic in structure, mingling spoken dialogue with song, the jig was homogeneously lyrical.

When we recall that the immature dramatic jig was simply a rhymed dialogue sung by two or more persons to the one tune, it is easy to see how street ballads for two voices came to be known and printed as jigs. But I think it is going too far to assume, as Professor Hyder E. Rollins has assumed, that all songs issued as jigs had originally been sung on the stage, though no doubt a few of them, in a slightly different form, were so sung.

Where history remains silent and research fails it is rash to conjecture, but to my mind all the circumstances point to that notable innovator, Richard Tarlton, the primal clown, as the creator of the dramatic jig. In this he would not have been acting disinterestedly, since the Clown figured prominently in most jigs, and was almost as fixed a character as the Arlecchino of the old Italian comedy. Nor is the matter purely one of conjecture. In 1590, shortly after the great clown's death, a pamphlet was issued bearing the revealing title, "Tarlton's Newes out of Purgatorie, onely such a jest as his jigge, fit for Gentlemen to laugh at an houre." On the whole, there seems to be no more fitting person to saddle the honours upon than the approved writer of topical ballads, that mad and merry wight who was also the author of a highly praised composite play, now lost, *The Seven Deadly Sins*.

---

[1] For which see W. J. Henderson, *Some Forerunners of Italian Opera*, chap. 13.

Perhaps we are entitled to associate another famous name with the history of the jig, but the point is doubtful. The man who introduced Tamburlaine and his high-astounding terms to an appreciative public by making the Prologue say,

> From jigging veins of rhyming mother-wits,
> And such conceits as clownage keeps in pay,
> We'll lead you to the stately tent of war,

fails to strike one as a likely person to have written jigs. Yet, if an extant manuscript be genuine and properly ascribed, Marlowe must be reckoned among the writers of early lyric farce. Primarily, however, the manuscript is suspect because it was first discovered and printed by Payne Collier,[1] though it is only fair to say that he did not claim it as a jig. Bullen, too, in reproducing the piece in his edition of Marlowe, is equally mystified as to its nature, and safeguards himself in styling it a dialogue. But, whether or not the work of Marlowe, it certainly is a dramatic jig. It is to be noted that the Clown figures among the characters, and that the characters, six or seven in all, are more numerous than in the average jig of the maturer order.

Nashe and Chettle are the first pamphleteers to make reference to the dramatic jig. In *Pierce Penilesse*, in 1592, Nashe has a sonnet in which we find the similitude:

> . . . like the quaint comedians of our time,
> That when their play is done doe fall to ryme.

This recalls what Spenser had written a year earlier in "The Teares of the Muses." Thalia laments how

> All places they with follie have possest,
> And with vain toyes the vulgar entertaine.

---

[1] *The Alleyn Papers*, p. 8.

And again, a little later:

> Instead thereof scoffing scurrilitie
> And scornful Follie with Contempt is crept,
> Rolling in rhymes of shameless ribauldry,
> Without regard or due decorum kept.

In Chettle's *Kind Hartes Dreame*,[1] the rogues of the town are made to complain of the players:

> "Out upon them, they spoile our trade: they open our crosse-biting, our conny-catching, our traines, our traps, our gins, our snares, our subtilties; for no sooner have we a trick of deceit, but they make it common, singing gigs, and making jeasts of us, that every boy can point out our houses as they passe by."

The reference here is somewhat ambiguous, but one takes it that it was rather in farce than in ditty that the comedians exposed the tricksters of the times.

In 1592 also Nashe wrote *Summer's Last Will and Testament* for private performance by boys at Croydon, a delightful piece of fantasy wherein, after the delivery of the prologue, Will Summers the jester is made to say of the author, "Why, he hath made a Prologue longer than his play. I'll be sworne, the Jigge of Rowland's Godsonne is a Gyant in comparison to it." Earlier in the year, at the end of April, "a proper new ballett intitled Rowland's godsonne, in two parts" had been entered on the Stationers' Register. This was probably identical with the "ballett" of the same name printed in 1907 in *The Shirburn Ballads*,[2] and in that case must have been the jig referred to by Summers, seeing that the Shirburn ballad not only calls for a stage but at a certain juncture indicates a change of scene. At stanza 21 the action passes to an orchard, a transference doubtless effected in those days of a bare stage by opening the back

---

[1] Signature E, 3b.   [2] Page 354.

curtains. From more than one source we are able to glean that "The Jigge of Rowland's Godsonne" was a reversion to type, and that it was entirely sung to the one tune, a tune known as "Loth to Depart." Deriving inspiration from the *Decameron* or the French fabliaux, its story dealt with the laughable misfortunes of a much-wronged husband, whose faithless wife adds insult to injury by combining and confederating with their man-servant to dupe and beat him.

The subsequent history of this particular jig has a curious interest. It happened that at the period with which I am now dealing the supply of London players was far in excess of the requirements, with the result that the surplus betook themselves to the Continent. Strange to say, success largely crowned their efforts, so much so that for many years on and off there were flows of a like emigration. Possibly because melody and dance speak a universal tongue, nothing these hardy itinerants included in their repertory proved half so popular as their jigs. As time passed, sundry foreign authors came even to adapt these happy buffooneries to the nascent German stage, and, not content to figure simply as translators, were stirred to imitation. Hence the origin of the German *Singspiel*.

Sometime before 1605, in which year he died, Jacob Ayrer wrote a jig for five characters entitled "Der Münch im Kesskarb," which was arranged to be sung entirely to "the melody of the English Roland," otherwise the tune already referred to as "Loth to Depart." In this we have sufficient indication of the Continental vogue of "The Jigge of Rowland's Godsonne." We have reason to be thankful for this foreign liking for the old English lyric farce, seeing that it led to the preservation of certain jigs that would have been otherwise lost to us. In 1620 a collection of translated English plays of various kinds was published in Germany, including the text and music of no fewer than five jigs.

From 1591 to 1595 a considerable number of "jigs" was entered on the Stationers' Register, but unfortunately it is not always possible to determine whether a particular entry deals with a theatre jig or a simple ballad. Even the association of a comedian's name with a jig proves nothing, since both Tarlton and Kempe had trolled substantive songs in the playhouse, as well as clowned in musical farces. One can do no more than note, therefore, that in 1591 there were entries of "a newe Northerne Jigge"; of "the second parte of the gigge between Rowland and the Sexton" (not to be confused with "The Jigge of Rowland's Godsonne"); and of "the third and laste parte of Kempe's Jigge." In 1592 we get slightly firmer foothold. On January 16 there was entered to Thomas Creede, with Kempe's name written in the margin, "a plesant new jigge of the broomeman." It may be that this is identical with the song, "Buy a Broom," preserved in *The Shirburn Ballads*. A few weeks later, we read of "a pleasant jigge between a tincker and a Clowne," and on February 17 comes the entry, "A ballad of Cuttinge George and his hostis being a jigge," the phrasing of which indicates that a ballad that was likewise a jig was essentially a dialogue ballad. Nothing is known of "Master Kempe's New Jigge of the Kitchen Stuffe woman," which follows on May 2, and the same has to be said of "Phillips his gigg of the Slyppers," entered a little later in the month. Augustine Phillips, the player, to whom the latter has been attributed, was then, in all probability, a member of the Admiral's company. Personally, I am of the opinion that "The Jig of the Slippers" was a farce, not a ballad, and that some faint clues to its existence on the stage are to be found later. Since there had been occasional visits from Italian players from 1574 onwards, it is perhaps as well for us to note that one of the stereotyped stage tricks of the *commedia dell' arte* players was known to them as "the lazzo of the slipper."[1] But I fear that to pursue this clue would be to go off on a false scent. The inclusion of a character called Slipper in Greene's *Scottish Historie of James IV* — a play registered in 1594 — fortifies me in the belief that Phillips's jig had nothing to do with footwear. One's mind here recalls what Chettle wrote about the disposition of the comedians to expose cross-biting and conny-catching in their jigs. If we assume that Phillips's farce dealt with the machinations of a couple of rogues who got clear away after perpetrating some swindle, then "the slippers" could be interpreted to mean "those who gave the slip." In Middleton's *A Mad World, My Masters*, as acted at Paul's about 1606, there is a scene in the fifth act showing the arrival of Follywit and his roystering companions at Sir Bounteous Progress's mansion, in the guise of strolling players. It is arranged that they are to give a performance of a piece called *The Slip*, and under the pretence that the things are required for "properties" Follywit borrows certain articles of jewellery from his fatuous, unsuspecting host. However, just as the prologue to the piece has been delivered, the Village Constable comes on, bringing with him most of the mock players as prisoners. But the quickwittedness of Follywit saves the situation. By adroit extemporising he succeeds in making the credulous old knight believe that the representative of law and order is the clown of the company. In spite of his struggles and remonstrances, the Constable is bound hard and

[1] Winifred Smith, *The Commedia dell' Arte* (1912), pp. 13, 14.

fast to a chair, as if the action were part of the play, and then the sham players slink off, thus giving Sir Bounteous "the slip" in all literalness. It seems to me that the whole point of the scene lay in the circumstance that there was an actual, well-known farce called *The Slip*, and that Follywit and his companions parodied its amusing "business." In Field's *Amends for Ladies*, a play of the period of 1611, Lord Feesimple, when asked in the second act what he intends doing that afternoon, says, "Faith, I have a great mind to see Long Meg and the Ship at the Fortune." The reference here to two pieces shows undoubtedly that the second was a jig. *Long Meg* was evidently *Long Meg of Westminster*, a play recorded in Henslowe's Diary as having been performed at Newington on February 14, 1594, the year in which a ballad bearing the same title was entered on the Stationers' books. "Ship," to my mind, is a misprint of "Slip," and "The Slip" the accurate title of Phillips's jig. The implication would be that in 1594 Augustine Phillips was a member of the Admiral's company, and not yet Shakespeare's associate.

Doubtless some of the old jigs had a satiric topicality. In a catchpenny of 1595, entitled "A Quest of Enquirie by women to know whether the Tripewife were trimmed by Doll, yea or no," we read:

> Alas, were you so simple
> To suffer such a thing:
> Your own maids set and mock ye
> And everie where doth ring,
> The trimming of the Tripe wife:
> It makes me in a rage,
> And doubt least that the players
> Will sing it on the stage.

Two identifiable stage jigs, registered in 1595, remain to be dealt with. On October 14 was licensed "a pretie newe jigge betwene Ffrancis the gentleman, Richard the farmer and their wyves," eventually printed (as Professor Hyder E. Rollins's reproduction shows [1]) as "Mr. Attowels Jigge." A variant, derived from a manuscript in the Earl of Maccesfield's library — notable for preserving the music of the four tunes used — is given in *The Shirburn Ballads*.[2] Unfortunately, Mr. Andrew Clark, the editor of this collection, has been ill advised enough to divide the jig into acts, equivalent to breaking a butterfly on a wheel. We know that the George Attewell who wrote it was a player, but there is no clue indicating with what company he was associated in or about the period of its composition. Dealing with less than the usual scabrous farcicality with a story of sex interest, this jig was devised for four characters and in four episodes, each of which was given to a separate tune.

Once upon a time it was orthodoxy to deny to Dick Tarlton the authorship of anything and everything attributed to him — as if the penning of doggerel were a rare accomplishment. That attitude, I take leave to think, can no longer be maintained. By a parity of unreasoning, however, Professor Rollins would deprive Kempe and Attewell of the jigs associated with their names. When one comes to psycho-analyse these insensate *obiter dicta*, one finds that they are due to an innate prejudice bordering on contempt held from time immemorial by most intellectuals for the genus player, a prejudice which helped to give rise to the Baconian heresy and still continues to fortify the anti-Stratfordians in their opinion. In the case of Attewell, Professor Rollins should have been given pause by the fact that the broadside from which he reprinted Attewell's jig has his name at the bottom, the usual place in these sadly ephemeral sheets for the name of the author.

---

[1] *A Pepysian Garland*, pp. 1 ff.   [2] No. 61.

Of equal interest is that broadly humorous farce entered on the Stationers' Register on October 21, 1595, as "Kempe's newe jigge betwixt a souldier and a miser and Sym the clown." Borne to Germany by the travelling English comedians not long after its production, this jig happens to have been preserved in translation among the five published in the German collection of 1620. It proves to be identical with *Singing Simpkin*, one of Cox's drolls published by Kirkman in 1663, in the collection called *The Wits, or Sport upon Sport*. Robert Cox, it may be noted, was a ripe Commonwealth comedian, who, in the days of Puritanical ascendency, strolled about the country with a little troupe of three or four players, giving these drolls at fairs and wakes. In this way the vogue of the jig survived the silencing of the theatres.

Comprising some one hundred and eighty lines of lively doggerel, *Singing Simpkin* may be pithily described as a salacious operetta of intrigue, written to be sung to a variety of well-worn tunes by five characters, a miserly old man, his wanton young wife, and her two lovers, Simpkin the clown and Bluster the roarer, and a servant.

The later title of this long-popular jig yields us a clue to the interesting circumstance that the old lyric farce was not permitted to die when the king came to his own again. In somewhat hole-and-corner way, it held its place in the esteem of the masses to the end of the century. Recall how Dryden, in dealing in *Mac Flecknoe* in 1682 with the quality of the fare provided at that Barbican school for players known as "the Nursery," wrote:

> Great Fletcher never treads in buskins here
> Nor greater Jonson dares in socks appear;
> But gentle Simkin just reception finds
> Amidst this monument of vanished minds.

Even when we take into consideration that money in later Elizabethan days had seven or eight times its present purchasing power, jig writing cannot be said to have been a very remunerative occupation. Henslowe, in his Diary on December 12, 1597, records the payment of a poor six shillings and eight pence for "two gigs for Shaw and his company to 2 young men."

The jig, it must be recalled, was purely a public-theatre characteristic. It was not looked for, and would not have been tolerated by the fastidious audience of the private theatre. Because of this restriction, there is a similitude in the second act of *Every Man out of his Humour* which is apt to give a wrong impression to the modern reader. "Its a project, a designment of his own," says Carlo Buffone, "a thing studied and rehearst as ordinarily at his coming from hawking or hunting, as a jig after a play." Apart, too, from this objection, we have to reconcile Jonson's comparison with a second, made much about the same time, in *Jack Drum's Entertainment:* "As the jig is called for after the play is done, even so let Monsieur go."

I should be inclined to deduce from this that the jig, though fairly regularly given at most public theatres, was not particularised in the bill, the audience having adopted the practice of calling for whichever jig in the company's repertory they were in the mood to hear. At a much later period, the gods reserved to themselves the right to call for the playing of particular tunes in the intervals, evidently a relic of some old practice. One can imagine the tumult there would have been in an Elizabethan playhouse when a difference of opinion existed as to the jig to be performed. Dekker, who is much given to indulging in quaint theatrical similitudes in his tracts, has incidentally drawn the scene for us in his *A Strange Horse Race*, published in 1613:

Now, as after the cleare stream hath glided away in his own current, the bottom is muddy and troubled; and, as I have often seen after the finishing of some worthy tragedy or catastrophe in the open theatres, that the sceane, after the epilogue, hath been more black, about a nasty bawdy jigge, then the most horrid sceane in the play was; the stinkards speaking all things, yet no man understanding; a mutiny being amongst them, yet none in danger; no tumult, and yet no quietness; no mischiefe begotten, and yet mischiefs borne; the swiftness of such a torrent, the more it overwhelms, breeding the more pleasure; so after these worthies and conquerors had left the field, another race was ready to begin, at which, though the persons in it were nothing equal to the former, yet the shouts and noise at these was as great, if not greater.

In 1611 the Fortune players enjoyed a remarkable spell of good luck, owing to their having hit upon the happy idea of inducing a well-known itinerant vendor of garlic to appear on the stage in a jig written around his idiosyncrasies. This created such a rage that other jigs were devised for the further exploitation of his personality. References pointing to the popularity and the coarseness of these "Garlic" jigs are rife in the plays and pamphlets of the time. In 1612, at a moment when the rage had abated, Dekker, in his Red Bull play, *If it be not Good, the Devil is in it*, made Scumbroth babble:

No, no, if fortune favoured me I should be full; but fortune favours nobody but Garlick, nor garlick neither now, yet she hath strong reason to love it; for though Garlick made her smell abhominably in the nostrils of the gallants, yet she had smelt and stunk worse but for garlick.

Still more vituperative is a passage in J. H.'s *This World's Folly; or a Warning-Piece discharged upon the Wickedness thereof*, a pamphlet issued in 1615, but apparently written somewhat earlier:

I will not particularize those Blitea dramata (as Laberius tearmes another sort) those *Fortune-fatted* fooles and Time's Idoets, whose garbe is the Toothache of witte, the Plague-sore of Judgement, the Common-sewer of Obscoenitie, and the Traine-powder that dischargeth the roaring Meg [not *Mol*] [1] of all scurrile villainies upon the Cities face; who are fain to produce blinde Impudence [2] to personate himselfe upon their stage, behung with chaynes of garlicke, as an Antidote against their owne infectious breaths, lest it should kill their Oyster-crying Audience.

So many disturbances took place at the Fortune during the vogue of these Garlic jigs that the matter came under notice of the magistracy. The result was that on October 1, 1612, the General Session of the Peace of Westminster issued an order for the suppression of jigs at the end of plays at all the Middlesex theatres indifferently, under penalty of silencing and imprisonment. In justification of this it was stated that

. . . by reason of certayne lewde jigges, songes and daunces used and accustomed at the playhouse called the Fortune in Goulding lane divers cutt-purse and other lewd and ill-disposed persons in great multitudes doe resort thither at the end of everye play many tymes causing tumultes and outrages whereby His Majesties peace is often broke and much mischiefe like to ensue thereby.[3]

There was a custom in vogue at the Restoration of free admission to the play at the end of the fourth act, and one takes it, from the stern opposition attempts to abolish it encountered, that this odd privilege had originated long before the Civil War, perhaps quite half a century earlier. It would appear as if the extraordinary popularity of the garlic seller in his rôle of player had caused all the tag, rag, and bobtail of London to wend its way belatedly to the Fortune and gain admission on these

[1] "Long Meg of Westminster" was at once the name of a well-known cannon and of an old Fortune play. "Mol" was the notorious Moll Cutpurse, the heroine of *The Roaring Girl*.
[2] The word "Garlicke" is here inserted in the margin.
[3] Chambers, *The Elizabethan Stage*, iv, 340.

easy terms. The phrasing of the magistrates' order indicates that it was not so much the acting of jigs that gave offence as the particular circumstances under which they were regularly acted. All that the players had to do, then, to evade the consequences of the order, and to get rid of the pest of a host of undesirable eleemosynary play-goers, was to transfer the jig from the end of the performance to one of its intervals. This course was not altogether unprecedented: we know from *The Knight of the Burning Pestle* and other sources that dances had already been given between the acts at the private theatres; and it would seem that at once the course was taken. The new system would naturally be adopted by the English troupes subsequently visiting the Continent; and, as it happens, there is abundant proof that within a few years of the magisterial pronouncement the English players in Germany were habituated to the intermediate performance of jigs.[1] On that score it will suffice now to say that, in the collection of translated English plays published in Germany in 1620, it is notified, relative to the five jigs included, that they "may be acted at pleasure between the comedies."

It has been sensibly surmised by the late Thornton Shirley Graves, whose early death brought a grave loss to Elizabethan scholarship, that, after the promulgation of the Westminster magisterial order, the players not only gave jigs between the acts, but sought to make them an integrant of the higher drama.[2] Some support can be given to this hypothesis. Coincident with the order, and

[1] See Mauermann, *Die Bühnenanweisungen im deutschen Drama bis 1700*, p. 109; Bolte, *Die Singspiele der englischen Komödianten*, pp. 9, 13, 26; also the facsimile of the old Nuremburg playbill given in the article on "The World's Oldest Playbills," in *The Stage Year Book* for 1920.

[2] Article on "The Act-Time in Elizabethan Theatres" in *Studies in Philology* for July, 1915, p. 115.

deemed therefore by some misconceiving commentators to have reference to the old terminal jigs, came Ben Jonson's complaint in the preface to *The Alchemist*, that "the concupiscence of Jigges and Daunces so raigneth so as to runne away from Nature, and be afraid of her in the only point of art that tickles the spectators."

Chambers [1] points out that for "Jigges and Daunces" in some copies of the quarto we get "daunces and antikes," an alteration which, to my mind, shows that Jonson, on second thought, saw that his use of the term "jigs" was liable to misconception, the very thing, indeed, which has so belatedly occurred. That he was referring to the current mode of play writing, a mode introduced before the Fortune trouble, is demonstrated by his variant treatment of his theme in *Discoveries*, wherein, under the heading "Ingeniorum discrimina," he writes:

The true artificer will not run away from nature as he were afraid of her; or depart from life and the likeness of truth; but speak for the capacity of his hearers. And though his language differ from the vulgar somewhat, it shall not fly from all humanity, with the Tamerlanes and Tamer-Chams of the later age, which had nothing in them but the scenical strutting and furious vociferation, to warrant them to the ignorant gapers.

By "jigges and daunces," or "daunces and anticks," Jonson, then, was plainly referring to certain new features of dramatic technique, not to something exterior to the play. Only a few months later he returned to the assault, introducing into *Bartholomew Fair* a puppet show in ridicule of the new fashion; and, so that his aim might be straight, outlined his intention in the induction to his piece. We are told that the author

[1] Chambers, *The Elizabethan Stage*, ii, 552, note 7.

is loth to make nature afraid in his plays, like those that beget tales, tempests, and such like drolleries, to mix his head with other men's heels; let the concupiscence of jigs and dances reign as strong as it will amongst you; yet if the puppets please anybody, they shall be entreated to come in.

What Jonson was here girding at was the satyrs' dance in *The Winter's Tale*, the masque in *The Tempest*, and, in all probability, the interpolated Witch songs and dances in the revised *Macbeth*.[1] Sundry other spectacular excrescences of the period may be noted, such as the May-Day interlude in *The Two Noble Kinsmen*,[2] and the Madmen's dance in *The Duchess of Malfi*. What we require to note is that it was customary at a later date, even so late as the post-Restoration period, to refer to these interpolations as "jigs." Thus "W. B.," in his lines prefixed to Massinger's *The Bondman* in 1623, writes:

> Here are no gipsy jigs, no drumming stuff,
> Dances or other trumpery to delight,
> Or take, by common way, the common sight.

So too Davenant, in his prologue for the revival of *The Wits* in 1661, has:

> So country jigs and farces, mixt among
> Heroic scenes, make plays continue long.

Assuming that substantive jigs were given wholly between the acts for some considerable time after the promulgation of the Westminster order, one has some difficulty in determining how long the practice lasted, and exactly when a return was made (as it certainly was made) to first principles. In this connection, we have to

---

[1] See my article, "The Mystery of *Macbeth*," in *The Fortnightly Review* for November, 1920.

[2] Cf. article entitled "New Light on *The Two Noble Kinsmen*," in the *Times Literary Supplement* for July 14, 1921.

consider what I take to be a highly misleading passage from the fourth act of Shirley's *The Changes*, a Salisbury Court play of 1632. This runs:

> Oh, sir, what plays are taking now with these
> Pretty devices? Many gentlemen
> Are not, as in the days of understanding,
> Now satisfied without a jig, which since
> They cannot, with their honour, call for after
> The Play, they look to be serv'd up in the middle:
> Your dance is the best language of some comedies,
> And footing runs away with all.

Here the reference to the old practice of calling for jigs induces one, at the first glance, to think — and to think wrongly — that one has lighted on proof that independent jigs were still being given between the acts, and at such junctures only. But that impression is nullified by an item of evidence advanced by a pamphlet belonging to the same year as the play. In the section on "Actors" in his *London and the Country Carbonadoed*, Donald Lupton writes: "Most commonly when the play is done, you shall have a jig or a dance of all kinds; they mean to put their legs to it, as well as their tongues. They make men wonder when they have done, for they all clap their hands."

One is safe in assuming, therefore, that the species of intermediate jig referred to in *The Changes* was the introduced jig, a species for which there is an abundance of contemporary evidence. At this period more than one dance or one song and dance were frequently given in a play. For example, in *The Northern Lasse* a masque occurs in the second act, and a round dance in the third, with Widgine singing in the middle. Similar extrinsicalities are to be found in *Hyde Park*, *The New Academy*, *The City Madam*, and *The Ball*. Features of this order, it is to be noted, figure more frequently in private-theatre than in public-theatre plays — one reason why there was no diminishment of the vogue of the independent jig. That the independent jig was still being given at the public theatres in 1638, and, as it would seem, at the end of the play, is indicated in the induction provided in that year for the revival of *The Careless Shepherdess* [1] at Salisbury Court, wherein one of the characters is made to say:

> I will hasten to the money box
> And take my shilling out again . . .
> I'll go to th' Bull or Fortune, and there see
> A Play for twopence with a jig to boot.

Doubtless, new independent jigs still continued to be provided, even in Caroline days, but of such there is very little trace. Judging by his silence, Professor Rollins, in reprinting "The Cunning Age," [2] a dialogue song for three women, registered in 1629, has evidently no suspicion that it either is, or was derived from, a stage jig. The line, "But stay, who comes yonder? tis well yt I tarry'd," surely savours of theatrical performance. The author was one John Cart, of whom we know nothing, and, idle as it may be, I feel disposed to speculate whether this man was the "J. C." who wrote the play of *The Two Merry Milkmaids*, printed in 1620, and usually assigned without any particular reason to John Cumber, the actor, who is not known to have written anything.

In Commonwealth days puritanical repression prolonged the life of the jig. Acting was still pursued, though in a necessarily furtive way, but, what with the dismantling of the theatres and the disorganisation of companies, little solid fare could be given. Anything in the nature

---

[1] For the date, see article on "The Authorship of *The Careless Shepherdess*" in the *Times Literary Supplement* for July 24, 1924.
[2] *A Pepysian Garland*, p. 239.

of a play could be presented in town only under pretence of giving an exhibition of ropedancing, and even then, as it was economically impossible for more than half-a-dozen players to hold together, the best that could be afforded was an old jig or two or a few comic scenes from a well-worn play. It was in this way that Robert Cox, the comedian-manager, fighting for long against heavy odds, contrived to give occasional surreptitious performances in the Red Bull, and, when things got too hot for him there, at country wakes and fairs. Cox's curious repertory of drolls was afterwards published by Kirkman under the general title, *The Wits, or Sport upon Sport*. Besides slices from Shakespeare and other old dramatists, *The Wits* presented two Elizabethan jigs, "Singing Simpkin," already discussed, and "The Black Man," which, so far from dealing with the colour question, simply illustrates the actions of a vendor of black tinderboxes and such ware. "The Black Man" had evidently been acted on the Continent by itinerant English players early in the century, as a Dutch variant of it exists.[1] Apart from its importance as historical evidence, the variant is chiefly of value for revealing to us what otherwise we should not know, namely, the names of the tunes to which the various phases of the jig were sung. On collating its tunes with those traceable in other jigs, one gets the impression of musical sameness: old airs such as "Walsingham" and "Fortune my Foe" were used over and over again. Written for six players, "The Black Man," as preserved for us in *The Wits*, is slightly corrupt. It breaks the rules. Towards the end we find a few mouthfuls of spoken dialogue, the first gleams, as it were, of later ballad opera.

When we come to consider how new life was given to the old jigs by the repressiveness of the Interregnum, it is

[1] Bolte, p. 180.

not surprising to find new jigs being written early in the Restoration. One of these, "The Cheaters Cheated," was the work of Thomas Jordan, an old Caroline actor-dramatist, and was devised by him for private performance. It has been preserved for us in Jordan's poetic miscellany, *A Rosary of Rarities*, published, without date, in 1664. Jordan had formerly acted with Robert Cox, under the veiled name of "Thomas Jay," and in Cox's collection of drolls is to be found a little piece called *The Cheaters Cheated*, taken from an old play, and bearing no resemblance to Jordan's jig. The title of the latter reads, "The Cheaters Cheated, representation in four parts to be sung by Nim, Filcher, Wat and Moll, made for the Sheriffs of London," showing that it was evidently written for some civic entertainment. The jigs ends with a sort of epilogue entitled "A Song of the 12 companies." Nine tunes were used in the piece proper, but their names are not specified.

Though the old dramatic jig survived for long in the theatrical booths of Bartholomew Fair, it boots not to pursue its history further. But something remains to be said of its illegitimate offshoot. With the advent of the picture-stage a new musico-dramatic mould, the serious opera, had swum into the English playgoer's ken, but, attractive as the genre proved, the difficulties of exemplifying it regularly in the wholesale could not at first be surmounted, and for long nothing better than petty retailing could be effected. Hence a very inartistic prolongation of the old convention of the intercalated jig. Operatic features became popular in drama before opera itself had been firmly established or its canons fully recognised. This proved bad for the opera and equally bad for the drama. The normal post-Restoration play was disfigured by vocal and spectacular excrescences.

Hardly any production of the period was reckoned complete without its lugged-in masque or operatic scena. The appetite for scenic gewgaws grew by what it fed on. Dramatists salved their consciences by an open profession of faith — faith in the drama, artistically pure and undefiled — and then servilely bowed the knee to Baal. In 1671 we find Edward Howard, in the preface to his comedy, *The Woman's Conquest*, sneering at the "scenes, machines, habits, jigs and Dances" then so *à la mode*, and complaining that they had even invaded the realms of tragedy; but when we turn to his own play we encounter among its features a masque of Diana and a dance of Nereids. Then, indeed, were laid the foundations of an ill taste that have only just ceased to be built upon.

V

"HAMLET" AS SHAKESPEARE STAGED IT

SHAKESPEAREAN production, after having been for some two hundred and fifty years on the wrong track, is now slowly and painfully retracing its steps. Once it came clearly to be recognised how few points of contact exist between Elizabethan dramaturgy and the dramaturgy of to-day, that the *ars celare artem* so characteristic of Shakespeare was largely inspired by a stage devoid of scenery and a front curtain, this right-about-face was inevitable. Though scholars might reasonably argue without erring on the side of pedantry that the neo-Elizabethanism of the hour makes but a halting approach towards pristine theatrical conditions and is apt on occasion to over-accentuate trivialities, the gain has been considerable. Shakespeare has demonstrated his capacity to work his spells without mumbo jumbo; his potency appears none the less when unaided by the conventional bolstering of "those gilt-gauds men-children swarm to see." What remains now to be determined is how far producers would be justified in prosecuting their zealous pursuit of first principles. The great public is so little antiquarian-minded that stage archaeology, when carried to extremes, is apt to defeat its own ends. On the other hand, a science-ridden age cannot remain content with the exploitation of half-truths, and it may be that a day will come, probably with the erection of an English national theatre, a rallying place for the cultured people of the English-speaking world, when there will be anxious

seeking, not so much for the broad principles of Elizabethan performance — which, after all, are readily deter-
minable — as for the correct methods of staging certain
classic dramas according to the original concepts. Doubtless, what we shall be curious to learn in such cases is
precisely how the action was suited to the word, or, in
stage parlance, what particular "business" should ac-
company each and every incident.

That quest will be one of exceeding difficulty. Old
stage directions tell us but little: not only do they tan-
talise by their brevity, but they have a trick of conveying
the exact opposite to what is intended. Then again, an
element of grave uncertainty attaches itself to traditional
records, valuable as they may prove as clues, since the
traditions attached to an old play rarely go back to the
period of its origin. In the great majority of cases they
sprang up intermediately through the happy innovative-
ness of some later player. When all is said, however, the
roots of Shakespeare's dramaturgy were firmly embedded
in the theatrical conventions of his time, and to steep
oneself in these is to go a long way towards solving the
problems of production that his plays present. Armed
with this knowledge, and aided by tradition (which, however, must be used with all the skill and caution with
which one handles edged tools), we can make both *a priori*
and *a posteriori* attack on the difficulties, and, by carefully
noting where the antecedent and the posterior evidence
agree, arrive in a good many instances at a satisfactory
conclusion. Unfortunately, it is impossible in the brief
time at my disposal to consider minutely, scene after
scene, the entirety of any of the greater Shakespearean
plays. In directing my batteries now on *Hamlet*, I have
no intention of attempting to sweep over the entire field.
I shall simply strive to elucidate some of the most diffi-

cult situations in the play, principally the scenes in which the Ghost appears (note that I said appears), and to clear up the mystery surrounding the "Look here upon this picture and on this" speech, which has for so long obscured from view the true correlative stage business. This, I hope, will prove a useful object lesson and convey the methods which should be pursued in all quests of a similar order.

Latterday playgoers are so accustomed to seeing the Ghost of Hamlet's father walk on and off the stage like a being of flesh and blood (that is, when they do see it: producers nowadays are inclined to deny us in whole or part its visible presence), they are so accustomed to seeing the Ghost use ordinary methods of locomotion, that they will be considerably surprised to learn that now and again in the original presentation of the tragedy the Ghost appeared and disappeared through a trap. It is true that no inkling of this can be found in the old stage directions, yet nevertheless it can be readily established. So usual, indeed, was the employment of trapwork for the coming and going of ghosts and devils in the plays in vogue immediately before and immediately after *Hamlet* that the surprise would be to find that trapwork was not resorted to in the great tragedy. On a double count we have a right to predicate some bowing to convention, not only because of the force of custom but from the circumstance that Shakespeare based on an earlier play and cannot be considered to have had entirely a free hand. Evidence of the use of trapwork in ghost scenes late in the sixteenth century and early in the seventeenth cannot be said to be abundant, but it is at any rate sufficient. As far back as 1587 or thereabouts the Shade of Calchas in Greene's *Alphonsus, King of Arragon*, came up from below and sank whence it came. So, too, in Peele's *King Edward the*

First, as performed a few years later, the Shade of Queen Elinor rose slowly through a trap, much to the consternation of the Potter's Wife, whose comment on the apparition happens to be remarkably informative. There can be little doubt that stage effects of this order were hugely delighted in by the mob and could have been omitted by the players only at their peril. Assuredly the Elizabethan ghost which refused to rise or sink would have been shorn of more than half its thrills. Of all the dramatists of the time Jonson was the least disposed to truckle to the many-headed beast, yet even he dared not innovate in the matter of spectral habitude. In his *Catiline*, as produced at Shakespeare's Globe in 1611, the Ghost of Sylla rises to speak the prologue and sinks after having fulfilled its mission.

Immediately on proceeding to investigate the staging of *Hamlet* one finds need to make microscopic examination of the circumstances in which the Ghost makes its first appearance, since the remarkable and not to say incongruous disposition of the sentinels has so frequently been altered by latterday producers. We are forced to begin by asking ourselves, why, in a scene representing the bleak battlements of a Danish fortress, was Shakespeare considerate enough to supply stools, not only for the watch but for everybody who might chance to come that way? It is only when we seek unremittingly for an answer to that question that we see that a strategic purpose was served by the provision of those stools. Let us visualise the situation. Bernardo asks Horatio to "sit down a while" till he relates again the story about which Horatio is so sceptical, and the two, together with Marcellus, group themselves on stools with their faces turned towards the front of the stage, or, in other words, towards the bulk of the audience. In this way they cannot per-

ceive the three entrance ways which are situated behind
them, yet, on the clock striking one, the narrative is
dramatically interrupted by the appearance of the Ghost.
It is obvious that there was absolutely no other way by
which the Ghost could suddenly make itself visible to
the three save by emerging in front of them through a
trap. Since resort here to the use of stools was at best but
a clumsy expedient and would have proved much clumsier
had the Ghost come on at the back, we are compelled to
conclude that the seated attitude was adopted so as to
concentrate attention on the spectre. The sciolist might
possibly object that the Folio merely says, "Enter the
Ghost," and gives no hint of trapwork; but scholars will
not need to be reminded that "enter" in the old stage
directions is often used with a perplexing ambiguity and
often means exactly the opposite to what it conveys. Not
infrequently it connotes a simple discovery, as in *George
a Greene*, where we have "Enter a Shoomaker sitting
upon the stage at worke, Jenkin to him," a bull excelled
only by the "Enter three Taylors on a shop-board" of
The Rebellion. Much more apposite, however, to our
present purpose is the misleading direction, "Enter the
Devill," to be found near the close of the anonymous
Rose comedy, *A Knacke to Know a Knave*, produced by
Strange's Men in 1592, a direction which might be taken
to mean what it says, were it not for the fact that the text
clearly conveys that Asmoroth, the devil in question,
emerges from a trap.

When challenged by Horatio, the Ghost "stalks away,"
evidently disappearing through the curtains at the back,
or through one of the entering doors. With its departure
the triad resume their seats and proceed to speculate
upon the portent. The second appearance of the Ghost
must have been made precisely in the same way as the

first — through the same trap, since Horatio and the watch have resumed their old position. Once more the three spring to their feet, and Horatio indulges in an ad-juration to which the Ghost seems about to respond, but just then the cock crows, and the spectre is compelled to slink away. We know from a direction in the First Quarto that originally the cock was actually heard crowing, and we also know from certain later theatrical records that this quaint cue for the Ghost's departure was religiously given in all subsequent revivals of the tragedy up to the close of the eighteenth century. More specific reference to these records will be made later, but the diuturnity of this practice requires to be emphasised now as proof of the evidential value of stage tradition in connection with this particular play and, possibly, the Shakespearean drama generally.

I take leave to think that, from the producer's stand-point, no greater puzzle is presented anywhere in the entire Shakespeare canon than the difficulty of determin-ing what was the exact "business" arranged for the situation developing out of Horatio's command, "Stop it, Marcellus." There have been few attempts at a solu-tion, and none has half the feasibility of the one neatly formulated by Louis Calvert in his book entitled *An Actor's Hamlet*. This I unhesitatingly adopt, since there can be no doubt that here a double for the Ghost was adroitly provided.[1] My reading would be that just as the Ghost disappeared at one of the two widely separated entering doors, Bernardo cried, "'Tis here," only to be astonished on hearing Horatio echo him as the spectre's

---

[1] Gifford finds an analogous scene in *The Virgin Martir*, V, 1, where analogy there is none. The only true parallel is in *The Witch of Edmonton*, V, 2, the scene of Frank's bedchamber, where the Ghost of Susan undoubt-edly appeared in duplicate.

double immediately came forth from the other door. Marcellus' ensuing ejaculation, "'Tis gone," read by the light of his later comment, "It *faded* on the crowing of the cock," indicates not only the moment of the double's disappearance, but the manner. One recalls the vision seen in *Cymbeline:* how Jupiter bids the kneeling ghosts "rise and fade," and how they "vanish." It may, I think, be safely assumed that when Marcellus said, "'Tis gone" the Ghost took a step forward and flung itself down the suddenly yawning grave trap, a trap not previously pressed into the service of the play but of whose existence we have evidence in the graveyard scene. Nothing that is subsequently to be found in the text seriously controverts this interpretation, not even Horatio's

> the morning cock crew loud,
> And at the sound it shrunk in haste away
> And vanish'd from our sight.

Obviously, if the exponent of the Ghost — traditionally said to have been Shakespeare himself — had been arrayed cap-a-pie in real armour, considerable danger would have attended the jump, a constant risk of bruises and broken bones. But there is good reason to believe that real armour was not employed. Curiously enough, the "business" just postulated by way of solution is not without its actual precedent. More than thirty years before *Hamlet* was produced, there was seen in Gascoigne and Kinwelmershe's Gray's Inn tragedy of *Jocasta* a dumb show in which Curtius fulfilled his destiny by leaping full-armed into the gulf. Even on the public stage at the end of the sixteenth century this method of disappearing was occasionally practised. Scholars will recall how, in Peele's *The Old Wives Tale*, the Ghost of Jack makes its final exit by jumping down a trap. If the play be, as often said, frank burlesque, it would be interesting to learn what this incident travestied.

Imitation armour was employed for stage purposes long before Shakespeare's day. It was probably made of silvered leather. In the accounts for the Court entertainments of 1574–75 one finds a payment to John Carow, a property maker, for supplying a great variety of requisites, including monsters, weapons of war, and counterfeit armour. As to the nature of the old imitation armour, we have but a single slender clue. In discussing the odd figure cut by a panoplied ghost in his *Fontainville Forest* at Covent Garden in 1794, Boaden, in his *Life of John Kemble*,[1] tells us that a leathern pilch had been "time out of mind the player's armour" and that it was once more worn by the ghost in his own melodrama. The scholarly mind will instinctively revert to the induction to *A Warning for Faire Women*, wherein sarcastic reference is made to

> a filthie whining ghost,
> Lapt in some fowle sheet or a leather pilch,

possibly a gird in part at the pre-Shakespearean *Hamlet*.

In the fourth scene of the great tragedy the Ghost doubtless rose through the stage again when Horatio interrupted with,

> Look, my lord, it comes,

though the stage direction, as before, points only to a normal entry. When the spectre lured Hamlet to a retired spot the two departed through one of the doors, and, after the scene had been finished by the others, returned by the other door. On the Elizabethan stage this procedure always indicated a change of locality. To con-

[1] Vol. ii, pp. 117–119.

vey the change it was necessary that the characters which finished the one scene should not commence the other.

Two forces have operated against the survival of the original "business" in those of Shakespeare's plays which have continuously held the stage. Some rearrangement necessarily took place at the Restoration, since action adapted for a platform-stage having all the entrances at the back was not always suitable for a stage encumbered with scenery. Much more destructive, however, to traditional observance was the nineteenth-century rage for fresh interpretations, the desire for novelty often overwhelming common sense. In whatever manner it was extirpated, the disappearance from the fourth scene of *Hamlet* of an essential bit of primordial "business" has created obscurity. The latterday spectator, who sees the Ghost stalk off after he has taken a sad and solemn farewell of his son, is mightily puzzled to know why he should speak immediately afterwards from beneath the stage. That bedevilment was not experienced by the Elizabethan spectator, since to him it was no surprise to hear the Ghost speak from the region to which he had seen him depart. There are variant readings of the last line in the Ghost's abortive leave-taking, but it would appear that originally the line ran:

Adieu, adieu, adieu! remember me;

that it was uttered while standing on a trap, and that with each *adieu* the spectre sank a little, and disappeared rapidly on saying, "Remember me." No doubt this was a matter of mere stage effect, but even to-day the disappearance of the Ghost is essential in order to make Hamlet's references to "this fellow in the cellarage" and "old mole" comprehensible. (Their grating flippancy, by the way, strikes the first note of the young prince's simulated

madness.) As for the sinking by degrees, it was a favourite piece of theatrical trick-and-shuffleboard in Shakespeare's day, and, as an incident in the fifth act of Dryden
and Lee's *Oedipus* betokens, held the stage to a considerably later period. Two early examples, the first synchro-
nising with the production of *Hamlet*, may be cited. In
the induction to Ben Jonson's *Poetaster* Envy, after
spitting out venom for a considerable period, begins sinking on the spot whence he rose, and when his chin
reaches stage level the Prologue enters and places his
foot on his head. So, too, in the last act of *The Virgin
Martir* we find Harpax first sinking a little and then disappearing. The inference is that stage mechanism in
Shakespeare's day was much more advanced than even
the ripest of scholars suspect.

When we come to the Closet scene, the only other
scene in which the Ghost appears, the main problem
which confronts us is the problem of the pictures. But
first of all it is requisite to note that in the spurious First
Quarto we get an inkling of a bit of stage business to
which there is absolutely no clue in either the Second
Quarto or the Folio. When the Queen echoes Hamlet on
his entrance by asking him, "How is 't with you?" the
Prince replies, "Ill tell you, but first weele make all safe,"
an intimation that shows he proceeded to lock the doors.
So resolute an act would obviously arouse suspicion in
the minds of the Queen and the eavesdropping Polonius,
and, viewed from the spectators' standpoint, it lends the
necessary plausibility to their subsequent alarm. It also
explains why Polonius contents himself by calling out,
"Help!" from his hiding-place, instead of tottering to the
door and summoning the guard. He really had not far to
run, and, with ready egress, that would have been the
natural course. Moreover, if Hamlet really locked the

doors — and I fail to see why any theatrical pretence should have been made in days when the stage doors were so often realistically locked — then his reference to the Ghost's disappearance "out at the portal" must receive a new interpretation, and be taken to apply to the large curtained opening, since the Ghost, having a human representative, would be denied any other method of departure.

I turn now to the more vital question of the two portraits. What precisely was their nature, and where were they placed? Some forty-odd years ago Sir Henry Irving lit upon a solution eminently satisfying to the exclusively modern intelligence when he made *his* Hamlet see the two portraits imaginatively on the invisible fourth wall of the stage. That admirably served the purpose of the hour, but Irving flagrantly overstepped the mark when he went so far as to maintain, in a paper in *The Nineteenth Century*,[1] that he had really done nothing more than restore Shakespeare's own method. Having no proscenium arch, the Elizabethan stage had no invisible fourth wall; besides which it was wholly uncustomary for the Elizabethan players to leave to the imagination anything that could be visibly presented. Nor can it be conceded that the use of miniatures — the expedient most frequently resorted to by nineteenth-century tragedians — solves the problem in a sound, archaeological way. Common sense rebels. Of a surety, Shakespeare had no mere miniature in his mind's eye when he wrote of

> A station like the herald Mercury,
> New-lighted on a heaven-kissing hill;
> A combination and a form indeed,
> Where every god did seem to set his seal
> To give the world assurance of a man.

---

[1] "An Actor's Notes on Shakespeare," in the issue of February, 1879.

As it happens, however, there is no need for us to flounder about helplessly in a quagmire of conjecture: two distinct clues, distinct yet harmonising, exist to the original method. One is to be found in *Fratricide Punished* (to give the play the title under which it was recently acted at Oxford), that curious old German version of *Hamlet*,[1] modernised, it is true, but made early in the eighteenth century from an earlier German play which had evidently been based partly on the pre-Shakespearean *Hamlet* and partly on the spurious First Quarto. One observes, for example, that Polonius figures in it as Corambus. In the counterpart to the Closet scene in this German version Hamlet says to the Queen:

> But look, in that gallery hangs the counterfeit resemblance of your first husband, and there hangs the counterfeit of your present husband. What think ye now, which hath more dignity and presence? Does not the first bear him with magnificent grace?

Uttered, as it was, on the eighteenth-century stage, this might be taken at a pinch to substantiate Irving's hypothesis regarding the invisible fourth wall, were it not that the other clue spoken of advances evidence demonstrating that the portraits, so far from being, as it were, subjective, were exhibited to the audience. In Rowe's *Shakespeare*, published in 1709, are to be found a number of remarkably curious illustrations, some of scenes in the plays which still held ground in the standard repertory and some of scenes in plays long shelved; but all showing the various characters in the contemporary eighteenth-century costume. Arguing from this peculiarity, that very distinguished theatrical antiquary, the late Robert W. Lowe, once maintained very sensibly that the illustrations of the Shakespeare plays which still

---

[1] The text and an English translation are given in A. Cohn's *Shakespeare in Germany in the Sixteenth and Seventeenth Centuries.*

held the stage were trustworthy records of the contemporary methods of performance.[1] If this be true of any, it is most likely to have strict application to so popular a play as *Hamlet*. Let us consider the cut of the Closet scene as given in Rowe. The two portraits, evidently half-length, life-size oil paintings, are shown hanging at the back, over the head of the seated Queen. The moment chosen is just at the entrance of the Ghost. There is no reason to doubt that such had been the disposition of the portraits ever since the Restoration, but there are good reasons for doubting that this had been precisely the original method. An important adjunct, which made for theatrical effectiveness in the acting of the scene, is missing.

In private life in Elizabethan days it was customary to provide oil paintings with a ringed curtain running on a rail, to protect them from dust, glass being then too expensive to use as a covering; and in most cases where oil paintings were used on the stage (probably as a mere matter of realism) the same practice was followed. Now and again we find Shakespeare making neat, metaphorical allusion to this shrouding of pictures. "Wherefore are these things hid? Wherefore have these gifts a curtain before 'em?" asks Sir Toby Belch. "Are they like to take dust, like Mistress Mall's picture?" So, too, Olivia, when about to unveil herself in response to Viola's request in a later scene, says: "Have you any commission from your lord to negotiate with my face? You are now out of your text; but we will draw the curtain and show you the picture." [2] Moreover, the same metaphor, similarly applied,

[1] See his illustrated article, "How the Old Actors dressed 'Shakspere' — II" in *The Illustrated London News* for February 18, 1893.

[2] The same metaphor is used in *Westward Ho*, II, 3, where Sir Gosling, addressing the three masked women, says: "So, draw those curtains and let's see the pictures under 'em."

THE CLOSET SCENE IN "HAMLET"

From Rowe's *Shakespeare*, 1709

is to be found in *Troilus and Cressida*, III, 2. It is curious that this image should have obsessed the great poet for a brief period only, the period of *Hamlet*.

Evidence exists to show the adroit use made on the stage of curtained pictures, not only in the days of Shakespeare's creative activity but for a considerable number of years afterwards. To cite the most apposite example, Webster has a scene in *The White Devil* wherein a vision is conjured up by a magician. A long stage direction begins with, "Enter suspiciously Julio and Christophero: they draw a curtain where Brachiano's picture is"; then they don "spectacles of glass," a sort of primitive gasmask, and burn chemicals, and oil the lips of the portrait with some deadly compound. On their departure, Isabella, being about to retire to bed, comes in with her attendants, prays before the picture, draws the curtain, kisses the portrait thrice, and is immediately poisoned. At a later period an analogous situation to that in the Closet scene in *Hamlet* is to be found in the opening act of William Heminge's Caroline tragedy, *The Fatal Contract*, where, as a direction indicates, the Queen draws a curtain and shows to the Eunuch a composite picture representing the murder of her brother.

There is no need, I think, to labour the point that curtained pictures were employed in *Hamlet*, but one question demands reply. Why did the tortured young prince begin his speech with "Look *here* upon *this* picture and on *this*," instead of saying simply, "Glance your eye over these two portraits"? Answer this and you solve the problem. On first thought one is inclined to jump to the conclusion that the portraits were placed far apart, but this impression is dissipated by maturer reflection. One is given pause not only by Hamlet's emphatic *here*, but by the subsequent

Here is your husband; like a mildew'd ear
Blasting his wholesome brother.

Clearly the two portraits were situated side by side at the back, and Hamlet was standing close beside them as he spoke. On the left was the picture of the dead king, on the right the picture of his brother, and both were curtained. "Look here, upon *this* picture," said Hamlet sternly, as he drew aside the curtain veiling his father's portrait, and then—jerking the other curtain away as his tones deepened suddenly into contempt — "and on *this*." It is plain to be seen that the whole was an effective bit of theatricality concentrating attention precisely where it was required.

One other deviation from the original method of staging the Closet scene is indicated in Rowe's illustration. In it we see the Ghost, not "in his habit as he lived," as the text demands, — a habit interpreted in an important, and, no doubt, accurate stage direction in the First Quarto as "a night-gown," — but, absurdly enough, armed cap-a-pie, as at the opening of the play. We must not delude ourselves into the belief that the Ghost came on in the Elizabethan equivalent for pyjamas, or what was then known as a "night-rail." The early seventeenth-century nightgown was merely a sort of dressing gown. It was generally made of silk or satin and faced with fur. This explains why Piero, when he visited the church at the dead of night in the third act of *Antonio's Revenge*, wore a nightgown and nightcap. The garb really symbolised the lateness of the hour.

Accordingly, in *Hamlet* the term *habit*, inaccurate so far as armour is concerned, was congruous. It was only when in the field that the old king could have lived in armour. Yet even to-day, just as in Rowe's time, when the elder Hamlet's Ghost is seen on the stage in the Closet

scene he still appears in panoply. One says *when he is
seen* advisedly, because there is a tendency among latterday producers to leave the Ghost here to our imagination, owing to the fact that the Queen's ignorance of its
presence has given rise to the impression that it is purely
subjective, an idle conjuration of Hamlet's distempered
mind. In the text as it stands we are afforded no clue as
to the reason why the shade of the dead king refrained
from making itself visible to its former consort, but in the
old German version of the play a reason, wheresoever derived, is very appropriately advanced in a rebuke. When
the Queen says that she sees nothing, Hamlet replies:
"Well, I believe you do see nothing, for you are no
longer worthy to look upon his form, out upon you, I
can no longer hold converse with you."

I take it that originally in this scene the Ghost emerged
through a trap and stood stock-still until Hamlet said,
"Look, how it steals away!" This was requisite in order
to convey at once to the audience knowledge of the
Ghost's identity, since its identity would be somewhat
obscured by its unexpected change of attire.[1] Nor can
there be any doubt that the Ghost's final departure was
made on foot; Hamlet speaks of it as going "out at the
portal." It is noteworthy, however, that the evidence of
tradition runs to the contrary. One is inclined to think
that some considerable deviation from the old routine
occurred in this particular scene at the Restoration,
doubtless for some good reason, though the reason is hard
to divine. It was not because of any serious alteration
of the text, since, of all the plays of Shakespeare which

[1] Probably the Ghost, following the precedent set by its prototype in
the pre-Shakespearean *Hamlet*, wore a white vizard; and this, combined with
the method of its appearance, would prevent any misconception on the part
of the audience.

contrived to maintain their pride of place on the stage, *Hamlet* was the last to suffer sophistication.[1] Bating some omissions, the tragedy was played much as it had been written until Garrick flung his atrocious variant at an unoffending public in 1772.

On the eighteenth-century stage we find relics of the pristine trapwork in the play, but the evidence is not a little puzzling, since the relics are not wholly what we should be inclined to expect. Apart from that, however, there would appear to be significance in the fact that all stage ghosts of the first part of that century, not excepting those who delivered prologues or figured in new plays, invariably made their appearance from below. The inference would be that the vogue of *Hamlet* had established a convention from which the players were afraid to depart. Not even the girdings of Lloyd[2] could induce them to alter their ways, and in *Hamlet* itself we find ghostly trapwork persisting up to the third decade of the last century.

On the score of the earlier procedure, Fielding affords us some notable evidence. In that neat precursor of *The Critic*, his dramatic satire of *Pasquin*, a Haymarket Theatre attraction of 1736, one finds in the rehearsal of Fustian's tragedy in the fourth act a delicious travesty of the cock-crowing incident in *Hamlet*, a travesty which would serve to show that at least one of the old traditions was being sturdily maintained, were we not already aware that the crowing remained a concomitant of the tragedy for at least another forty years. The Ghost of Tragedy rises to deliver a message to Common Sense, but before

[1] Cf. Allardyce Nicoll on "The Editors of Shakespeare from First Folio to Malone" in *Studies in the First Folio* (by members of the Shakespeare Association), pp. 168–170.

[2] In his poem entitled "The Actor," which created considerable stir.

it has proceeded far it suffers infinite annoyance through the inopportune crowing of a cock, and descends precipitately with the remark:

> But ha! the cursed cock has warn'd me hence;
> I did set out too late, and therefore must
> Leave all my business to some other time.

The delight taken in this quaint episode by patrons of the Haymarket was at once commemorated in a cartoon dedicated to Fielding and entitled, "The Queen of Common Sense," in which a cock is shown crowing lustily at an armoured ghost half-sunk beneath the stage, while Shakespeare stands by looking complacently at the contretemps.[1]

Elsewhere, in the famous chapter on "Partridge at the Play" in *Tom Jones* (Book XVI, chapter 5), Fielding has embalmed for us a few of the other characteristics of the contemporary *Hamlet*. It may be that we are not entitled to take seriously this humorous exposition of Partridge's naïvety, to view it as scientific evidence regarding the method in which the tragedy was presented at old Drury, but it is certainly remarkable that the only allusion to the use of trapwork in the play is Partridge's ejaculation in the middle of the Closet scene, "Bless me! what's become of the spirit? As I am a living soul, I thought I saw him sink into the earth." One is half inclined to believe that in making the Ghost descend at the one particular juncture when the text expressly forbids it, and at that juncture only, Fielding has contorted the truth for his own particular ends. If the earlier descents had been abandoned, it is amazing that they should have recurred at a considerably later period. Boaden, in discussing

[1] For reproductions see George Paston, *Social Caricature in the Eighteenth Century*, p. 40, and Godden's *Life of Henry Fielding*, p. 70.

Kemble's début as Hamlet at Drury Lane in 1783, tells us that at the close of this interview with the Ghost he fell to his knees as the Ghost descended, an innovation which the sticklers for conventionality resented, but which Henderson thought so sensible that he immediately adopted it.[1]

On the other hand, there is a possibility that Fielding, in *Tom Jones*, simply ignored the earlier descents of the Ghost for the purposes of his narrative, and that, moreover, he was strictly accurate in representing it as disappearing through a trap in the Closet scene. We have much later evidence of an equally amusing order relative to the use of trapwork in this particular scene. In Poole's *Hamlet Travestie*, as performed at Covent Garden in 1813, we find Hamlet and the Ghost and the Queen engaging in a trio. Gertrude asks her son, "On what art thou looking? To whom art thou talking?" and Hamlet sings in reply:

> Whom 'tis I look at, fain you'd be knowing;
> Straight through the trapdoor now he's going,

on which the Ghost sinks. But Poole's burlesque was written and published a few years before its production, and already there were indications that the employment of trapwork, not only in this particular scene but in the tragedy generally, was falling into desuetude. John Finlay, in reviewing Edmund Kean's performance of Hamlet at Dublin in 1814, takes exception to certain features of the Closet scene:

At the exit of the ghost he slapped the door in Hamlet's face. This, though very usual, is very absurd. Shakespeare regulated his fancy, even in his flights, by a certain degree of propriety which

---

[1] *Memoirs of John Philip Kemble*, i, 98.

never would permit him to give directions to any of his ghosts *to shut the door after them*.[1]

One finds what is here animadverted upon fully elucidated in the account of Kean's Hamlet written by Tieck after seeing the tragedian in London in 1817. After expressing his profound contempt for the exponent of the Ghost, the great German critic proceeds to find fault with the Ghost's conduct:

> Worst of all is its appearance in the Queen Mother's chamber, when the Ghost with great complacency enters by one door, totters across the stage, and, not looking particularly either at Hamlet or the Queen, goes off through the opposite door, which closes behind him, while Hamlet, inaptly enough, hurries after him, and is only kept back by the door slamming in his face. At this passage it is difficult not to laugh. Quite lately a friend of mine in the pit could not contain himself when Kemble played the part in the same way and with the same absurd effect; but the English, who, although they do not believe in ghosts, do not like to have them laughed at, took his conduct much amiss.[2]

What needs further to be grasped is that there was in those days a proscenium entering door on either side of the fore-stage projecting beyond the curtain line, and that the Ghost entered by one of these doors, walked straight across, and departed by the other. Hamlet and the Queen were stationed farther back in the scene proper.

Tieck is in more than one way illuminative. The principle of the descending ghost had been reduced to absurdity by its frequent exposition in innumerable melodramas, and it was precisely because the English did not relish Shakespeare's ghosts being laughed at that the old traditions had had to walk the board.

---

[1] John Finlay, *Miscellanies* (Dublin, 1835), p. 229.
[2] See Sir Theodore Martin on "An Eye-Witness of John Kemble," *The Nineteenth Century* (February, 1880), pp. 293, 294.

VI

THE ELIZABETHAN NOCTURNAL

I TAKE leave to think that there is a good deal more topical allusiveness in *Hamlet*, especially in regard to theatrical matters, than has hitherto been suspected.[1] Shakespeare was writing for his immediate audience, and not worrying about posterity, when he made the young prince tell Polonius that the players were "the abstract and brief chronicles of the time," and that he had "better have a bad epitaph than their ill report" while he lived. It was only at a period when the stage was dealing in gross personalities that such a definition and such a reflection upon it could have had any pertinency. So, too, I am inclined to believe that there is lurking satire in Polonius's extraordinary outpouring of play classifications, so pretendedly scientific and exhaustive in its array of unwonted compounds, and withal so curiously incomplete. Following the perplexity which arises from the enumeration of categories not commonly recognised[2] comes a further mystery due to the absence from the list, of two technicalities then current in theatrical circles and familiarly used in synchronous plays.

[1] See my elucidation of "the humorous man shall end his part in peace," in the article on "The Date of *Hamlet*" in the *Times Literary Supplement*, April 15, 1926.

[2] Echoes of Polonius's phraseology occur in Day's *The Isle of Guls* (1606). In Act III, scene 1, Manasses says, "You shall have some Poet (Apollöes vicar especially) write you a comicall Pastorall Tragicall Musical historie in prose will make the auditors eyes runne a water like so many water spouts." Again, in Act IV, scene 2, we find Philanax inquiring, "Hath he no fellow actors in his most lamentable comicall, historicall, tragicall, musicall pastorall?" Both examples out-Herod Herod in adding the word "musicall."

In the induction to Marston's *What You Will*, a comedy
which remained unprinted until 1606, though deemed by
most scholars to have been acted by the Paul's Boys in
1601, we find Doricus inquiring whether the piece about
to be presented was "a comedy, tragedy, pastoral, moral,
nocturnal, or a history." Here is afforded a more sensible list than the garrulous old chamberlain's, and a list,
moreover, which includes a certain type of play that he
ignores, and upon whose significance Elizabethan scholars are unanimously silent. As it happens, the only way
to solve the problem, to arrive at the nature of a nocturnal, is to seek out instances of the contemporary use
of the word. They are not abundant. One is to be found
in a mysterious anonymous play called *Histriomastix, or
The Player Whipt*, first published in 1610, but evidently
dating from before 1599, since allusion is made to it in
Every Man out of his Humour.[1] Unfortunately this silly
satire bears signs of revision, and we have consequently
no means of determining when any particular part of it
was written. But it is to be noted that in its second act
there is a scene in which the Usher asks the strollers for
a list of their plays, and is told by Post-Haste, their
spokesman, that they are ready to act "*Mother Gurton's
Needle* (a tragedy); *The Divel and Dives* (a comedie); *A
Russet Coat and a Knaves Cap* (an infernall); *The Widow's
Apron-Strings* (a nocturnal)." As at least one of these
plays, the primitive comedy of *Gammer Gurton's Needle*,
was a real play, and another, even if not wholly identifiable with *The Dialogue of Dives* mentioned by Greene in
1590,[2] is self-classifying, there is a sort of Dogberryan

[1] Act III, scene 1.

[2] Fleay, *The Shakespeare Manual*, p. 292, identifies *The Divel and Dives*
with *The Dialogue of Dives*, mentioned by Greene in *Never Too Late* (1590)
and again, two years later, in *Greene's Groat's-worth of Wit*, but a *Dives and
Lazarus* is also referred to in the play, *Sir Thomas More*.

humour in the list, inasmuch as Post-Haste justifies his name by indulging in a patent misapplication of terms. *The Divel and Dives* must assuredly have been an infernal, and not a comedy, for it needs no ghost from the grave to tell us that an infernal was a play in which devils figured.[1] Though no other instance of the use of this technicality is traceable, I feel assured that it was a common tiring-house term, and not a mere coinage of the moment; and my reason for this assurance is that derivatives from it were in vogue. In Marston's *The Wonder of Women, or Sophonisba*, IV, 1, we get the direction, "Infernall musicke playes softly, whilst Erictha enters, and, when she speakes, ceaseth." This instruction is otherwise noteworthy because it indicates that certain strains of music were conventionally associated with the appearance of evil spirits, thus forming a sort of crude *leit-motiv*.

As Elizabethan investigator, I have often deemed it providential that Dekker, as pamphleteer, delighted so much in theatrical metaphor, but never more so than now, since one of his tropes in *The Seven Deadly Sinnes of London*, which appeared in 1606, not only indicates that the nocturnal was still in vogue but enables me to arrive at its characteristics. Presenting Candlelight as a personification in his section entitled "Candle-light, or the Nocturnal Tryumph," he says of him:

No sooner was he advanced up into the moste famous streetes, but a number of shops for joy beganne to shut in: mercers rolled up their silkes and velvets; the goldsmithes drew backe their plate, and all the Citty lookt like a private Play-house, when the windows are clapt downe, as if some *Nocturnall*, or dismall *Tragedy* were presently to be acted before all the Tradesmen.

---

[1] For some account of "infernals" (without use of the term) see Herford and Simpson's *Ben Jonson*, ii, 153–158.

In the original quarto two words in this passage are italicised, indicating, what their capitalisation also indicates, that both words were substantives. Basing, however, on a misquotation of Malone's, scholars persist in reading "nocturnal" in an adjectival sense, as if the reference were simply to a nocturnal tragedy, thus checking all progress towards a comprehension of the writer's meaning.[1] And just here I may pause for a moment to say that, three years later, Dekker indulges in another allusion to nocturnals — this time a somewhat cryptic punning allusion — in a passage dealing with the players' recent sufferings through plague, in his tract entitled *Worke for Armorours, or the Peace is Broken*.[2] This, however, I must refrain from discussing, lest I get entangled in a side issue.

Apart from scholastic misinterpretation of Dekker's use of the word "nocturnal" in *The Seven Deadly Sinnes of London*, there is another phrase in the same passage which generally proves a stumbling-block to all those who have not put back the clock and transferred themselves imaginatively to Elizabethan times. It is not too much to say that hardly any term in common use in Shakespeare's day is more liable to be miscomprehended than the term "private playhouse." The average reader generally takes it to mean a theatre for amateurs where admission is by invitation only, the latterday acceptation; but one needs to stress the fact that this was a type of house utterly unknown in Dekker's time. At that period there were two kinds of London theatres, usually distinguished as the public and the private. Broadly speaking,

---

[1] Malone (*Variorum Shakespeare*, iii, 61) has "nocturnal *and* dismal tragedy," and Creizenach (*English Drama in the Age of Shakespeare*, p. 366, note), in citing from him, gives renewed life to the blunder.

[2] Grosart's *Dekker*, iv, 96.

the one was a summer, and the other a winter, resort. The public theatre (sometimes referred to also as the "common" or "open") was a large, open-roofed building, where acting took place in the afternoon and by natural light. The private theatre was small and covered in, and although its auditorium was almost wholly sunlit the regions of the stage were provided with lamps and candles. But perhaps what we most require to bear in mind is that the smaller houses were equally public with the larger, the only difference being that the private theatre, in levying higher rates of admission, secured a superior type of audience.

Dekker's quaint simile does not imply that nocturnals were given in the private theatres only: that, as I hope to show, is against the facts. What it does imply with regard to them is that it was in them alone that the windows were clapped down for the better performance of nocturnals. But, as we must pick our steps warily so as to avoid the risk of constantly tripping over familiar terms unfamiliarly employed, we are forced to pause and ask ourselves what Dekker really meant by the clapping down of windows. Exercise of the purely modern intelligence would here wholly obscure the issue. In Elizabethan days the word "window" had a much wider significance than it has to-day, and was more loosely employed. Sometimes it was used to imply an opening, and sometimes a shutter. Marlowe uses it in the latter sense in *1 Tamburlaine*, V, 1, where Bajazeth, before killing himself, says:

> O highest lamp of ever-living Jove,
> Accursed day! infected with my griefs,
> Hide now thy stained face in endless night,
> And shut the windows of the lightsome heavens!

Shakespeare employs the word in both senses, but more commonly in the sense of shutter. He was thinking of orifices when he wrote, in *King Richard III*, I, 2, 12, "these windows that let forth thy life," and of shutters when he made the Fourth Plebeian cry, in *Julius Caesar*, III, 2, 276, "plucke downe Formes, Windowes, anything." He has a trick (one which has proved highly puzzling on occasion to the commentators) of making metaphoric reference to the eyelids as the windows of the eye, as in *Romeo and Juliet*, where we find Friar Laurence saying:

> . . . thy eyes' windows fall
> Like death when he shuts up the day of life.

To recognise this propensity of his is to read the riddle set by Iachimo's beautiful lines in *Cymbeline*, II, 2:

> The flame o' th' taper
> Bows toward her, and would underpeep her lids,
> To see th' enclosed lights, now canopied
> Under these windowes, white and azure-lac'd
> With blue of Heavens own tint.

The windows, white and azure-laced, were the blue-veined eyelids of the sleeping woman, an equivalent of the "two blue windows" of *Venus and Adonis*, line 482. Here the poem and the play are mutually complementary, and both are elucidated by Keats's

> And still she slept an azure-lidded sleep.

The kind of shutter we have to picture in order to grasp what Marlowe, Shakespeare, and Dekker were driving at is the solid wooden shutter with which the old London shopkeeper was accustomed to close up his stall. The source of the Shakespearean metaphor becomes apparent when we turn to Ford's *The Fancies Chaste and*

Noble, V, 2, and note what Secco, the barber, says to Spadone before proceeding to operate upon him:

Wink fast with both your eyes; the ingredients to the composition of this ball are most odorous camphire, pure soap of Venice, oil of sweet almonds, with the spirit of alum; they will search and smart shrewdly, if you keep not the shop-windows of your head close.

It was a window of this order, you will recall, that the Prentice let down in *Arden of Feversham*, and by so doing broke Black Will's head. There are some things that can never be determined, and I do not pretend to know what was precisely the nature of the shutters fitted up in the private theatres for darkening purposes. But I *do* know that elsewhere they could have been of no utility: to darken the windows in a large, unroofed summer theatre would hardly have caused any serious diminution of the light. I am by no means ignorant of the fact that it has been suggested more than once that these open houses were specially equipped with a movable canvas awning for darkening purposes.[1] But this I can only characterise as mere miserable guesswork: not a tittle of evidence has been advanced in support of it. The Elizabethan public theatre undoubtedly laboured under one of the disadvantages of the ancient Greek theatre, in having to present on occasion a night or stormy scene under a serene blue sky. But where realism could not be attained, symbolism came into play. It did not remain for modern psychology to demonstrate the powers of suggestion: the Elizabethan players were past masters of that science. In night scenes they had a dual method of attack, by textual insinuation and by the bringing on of lights. Textual reference not only comprised reflective poetic descriptions of nightfall, — of which, by the way, a

[1] Henry Thew Stephenson, *The Study of Shakespeare*, p. 187; Sir Arthur Quiller-Couch, *Shakespeare's Workmanship*, p. 45.

remarkable anthology could be compiled,[1] — but repeated allusion to the prevailing darkness. Assuredly, a convention of this order would have been utterly superfluous if the light could have been appreciably diminished in the public theatre. That fine Shakespearean scholar, Sir Walter Raleigh, showed his thorough grasp of Elizabethan methods when, in analysing the conspiracy scene in *Julius Caesar*, he wrote: "The whole scene is heavy with the sense of night and the darkness of conspiracy, yet the effect is produced by nothing but the spoken words and the gestures of the players."[2]

In substantiation of this, it remains to be noted that Shakespeare conjures up the darkness imaginatively, without bringing on a single light. Nothing is done to mar the illusion of the scene. Brutus even reveals how it chances that he is enabled to read the letter in the dark:

> The exhalations whizzing in the air
> Give so much light that I may read by them.

In a few old plays the stage directions make reference to this imaginary darkness. In Part II, Act II, of *The Iron*

[1] See *Arden of Feversham*, III, 2; *A Knack to Know an Honest Man* (Malone Society reprint), line 1000; *A Knacke to Know a Knave*, passage cited by Collier, *Annals* (1831), iii, 31; *The Insatiate Countess*, III, 1; *The Two Angry Women of Abington*, IV; *How a Man may Choose a Good Wife from a Bad*, IV, 1 (Dodsley's division); *The Dumb Knight*, II, 2, Philocles' soliloquy; *The Valiant Welshman*, V, 1.

For iterated references to the darkness throughout a scene, see *Antony and Cleopatra*, IV, 9; *Henry V*, III, 7 (four references); *Romeo and Juliet*, II, 1, balcony scene (over seven); *The Merchant of Venice*, V; *Measure for Measure*, IV, 2 (five); *The Two Angry Women of Abington* (nocturnal, Mermaid edition), III (seven), IV (sixteen), V (eleven). In *Macbeth*, II, 1, note the grim humour of Banquo's

> There's husbandry in Heaven,
> Their candles are all out.

[2] Raleigh, *Shakespeare*, pp. 121, 122.

Age, we find, "Pyrrhus, Diomed and the rest, leape from out the Horse, and, as if groping in the darke, meete with Agamemnon and the rest." So, too, in Brome's *A Mad Couple Well Match'd*, IV, 4, the opening direction reads, "Phebe passes over the stage in night attire, Carelesse follows her as in the darke." Remark also what the Prologue begs of the audience in introducing Peter Fabell in *The Merry Devil of Edmonton*:

> Suppose the silent, sable-visag'd night
> Casts her black curtaine over all the world.

Though, as we have seen, the private theatres had a method of procuring darkness by clapping down the auditorium shutters, it was too elaborate a process to be resorted to for momentary effects, the main reason why we find the private-theatre dramatist so often adopting the public-theatre principle, and indulging in poetic descriptions of nightfall and iterative references to the prevailing darkness. But it is noteworthy that the public theatre, though lacking these shutters, could, on occasion, obscure the action, though not for any length of time. This was done by emitting a volume of smoke through a stage trap, an effective enough expedient, but one which was apt to prove offensive to the audience if prolonged. Finding a direction in the opening scene of *Cataline* stating that "a darkness comes over the place," and believing that effects of sudden darkness were wholly unattainable in the public theatre, Creizenach [1] thinks that the play was exclusively a Blackfriars play. But he overlooks the likelihood of resort to this smoke effect, an effect seldom, if ever, attempted in a small, enclosed theatre. There is a textual reference to the coming of "sudden shade" just before the thunder and lightning

---

[1] Creizenach, *English Drama in the Age of Shakespeare*, p. 366.

in Chapman's *Caesar and Pompey*, II, 4, but, in the absence of an accompanying stage direction, and owing to the circumstance that the play is not known to have been acted, nothing can be deduced from it. A trifle more definite is the evidence presented by Kirke's *The Seven Champions of Christendome*, a play published in 1638, as "acted at the Cockpit and at the Red Bull in St. John Street with a generall liking." In the third act of this showy piece there is a scene of enchantment, with manifestations of thunder and lightning but no note of darkening. After a fight between demons who wield fiery clubs, a wand is waved, and we get the direction, "The day cleares, enchantments cease; sweet musicke." Here the effect does not seem to have been an effect of smoke but one of shuttering, and the question immediately arises, how was this managed at a public theatre like the Red Bull? The answer will be found, I think, in my article entitled "New Light on the Elizabethan Theatre" in *The Fortnightly Review* for May, 1916. Reasons are shown there for believing that sometime before 1630 the Red Bull and the Fortune had been roofed, thus making architectural approximation to the characteristics of the private theatres. Uniformity was now being aimed at, and with this approximation would doubtless come some adoption of private-theatre methods.

The Atheist's Tragedie of Cyril Tourneur was published in 1611, "as in diuers places it hath often been Acted," but unfortunately we have no clue to the whereabouts of any of these divers places. In the second act are several scenes of continuous darkness, and at the opening of the act we get the curious direction: "Musicke. A banquet. In the night."[1] This is undoubtedly a prompter's

[1] In Carliell's Caroline play, *The Deserving Favourite*, II, 2, we have, at the beginning, "Enter Clarinda and Lysander (as in an Arbour) in the night." But, although this was a Blackfriars play, and the house might possibly

memorandum, since the music is not heard until the ninth speech, when it is called for. If the play were distinctively a private-theatre play, I should take "in the night" as a warning to clap down the windows, but it may mean nothing more than "place torches on the stage." After the banquet three drunken servants enter, and one of them refers to the lights, suggesting that they be extinguished while they carouse in the dark. In scene 4, a night scene in the open, adroit constructiveness is evinced in the fight between the two light-bearing servants, since, in the absence of anything better, they use their torches as weapons and naturally extinguish them in the struggle, thus accidentally leaving Montferrers helpless in the dark and an easy prey to the assassins. But Tourneur was by no means singular in his knowledge of the art of extracting dramatic effect out of skilful manipulation of lights. Webster, Ford, and Massinger were equally gifted in that way.

This has been a long digression, but I make no apology for it, because the details are essential if we hope to deduce from Dekker's simile the main characteristics of the nocturnal. Assuming that the clapping down of the private-theatre windows was too elaborate a process to be undertaken for the procurement of a momentary illusion, more particularly as the principle involved double work, we are debarred at the outset from reckoning as nocturnals a very considerable number of pre-Restoration plays which present an occasional night scene, or several disjointed scenes of the sort. This nar-

have been darkened, stress is laid, in the opening speeches, on the prevailing obscurity.

Cf. Mahelot's inventory relative to the properties, etc., required for the staging of du Ryer's *Lisande et Caliste* at the Hotel de Bourgogne in 1636. The list of desiderata ends with, "*Il faut aussy une nuict.*" (H. C. Lancaster, *Le Mémoire de Mahelot, Laurent*, etc., pp. 67, 68.)

rows the issue very materially. Labour can also be legitimately minimised by confining our investigation for the time being to plays belonging to the last two decades of Elizabeth's reign. Next I make bold to discard all tragedies from the list, since Dekker, in speaking of "dismall Tragedy" in the same breath in which he speaks of nocturnals, clearly shows that tragedy, while admitting on occasion of being staged after the manner of nocturnals, was not of their nature. A careful examination of the residue for night scenes of prominence, together with a minute noting of points of resemblance in such scenes, where they were to be found, leads me to the conclusion that the nocturnal was a species of comedy, either rustic or urban, presenting an unbroken sequence of more or less complicated night scenes, and monopolising (where act divisions can be determined) at least one entire act of the play. At a pinch, that would possibly answer for a working definition, but it is likewise my opinion that the nocturnal element was generally infused about midway — say, rather towards the end than at the beginning; and, furthermore, that the humorous embroilment of the piece was almost wholly due to a variety of blunders committed in the dark. If more needs to be said, it is that implicit in the scheme was the understanding that the audience was from first to last to be in the secret, a tacit agreement which obviated the necessity for any deep realisation of the gloom of night.

As I shall have occasion more than once in these studies to point out, certain important facts relative to the productiveness of the last decade of the sixteenth century have been blandly ignored by all our theatrical historians. It was a period of remarkable dramatic innovation, yet on that score we have been told little: so little, indeed, that the circumstances which brought about a constant, if one-sided, seeking after novelty have escaped us. Personally, I am inclined to believe that this fructification was due to a hitherto unsuspected rivalry between the Admiral's Men and the Chamberlain's Men, a rivalry which grew keen about 1594, at a time when each of the two companies was settled at its own theatre, on opposite sides of the Thames. Viewing both purely as creative organisations, it would seem that the Admiral's Men were the more enterprising and fertile-minded, since they gave employment to a far greater number of dramatists. It was not the policy of the Chamberlain's Men to provide ideas for others; rather was it their policy to await the coming of new ideas and give them fuller and more artistic exploitation. They had Shakespeare at their beck, and Shakespeare was a consummate betterer.

To this tense rivalry between the two companies we owe the abundance of Welsh characterisation which marks the drama of the last decade of the sixteenth century and the first lustrum of the seventeenth.[1] Out of it sprang one of the immortals — Fluellen. Then the Admiral's Men invented the complex-disguise play, that type of theatre piece in which one of the chief characters assumes a variety of disguises in the course of the action, thus providing the machinery of the plot; and at their hands it received capital exemplification in Chapman's *The Blind Beggar of Alexandria* and the anonymous *Look About You*. For once Shakespeare failed to respond; he believed in employing disguise in moderation, not in dealing in it in the wholesale. For him the mould was too artificial. But the Chamberlain's Men were not wholly defeated; Ben Jonson saved the situation by providing them with *Every Man in his Humour*.

[1] See my article on "Welsh Portraiture in Elizabethan Drama" in the *Times Literary Supplement* for November 9, 1922.

I feel assured that it is to this rivalry, this lopsided seeking after novelty, that we owe the upspringing of the nocturnal, and that, as usual, the Admiral's Men were the innovators. Unfortunately, many of their early plays are lost, and it would be idle, I fear, in the circumstances, to attempt the identification of the first nocturnal. Two Rose Theatre comedies of the type have come down to us, Haughton's *Englishmen For My Money; or a Woman will Have her Will*, and Porter's *The Two Angry Women of Abington*, but even the former and earlier came too belatedly to be taken as the archetype. I shall have occasion soon to speak at length of an antecedent nocturnal produced by the Chamberlain's Men. Meantime, I may say that William Haughton's urban comedy, *Englishmen For My Money*, was originally brought out at the Rose under its sub-title in the spring of 1598, but, though registered in 1601, apparently was not printed until 1616. It is undivided, but it is curiously significant that in Dr. Albert Croll Baugh's recension of the play (published at Philadelphia in 1917, at a time when no one had made any attempt to determine the nature of the nocturnal), the night scenes monopolise the whole of the third and fourth acts. *The Two Angry Women of Abington* was issued in 1599, as "lately playde" by the Admiral's Men, and must have seen the light very soon after Haughton's play. This amusing rustic comedy is also undivided, but it is interesting to note that in Mr. Havelock Ellis's recension of its text [1] the nocturnal characteristics begin to develop with the opening of the third act and last until the end of the play, a considerably longer period than that devoted to them in its predecessor.

The manifold difficulties of play dating unfortunately

[1] In the volume of *Nero and Other Plays* in the Mermaid Series.

preclude any attempt at outlining the rise and progress of the nocturnal. Thus, though there are sound reasons for believing that *The Merry Devil of Edmonton* was distinctly of the order, we cannot do more than approximate the period of its production. This long-popular play was published in 1608, "as it hath beene sundry times Acted, by his Maiesties Seruants, at the Globe, on the bankeside." It had then been at least five years in existence, as there is a reference to it in *The Black Book* of "T.M.," published in 1604.[1] Fleay, basing on a guess of Coxeter's, assigned it to Michael Drayton, and believed it was brought out at the Curtain by the Chamberlain's Men in 1597.[2] More recent judgement sees the good right hands of Dekker and Heywood in the play. The text is not only undivided but hopelessly corrupt, circumstances which render analysis difficult; but, according to the divisions in latterday reprints, the whole of the fourth act was devoted to the nocturnal element.

I have hinted already of the existence of a Chamberlain's Men's nocturnal which preceded any known nocturnal belonging to the Admiral's Men. Will it surprise you to learn that Shakespeare wrote it, and that it is known to us as *A Midsummer Night's Dream?* It is as well for us to recall in this connexion what Schelling so well says about the master's prime quality as a working dramatist. He rightly attributes to him "the seizure on a variety of drama already tried in the popular taste, with a glorification of it by the strength of his genius to a position above its class."[3]

Because of this principle and this capacity, unless we can assume that for once Shakespeare grew boldly in-

[1] A. H. Bullen, *Middleton's Works*, viii, 36.
[2] Fleay, *Biographical Chronicle of the English Drama*, ii, 313.
[3] F. E. Schelling, *Elizabethan Drama*, ii, 21.

novative, the *Dream* must rank as the sublimation of cruder elements collocated by an inferior mind. That it was designed initially as a nocturnal, notwithstanding the fundamentally disharmonic nature of its parts and the intricacies of its opening movement, becomes assured once one has made a time-and-locality analysis of the whole. One sees then that not only the entire second act, but the entire third act and a fragment of the opening scene of the fourth act, — or, reckoning by lines, something more than half the play, — pass in the enchanted wood by night. The response to the acid test afforded by my formula for the nocturnal is immediate and convincing. It is not too much to say that, amidst all the motley elements surging in the poet's brain when the play was in process of incubation, the nocturnal motif must have been paramount. The wood scenes are all dark scenes, and the action in the wood brings into close association the unrelated threefold action of the opening. To prevent his night scenes from falling into the common rut, as well as adequately to motivate the crisscross action in the wood, the poet was compelled, not to tap the resources of that invisible world of which Spenser had the freedom, but to create that freakish, non-moral, ever-beckoning world of fairydom. Such is the measure of our indebtedness to that fleeting, forgotten thing, the nocturnal. But this alone is not the sole differentiation of the *Dream* as a play of its particular class. In sublimating the nocturnal it incidentally pokes fun at it. We must not overlook the play within the play. The "tedious brief scene of young Pyramus, and his love Thisbe; very tragical mirth" is not only a burlesque but a burlesque nocturnal. Shakespeare showed in the same breath how to do it and how not.

The routine opinion about the *Dream* is that it was

written in honour of, and for performance at, some noble
wedding about the year 1595. This, to my mind, is contemptible guesswork. Masques were much more apt to
be given at weddings in those days than plays, and there
is absolutely no trace of the writing of a play for special
performance at a wedding before 1614, in which year
Daniel's *Hymen's Triumph*, never afterwards acted
publicly, was given at Denmark House in honour of Lord
Roxborough's nuptials. For this reason I have no belief
in the conjectured origin of the play; and for another I
am not inclined to date it any earlier than 1597. The
vogue of the nocturnal began about that year, certainly
not before it, and the *Dream* was the nocturnal *in excelsis*.
Time does not permit me to go fully into the matter now,
but for a preliminary statement of my views on the subject I may refer you to the study entitled, "A Plummet
for Bottom's Dream," published in *The Fortnightly Review* for May, 1922. Something, however, requires to be
added to that study in substantiation of the opinions expressed. There can be little doubt that the *Dream*, as we
now have it, is not in its original state. I am in hearty
agreement with that ripe scholar, Mr. E. H. C. Oliphant,
when he says of it:

> There are many signs of the play having undergone revision and
> abbreviation. If in its present form it be of as early date as some of
> the critics have supposed, Shakespeare's style must have been formed
> early.[1]

My belief, as outlined in the *Fortnightly* article just
referred to, is that the play was written for ordinary
theatrical performance late in 1597, and that it was
subsequently abbreviated and altered for performance
before the Queen at the Russell mansion in Blackfriars

[1] *The Modern Language Review*, iv, 347.

on June 16, 1600, the day of Anne Russell's marriage. According to this theory, the version of the play then given was the version shortly afterwards published. Something more, something of importance, requires now to be said in support of this view.

Shakespeare was not the man to indulge in superfluities. When we find two speeches expatiating on the one theme, cheek by jowl in the same play (as we find, for example, in *Love's Labour's Lost*), we may suspect rewriting, and not only rewriting but reprinting from an ill-arranged manuscript, in which discarded passages were somehow allowed to remain uncancelled. So far, so good; but in the *Dream* there is a remarkable superfluity that cannot thuswise be explained away. When one comes to think of it, the conjuring up of the fog in Act III, scene 2, in no way furthers the action and is not demanded by the exigencies of the plot. Dowden once characterised the play as "a comedy of errors — the errors of a night," and thereby made apt definition of the genus nocturnal. The fact that the action passes in the wood at night in itself establishes all the necessary obscurity. Puck's misapplication of the flower love-in-idleness accounts for all the rest. Nothing is gained by the supernatural raising of the fog. Moreover, popular superstition attributed that prerogative to witches, not to fairies, and Shakespeare followed popular superstition in that respect in *Macbeth*. My own belief is that originally the fog had no place in the scheme of the play, and that it was interpolated for wholly extrinsic purposes when the play was revised for performance at the Herbert–Russell wedding in 1600. At that period there was a device of censing, known as "a mist of delicate perfumes," much employed for refreshing the atmosphere of crowded assemblies. Exactly when it became customary to make it part of the play at court and at other distinguished private performances I cannot say; but use of it in this way can be traced at Whitehall early in 1606, in Ben Jonson's *The Barriers*.[1] Note that in the *Dream* the fog is raised precisely in the middle of the play, a juncture when a sweetening of the atmosphere would be best appreciated.

One difficulty in the hunt for nocturnals is to determine how long the taste for this particular kind of play proved procreative. There are reasonable grounds for suspecting that one or two nocturnals held their place on the stage for some years after nocturnals had ceased to be written. We know, for example, from a reference of Jonson's in the first "intermean" of *The Staple of News*, that *The Merry Devil of Edmonton* was still enjoying a large measure of popularity in 1625. On the whole, I think we are safest in seeking our quarry a few years before, and a few years after, the dawn of the seventeenth century. Nor is there any reason why we should restrict ourselves to an examination of public-theatre plays. After Marston's hint in the induction to *What You Will*, it is by no means surprising to find that the principle of the nocturnal had exemplification in the private theatre, notwithstanding that it had proved the "dear delight" of the masses. My first trace of it in the private theatre is in 1601, when Middleton's *Blurt, Master Constable, or The Spaniard's Night-Walke* was acted by the Paul's Boys. I think that, if you examine the fourth act of this piece, you will conclude that I am justified in placing it among nocturnals. It was probably the success of this venture which encour-

---

[1] *Jonson's Masques and Entertainments* (Carisbrooke Library Series, edited by Henry Morley, 1890), p. 81. The practice was long continued. An old shepherd enters with a censer and perfumes at the beginning of *Pan's Anniversary* (Great Hall, Whitehall, January 17, 1620). Note also the direction in *Love's Triumph Through Callipolis* (Whitehall, 1631): "Here the Chorus walk about with their censers."

aged Middleton to write another play of the same type for the same boys, the result being *The Phoenix*, produced about 1603. Remark that in both pieces the nocturnal element is confined to the fourth act.

So far we have pretty sure foothold, but unless we can make up our minds that there was some loosening of the bonds, some departure from the old formula, — a thing not at all unlikely, — it is sheer waste of time to search for later private-theatre examples. Because of hesitation on this point, I find myself halting between two opinions about Marston's *The Dutch Courtezan*, a Blackfriars play of 1602 or 1603. In this the nocturnal element is not continuous. Two of the acts, the first and the fourth, pass in the night, but it is only in the latter that a dark scene occurs, and it is doubtful whether, on the strength of this, we should be warranted in placing it on the list. And the further we proceed along the years, the greater the difficulties that arise. When one reads in Greg's *Pastoral Poetry and Pastoral Drama*,[1] at the close of his fine analysis of *The Faithful Shepherdess*, that "what we have witnessed was no more than the comedy of errors of a midsummer night," one's mind suddenly reverts to Dowden's epigrammatic description of the *Dream*, and one cries involuntarily, "Eureka! a nocturnal!" Easier said than proved, however. Even if we concede what has been more than once claimed, that the one play inspired the other, does that entitle us to draw the analogy? Fletcher's piece, we know, had been produced (and most unaccountably damned) at the Blackfriars in 1608 or 1609, a period at which, as Dekker's cryptic reference to nocturnals in his *Worke for Armorours, or the Peace is Broken* shows,[2] the nocturnal was still commonly recog-

---

[1] Page 269.

[2] Dekker tells us that, as a result of the plague of 1608-09, "*Playhouses* stand (like *tavernes* that have cast out their *Maisters*) the dores locked vp,

nised as a specific type. Following Polonius's lead, one feels inclined to style *The Faithful Shepherdess* a nocturnal-pastoral-tragi-comedy. Its principal action passes in the night, but the complications are not due to the darkness. Perigot would have taken the magically transformed Amarïllis for Amoret equally as well in the daytime as in the night. But, as the darkness lasts for almost the whole of two acts, it is quite possible that the Blackfriars auditorium was shuttered from the end of Act II to Act IV, scene 4, or where the Satyr, in a beautiful speech, says:

> See, the day begins to break,
> And the light shoots like a streak
> Of subtle fire.

Indeed, we are almost warranted in assuming that the house was thus darkened, for such a course would account for a reference in Ben Jonson's lines "to Mr. John Fletcher, upon his 'Faithful Shepherdess'" in a much better way than it has hitherto been interpreted. In quoting these, I desire to draw your attention to the expression "cauk'd in the dark":

> The wise, and many-headed bench, that sits
> Upon the life and death of plays and wits,
> (Compos'd of gamester, captain, knight, knight's man,
> Lady or pusil, that wears mask or fan,
> Velvet or taffata cap, cauk'd in the dark
> With the shop's foreman, or some such brave spark
> That may judge for his sixpence) had, before
> They saw it half, damn'd thy whole play, and more:

the *Flagges* (like their *Bushes*) taken down; or rather like *Houses* lately infected, from whence the affrighted dwellers are fled, in hope to live better in the *Country*. The *Players* themselves did never worke till nowe, their Comedies are all turned to *Nocturnals*, and the best of them are weary of playing these *Nocturnal Tragedies*."

Their motives were, since it had not to do
With vices, which they look'd for and came to.
I, that am glad thy innocence was thy guilt,
And wish that all the Muses' blood were spilt
In such a martyrdom to vex their eyes,
Do crown thy murder'd poem: which shall rise
A glorified work to time, when fire,
Or moths shall eat what all these fools admire.

Latterday experience shows that an audience asked to sit for long in the dark at a play is apt to prove restless and noisy — a remark, by the way, which has no application to a picture-house assembly. I mention this fact because there is a reference in Jonson's lines which admits of the reading that, when the trouble came, the offending Blackfriars crowd was seated in the dark. We are told that the discontent was shown early, that the row started before the play was half over — assertions which clearly point to shuttering, since the dark scenes commence with the third act. It is noteworthy also that Jonson's reasons for the failure of the play are not in harmony with the reasons advanced by Fletcher himself. Might it not have been that the manner in which the piece opened, together with the ensuing darkness, aroused expectations of an amusing nocturnal imbroglio, which, on being baulked, led to the assumption of a hostile attitude? It was not in human nature for an audience in the *Merry Devil of Edmonton* mood to enjoy a highly poetic pastoral.

By the close of James I's reign the term "nocturnal" had lost its prime theatrical significance, so ephemeral was the type. In 1620 a prospectus was drawn up, setting forth all the projected new entertainments that certain promoters proposed to give in a contemplated new London amphitheatre, including realistic sea-fights and firework exhibitions. Cornelius Drebbel, memorable as the inventor of a perpetual-motion machine and a submarine boat, was to be the chief artificer, and among the enumerated novelties he was to present was a sort of magic-lantern device, showing "Nocturnalls of vnexpressable Figures; Visions and Apparitions. Figuring deepe Melancholly and Vnvsuall Representations." [1] Doubtless, had not the project proved abortive, the transient, mid-Victorian delights of Pepper's Ghost would have been long forestalled.

Later on, poetry momentarily adopted the abandoned and abused term. In 1631 we find Donne writing "A Nocturnal upon St Lucy's Day being the shortest Day." The day of the stage nocturnal had been equally short.

[1] Cf. *Notes and Queries*, 11th series, x, 481, 482, and J. Q. Adams, *Shakespearean Playhouses*, pp. 412–417.

VII

STAGE TRAPS IN THE EARLY ENGLISH THEATRE

ALTHOUGH for fully a score of years there has been a world-wide investigation of the physical conditions of the Elizabethan theatre, it is at once astonishing and humiliating how little we really know about the characteristics, the number, and the working of early stage traps. We have been vouchsafed no reasoned conclusion on the subject; the space devoted to it by Brodmeier, Albright, Thorndike, and others has been of the startling brevity of the famous chapter on snakes of Iceland. Excuse might be found for this perfunctory handling of an important matter if a sufficiency of data were lacking, but that cannot for a moment be maintained. It requires no very exhaustive research to determine that the old platform-stage never had less than two traps and in its later period possessed at least five; yet Brodmeier, in drawing up his plan of the Shakespeare stage in 1904,[1] could conceive of only one. To pillory Brodmeier now is, of course, equivalent to flogging a dead horse, so far has he become a creed outworn, but those who came after him, while avoiding his particular error, are in no better case. All stood aghast before the complexities of a subject with which not all their scholastic training had made

---

[1] *Die Shakespeare-Bühne nach den alten Bühnenanweisungen* (Weimar, 1904). For a reproduction of the plan, see William Archer's article on "The Elizabethan Stage" in *The Quarterly Review* for April, 1908, p. 450.

them competent to deal. The problem was not for them, but for the seasoned theatrical antiquary, the man who had striven to fathom the mysteries of early stage mechanics, who was something more than an Elizabethan specialist, whose labours were not confined to any particular period or any particular country. Not all Elizabethan specialists have been honest with themselves about this matter: some have endeavoured to conceal their deficiencies by crying out, "Sour grapes." Albright, who says all that he has to say about traps in a meagre nineteen lines, is of opinion that

the outer stage, inner stage, and gallery each contained one or more traps. The number and exact location of these are of no consequence even if it were possible to determine the matter with certainty.[1]

To my mind, any Elizabethan investigator who expresses belief that any new fact regarding the disposition of the Elizabethan stage could be of no importance is lacking in a proper sense of vocation. Facts that have no substantive value are often contributory to knowledge through the light they throw on other facts. Albright's cavalier dismissal of the subject is calculated to obscure what I hope shortly to demonstrate, namely, how large and vital a factor of early stage effect was trapwork. But I take leave to say now, before entering upon that task, that I have very grave doubts about the permanence of his postulated gallery, or upper-stage, trap. If the contrivance to which he refers were permanent, it cannot fittingly be reckoned in the category of stage traps. He himself advances only a single item of evidence in support of his assumption, and it is a remarkable, and surely significant, fact that no other can be found in the

[1] Albright, *The Shaksperian Stage*, p. 74. Thorndike, *Shakespeare's Theater*, pp. 92, 134, merely summarises Albright.

whole corpus of what is broadly known as the Elizabethan drama. A permanent stage trap which had so
little employment would have been a very curious sort
of contrivance. The Elizabethan players were not given
to the provision of superfluities.

It is solely upon Marlowe's *The Jew of Malta*, V, 6,
that Albright bases. This is the highly melodramatic
scene in which Barabas sets a death trap for Calymas and
is hoist with his own petard. On a gallery, as he calls it,
he has constructed a trap held in place by a rope and
pulley, and beneath it he has placed a boiling cauldron.
The rope is to be cut below at a given signal, but Fer-
neze severs it prematurely, and the Jew meets the end
that he had designed for the Turk. Here, in reverting to
the stage directions, one must be careful to consult the
original and very belated quarto of 1633, and to ignore
the sophistications of latterday editors. Note that the
cauldron was revealed only at the moment of Barabas's
precipitation, a fact showing that it must have been
stationed on the rear stage. Accordingly, Albright errs
in describing the trap as a gallery trap, seeing that the
gallery was in front of, not over, the rear stage. There is
absolutely no other place for the trap, save on the floor of
the upper curtained room, otherwise the upper stage.
We could suppose it to be permanent there only on the
assumption that its main office was of a non-dramatic
order, or, in other words, that it was primarily constructed to admit of the lowering of properties from
above. No clue, however, to any such lowering can be
found. Moreover, one suspects that the trap was a specially provided feature, not a permanent appurtenance,
on one's failure to find, after prolonged searching, any
analogous effect in pre-Restoration drama. Had the
effect admitted of facile imitation, it would surely have

been reproduced in some other play; it is, I think, the only Elizabethan effect that remains uncopied.

What we have first to bear in mind in entering upon our investigation, while confining our retrospect strictly to modern times, is that trapwork ranks among the oldest of stage sciences. Much thought had gone to the perfecting of stage traps long before the first modern theatre had been built. In the old French mysteries, reliance upon their adroit use was largely placed in order to create a supernatural atmosphere. It was certainly fitting that the stage mechanists of those days should have denominated trap effects *secrets*, for, so little do we know of the *modus operandi*, secrets they remain. Illusion seems to have been carefully fostered. In Jean Michel's *Le Mistere de la Resurrection de Nostre Seigneur*, produced I know not where in 1491, Jesus suddenly rose through the stage, leaving no trace of the place of his emergence. This effect was procured by placing earth and sods all around the trap, as well as on the trap itself. Afterwards there was a reversal of the process: Jesus suddenly vanished from the eyes of sundry pilgrims by means of an engine.[1] It will be as well for us not to forget that engine.

In the old French mysteries one finds also the prototype of a popular Elizabethan stage effect. That its performance was not without risk an early record goes to show. At Seurre, in 1496, when the Devil came up a trap in the *Vie de Saint Martin*, the flames of Hell darted after him a little too fiercely, with the result that his tail and some part of his nether garment got badly burned, and his Satanic Majesty had perforce to return below for alterations and repairs.[2]

Remote and foreign as are these records, they are not

[1] L. Petit de Julleville, *Les Mystères*, i, 399.   [2] *Ibid.*

EARLY STAGE TRAPS

without their relevancy. They suggest the question whether in matters of trap making the English stage builders of the latter half of the sixteenth century — by which I do not mean solely the theatre-stage builders — had been handed on the torch, or whether they had had laboriously to work things out for themselves. Personally, being thoroughly convinced that the English guild plays now commonly known by their purely modern designation of miracle plays were largely derivative, and that they drew inspiration from France, I am firmly of the opinion that the Continental stage mechanists yielded their *secrets* to the English guilds and that in process of time the knowledge thus acquired became the heritage of the secular-stage builders. Unless one postulates some such transference, one must stand amazed before the technical expertness in matters of trap making shown by the English stage builders in less than a decade after the erection of the first London theatre. But, in this connexion, it requires to be grasped that the little resort to trapwork made in the moralities, — and that despite the frequent appearance of the Devil among the dramatis personae, — so far from indicating an early lack of technical knowledge, goes to confirm the common belief that the moralities were devised indifferently for either indoor or outdoor performance, anywhere or everywhere, now on an improvised stage and now without any stage at all. Progress was made, however, even with the morality, and in some of the later examples we find traces of elementary trapwork. In Lupton's *All for Money*, as issued in 1578, we find the instruction:

Money commeth in, having one halfe of his gowne yellowe and the other white, having the coyne of silver and golde painted upon it, there must be a chair for him to sit in, and under it or neere the same, there must be some hollow place for one to come up in.

This indicates the manner in which Pleasure appears when vomited by Money. The direction merely says, "Here with some fine conveyance, Pleasure shall appear from beneath." Afterwards Pleasure similarly vomits up Sin, and Sin, Damnation. Payne Collier[1] expresses his doubts whether a trap was used in the play, but it is difficult to see how the "fine conveyance" could otherwise have been made.

No greater mistake could be made than to assume that the impermanent stage scotched the wheel of technical progress. Much depended on the kind of impermanent stage; we must discriminate. There was no permanent theatre at the English court before the meridian of the Caroline period; and the court masque, which, even in Jacobean days, demanded a greater wealth of stage mechanism than any contemporary play, was not given on a permanent stage until a year or two before the Civil War. These conditions, so curiously analogous to those of the old Italian ducal courts, actually made for scenic progress. The dramatist or masque-writer who set himself to write for a specific permanent stage would have had to restrict himself to the effects readily procurable on that stage.[2] There would be certain limitations. Reverse the process, give the author a free hand, construct the stage specially for his play or masque, and the odds are that in giving rein to his imagination he will stimulate the stage mechanist to further effort. As a matter of fact, this is what really happened. All early progress in matters of pictorial embellishment and spectacular stage effect was made sporadically on various temporary court and academic stages. It was on a tem-

[1] *History of English Dramatic Poetry* (1831), iii, 364.
[2] For a partial demonstration of this see my subsequent study of the independent theatre masque.

porary stage at Oxford in 1605 that the first movable scenery ever seen in England was shown.

These are simple facts, but they have not yet been thoroughly digested. Knowledge of their cogency has impelled me to look for evidence of trapwork in the court and cognate drama of the early years of Queen Elizabeth's reign, or a decade before the building of the first two London theatres; and my search has not been without its reward. In the tragedy of *Gorboduc*, as given at Whitehall early in 1562, one finds, in the fourth dumb show, an effect afterwards frequently repeated in court plays, the coming of the Furies from the nether regions. We have in this convention some justification of Cunliffe's theory that the dumb show was derived from the Italian court *intermedi*,[1] since the *intermedi* had no commoner feature than a dance of Furies.[2] If, in this particular connexion, Italy was the immediate source, it may be that the Italian procedure, as revealed at a later period by Sabbattini,[3] was adopted, and that the Furies, instead of being elevated by mechanical means to stage level, simply ran up a step-ladder.

Four years later came two other court plays, *Tancred and Gismund* and *Jocasta*. In the prelude to Act IV of the first-mentioned tragedy, Guiszard ascends "from underneeth the stage" and helps up Gismund, a simple use of a simple opening. Shortly afterwards, "Megaera ariseth out of hell with the other furies, Alecto and Tysiphone, dancing a hellish round," as the direction has it; and, the dance done, Megaera dismisses the other Furies, who "depart down." Evidently the two had neither

---

[1] J. W. Cunliffe, *Early English Classical Tragedies*, Introd., p. xl.

[2] See *Ibid.*, for De Sommi on *intermedi*.

[3] *Practica de Fabricar Scene e Machine ne' Teatri* (Ravenna, 1638), Bk. II, pp. 94–101.

entered nor left through the opening by which Guiszard and Gismund had emerged, since such a course would have led to a sad confusion of localities. Hence the stage was provided with at least two trapdoors. On the other hand, in Gascoigne and Kinwelmershe's *Jocasta* we have evidence of the use of one trap only, a large, oblong trap, still employed on the stage and still known by the old name of grave trap, a name which indicates the most usual of its services. This trap was resorted to in two of the dumb shows given in the tragedy, first in the one where two coffins are lowered into a grave and burnt, and afterwards to represent the great gulf into which the panoplied Curtius jumps.[1] Even thus early was it proving of a very grateful utility. Though there is reason to believe that, on the regular stage, mechanism was afterwards occasionally associated with it, fundamentally the grave trap was an opening and nothing more — a device of no more intricacy, and calling for no more manipulation, than the trap through which the golden and bejewelled tree in the second act of Peele's court pastoral, *The Arraignment of Paris*, rose up and sank again, when the play was acted before the Queen in or about the year 1583.[2] Not, however, that trapwork of some complexity was not demanded by this dainty play. Recall the situation in the fourth act, where Pluto, while seated on his throne, comes from below. Here, for the first time, we get into grapples with the knotty problem of mechanical trapwork, since it is difficult to see how the elevation of the throne could have been manually accomplished.

In another court play of practically the same period,

[1] Cunliffe, *op cit.*, points out that the story of Curtius had occasionally been dealt with in the Italian *intermedi*.

[2] A similar effect was seen in an intercalated dumb show in *A Warning for Women*, a public-theatre play of a decade later.

The Rare Triumphs of Love and Fortune, there was a mild recurrence of the Fury convention. A single Fury emerged from a trap at the beginning of the play. Five years later, or by 1588, the court had not wearied seemingly of the old device, judging by the fact that it was pressed into service in a dumb show in *The Misfortune of Arthur*.

On the old platform-stage, the grave trap proved so useful in a variety of ways that its provision in every theatre, early or late, public or private, was indispensable. Locations of early traps are difficult to determine, particularly as stage building was progressive and we cannot even be sure that all the theatres of the one narrow period pursued the one system. Superficial area would be in part a determining factor, and it is conceivable that the small stages of the private theatres would be somewhat differently arranged to the large stages of the public theatres. But it is not on these counts alone that the evidence for the position of the grave trap proves to be of a curiously contradictory order. How far the problem bristles with difficulties will become apparent on a minute examination of the grave scene in *Hamlet*. If we assume that the generally accepted divisions of the play are authentic, and agree that the fifth act opened with the graveyard scene, then there would appear to be some necessity for the placing of the grave trap on the rear stage. To mark the break between scene and scene, it seems requisite that the curtains should close at the end and obscure the grave from sight. It all depends on whether the First Gravedigger, before taking his departure, had had time to make everything clean and tidy. In those days the business of grave digging and grave filling was always more or less realistically performed. One finds a notable scene of the sort in *Two Maids of More-Clack*, a private-theatre play of a period slightly subsequent to *Hamlet*. First we get: "Enter two sailors with a truncke, wherein is Mistresse Mary in her winding sheet, others with pickaxe and spades, as on the sands." Toures, who laments that "this night's tempest" has taken Mary from him, bids the sailors

> Dig ho! this golden beach, whose glittering sands
> Shews with sunne as diamonds set in gold;

and the men bury her in haste, lest the wind should veer to the south and carry their vessel away. Nevertheless some ninety lines are uttered between Toures's "Dig ho!" and the completion of their task. Called for suddenly by their messmates on shipboard, the sailors depart precipitately, leaving the pickaxe and spades behind them. Then enter the Governor and a Gentleman. The Governor welcomes the stranger to Scilly, and, after showing him France, Ireland, Britain, and Jersey through a spyglass, suddenly breaks off with:

> Ha, what scrambled ends heape up confusedly?
> New digg'd and ript up in this plot of ground.

On the Gentleman's suggestion, the two set about digging up the sands, and, discovering the trunk, lift it out and break it open. And behold! the comatose Mary suddenly comes to life.

This elaborate scene would serve to fortify one in the belief that the grave trap in *Hamlet* was situated on the rear stage, were it not for one confounding circumstance. When Hamlet and Horatio enter it is, as the direction tells us, "afar off," meaning that they come on through the door at the back of the rear stage and pause there. They listen for long, unseen, to the singing of the First Gravedigger, and watch him as he throws up the skulls. In the circumstances, it is impossible that the trap can have been situated on the rear stage.

If this leaves us in doubt as to the arrangement at the Globe, there is, on the other hand, some slight evidence to show that on the smaller stage of the Blackfriars the grave trap was on the rear stage. Hardly otherwise than by this trap could the cave-mouth opening into the King's bedchamber in Marston's *The Wonder of Women, or Sophonisba* have been represented. It was evidently no small orifice, since Vangue, when given the drugged wine in Act III, scene 1, says warningly, "Close the vault's mouth lest we do slip in drink." Down it Sophonisba, Zanthia, and Syphax afterwards severally "descend," presumably going down unseen steps. All the indications are that this was a rear-stage scene.

There were many situations of a wholly different order in which the grave trap proved equally serviceable. After a purposeful study of the various texts of *Romeo and Juliet*, I have arrived at the conclusion that Juliet's tomb was represented by a trap of this order, that it was a trap, and not a property tomb, which Romeo prised open, and that it was down the trap he afterwards put Paris's body. Note that Juliet, on making her appearance, "rises." The common idea of a property tomb on the rear stage does not seem to me to meet all the requirements.

Because of its prime adaptability, there are many situations in the old drama in which the employment of the grave trap is apt to be overlooked through not being suspected. Though, fundamentally, it was nothing more than a trapdoor covering a capacious opening, we must bear in mind that it lent itself readily to alliance with stage mechanism, and in this way admitted of the procurement of elaborate effects. It must be confessed that this bold assertion is not unmixed with surmise, but at least, I think, I am surmising intelligently. For the reason that from Jacobean times onwards the players were profuse in the provision of small traps, they must of necessity have economised in large traps. The line had to be drawn somewhere, since they had not wholly a free stage. I think therefore that the grave trap was made to work on the *multum in parvo* principle. Nothing could be gained by predicating the provision of a large, mechanical, permanently fitted-up trap, since no trap of the kind could have been so devised as to serve for all the various intricate effects from time to time procured, effects which could be best arranged for in connexion with an elementary, adaptive trap.

But we are proceeding a trifle too quickly. Let us first consider the simple uses of the grave trap, over and beyond those already indicated, and then proceed to discuss the more and more complex. It is important to note that in every case where a character falls, jumps, or is pushed into a gap, resort to this trap is implied. Instances occur in the last act of *The Old Wives' Tale*, where the Ghost of Jack says farewell and leaps down into the ground; in *Arden of Feversham*, IV, 3, where Shakebag falls into the ditch; and, similarly, in *The Valiant Welshman*, II, 5, where Marion has a mishap while engaged in chasing the fairy.[1] In the last-mentioned case, the fairy disappeared perpendicularly down a small trap, and her pursuer fell headlong down a large one. So, too, we may be sure that the grave trap did duty in *Titus Andronicus* for the pit where the body of Bassanius is hidden, and into which two of the other characters subsequently fall.

Over the employment of this trap in *Grim the Collier of*

[1] See also *A Larum for London*, Signature F; *The Wonder of Women*, V, 1, direction, "Erectho slips into the ground as Syphax offers his sword to her"; *Hogge Hath Lost his Pearle*, V, 1; and *Blurt, Master Constable*, IV, 2.

Croydon, W. Carew Hazlitt curiously blunders.[1] In the
last scene of the play Castiliano, alias Belphegor, recognising that the hour has come for his return to Hell, calls
out:

> And now, my servant, whereso'er thou be,
> Come quickly, Abericock, and follow me.
> Lordings, adieu, and my curs'd wife, farewell,
> If me ye seek, come follow me to hell.

Abericock has already made his last appearance and
said his last say: despite his master's command, there is
no reason why he should again show himself. Though
Hazlitt is loth to admit of competitive routes, it is still
pretty generally conceded that there is more than one
way of going to Hell. In his eyes, there was no road for
poor Abericock save by the grave trap. Hence, when he
found at the close of Castiliano's speech the direction,
"The ground opens, and he falls down into it," he considered it incorrect, and altered "he falls" to "they both
fall," ignoring the patent fact that the rapid falling of
two people down the same trap would have resulted in
broken bones. To see the absurdity of his emendation
one has only to read a little farther. No sooner has
Castiliano disappeared than Earl Morgan says, "The
earth that opened now is clos'd again"; and a little
later Clinton asks, "Was there a quagmire that *he* sank
so soon?"

Though two people could not with safety have jumped
down a grave trap the one immediately after the other,
I think it was possible, by some special arrangement of
the trap, for two persons who stood at either end of it to
be quickly lowered wholly or partly out of sight. This is
my reading of the action at that juncture in the twenty-
sixth scene of the anonymous, undivided play, *Look*

---

[1] *Dodsley's Old Plays*, ed. Hazlitt, vol. viii.

About You,[1] where Prince John asks the disguised Skink whether there are not caves thereabouts, and gets the reply, "Yes, sir; tread the ground, sir, and you shall hear their hollowness; this way, sir, this way." No direction follows, but, judging from their immediate exclamations, John and Fauconbridge must have fallen down the one trap, almost side by side, with only their heads remaining in sight. After they have been robbed by Skink, Fauconbridge scrambles out and helps the Prince up. Note that the date of the play is *circa* 1600, certainly not later than that year, a period which yields us no proof of the provision in any theatre of as many as two traps of the smaller order. Even if this were forthcoming, the likelihood then or later of the employment of two small, contiguous traps is inadmissible.

It is not difficult to determine that the grave trap represented the gravel pit into which, in *The Atheist's Tragedie*,[2] Borachio descends to await D'Amville's treacherous thrusting-down of Montferrers. But it is not so easy to see that it also stood, later on,[3] for the charnel house in the churchyard scene. Charlemont, fearing pursuit after having killed Borachio, says:

> Ile hide me heere i' th' charnell house,
> This convocation-house of dead men's sculles.

Then comes the direction, "To get into the Charnell house he takes holde of a Death's head; it slips and staggers him." After two lines of sombre reflection, he "hides himselfe," according to another direction, "in the Charnell house." At first one is inclined to think that the curtained rear stage was made to answer for the charnel house, but this impression is dissipated when

---

[1] *Dodsley's Old Plays*, vii, 465.   [2] Act II, scene 4.
[3] Act IV, scene 3.

D'Amville assails Castabella, and, as a further direction reads, "Charlemont rises in the disguise, and frights D'Amville away." The word "rises" surely implies emergence from a trap.

It must be further noted that there was a certain kind of realistic river scene in which the employment of the grave trap, together with a particular concomitant, was indispensable. No fewer than three examples of this effect occur in *Locrine*, a play printed in 1595 and probably then about four years old. In the dumb show preceding the third act a crocodile was seen sitting on a river's bank with a snake in the act of stinging it. After both had fallen into the water, Ate proceeded to expound the symbol. The curtains must have been drawn open at the beginning, as the spectacle was obviously a discovery; and it would appear that these river scenes were generally acted on the rear stage. Some might take this as indicative of the normal position of the grave trap, but to me the general evidence on the point is too confusing to permit of a decision.

The river scenes were mostly used for drownings, and there are two subsequent examples in *Locrine*. In nearly all instances where they occur we have mention of the river's bank, evidently a "property" designed to hide the grave trap from view. Remark the description of the opening dumb show in *The Weakest Goeth to the Wall*, a late sixteenth-century play:

After an Alarum, enter, one way, the Duke of Burgundy; another way, the Duke of Anjou with his power; they encounter; Burgundy is slain. Then enter the Duchess of Burgundy with young Frederick in her hand, who, being pursued by the French, leaps into a river, leaving the child upon the bank, who is presently found by the Duke of Brabant, who comes to aid Burgundy when it is too late.

Here, since the front stage had to be kept clear for the fight, the river must have been on the rear stage. No difficulty was ever encountered in masking the grave trap from view, because every theatre had in its property room an imitation moss bank or flowery bank for ready use.[1] The jumping down the trap had, of course, to be neatly accomplished, but then most players of the time were trained acrobats.

A diversion from the orthodox river scene occurs in *The Divil's Charter*, a highly coloured Globe play of Jacobean days. In a night scene on the banks of the Tiber, Caesar Borgia, aided by a bravo, murders the Duke of Candy, his brother, and throws his body into the river. No sooner is this done than Borgia, to get rid of all evidence of the crime, throws in the stooping, unwary bravo likewise. So much care was commonly taken on the Elizabethan stage to procure all the necessary illusions of sound that one is apt to wonder whether or not in these river scenes an accompanying splash was heard. Something of the sort seems requisite, even after due allowance has been made for the exercise of imagination.

Among effects of some elaboration procured by means of a specially equipped grave trap, two call for particular mention, one in *A Looking Glasse for London and England*, and the other in *Macbeth*. As illustrative of the difficulties which have to be surmounted before accepting the evidence of river scenes and assigning to the grave trap a rear-stage position, it requires to be noted that the trap effect in *A Looking Glasse* cannot possibly have been performed on the rear stage. Immediately before its representation Remilia had been hidden behind the cur-

[1] In Henslowe's inventory of the Admiral's Men's properties, taken on March 10, 1598, there is an item which includes "ij moss banckes and j snake."

tains, and immediately afterwards the curtains are with-
drawn and her thunderstricken body revealed. The
effect itself is indicated in the direction, "The Magi with
their rods, beat the ground, and from under the same
riseth a brave arbour." The same trap was doubtless
used again later where we have the direction, "A flame of
fire appeareth from beneath, and Radagon is swallowed."
The whole play is remarkably spectacular for its period
— that of 1590 or thereabouts — and reads as if fashioned
for court performance, or as if, at least, it had come down
to us in its special court form. But, unlike another play
of Greene's, *Orlando Furioso*, printed in the same year
and probably acted by the same company, we have no
record of its performance at court.

It was fitting, of course, that the Magi, when asked to
conjure up a magic bower, should beat the ground with
their wands by way of incantation, but the act served
quite another purpose in giving the cue to the trap-men
below to send up the bower. Everything had to be carefully pre-arranged. We learn from the revealing prompt-
copy of Massinger's *Believe as You List* that two men
had to be sent into the cellar to open the simple trapdoor
when Antiochus came up from below, and can surmise
from this how many hands would have been required for
a more complex trap effect. By no means so appropriate
was the cue given for the opening of the grave trap in
the fourth act of *Antonio's Revenge*, a Paul's play of 1601.
Pandulpho, referring to his slain son, says:

> Let's dig his grave, with that shall dig the heart,
> Liver and entrails of the murderer.

And then comes the direction, "They strike the stage
with their daggers, and the grave openeth." Surely the
rapidest case of grave digging on record, whether on or
off the stage.

The usual cue for the opening of a trap was a stamp of the foot, though we find Jonson, in *Cynthia's Revels*,[1] following Greene's example in making Mercury strike the ground three times with his caduceus to bring up Echo. We encounter the orthodox warning in the fourth act of *The Whore of Babylon*, where Falsehood strikes the earth in several places with her foot, and, in one spot or another, several characters rise. So, too, in *A Mad World, My Masters*, IV, 1, the succubus, on being conjured to depart, "stamps and exit" — a succinct direction which clearly conveys to the initiated that she disappeared down a trap. Again, in that composite court play, *Four Plays in One*, we get, in scene 4 of the terminal masque, an apposite instruction which reads as if capital and labour had begun to quarrel as early as the first half of the seventeenth century. It runs: "Plutus stamps, Labour rises." It is noteworthy that the stamp often reveals the trapwork when the direction is otherwise silent upon the point. Thus in *The Witch of Edmonton*, II, 1, we learn that Mother Sawyer "stamps on the ground; the Dog appears, and fawns upon her" — an indication that the dog came up from below. It is rare to find directions of this order as explicit as the one in the fourth act of Rawlins's Caroline play, *The Rebellion*, where Aurelia "takes a dogge and tyes it to the chaire: shee stampes. The Chaire and Dogge descends, a Pistoll shot within," and so forth. Even in much later days the old method of warning the cellarmen obtained. In Ravenscroft's *Dame Dobson*, a Duke's Theatre play of 1684, the Dame is to be found disappearing after stamping her foot.

On the old platform-stage there can have been few, if any, more elaborate trap effects than the one presented in *Macbeth*, in the opening scene of the fourth act. Here

[1] Act I, scene 2.

we have a capacious cauldron standing on a trap, down which it eventually descends. The trapdoor itself cannot have been solid, seeing that not alone do flames emerge through the cauldron but three apparitions rise above it. Note that the cauldron sinks to a music cue: the hautboys start to play just before its disappearance. This was not wholly without precedent. In the induction to Jonson's *Poetaster*, Envy began to sink with the third sounding, that is to say, at the cue given by a trumpet call. But why did the cauldron disappear? Its sinking served no dramatic purpose, and was apparently necessitated by the subsequent "business" of the scene. The puzzle is to determine the precise nature of this business. If the cauldron was situated on the rear stage, as seems probable, it might have been requisite to clear it away, in order to afford an unobstructed view of the Show of the Eight Kings. It has been suggested to me that the trap on which it stood might have been wanted to serve in part for the subsequent disappearance of the witches. But this, I fear, begs the question. It was usual, we know, for ghosts and devils to come and go through traps, but it is by no means so assured that that was the common mode of transit adopted by witches. And even if it were, it is difficult to see how four witches could have disappeared simultaneously. No single trap could have sufficed. Moreover, the text runs counter to the theory of downward disappearance. Macbeth asks Lennox shortly afterwards, "Saw you the weird sisters? . . . Came they not by you?" and, on getting an iterated negative, spits out the malediction, "Infected be the air whereon they ride."

This is only one of the many problems which confront, fascinate, and baffle every investigator who concerns himself with early theatrical conditions and the mysteries of staging. Of the others, none is more formidable than the much-vexed question of the removable stage. Until it is answered, we shall never be able to speak with any decision as to the precise number of sixteenth-century traps, where they were placed, and how they were worked. Little evidence exists to warrant the often-expressed belief in the early prevalence, in inn-yard and theatre, of the removable stage. No one can say positively that it was employed anywhere save at that playhouse-*cum*-bear-garden, the Hope, from 1613 onwards. According to the building contract for that house, the stage was to be so constructed that it could be "carryed or taken awaie, and to stande vppon tressells good, substanciall, and sufficient for the carryinge and bearinge of suche a stage." [1] Obviously, no such contrivance could have admitted of the provision of the number and variety of traps then in vogue at the public theatres; but the Hope had at least a permanent tiring-house, which included the rear stage and was therefore not entirely debarred from the use of trapwork.

Try as one may, one cannot wholly rid oneself of the suspicion that there was precedent for the principle adopted at the Hope. It has frequently been surmised that the removable stage originated in the inn-yards and was transferred thence to the early theatres, but, apart from the fact that the necessity for such transference has not been demonstrated, there is good reason to doubt the regular impermanency of the inn-yard stages. [2] Having probed pretty fully into this matter in a previous paper, I need say now only that several inn-yard and public-theatre plays published before 1600 present trap effects

[1] Chambers, *The Elizabethan Stage*, ii, 466.
[2] See my lecture on "The Inn-Yard Playing-Places: Their Uprise and Characteristics."

of some complexity, demanding the use of mechanism such as could not be employed on so primitive a contrivance as a removable stage. Elaborate trapwork connotes excavation for cellar space. No early public stage could have been more than five feet high, more particularly as in most Elizabethan theatres the stage was surmounted on its sides by a balustrade. The fact that the balustrade is missing in the well-known Dutch sketch of the Swan suggests the necessity to make close examination of the stage depicted in that sketch. One notes that it is unenclosed and is borne up near its front by two supports. If its raw, primitive aspect indicates anything, it indicates removability, but, assuming that that was the aim, all that it admitted of at best was a partial clearance. Only the portion in front of the pillars of the heavens could have been taken away, or not more than one half of the stage. There is no evidence to show that the Swan was built with the intention of using it otherwise than as a playhouse, but, assuming that occasional bear-baiting called for the removal of the front part of the stage, the permanent back part would have admitted of the provision of one or two traps, together with some excavation. I take leave to think, however, that, even if we could arrive at a definite conclusion on this point, it would be perilous to deduce all the characteristics of the Theater and the Curtain from the old drawing of the Swan.

Apart from the question regarding to what extent the principle of the removable stage was practised, there are some grounds for believing that the first theatre to boast an enclosed stage was the Rose, and that the palisading there was a belated improvement, probably among those made by Henslowe at very considerable expense in 1592. All we know for certain, however, is that the Globe in 1599 and the Fortune in 1600 had enclosed balustraded stages. The argument in support of the surmised innovation at the Rose is as follows. Speaking in the cellar is peculiar to the enclosed stage, since an open stage could hardly be said to possess a cellar. Speaking of this order is first to be traced in 1596, in Anthony Munday's *John a Kent and John a Cumber;* and it is remarkable that for a little over a lustrum it remained a popular stage effect, popular, that is, at both the public and private houses. Before 1603 it was practised in *Cynthia's Revels* at the Blackfriars, in *Antonio's Revenge* at Paul's, and in *Hamlet* at the Globe.[1] We do not know for what company *John a Kent and John a Cumber* was written or where it was produced, but we do know that at the period of its composition Munday was one of the stock dramatists of the Rose, devising plays strictly to measure — the measure of the players, the house, and the audience.

If sheer lack of data prevents us from determining whether the first two public theatres began with a removable or a permanent stage, there is, on the other hand, reason for entertaining the belief that, assuming for argument's sake that they originally had removable stages, progress to permanency took place within some fifteen years, and that, too, despite the seeming denial of the Swan sketch. Reactionary principles were exemplified later at the Hope, and, for a similar reason, may have previously exercised their influence at the Swan. My main reason for postulating the early prevalence of the permanent stage is that from 1590 onwards we have regular trace, both in public-theatre plays and in a few plays written for inn-yard performance, of trapwork of a complexity incompatible with any kind of primitive stage This points to resort to mechanical appliances, and, in some instances, to the provision of an excavated cel-

[1] *Cynthia's Revels,* I, 1; *Antonio's Revenge,* III, 3; *Hamlet,* I, 5.

larage. There are clear indications of the use of a small trap for the ascensions and descensions of a single character either in a slow or rapid way, a graduation and control of movement hardly obtainable by pure manual working. Look, for example, at Greene's *Alphonsus, King of Arragon*, a play which has been conjectured to date from 1587, and was probably written for inn-yard performance. In the third act the Ghost of Calchas comes up from below "in a white cirples and a Cardinal's Myter," and disappears later through the same trap.[1] In this we are afforded a fairly satisfactory *terminus a quo* for the convention of ghostly approach so rigorously followed throughout the seventeenth century; but, in point of scientific evidence, a much better example comes to hand in Peele's *King Edward I*, a play of a lustrum later. Queen Elinor, having rashly wished that her soul might sink to Hell if she were the author of the Mayoress's tragedy, "the earth," according to the direction, "opens and swallows her." Later on, when we get to Potter's Hive, the Queen's Ghost rises slowly out of the ground, occasioning the Potter's Wife to exclaim affrightedly: "But stay, John: what's that riseth out of the ground? Jesus, bless us, John, look how it riseth higher and higher."

A few examples of this measured progression, both up and down, so eloquent of mechanical control, are to be found at a subsequent period. In the induction to Jonson's *Poetaster*, a Blackfriars play of 1601, Envy rises "in the midst of the stage," as the direction has it, and after delivering a long soliloquy proceeds slowly to make her return journey. When she has almost disappeared, the Prologue enters, and, placing his foot on her head, says:

---

[1] The textual admonition to the player, "Calchas sink down where you came up" means "be careful to stand on the trap."

Stay, monster, ere thou sinke, thus on thy head:
Set we our bolder foot; with which we tread
Thy malice into earth.

An effect of this order depends upon the scientific precision with which it is executed — another indication of mechanical means. Remark further the central position of the trap. The Paul's private playhouse of exactly the same period had a similar arrangement. In William Percy's *The Aphrodysiall or Sea Feast*, which was intended for that house, the action at one juncture calls for "a trap-door in the middle of the stage." Ben Jonson's effective bit of stage business brings to mind what Dekker wrote a lustrum later about the Devil in his *Newes from Hell:*

At sword and buckler little *Davy* was no bodie to him, and as for Rapier and dagger, the *Germane* may be his journeyman. Marry, the question is, in which of the *Playhouses* he would have performed his Prize, if it had grown to blowes, and whether the money being gathered he would have cozened the Fencers, or the Fencers him, because *Hell* being vnder everie one of their Stages, the Players (if they had owed him a spight) might with a false Trappe doore have slipt him downe, and there kept him as a laughing stocke to all their yawning spectators.

A later example of this nicety of control occurs in the fifth act of *The Virgin Martir*, a Red Bull play of 1620. When Theophilus raises the cross of flowers in self-defence, the fiend Harpax, according to the direction, "sinks a little," on which Theophilus says, "Art posting to thy centre? Down, hell-hound, down!" And then Harpax disappears. Equally significant is the direction to be found in Act V of Richards's *Messallina*, a tragedy of the late Caroline period: "Thunder and lightning. Earth gapes and swallowes the three murderers by degrees. One of them before sinking is shot with a thunderbolt." It is noteworthy that, years after the Restoration, the

MANIPULATION OF A STAGE TRAP

From E. M. Laumann's *La Machinerie au Théâtre*, Paris, [1897], page 89

old convention, and doubtless the old mechanism, was still to the fore. A direction in the fifth act of Dryden and Lee's *Oedipus* notifies us that "the Ghost of Laïus ascends by degrees, pointing at Jocasta."[1]

My belief is that if we can determine the characteristics of what was known as the ghost trap in and after the eighteenth century, we shall have arrived at the mechanism and *modus operandi* of these early graduated trap effects. This is by no means an easy task, for, though the fundamental principles of trapworking still hold, latterday science has revolutionised methods in simplifying them. Thus, though the round star trap of to-day is the lineal descendant of the square ghost trap of yesterday — the one having exactly the same relationship to the other as the vampire trap has to the old grave trap — *a posteriori* deductions from existing usage would be dangerous. But there is an illustration in George Raymond's *Life of Elliston*, dealing with a trick once played upon an actor of the Ghost in *Hamlet*, which affords us a clue to the early *modus operandi*. It is an etching by George Cruikshank entitled, "Alas, poor Ghost," and dates from 1843, when *The Elliston Papers*, as the biography was first called, were published in *Ainsworth's Magazine*. This, however, is not of the nature of a technical drawing, and to gain a better idea of the characteristics of the primitive ghost trap one must turn to Laumann's *La Machinerie au Théâtre* and make minute examination of Figure 18.[2] After brooding over the matter, my impression is that the Elizabethan ghost trap

[1] Cf. Davenant's *Circe* (1677), V, 4, Orestes' visualised dream, where "the Dreams and Ghost sink down by degrees."

[2] E. M. Laumann, *La Machinerie au Théâtre*, p. 89. For the *modus operandi* of nineteenth-century English traps, see Contant et Filippi, *Parallèle des Principaux Théâtres Modernes*, 2d edition (Paris, 1870), vol. i, Plates 31–33.

consisted of a base the exact size of the trap opening, which worked up and down in four vertical, grooved beams by means of cords and pulleys. Friction, and the necessity for severe manual exertion, may have been lessened by counterweighting the trap. The principle of counterweighting was then well known, but nothing exists to show that it had already been exercised in the theatre. One notes its employment for scene-shifting purposes in Paris in 1673, in the first French Opera House. By using counterweights, the old ghost trap could have been worked by a couple of men, but without them probably four stage hands would have been required for the task. A study of the illustrations referred to, particularly of the French woodcut, reveals that a cellar depth of at least ten feet would have been demanded for the proper manipulation of the trap. This conclusion is wholly inimical to the idea that graduated ascents and descents could have been made on a removable (otherwise an unexcavated) stage.

There were a good many more of these mechanical trap effects in sixteenth-century drama than are superficially apparent. Old stage directions are often extraordinarily misleading. "Enter" does not always mean that the character referred to walked on. Sometimes he was discovered by the drawing of a curtain, and sometimes he was brought up on a trap. In *A Knacke to Know a Knave*, the text clearly conveys that Asmoroth, after the manner of all self-respecting stage demons, emerges from below, but the direction simply says, "Enter the Devill." So, too, in Lodge's *The Wounds of Civil War*, the Genius, according to the preliminary direction, enters to warn Sylla of his impending fate, but it is only later on that it dawns upon the reader how he entered. The "*evanescit subito*," affixed to his Latin speech, in indicating that he disappeared down a trap also indicates that he must have come up one.

The influence of the Stuart masques on the spectacular side of theatrical production could easily be exaggerated, but that they exercised some considerable influence is beyond all doubt. In a sense, masque and play were curiously interlinked. In the gorgeous Christmas fantasies at court, the antimasques were almost invariably executed by professional players, and the players soon acquired the trick of repeating these ingeniously contrived dances in their new plays.[1] We may be sure, indeed, that, while performing at Whitehall, the players kept their eyes widely open, and were not averse from appropriating any novelty that they could publicly utilise without incurring any serious outlay. In this connexion, it is noteworthy that the first trace we have of the employment of under-machinery in masques occurs in Campion's *Masque in honour of Lord Hay's Marriage*, as given before the King on Twelfth Night, 1607. Remarkably enough, Inigo Jones was not the artificer.[2] Intended as the most striking feature of this entertainment was the scene of a verdant glade, in the midst of which, according to the book, were "nine golden trees of 15 foot high, with arms and branches very glorious to behold." After Hesperus had descended, a song was heard, to which

the trees of gold instantly at the first sound of their voices began to move and dance according to the measure of the time which the musicians kept in singing, and the nature of the words which they delivered.

---

[1] Cf. Thorndike, *Shakespeare's Theater*, pp. 194, 195.
[2] As a matter of fact, though the point has never yet been demonstrated, Jones was then in Italy. More than this I cannot say, as the secret is not mine.

Then the trees ranged themselves in ranks of three, Night performed an incantation, and there was a song of the Sylvans

at the beginning whereof that part of the stage whereon the first three trees stood began to yield and the formost trees gently to sincke, and this was effected by an Ingin plac't vnder the stage. When the trees had sunk a yard they cleft in three parts and the Masquers appeared out of the tops of them, the trees were suddenly convayed away, and the first three maskers were raysed again by the Ingin.

Afterwards, the effect was repeated until the whole nine masquers had been disclosed. In the performance, however, there was some sad bungling; and, concerning this, Campion takes occasion to say in a marginal note:

Either by the simplicity, negligence or conspiracy of the painter, the passing away of the trees was somewhat hazarded; the pattern of them the same day having been shown with such advantage and the nine trees being left unset even to the same night.

Viewed purely with ultra-modern eyes, as at least one able investigator has viewed it,[1] this iterative effect looms clumsy, but surely here, if anywhere, historical criticism should come into play. As pure spectacle, forgetting for the moment its tardy coming-off, nothing quite so elaborate had been seen in England before. The impression I get from Campion's description (to which the reference to the single engine largely contributes) is that only one trap was employed, and that necessarily a large one. Counterweighting, I think, would have been indispensable. My reason for drawing attention to this particular effect is not that I believe it evoked any imitation on the public stage, a most unlikely contingency in

---

[1] Lily B. Campbell, *Scenes and Machines on the English Stage during the Renaissance*, p. 169.

the circumstances, but simply to indicate the degree of attention being paid to under-stage mechanism at a period when, spectacularly considered, the Stuart masque was in its crudity. Even, however, on the public stage, the subject had begun to receive special attention. There, only a few months previously, the first conjunctive use of two or more traps had been made. Beyond the fact that it was entered on the Stationers' Register on April 29, 1607, we have no clue to the date of production of Dekker's undivided Fortune play, *The Whore of Babylon*, but it does not seem likely that the event was then of any particular remoteness. In this play one finds a dumb show [1] in which Falsehood comes out of her cave, and, striking the earth in several places with her foot, summons up five characters,[2] the inference being that five traps were used. A stage effect in a somewhat later play, produced at another public theatre, indicates that four of the traps were situated at the corners of the stage, and the fifth was probably in the centre. The play referred to was Heywood's *The Silver Age*, a Red Bull production of 1612. In the fifth act of this, sundry devils appeared (to quote the direction) "at every corner of the stage with severall fireworks." As the devils could not have appeared at the front corners without coming up from below, we have here clear proof not only of four small traps, but of their precise localisation.

No student of pre-Restoration staging can afford to ignore the remarkable spectacular outburst at the Red Bull at this period, evidence of which is particularly rife in Heywood's plays of the Ages. Consider some of the features of *The Brazen Age*. In the fourth act Gallus

---

[1] *Dekker's Dramatic Works*, ed. Pearson, ii, 243.

[2] Albright, *The Shaksperian Stage*, p. 74, misreads the direction, and says eight.

sinks, and in his place rises a crowing cock. In the fifth, Hercules, after being struck with a thunderbolt, disappears into the ground, and a hand in a cloud comes down from above and from the gap left in the ground brings up a star which it fixes in the firmament. Other Red Bull dramatists showed equal resourcefulness. In *If it be not Good, the Devil is in it*, Dekker gave the audience Hell — in an epilogue. We read that

the play ending, as they goe off, from under the ground in severall places, rise up spirits. To them enter, leaping in great joy, Rufman, Shackesoule and Lurchall, discovering behind a curten, Ravillac, Guy Faulx, Barterville, a Prodigall, standing in their torments.

To this period also am I inclined to assign the anonymous Red Bull play, *The Two Noble Ladies; or The Converted Conjuror*, of which the manuscript is in the British Museum.[1] In Act V, scene 2, of this, we read that "The Devills sinck roaring; a flame of fier riseth after them." This was a common accompaniment of arriving or departing devils,[2] but it is difficult to say how the effect was procured. Sabbattini's receipt for hell-fire involved the blowing of Greek pitch and rosin through a torch by means of long tubes.[3] On the Elizabethan stage, the chances are that, save for the absence of thunder and the addition of smoke, the effect was procured in much the same way as the lightning effect,[4] or by simply blowing rosin through a candle. Old as this method then was

---

[1] Egerton MSS, 1994.
[2] Chapman's *Caesar and Pompey*, II, 1; *The Divil's Charter*, IV, 1; *The Silver Age*, V.
[3] *Practica*, Bk. II, chaps. 22, 23.
[4] Cf. Lawrence, *The Elizabethan Playhouse and Other Studies*, ii, 18. Note how, in Act V of *The Honest Lawyer*, a Red Bull play of *circa* 1616, Robin, while hiding in a bush, pretends to be a spirit. A direction says, "Rob. flashes powder." Cf. *The Virgin Martir*, V, 1: "Enter Harpax in a fearful shape, fire flashing out of the Study."

— it had served in a Resurrection play given at Reading in 1507 [1] — no better method of flashing lightning was known even in the mid-eighteenth century. To be convinced of this, one has only to read Rousseau on the absurdities of contemporary French opera.

To that rare type of scholar who is capable of appreciating Elizabethan drama as literature and of visualising it in action under the original conditions, Goldsmith's ever-green phrase,"Shakespeare and the musical glasses," has none of that antithetical significance it possesses for the ordinary man of culture. He knows that in Shakespeare's day the sublime and the ridiculous were not kept in water-tight compartments. Whether at its best or its worst, the Elizabethan drama is a jumble of opposites. Immortal poetry and inspiring thoughts stand cheek by jowl with the leer of the satyr and the puerile conceit of the witling. And inextricably mingled with these motley elements are the tricks of the mountebank, the "hey presto-pass!" of Hocus Pocus and his clan.

[1] Chambers, *The Mediaeval Stage*, ii, 393.

VIII

EARLY COMPOSITE PLAYS

ONCE more I find myself compelled resolutely to grapple with the manifold difficulties commonly encountered by those who, wearied with the tilling of exhausted fields, turn with relief to the disruption of virgin soil. Happily, I feel assured that at worst my labours will not have been wasted, for experience holds out the bright possibility that, no matter how meagre my crop, those who undauntedly take up the task may profit by my mistakes and reap "earthës increase, foison plenty."

The composite play may be tersely described as a play whose acts are composed of other plays, whether separate or deftly interlinked. No investigation has been made of the rise and progress of this scheme, and one is at a loss to trace it to its source. Though an example of the type can be traced on the English stage as early as 1585, it is by no means assured that the type was of English origin. Rather would it appear that the mould had been made in Italy. When we find that the principle of the composite play was practised by the Italian comedians both at home and abroad in the declining years of the sixteenth century, it is much more rational to suppose that England derived inspiration from Italy than Italy from England. In 1611 Flaminio Scala, chief comedian to the Duke of Mantua, published in Venice fifty scenarios from his own pen,[1] most of which had been utilised

---

[1] "Il teatro delle favole rappresentative overo la ricreatione comica, bosareccia e tragica, divisa in cinquante giornate composte da Flaminio Scala detto Flavio, comico del serenissimo signor duca di Montova."

in stage practice during the last quarter of the previous century.[1] One of these, entitled *L'Alvida*, is for a composite play. It consists of an outline of three plays in one, a comedy, a pastoral, and a tragedy, all interlinked.[2] It is known also that Giambattista Andreini, a distinguished actor-author who was born at Florence in 1579, wrote one or two composite plays, not scenarios, notably *La Centaure*, published in 1622 with a dedication to Marie de Medicis. This is in three acts, in prose, and with songs. Evidently following a prescribed formula, it consists of a comedy, a pastoral, and a tragedy, the sequence being the same as in Scala's scenario. Some idea of the fantastic nature of the pastoral may be gleaned from the fact that its dramatis personae consisted of a number of male and female centaurs, all members of the one family. The play is conjectured to date from about 1602.[3]

To watch the parachute of the dandelion sailing lightly along is to be reminded that seeds can travel afar and germinate without being planted. Assuming the Italian origin of the composite play, it is unnecessary to postulate practical exemplification of the principle in England by Italian players, to account for its transference across the Channel. The seed could have been borne in divers ways. Yet, withal, I cannot but think there is some significance in the fact that from 1571 onwards, for at least a decade, several troupes of Italian comedians were strolling in France,[4] and that within that period two of them visited England. In 1574 some Italian players accompanied Queen Elizabeth on her progress, and acted

[1] Moland, *Molière et la Comédie italienne*, p. 81.
[2] For analysis, see Winifred Smith, *The Commedia dell'Arte*, pp. 120–122.
[3] See Charles Magnin on the "Teatro Celeste" in the *Revue des Deux Mondes*, xl, 855, 856.
[4] Armand Baschet, *Les Comédiens italiens à la Cour de France, passim*.

before her at Windsor and Reading. But if English cultivation of the composite play was due directly to foreign initiation, more importance would appear to attach itself to the visit paid to London in 1578 by Drusiano Martinelli's troupe of *commedia dell'arte* players, especially as they were permitted to give public performances within the city.[1]

To my mind it is not at all improbable that Edmund Spenser wrote the first English composite play. Writing to him in April, 1580, Gabriel Harvey said, "I imagine your Magnificenza will hold us in suspense . . . for your nine English Commedies," and again:

I am void of all judgment if your Nine Comedies, whereunto in imitation of Herodotus, you give the names of the Nine Muses (and in one man's fancy not unworthily) come not nearer Ariosto's Comedies, either for the fineness of plausible elocution, or the rareness of Poetical Invention, than that Elvish Queen doth to his Orlando Furioso.[2]

As it does not seem to me at all likely that Spenser had written nine full-length comedies in illustration of the characteristics of the Muses, I can only conclude that what he had done was to write a composite play arranged in two parts, with five plays in the one and four in the other. All trace of these nine comedies is now lost, but it would be arguing against the probabilities to infer that they never reached the stage.

Records of the acting of English composite plays begin in 1585, but the earliest identified play of the type, Tarlton's *The Seven Deadly Sins*, not only is of unknown date but is unhappily lost to us. The first references we have to it occur four years after the famous clown's

[1] Chambers, *The Elizabethan Stage*, ii, 262.
[2] Harvey, *Two Other Very Commendable Letters*, in Works, ed. Grosart, i, 67, 95.

death. In 1592 Gabriel Harvey, acting on the principle that any stick is good enough to beat a dog with, commits the absurdity, in his *Foure Letters*, of accusing Nashe of stealing ideas, and characterises his *Pierce Penilesse* as not Dunsically botched-vp, but right formally conuied, according to the stile, and tenour of Tarleton's president, his famous play of the seauen Deadly sinnes; which most deadly, but most liuely playe, I might haue seene in London; and was verie gently inuited thereunto at Oxford by Tarleton himselfe.

Making reply shortly afterwards in his *Strange News*, Nashe, while acknowledging the excellence of Tarlton's play, had no difficulty in rebutting the charge of plagiarism. Preposterous as was that charge, it would have been still more so if, as Payne Collier maintained [1] and scholars for long after him believed, *The Seven Deadly Sins* had been a mere extemporisation, with no more material basis than a scenario.

All that we know of the characteristics of Tarlton's bisected play is due to Malone's discovery of the "plott," or players' guide, for the Second Part, commonly assumed by latterday Elizabethan investigators to have been made for a revival of the play by Strange's Men *circa* 1591.[2] It may be safely surmised from this that there were four plays in the First Part and three in the Second, each typifying a particular sin. All were contained within a neat framework, since, with Lidgate as presenter, the plays were supposed to be performed for the entertainment of the imprisoned King Henry VI.[3]

[1] Collier, *History of English Dramatic Poetry* (1831), iii, 393–400.

[2] Chambers, *The Elizabethan Stage*, ii, 125, 199; *The Review of English Studies*, i, 257, Greg on "The Evidence of Theatrical Plots for the History of the Elizabethan Stage," *passim*.

[3] Note that Munday's *Downfall of Robert Earl of Huntington*, Peele's *The Old Wives' Tale*, and the two Taming of the Shrew plays are all simplifications of this form.

There has been a good deal of wild conjecturing over Tarlton's composite piece. On the strength of the fact that Tarlton was an original member of the Queen's company, it has been assumed that the play was written for that company,[1] but the comedian had been on the stage for some years before the establishment of the Queen's Men in November, 1583, and had been known as early as 1570 as a writer of ballads. It seems not at all unlikely that the Queen's Men acted the play, but proof of acting is not necessarily proof of original ownership. This assumption was made by Fleay[2] with the aim of approximating the date of the play, and gave rise on his part to an untenable identification, which, strange to say, has been viewed with complacency by more than one capable scholar. In the Revels Accounts for 1585 Fleay found evidence that "an Invention called Fyve playes in one" was played by the Queen's Men "before her Matie on Twellfedaie at night in the hall at Grene-wiche," and that "an Invention of three playes in one" was to have been acted before the Queen by the same company at Somerset Place on the following Shrove Sunday night, but was not given.[3] Ignoring the circumstance that the seven cardinal sins were much more likely to have been dealt with in seven than in eight associated plays, he at once jumped to the conclusion that here were records of the incompleted court performance of Tarlton's composite piece. Obsessed by that belief, he sought to bolster it by specious reasoning. He remarked an induction in the plot of the Second Part, and sensibly surmised that Part I had also an induction. Hence, according to his view, Part I, otherwise

[1] Chambers, *The Elizabethan Stage*, ii, 342.
[2] Fleay, *Biographical Chronicle of the English Drama*, p. 83.
[3] Cunningham, *Revels Accounts*, p. 189.

Five Plays in One, consisted of an induction and four plays, and Part II, otherwise *Three Plays in One*, of the old induction and three plays. That is to say, for the purpose of his identification and no other earthly reason, we must reckon as a play the induction to Part I, but not the induction to Part II.

Detecting the falsity of Fleay's reasoning and at the same time desirous of supporting his hypothesis, Professor J. Tucker Murray [1] argues that when both parts of the play were acted together "the induction would, of course, precede the first part of the play," leaving us to assume that the Second Part had no individual induction, and that the induction was transferred to it when it happened to be played separately. But the invalidity of that contention becomes apparent when we find in the plot of the Second Part clear proof that that part had a particular induction of its own, one that could not possibly be played before the First Part. It will suffice to cite the opening details:

A tent being plast one the stage for Henry the Sixt. he in it Asleepe. to him The Leutentennt. A purcevaunt R. Cowley Jo Duke and i warder R. Pallant — to them Pride, Gluttony, Wrath and Covetousness at one dore, at an other dore Envie Sloth and Lechery. The Three put back the foure and so exeunt. [2]

Obviously, the induction was a visualised dream, in which Pride, Gluttony, Wrath, and Covetousness, whose ill qualities had already been exemplified in the First Part, indicate their desire to take possession again of the

---

[1] *English Dramatic Companies*, i, 78. Much water has since run under the bridge. Unfortunately, in 1910, when this was written, Mr. Murray was sharing the old belief that *The Seven Deadly Sins* was a mere extemporisation, and probably thought the two parts could, if necessary, be acted as a whole. I feel assured that he knows much better now.

[2] Collier, *History of English Dramatic Poetry* (1831), iii, 394.

stage, but they are indignantly expelled by Envy, Sloth, and Lechery, who have not yet had their innings.

It is not surprising to find Fleay committing himself to a fallacy of this order (he had rather a weakness in that way), but it shocks one to find cautious, full-armed scholars of the rare type of Greg and Chambers endorsing his fallacy.[1] What they have failed to grasp is that, so far as composite plays are concerned, there is absolutely no warrant for reckoning the induction, when it occurs, as one of the constituent plays. The little evidence we have on the point goes to prove the contrary. Yarrington's *Two Tragedies in One* is furnished with an induction, but, most indubitably, it is neither of the two tragedies. If it be argued that this play was not moulded on the Tarlton plan, I should instance a much later play that was so moulded, namely, the so-called Beaumont and Fletcher *Four Plays in One*. Here, as in practically all cases, the induction is almost extrinsic, certainly not an integrant of the work proper.

It has not been proved that *The Seven Deadly Sins* was originally produced by or ultimately belonged to the Queen's Men, but, viewing Tarlton's membership of that organisation, there are fair grounds for believing that they had acquired possession of and acted the play. But with their decline in court favour, and their departure into the country late in 1591, they apparently disposed of a number of their old plays to Strange's Men, a circumstance which has been advanced to explain the existence of a plot of the Second Part of *The Seven Deadly Sins* — the plot already referred to — in which the names of most of the contemporaneous members of Strange's

[1] Greg, *Henslowe Papers*, p. 129; Chambers, *The Elizabethan Stage*, iii, 497. *Per contra*, R. Crompton Rhodes, in a letter published in the *Times Literary Supplement* for October 23, 1919, showed the absurdities of Fleay's reasoning.

Men figure. But Fleay and his prominent latterday supporters [1] ask a little too much when they expect us to believe that *Four Plays in One*, acted by Strange's Men at the Rose on March 6, 1591–92, was identical with Tarlton's Second Part. To concede that, we should have to reckon the induction as a play, a course which, as I have shown, cannot be legitimately taken. What surprises one, in these fertile days of wild conjecture, is that nobody has argued that the piece then really played at the Rose was Tarlton's First Part, viewing the coincidence in the number of constituent plays. Apart from that, it surely argues a woeful lack of imagination on the part of investigators not to be able to postulate that Strange's Men had more than one composite play in their repertory. Why consider them rarities?

Bubbles charm the eye with their iridescence, but they are fated to burst. The truth of the matter is that it is highly absurd to identify *The Seven Deadly Sins* with any play recorded in the Revels Accounts or in Henslowe's Diary under any such title as *Four Plays in One*. Composite plays in two parts would not be titled in this indefinite way, since it was essential in the titling to link Part II with Part I. The whole point of Tarlton's play lies in its title: alter that, and it has no *raison d'être*. We know for certain that it was called *The Seven Deadly Sins:* on that score the evidence of Gabriel Harvey and of the plot of Part II is equally valuable.

In connexion with the production of a new composite play at the Rose in 1597, Henslowe's Diary yields information serving to show in what manner a new play ran its course in those days. On April 7 of that year the Admiral's Men produced there a new piece by an un-

---

[1] Fleay, *Biographical Chronicle of the English Drama*, p. 83; Greg, *Henslowe's Diary*, ii, 153; Chambers, *The Elizabethan Stage*, iii, 497.

known author, entitled *Five Plays in One*, and acted it, in all, ten times. This would have been reckoned then a fairly successful production. To become convinced that runs had not yet come into existence we have only to note the dates on which this play was given: April 7, 15, 20, 25, May 6, 14, 23, June 10, 28, July 27. Remark that at no period during the four months were two consecutive performances given. There was an interval of eight days between the first and second performances, time enough for the first-day audience to spread the news concerning the merits of the play. Fleay, the indomitable, in dealing with the production, gives it as his belief that the five constituent plays were Heywood's *Deorum Judicium*, *Jupiter & Io*, *Apollo and Daphne*, *Amphrisa*, and possibly *Misanthropos*, all first published in his *Pleasant Dialogues and Dramas* in 1637, but none spoken of as having been ever acted. On this score Dr. Greg has yielded him a tepid allegiance, but otherwise he has met with no support.[1] Personally, while agreeing with Bang that Fleay's theory is hazardous, I am of the opinion that Heywood had written a composite play or two in his early days and grown to like the form. It has escaped notice that two of his Jacobean plays, *The Silver Age* and *The Brazen Age*, are of this particular order. Each act, in both, deals with a different theme and has an entirely new set of characters.

Occasional attempts were made to put the old wine into new bottles. In 1601 there was published, under the running title of *Two Tragedies in One*, but without mention of the place of performance or the producers, a play with a long-tailed title reading: *Two Lamentable Tragedies. The one of the murder of Maister Beech a Chaundler in Thames-streete, and his boye, done by Thomas*

---

[1] Cf. Chambers, *The Elizabethan Stage*, iii, 346.

*Merry. The other of a young childe murthered in a Wood
by two ruffins with the consent of his Vncle. By Rob.
Yarington.*

There has been a good deal of controversy, much cry
and little wool, as to what relationship this play bears
to the *Beech's Tragedy* for which Henslowe, on behalf of
the Admiral's Men, made payments to Day and Haughton in 1597, and whether it was in any wise connected
with *The Orphan's Tragedy* of 1601.[1] Nothing is known
of Yarington, and the attribution of the play to him has
been doubted. As its title indicates, it discusses two
separate themes, the murder of Beech, the chandler, in
London in August, 1594, and the old, old story of the
Babes in the Wood, but with the scene, probably for
distinction's sake, laid in Italy, and, alas, with only one
babe. The two themes are treated in alternate scenes,
somewhat after the manner of a plot and sub-plot, but
without interlinkment. A plausible pretext for their
dramatic juxtaposition is given in the induction, in which
Homicide and Avarice conspire and Truth takes upon
herself the duties of expositor, appearing afterwards as
Chorus. A sort of framework to the whole is thus afforded, since the three come on again at the end to settle
conclusions. The verdict on the play, assuming that it
was ever acted, must have been unfavourable, for its
mingled method evoked no emulation.

Shakespeare was an opportunist and gave his public
what it wanted when it wanted it, but there were some
crazes against which his profound good sense rebelled, and
the composite play was of them. By an irony of circumstance, however, a self-contained fragment of a composite
play was published as his by the contemptible Pavier
in 1608. Its title ran: *A Yorkshire Tragedy. Not so New*

[1] Chambers, *The Elizabethan Stage*, iii, 518.

as Lamentable and true. Acted by his Maiesties Players at the Globe. Written by W. Shakespeare.

We should not know that this was a fragment but for the happy presence of a head-title which reads:

ALL'S ONE,

or, one of the Four Plaies in One, called

A YORK-SHIRE TRAGEDY

As it was plaid by the Kings Maiesties Plaiers.

Its production cannot have taken place more than a year or two, at most, before publication, since it dealt with the story of Walter Calverley, who was executed for murder in August, 1605. Having a long row to hoe, I must refrain from taking a hand in the lively game of conjecture that is being played concerning it, and refer those interested to Professor Tucker Brooke's introduction to *The Shakespeare Apocrypha*,[1] and to the invaluable Chambers.[2]

It would appear that by this time the taste for the composite play was rapidly decaying, though occasional attempts to re-create it were made in the latter half of the century. Only one other pre-Restoration play of the type remains to be discussed, the *Four Plays in One* of the Beaumont and Fletcher folio of 1647. There has been much controversy over the authorship of this mysterious piece, but I shall not contribute to it beyond saying that its publication in the Folio is *prima facie* evidence that either Beaumont or Fletcher, if not both, had a hand in it. One thing is certain: though the bulk of the Beaumont and Fletcher canon belonged to the King's Men, it was not a King's Men's play. In the first place, all the plays produced by them and published in the folio have casts, a feature of which it is devoid; and

[1] Pages xxxiii–xxxvi.   [2] *The Elizabethan Stage,* iv, 54.

secondly, it has no mention in the list of their plays printed in the Malone Society *Collections*.[1]

Four Plays in One consists mainly of three plays bearing the titles, *The Triumph of Honour*, *The Triumph of Love*, and *The Triumph of Death*, all dealing with themes taken from the *Decameron*, together with an original masque entitled *The Triumph of Time*. The whole is in a neat framework. An induction reveals that an entertainment is about to be given in celebration of the nuptials of Emanuel, King of Portugal, and Isabella of Castile, and in their presence. This explains why, between the constituent plays and at the close, the royal pair make their appearance and discuss what they have seen. As I shall point out later in full detail, the piece itself presents irrefragible evidence that it was written initially for court performance; and it seems not unlikely that the induction has topical allusiveness to an event that has just taken place or is foreshadowed. But at this juncture I must cry *peccavi*. In an article entitled, "The Date of *Four Plays in One*," published in the *Times Literary Supplement* for December 11, 1919, I sought to show that the play was written in 1613, in honour of the nuptials of the Prince Palatine and the Lady Elizabeth, but I have since seen the error of my ways, and am therefore perfectly reconciled to the fact that Sir Edmund Chambers finds my argument unconvincing.[2] On the principle, however, that an Irishman is always allowed to speak twice, I claim another hearing.

In his interesting paper on "Nathaniel Field's work in the Beaumont and Fletcher Plays," forming part of his *Sidelights on the Elizabethan Drama*, Mr. H. Dugdale Sykes makes a move in the right direction in dating *Four Plays in One* considerably later than it has hitherto been dated.

[1] Vol. i, part 5, p. 364. [2] *The Elizabethan Stage*, iii, 231.

He thinks it cannot have been written before 1617, and belongs to close on that year. Emboldened by his example, I am inclined to go still further ahead, and assign the play to the period of 1623-25. To begin with, one gets faint clues to this period in the induction, where Frigoso, the court usher, is shown exerting himself to keep back a crowd of unseen people who are struggling to get in to see the performance. This situation, it may be noted, is a prime favourite of Fletcher's. In his *A Wife for a Month*, as licensed for the King's Men in May, 1624, there occurs in the middle of the second act a scene before the masque, in which the Second Servant says:

> Look to that back door,
> And keep it fast; they swarm like bees about it.

And presently the citizens' wives troop in to see the entertainment. But it is perhaps more important to note that there is an allusion in the induction of *Four Plays in One* to a recently introduced custom of giving occasional court performances to the fair sex only. Frigoso says: "You see how full the scaffolds are, there is scant room for a lover's thoughts there. Gentlewoman, sit close for shame: has none of ye a little corner for this gentleman?"

We get a clue to the period when this practice began in an entry in Sir Henry Herbert's Office Book, dealing with November 2, 1624, and reading: "The night after, my lord Chamberlin had *Rule a Wife and Have a Wife* for the ladys, by the kings company." [1]

One of the puzzles presented by the composite play under discussion is that, while the epilogue sounds as if addressed to an ordinary audience, the whole production smacks of the court. Not since the first success of *Tamburlaine* had there been such a profuse employment of

[1] Adams, *Dramatic Records of Sir Henry Herbert*, p. 52.

chariots as is to be noted in this piece, but it must be borne in mind that they had been frequently introduced into the court masques and triumphs of the Jacobean period.[1] Then again, in very few pre-Restoration plays can the number and variety of aerial ascents and descents seen in this play be paralleled. Consider, particularly, the simultaneous descents of Jupiter and Mercury in the second scene of *The Triumph of Time*. This was a feat unaccomplished in any of the Jacobean court masques, and, if a theatre feat, must belong to a later period. Court scenic machinery must have reached some considerable degree of perfection before that precise spectacular effect could be attained. Moreover, in the first of the constituent plays, *The Triumph of Honour*, there is a magical transformation unlike anything to be found in the whole range of early seventeenth-century drama, but bearing resemblance to sundry scenic transformations seen in the court masques. Scene 2 represents a rocky view near Athens. The transformation comes near its close, and is indicated by the direction, "Solemn music. A mist ariseth, the rocks remove."

It is noteworthy also that in the concluding masque, *The Triumph of Time*, another rock effect was seen. The stage was occupied by a symbolical golden rock, evidently a massive "property," which spurted fire when Plutus struck it. One has only to turn to the early Revels Accounts to see that this had long been a conventional court effect.[2] Evidently, on Reyher's showing, large property rocks were still being used in court entertainments at the close of the Jacobean period. In his excel-

[1] See *The Masque of Oberon* (1611), *Love Restored* (1612), and Jonson's *Challenge at Tilt*, Second Part (as given on January 1, 1614, at the Earl of Somerset's marriage).

[2] Cunningham, *Revels Accounts*, pp. 144, 146.

lent book on masques Reyher, in discussing *Neptune's Triumph*, Jonson's aborted Whitehall masque of January, 1624, quotes from a carpenter's account preserved in the Audit Office,[1] detailing the "makeinge of a rocke in the vault vnder the banquetting house, setting vpp degrees and making ready the banquetting house for the maske," and so forth.[2] But the rock referred to can hardly have been prepared for *Neptune's Triumph*. An examination of the text of that masque and of *The Fortunate Isles and their Union*, the later masque which absorbed all of its scenic features, reveals no necessity for the provision of a rock. On the other hand, one cannot conclude that the property was prepared for *Four Plays in One*. No event took place in the period of 1623–24 that that composite piece could be supposed to celebrate. It could scarcely have been written in honour of the intended nuptials of Prince Charles and the Infanta of Spain, since by October, 1623, it was well known that all idea of the match had been definitely abandoned. If we are to date the play anywhere about this period, we have no option but to assume that it was written in celebration of the Prince's marriage with Henrietta Maria early in 1625.

To my mind, the clearest indication that *Four Plays in One* was written for court performance occurs in a stage direction in the last scene of *The Triumph of Time*. It reads: "One half a cloud is drawn. Singers are discovered: then the other half drawn."

The withdrawal of the second half reveals Jupiter in all his glory. Obviously, this was designed for a masque stage of the middle period. A disclosure of this order was

---

[1] Reference "(W) B. 2424 R 54."

[2] Reyher, *Les Masques Anglais*, appendix, p. 528. For details of the genesis and suppression of *Neptune's Triumph*, see *Ibid.*, pp. 303–305.

attainable only on a stage·fronted by a proscenium arch, a court-masque stage as contradistinguished from the open platform-stage of the theatres. The *modus operandi* can be readily deduced from Inigo Jones's maturer scheme of mounting, and particularly from the sectional design for *Salmacida Spolia*, preserved among the Lansdowne MSS.[1] As in our latterday theatre, the masque stage of the middle period was equipped with sky borders, but the arrangement was wholly different from that which recently obtained. Instead of being all of a piece and working perpendicularly, the old borders were in two or three sections and worked laterally. In this explanation lies the secret of the common masque direction, "The clouds divide." This arrangement afterwards became part of the scheme of mounting adopted on the Restoration picture-stage, and held good in the English theatre until the meridian of the eighteenth century. Hence, in the fifth act of Duffet's *Psyche Debauch'd*, a burlesque of 1678, we have the direction: "Trumpets are heard afar off, the Heavens divide; and from the farthest end Mercury flies down attended by Fame, and the whole Heaven appears adorn'd with Angels and Musick."

The old name for these sky borders was "cloudings," and it is significant that in an extant inventory made in Covent Garden in 1743 we have mention of "a hook to draw off the cloudings." [2]

One reason why I formerly fixed the date of *Four Plays in One* as 1613 was a certain similarity of theme between *The Triumph of Time* and Chapman's masque of the Inner Temple and Lincoln's Inn in honour of the Lady

---

[1] For a reproduction, see Thorndike, *Shakespeare's Theater*, p. 188; cf. Simpson and Bell, *Designs by Inigo Jones for Masques and Plays at Court*, pp. 119, 120.

[2] Wyndham, *Annals of Covent Garden Theatre*, ii, 312.

Elizabeth's wedding. In the play, Plutus enters, surrounded by singing and dancing Indians who acknowledge him as master. Labour, Industry, and the Arts emerge. Anthropos is borne to a rock, which Plutus strikes; flames fly out, and Anthropos gives thanks to Jupiter on beholding a mine of gold. Plutus then departs for Virginia, accompanied by Industry and Labour. My early mistake was in not seeing that Virginian affairs were quite as much on the *tapis* at the close of James's reign as in its meridian. In August, 1623, Herbert licensed for the Curtain players "A Tragedy of the Plantation of Virginia." [1]

With the Puritans in the ascendant at the interregnum, one gets time to turn one's eyes to France, where, in 1655, Quinault had his composite play, *La Comédie sans Comédie*, successfully produced at the Théâtre du Marais. This was a piece of five acts, of which the first was introductory and binding. Act II was a pastoral entitled *Clomire*; Act III, a comedy, *Le Docteur de Verre*; Act IV, a tragedy, *Clorinde*; and Act V, a spectacular tragicomedy, *Armide et Regnault*. I cannot pretend to have any profound knowledge of the French drama of the late seventeenth century, but I have sought in vain for proof that the success of Quinault's composite play raised a crop of plays precisely of the same type. I say, precisely of the same type, because there came into vogue a few years later a wholly different kind of composite play, the comedy or tragedy with *intermèdes*. I find, however, that Le Bas des Isles, a Norman gentleman who flourished between 1663 and 1700, wrote a play of the Quinault order, which was published sans date or place of

[1] Adams, *Dramatic Records of Sir Henry Herbert*, p. 24. Note that in *The City Madam* (1632), III, 3, three of the characters disguise themselves as Virginian Indians.

issue. Bearing the title *L'Air Enjoué*, and described as a comedy, it is in five acts and in verse. The first act comes by way of introduction and the last act as a sequel to it, but the intermediate acts are substantive and independent. Embedded in the whole are two comedies, *Les Valets Deguisés* and *Les Grippes*, and a tragedy, *Valentinian*.

Quinault exercised a good deal of influence on the trend of Restoration drama, and it is not at all unlikely that *La Comédie sans Comédie* was the inspiring cause of Davenant's *A Playhouse to be Let*, an ingenious composite play first published in the Davenant folio of 1673. Slender as are the clues, the date of Davenant's piece can be readily approximated. Reference is made to it in the prologue to Stapylton's *The Stepmother*, a tragi-comedy licensed for printing on December 26, 1663, and without doubt produced a month or two earlier. On bringing this clue to bear on the fact that Davenant in his epilogue speaks of the severer critics as being out of town, I find myself forced to conclude that *A Playhouse to be Let* saw the light in the Long Vacation of 1663. Moreover, it would appear that there was humorous topicality in its title, seeing that in the May previous the King's Players had abandoned their Vere Street house, on opening the new Theatre Royal in Bridges Street.

Davenant's first act, following the French mode, is introductory, the scene being laid on the stage of a playhouse during the Long Vacation, with the Tirewoman and the Chairwoman in occupation. To them comes a French player, who expresses his desire to take the house for the off-season and is permitted to rehearse his farce by way of giving a taste of his company's quality. The subsequent acts are composed of pieces rehearsed by the various players, who are rivals for the possession of the playhouse. It has been argued by Gillet [1] that the idea of Davenant's introduction was taken from *L'Impromptu de Versailles*, which was first acted privately at the French court on October 15, 1663, and first given publicly on November 4 following. To concede this would be to date *A Playhouse to be Let* no earlier than the ensuing December, an impossibility in the circumstances. Yet French influence of more than one kind there undoubtedly was. We stand on much safer ground when we see in *Sganarelle, ou le Cocu Imaginaire*, the prototype of the quaint French farce — French only in being spoken in broken English — which constitutes Davenant's second act. But, in truth, the play was an extraordinary hotch-potch. The third and fourth acts were made up of sorry old stuff — nothing less than the knight's so-called interregnum "operas," *Sir Francis Drake* and *The Cruelty of the Spaniards in Peru*. Nothing, however, seems to have made much impression save the burlesque tragedy of *Antony and Cleopatra*, which formed the last act and was the only part of the composite that survived. Later on, when the resplendent Duke's Theatre in Dorset Garden came to be built, it was revived there as an afterpiece.

Once again, in proceeding on our chronological journey, we find ourselves compelled to hie to Paris. Here, as personal conductor of the tour, I have no option — despite the risk of mixing up categories in inextricable confusion — but to reckon among composite plays a few plays with *intermèdes*, though, strictly speaking, they belong to an older and different order. The reason for this will at once become apparent. Take, for example, Montfleury's *L'Ambigu Comique, ou les Amours de Didon et d'Enée*,

[1] J. E. Gillet, *Molière en Angleterre, 1666–1670* (Mémoires de l'Académie Royale de Bruxelles, N. S., 1913; ix, 32).

otherwise a tragedy in three acts interspersed with three farces, *Le Nouveau Marié, Dom Pasquin d'Avolos,* and *Le Semblable à soi-même,* the third of which concluded the entertainment. The author states in his address to the reader that he had fastened upon the familiar story of Dido for his main plot in order that its threads might not be lost in the complicated interweaving. His piece saw the light early in 1673. Afterwards he wrote, in conjunction with Thomas Corneille, a much neater and more ingenious composite play entitled *Le Comédien Poète,* which was produced in the following November with very considerable success. This deals with the so-called (but interrupted) rehearsal of a one-act farce and a five-act comedy, in a crisply connective way. The play opens with a prose prologue, in which a conversation between a poet and an actor reveals that a rhymed farce by the poet, taken from the *Mostellaria* of Plautus, is about to be rehearsed. Only one act — in reality all — of this is given. In the absence of Damon *père,* Damon *fils* turns the family mansion into a private theatre, and is about to perform an opera for the amusement of his friends when Crispin, the young man's servant, learns of the old man's unexpected return, and sets his wits to work to save the situation. Damon *père* is told a cock-and-bull story about the house having become haunted by devils and having to be abandoned. In spite of his fears, the old man is so desperately anxious about the safety of his strong boxes that he sallies into the house, where he is seized by the rehearsing players, who are arrayed as demons, and borne up into the air. When the second act is about to follow, the poet and two of the actors come on. The poet reprimands the second actor for not being dressed for his part, and the rebuked one tells him in reply, not only that he is not going to play the part, but that the rehearsal will not take place, as he has arranged for the rehearsal of a play of his own. And then a new five-act comedy is represented.

Few people know that Offenbach's *Tales of Hoffman* has a very respectable ancestry. Its genealogical tree first began to sprout in 1697, when André Campra's French opera, *L'Europe galante*, saw the light. This novelty was the earliest of a long series of composite operas, specifically known as *spectacles coupés*, each act of which was complete in itself.

It was in 1697 also, though in London, that Motteux and Oldmixon's olla-podrida called *The Novelty, or Every Act a Play*, was brought out in the Long Vacation at the Lincoln's Inn Fields Theatre. Oldmixon's sole contribution to the medley was a pastoral called *Thyrsis*, which formed its first act. All the rest, with the exception of the fourth act, was the work of Peter Motteux. The second act consisted of a comedy of London life entitled *All Without Money*, and the third, of a masque of *Hercules*, with music by Eccles. The masque was deemed the most important feature of the production, and printed copies of it were distributed to the first-day audience. Act IV was a tragedy called *The Unfortunate Brother*, and proved to be nothing more than the latter part of Filmer's *Unnatural Brother*, a piece which had been summarily condemned on its production at the same house about seven months earlier. But, in all conscience, there was variety enough and to spare in the conglomeration. The fifth act consisted of a harlequinade, fashioned after the reigning Franco-Italian mode and bearing the title, *Natural Magic*. In this, Clown, Pantaloon, and Columbine were all seen, but, strange to say, there was no Harlequin. The particoloured mime, however, was only lurking round the corner, as it were; and all the motley elements of Christ-

mas Pantomime were already in the land, awaiting precipitation.

Neither in England nor in France had the composite
play any particular vogue during the eighteenth century.
One notes, however, that in July, 1729, there was acted
in Paris, and subsequently published, a play of this
order by M. Dumas d'Aiquebert, entitled *Les Trois
Spectacles*. Besides a prologue in prose (or what the
Elizabethans would have styled an induction), this piece
comprised a one-act tragedy in verse, entitled *Polixène*,
an equally short comedy, also in verse, entitled *L'Avare
Amoureux*, and an heroic pastoral operetta, with music
by Mouret, entitled *Pan et Doris*. So far as England was
concerned, it would seem that any likelihood of a revival
of interest in the type was extinguished by the unhappy
fate of Sir Hildebrand Jacob's *Nest of Plays*, on its production at Covent Garden late in January, 1738. The
eggs in Jacob's nest were three comedies, and all, when
put on the market, were deemed addled. It happened
that the piece was the first play licensed under the new
and highly unpopular Licensing Act, and the fact that it
had found favour with the Lord Chamberlain effectually
damned it in the public mind. Accordingly, it was given
but short shrift. Over this there need be no lamentation:
the composite play had already enjoyed an innings more
than commensurate with its merits. Afterwards, on the
rare occasions when it emerged from obscurity, it was in
unpenetrated disguise. As an exemplification of this, one
may point to Edward Knoblock's absorbing play, *My
Lady's Dress*, which has borne occasional revival at home
and abroad since its original production at the Royalty
Theatre in April, 1914. Nobody has ever dreamt of its
high and distinguished lineage, but one anonymous critic
got near the mark when he described it as "a connected

and cumulative group of one-act plays built round a central idea." Interpreted by the flashlights of history, this means that it remained for a twentieth-century dramatist to carry the type to its highest artistic form. May we not say that, in evolving homogeneity out of a scheme fundamentally heterogeneous, Mr. Knoblock has practically squared the circle?

IX

ILLUSION OF SOUNDS IN THE
ELIZABETHAN THEATRE

POPULAR impressions are never scientifically accurate, and the prevailing idea that an Elizabethan theatrical performance demanded excessive powers of make-believe is about as far from the mark as a popular impression could well be. It denies to Shakespeare's stage the extraordinary complexity that proved to be its glory. Not by one principle but by a jumble of principles was it ruled. Ever striving after the real, it was compelled by its shortcomings to make constant resort to the ideal. Everything that could be shown was shown, and what could not be shown was conveyed imaginatively.

With all his resourcefulness, there were problems that baffled the Elizabethan producer, and these he left by tacit understanding to be solved by the poet's pen. Backgrounds which conveyed a hundred different impressions to a hundred different minds were imperishably built up in a mosaic of scintillating phrase and glowing imagery. But if the prime conveyance of atmosphere was the poet's prerogative, none the less was it the producer's duty to prolong its vibrations. He had at his beck a rich comprehension of the science of the illusion of sounds, that subtler kind of realism which, when deftly brought into play, proves such a quickener of the imagination. As procured by him, it reënforced the pen-picture sketched in by the poet and gave it colour. Thunder, the muttering of the storm and the whistling of the wind, the singing of birds, the lowing of cattle, the baying of hounds, the pealing of bells, the galloping of horses, the boom of cannon, and the rattle of musketry — all were well and truly imitated. He had no electric lights to enable him to convey the gradations of the dawn, but he was able, as in *Hamlet*, to conjure up all its eeriness by the simple crowing of a cock.

One important fact in connexion with Elizabethan stage presentation, involving a subtle distinction, has never yet been grasped. Not all sights seen in the course of the action by the characters were (or could be) shown to the audience, but all sounds heard by the characters could be, and were, heard by the audience. In other words, sights were sometimes imagined, but sounds never. In the absence of fully corroborative stage directions, this will doubtless take some proving, but I face the task with happy intuitions and supporting optimism. Instructions for the procuring of certain effects were often confined to prompters' marginalia, excrescences usually ignored in the printing; but now and again, by some stroke of good fortune, an odd jotting of the sort managed somehow to get into type. It is largely on the strength of one or two providential blunders of this kind that I venture to predicate that all textual references to the hearing of bird song were accompanied by imitative warbling. To prove one or two instances at different periods and different theatres, as I hope to do, is to afford grounds for reasonable belief in the existence of a custom. Nor will it suffice, for doubting Thomases, to protest that a considerable variety of bird song was heard by the old dramatis personae, sometimes solos and sometimes concerted; that objection might hold, were we not in a position to know that the Elizabethan players had ways and means of imitating, not alone the pipe of all indigenous singing birds, but the call of several ungifted with melody.

It would be rash to assume that any elaborate mechanical device was utilised for the purpose, though a device of the sort was certainly known. There is reason to believe that this had been resorted to in foreign pageants and native court masques, but the Elizabethan players undoubtedly adopted simpler means. The *modus operandi* of this curious hydraulic machine is discussed by Salomon de Caus in his *Les Raisons des Forces Mouvantes*, published at Frankfort in 1615. A score of years later John Bate, in his interesting little book, *The Mysteries of Nature and Art*, also deals with the machine, referring to it as "a device whereby several voices of birds chirping may be heard." [1] One recalls in this connexion how, on the entry of Henri II and Catherine de Medicis into Lyons in 1548, there was seen at the Bridge of St. Paul a golden triumphal arch, behind which was a grove in which artificial birds sang. [2] Again, in Dekker's description of the London pageant of 1604, given in honour of King James's coronation, we read that at one haltingplace a song was sung "to a loude and excellent musicke, composed of violins, and another rare artificiall instrument, wherein, besides sundrie severall sounds effused (all at one time) were also sensibly distinguisht the chirpings of birds." [3]

It has been sensibly argued by Mönkemeyer [4] that the use of bird song in early Elizabethan court plays indicates

[1] Bate, *The Mysteries of Nature and Art* (2d edition, London, 1635), p. 24. See also Conrad W. Cooke, *Automata Old and New*, p. 55.

[2] Albert Baur, *Maurice Scève et la Renaissance Lyonnaise* (doctoral thesis; Paris, 1906), p. 99.

[3] Nichol, *Progresses of Elizabeth*, iii, 64, 65.

[4] *Prolegomena zu einer Darstellung der englischen Volksbühne zur Elisabeth- und Stuart- Zeit* (Hanover, 1906), p. 82.

a desire to heighten the illusion of actual wood settings, rather than an effort to compensate for their absence. As a corollary of this, one would be disposed to think that, contrarily, the players had adopted the court convention with the view of thus conjuring up the entire scenic effect, were it not for the circumstance that bird song had been heard on the public stage quite as early as at court, if not earlier. The first trace of the effect at court occurs in Peele's *The Arraignment of Paris*, in which, to quote from the book, "an artificiall charm of birds" lent illusion to the woodland effect. Peele's play cannot be dated earlier than 1584, but in July, 1576, there was entered in the Stationers' Register an ordinary play called *Common Conditions*, no doubt a year or two old, in which, at the beginning, Sedmond is to be found listening to the carolling of birds, notably of the nightingale.

What reason have we to believe that what he heard the audience failed to hear? Remember that, of all bird songs, the song of the nightingale admitted of the readiest imitation, was indeed the one song most commonly imitated on all European stages. Once we arrive at an old and simple method of nightingale simulation, we shall, if I mistake not, have read the riddle which has so long proved perplexing to the most erudite of French theatrical historians: namely, what were the *rossignols* so frequently mentioned in connexion with woodland and garden scenes in Mahelot's famous list of the scenes and properties requisite for the plays performed at the Hôtel de Bourgogne in the early seventeenth century?[1] I believe we have a clue to that old and simple method in

[1] H. C. Lancaster, *Le Mémoire de Mahelot, Laurent et d'autres décorateurs de l'Hôtel de Bourgogne et de la Comédie-Française au XVIIe siècle*, pp. 70, 82.

what Bacon writes in his *Sylva Sylvarum* concerning the old portable organ known as the regalls. "In regalls," he says, "(where they have a pipe they call the Nightingale-pipe, which containeth water) the sound hath a continual trembling." Whether or not the pipe when used alone gave a good nightingale imitation, the fact remains that the regalls was an instrument much employed by the Elizabethan choir-boy players. We find specific mention made of it at the second Blackfriars, in Marston's *The Wonder of Women, or Sophonisba.* Moreover, evidence of the simulation of bird song in the early private theatres is to hand, and, if not abundant, is at any rate sufficing. Middleton's *Blurt, Master Constable* was acted by the Paul's Boys late in 1601. In Act IV, scene 2, to be noted as an interior, we have the direction, "Musick suddenly plays and birds sing." The idea is to convey to Lazarillo the impression that he is in a haunted bedchamber. Again, in Marston's *The Dutch Courtezan*, a Blackfriars play of 1604, Malheureux, in the opening scene of the second act, says:

> The studious morn, with paler cheek, draw on
> The day's bold light. Hark how the free-born birds
> Carol their unaffected passions!
> Now sing their sonnets — thus they cry, we love!
> O breath of heaven! Thus they, harmless souls,
> Give entertain to mutual effects.
> They have no bawds, no mercenary beds,
> No polite restraints, no artificial heats,
> No faint dissemblings; no custom makes them blush,
> No shame afflicts their name.

For all that to be said without any singing heard would have been the height of absurdity; but happily we are relieved from all doubt on the point by a direction after the third line, notifying that "the nightingales sing."

While I am far from suggesting that Bacon's observation concerning the nightingale pipe indicates the precise manner in which nightingale song was imitated even in the private theatres (where the regalls were almost exclusively employed), still I am inclined to believe that his description of the pipe affords a clue to the means whereby the song was rendered. The thing was simple: apparently all that was wanted was a whistle, a bowl of water, and the exercise of some discrimination. Certainly the nightingale effect was an effect of too great frequency to be procured in an elaborate way. When the sweet strains of the immortal bird were heard in *The Spanish Tragedy*, they so worked upon the lovers as to induce them to pay each other pretty compliments. Horatio averred that the bird sang "for joy that Bel-imperia sits in sight," and Bel-imperia, not to be outdone, replied:

> No; Cupid counterfeits the nightingale
> To frame sweet musick to Horatio's tale.

One recalls, also how, at the opening of *The Taming of the Shrew*, the Lord asks of Sly:

> Wilt thou have music? Hark! Apollo plays,
> And twenty caged nightingales do sing.

We find later instances of this delightful combination. In Fletcher's comedy, *The Pilgrim*, a King's Men's production of 1621, there is, in the fifth act, a notable woodland scene in which Roderigo and Pedro lie down and listen to the warbling of the birds. Here the prompter inserted two warnings in his book, and, the book having been sent to the printer's, both have been happily preserved to us. The first reads, "Musick and birds," and the second, "Musick afar off. Pot Birds." Mönkemeyer very shrewdly maintains that "pot birds" signifies that well-known device, so alluring to all well-ordered boyhood, of producing warbling sounds by blowing into a bowl of water through a pipe.[1]

Let me repeat again that we must not make the mistake of imagining that in the old days one kind of imitative bird song sufficed for any and every bird whose pipe was heard in the theatre. Generalisation of this order would not have sufficed in times when town and country almost mingled and when the public theatres actually stood in the fields. No Elizabethan gamin could have displayed the ignorance shown by the boy in *Punch* who, on hearing a skylark, ran excitedly up to a passer-by and said, "Hi, mister, there's a bloomin' bird over there, and he cawnt get up and he cawnt get down — and ain't he a-hollerin!" We may be sure that, when Puck said warningly to Oberon:

> Fair king attend, and mark
> I do hear the morning lark,

it was the lark, and no other sort of bird, that was imitated. All our pre-conceptions of a generalised bird-song become dissipated once we come across evidence of divers kinds of birds singing separately in the one scene, while comment is made on their several songs. For this we need not seek beyond *Every Woman in her Humour*, an anonymous play of which little is known save that it was printed in 1609. In the course of the action a short masque is introduced, in which various birds are imitated off the stage as illustrative accompaniment to a song.[2] The birds mentioned in the song are the blackbird, thrush, nightingale, mavis, wagtail, linnet, and lark. At a considerably later period we get some clues to the manner in which the various kinds of song were distinguished.

[1] *Prolegomena*, p. 83.
[2] Cf. Edward Bliss Reed, *Songs from the British Drama*, pp. 105, 294.

Writing in his *Memorials*, Sir Bulstrode Whitelock gives intimate details of the performance of Shirley's masque, *The Triumph of Peace*, at Whitehall in 1634, and, in describing the preliminary public pageant, says:

After the Beggars' antimasque, came men on horseback playing upon pipes, whistles and instruments sounding notes like those of birds of all sorts, and in excellent consort, and were followed by the antimasque of Birds.

Probing still further, I find, by a useful little book of the period, Bate's *The Mysteries of Nature and Art*,[1] already referred to, that many of the Caroline shopkeepers had for sale mysterious, long white boxes containing a number of devices for imitating the song or cry of sundry birds and animals, such as the quail, cuckoo, peacock, stag, and fox. Nearly all these contraptions were of the nature of whistles, and some of them are depicted in an accompanying engraving. It is difficult to say how long they had been in vogue, but contemporary use of a few of them in the theatre can be traced. Thus, in Randolph's *Amyntas*, V, 5, Mopsus deludes himself into believing he is getting a message from the birds when he proceeds to play, unseen, on a quail pipe. The accompanying direction indicates that here a quail pipe was really used.

According to Bate, the cuckoo pipe could be so manipulated as to imitate also the hooting of an owl and the crowing of a cock. One wonders whether it would be safe to deduce from this that Chanticleer's heralding of the morning in *Hamlet* was not effected by an unaided human mimic. Cock-crowing was a very old and very popular stage effect. At Coventry, in 1573, a man was paid fourpence for imitating the cock that shamed Peter in a miracle play.[2] Afterwards, Shakespeare put cock-

---

[1] Page 82.   [2] Allardyce Nicoll, *British Drama*, p. 27.

crowing to equally dignified use, and Jonson made resort to it at court in his *Masque of Oberon*. But it seems curious that a pipe should have been contrived for the imitation of the cuckoo and the cock when both could be readily imitated by human means. To-day, any English country lad can give you the melodious song of the cuckoo by simply blowing into his hollow fists. But primitive methods of this order apparently did not suffice in early theatrical representation. It is surely significant that, just about the time Bate was describing the cuckoo pipe and other devices, the cuckoo's note was heard at the Cockpit iteratively in *The Sun's Darling, Hyde Park,* and *The Jovial Crew,* three pieces, it is to be noted, by three different authors.

Perhaps, on the whole, one would not err far in concluding that these long white boxes had not been many months on the market when Bate wrote. The frequency with which the effects that their contents were designed to procure recurred, shortly afterwards, in masque and play, seems to warrant that supposition. In Kynaston's *Corona Minervae*, a court masque of 1635 which dealt with the four seasons of the year, we read early in the book: "Here several noyses and voyces are heard confusedly of birds and beasts as exactly performed to the life, that no man could distinguish them."

Later on in the masque, Time has a long speech describing the salient characteristics of each season, and as these are mentioned illustrative sounds are heard. Lambs bleat, the lark, cuckoo, swallow, and thrush sing, boars grunt, and owls give their "too-whit, too-whoo."

So, too, in Nabbes's masque in honour of the Prince's birthday, given in May, 1638, the second scene, described as "a pleasant garden," opens with "a symphonie of musicke with chirping of birds, singing of nightin-

gales and cuckoos," an effect repeated in a subsequent
scene. The chirping of birds was also heard—somewhere
about the same period—in the third act of Brome's
The Queen and Concubine, where the wandering, ill-used
Queen soliloquises upon her distresses. Interrupted by
their chirping, she reflects:

> What Musick had the Court compar'd with this,
> Or what comparison can all their sports
> And Revells hold with those of kids and fawnes,
> And frisking Lambs upon the country Lawnes
> Which are my hourly pleasant entertainments
> In all my wanderings.

In Elizabethan days the theatrical barometer seldom
stood at set fair. There was generally storm of one kind
or another, either in the tiring-house or among the stinkards in the yard. When you come to think of it, that
latterday term of contempt, "blood-and-thunder drama,"
pithily characterises the bulk of the heavier fare of the
time. There was then no commoner illusion of sound
than that which pictured the battling of the elements.
Its recurrence is indicative of the early rise of the pathetic
fallacy in its broader aspects: the assumption for dramatic purposes that Nature concerned herself not only
with the woes but with the ill deeds of man. She could
echo rage as in *King Lear*, and she could act retribu-
tively. In olden times, no arch-villain or blatant atheist
was satisfactorily dispatched without an accompaniment
of thunder and lightning. *Doctor Faustus* was the great
archetype. Both the vogue and the *modus operandi* of
these early storm effects are clearly revealed in Jonson's
biting prologue for a Jacobean revival of *Every Man in his
Humour*, those familiar lines wherein rare old Ben very
absurdly claims praise for eschewing certain facile popular effects which the very nature of his play precluded

him from introducing. The play, in his estimation, is a model play, because he brings on no Chorus to fill up the gaps, lets off no fireworks to please the unthinking,

> nor roul'd bullet heard
> To say, it thunders; nor tempestuous drumme
> Rumbles, to tell you when the storm is come.

For much too long a period there has been a widespread belief that Jonson's prologue was one prolonged gird at Shakespeare — as if any attack of the sort could possibly have been made in the theatre identified with Shakespeare's greatest triumphs! Thank goodness, Professor Tucker Brooke has at last burst that glamorous bubble by demonstrating that Jonson's sneers were levelled at the King's Men's old rivals, the Prince's Men, for daring to revive *Doctor Faustus* in revised form at the Fortune.[1] It is noteworthy that John Melton, in making allusion to the same play at the same theatre a few years later in his *Astrologaster, or The Figure Caster*,[2] indicates that thunder then was simulated wholly and solely by the method spoken of by Jonson as adopted to give the illusion of the monitory muttering of the storm. Here is the passage:

Another will foretell of Lightning and Thunder that shall happen such a day, when there are no such inflammations seene except men goe to the *Fortune* in *Golding lane* to see the Tragedie of Doctor Faustus. There indeed a man may behold shagge-hayr'd devills runne roaring over the stage with squibs in their mouthes, while Drummers make Thunder in the Tyring-house, and the twelve-penny Hirelings make artificiall lightning in their Heavens.

---

[1] Cf. my paper on "Early Stage Properties." For the latest instance of the fallacy, see Simpson and Herford, *Ben Jonson*, ii, 115.

[2] Issued in 1620. A garbled version of the passage recurs, in *Crete Wonders Foretold*, in 1643 and again in 1647.

On this score, however, Jonson is infinitely the better authority, not only because of his intimate acquaintanceship with theatrical trick-and-shuffleboard, but because his statement admits of sound collateral corroboration. We know from Sabbattini that the usual method of procuring thunder on the early seventeenth-century Italian stage was by rolling an iron bullet down an inclined wooden trough provided here and there with slight obstructions over which it crashed.[1] Afterwards known in France as the *trémie*, or mill-hopper,[2] this device is still employed in a few old Continental theatres. But it cannot have been long in vogue when Jonson wrote of it, since it called for some considerable space in the working. In the Elizabethan public theatre it must have been situated in the tiring-house garret; in the inn-yard playing places it can have had no existence. There, resort was most likely to the old method used in the mysteries and in the Spanish secular drama of the late sixteenth century,[3] namely, simulation of the thunderclap by rolling a barrel half filled with stones. It may be, however, that Melton was referring to an alternative contemporary method. We get suggestions of its nature in our latter-day system of musical thunder, as applied operatically. Thus, in the overture to Herold's *Zampa*, thunder is procured by a roll on the bass drum. This drum is usually played with one stick, but for the thunder effect a short stick with two heads — otherwise round nobs covered with tow and chamois leather — is provided. It is held in the middle and the roll given by alternate twists of the wrist.[4]

[1] *Practica*, Bk. II, chap. 53.   [2] M. J. Moynet, *Trucs et Décors*, pp. 266, 267.
[3] Sismondi, *Historical View of the Literature of the South of Europe* (1846), ii, 240. For the thunder barrel at Westminster School in 1565-66, see Chambers, *The Elizabethan Stage*, ii, 73, note 1.
[4] Groves's *Dictionary of Music*, under "Tonnerre, Grosse Caisse en."

We have no proof that the Elizabethan stage possessed, what we possess to-day and what has long been known, a wind machine. For storm effects, unaccompanied by thunder, the rolling of the drum apparently sufficed. Wind was rarely simulated separately, but as it was commonly a forerunner of thunder, — as in *The Tempest*, II, 2, where Trinculo hears it singing just before he is drenched by the thundercloud, — thunder must have been mostly procured by the iron bullet. Of the wind effect alone we get a trace in *The Second Maiden's Tragedy*, a Globe play of 1611. A direction in Act IV, scene 4, reads: "On a sudden, in a kind of noise like a wind, the doors clattering, the tombstone flies open, and a great light appears in the midst of the tomb."

Somewhat more definite is the evidence of the Caroline period. In Heywood's *Love's Maistresse*, III, a direction occurs for "a storme," without any indication of thunder and lightning, and the textual reference is solely to the boisterousness of the wind. In *The Captives* of the same author, we find in the margin of Act II, scene 1, a double prompt warning, "Tempest, Thunder," proof positive that the two effects were not procured by the same medium.

Almost as vivid as the battle of the elements was the illusion of a fight by sea or land. Chorus in *Henry V* indulges in a needless moan over the poverty of theatrical resource, the hopelessness of giving an idea of the glories of Agincourt by the skirmishing of half-a-dozen men. But is it not a fact that, no matter what the stage or how well equipped, battle can be much better conveyed to the imagination than to the eye? With all our modern improvements, we have not advanced a tittle upon the Elizabethan method. Look, for example, at Beaumont and Fletcher's *Bonduca*, III, 5. Here, the spectators were given all the illusion of a mighty struggle without a single blow being struck. Interspersed between the vivid descriptions given by eye-witnesses viewing the battle from a height came a variety of stirring sounds off, "alarms, drums and trumpets in several places afar off," "loud shouts," "drums loud again," more shouting. There was virtually only one spectacular concession: when the battle was over, a fight took place on the stage between Junius and Catarach. Equal restraint, and equal imaginative use of sounds, are to be noted in the conflagration scene in the third act of Fletcher's *The Island Princess*. First the explosion of the train is heard, an alarm bell rings, there are cries of "Fire! fire!" both on and off the stage, intermingled with much hurrying and scurrying.[1] The principle followed in both cases is of the soundest: no veteran playgoer but will agree that the best-staged horse-race within his experience was the race he never saw!

In siege scenes and sea-fights a measure of realism was attained by the firing of chambers from the turret of the tiring-house. Chambers were small pieces of ordnance which stood on their breeching, without other support. The small private theatres of the sixteenth century had no turret, and partly for this reason and partly because the noise and reek of gunpowder in a small enclosed building was "most tolerable and not to be endured," the use of chambers in those particular houses was avoided. In an unpublished play of that period, *The Aphrodysiall*, the author, William Percy, gives instruction at one juncture for the firing of chambers, with the

---

[1] So, too, in *The Two Noble Kinsmen*, the whole excitement of the tournament is conveyed by noises, cries, and the ceremonial sounding of the cornets. This is a distinctive Fletcher touch; and it is noteworthy that the play belongs to the period of *Bonduca*.

reservation that if the play be acted by the Paul's Boys, the noise can be supposed.[1] But it is doubtful whether the boom of cannonading was always supposed at Paul's, and it would appear as if some cognate minor noise was substituted, probably a pistol shot or two. The First Part of *Antonio and Mellida* was produced at that house in 1601, and in Act I, line 340, we have the direction, "Exeunt all on the lower Stage: at which the Cornets sound a florish, and a peale of shot is giuen."

It is noteworthy that, besides their normal dramatic use, chambers were employed illustratively. When Gascoigne and Kinwelmershe's *Jocasta* was performed at Gray's Inn in 1566, "a peale of ordnance" was shot off in one of the inter-act dumb shows. The most striking instance, however, occurs in association with the Chorus before the third act of *Henry V*, where an alarm is given and chambers go off just as the speaker reaches the word "touches," a highly effective accompaniment of the lines:

> the nimble gunner
> With linstock now the devilish cannon touches,
> And down goes all before them.

Shakespeare has been credited here with a new device,[2] but I am inclined to believe it was an old convention. If new, it established a precedent, since in *The Travailes of the Three English Brothers*, a Curtain play of *circa* 1605, "a chamber" is "shot off" near the close of a chorus.

The ample theme of early stage bells having been dis-

[1] *Modern Philology* (1914), xii, 126, G. F. Reynolds on "William Percy and his Plays."
[2] See Charlotte Porter, Introd. to *Henry V* in *The First Folio Edition of Shakespeare* (1906), pp. xv, xvi. Cf. Albert H. Tolman's essay on "The Epic Character of *Henry V*" in his *Falstaff and Other Shakespearean Topics*.

cussed by me elsewhere,[1] there is little need for me to do more now than dwell upon its main aspects. What requires chiefly to be noted is that the large bell so commonly used for tolling, alarm, and clock-striking effects was situated above in the tower, though it is not improbable that it was rung from stage level by means of a rope descending through the tiring-house. But there were certain bell effects for which a single bell would not answer, and we have to ask ourselves how these were procured. The tower had divers other theatrical uses besides serving as a bell tower: thunder had to be made there, chambers fired, and gods and goddesses lowered; room would have been lacking for the instalment of a peal of bells. Nevertheless, melodious pealing was heard on occasion in the old playhouses. In the extant manuscript of Munday's *John a Kent and John a Cumber*, a play belonging to *circa* 1596, one finds in the fourth act a marginal warning for "Musique chime," and afterwards there occur two directions, the one reading "the chyme playes," and the other, "the chyme agayne." We cannot be certain that a chime of bells was here intended, but, judging by other evidence, that would be the inference. Regarding pealing at a slightly later period there is no room for doubt. Take Day's *The Isle of Gulls*, a Blackfriars play of the early Jacobean period. In Act II, scene 5, we have the direction, "Musicke of Bels &c," signifying the arrival of strangers at the fortified island. Then again, in Brome's *The Queen's Exchange*, another Blackfriars play but of a much later time, a direction occurs in Act I, scene 2, for "a shout within, the Musick, sound the bells." More interesting still is the bell-ringing competition in Act IV of Fletcher and Shirley's

[1] See *The Fortnightly Review* for July, 1924, my article on "Bells on the Elizabethan Stage."

Caroline comedy, *The Night Walker*, a piece often acted in Restoration days as *The Little Thief*. The scene being laid outside the church, the ringing is not seen, but betweenwhiles the ringers come out and discuss matters with the sexton, who is acting as judge.

When we come to ask ourselves how the thing was done, we get a clue to the mystery in Henslowe's Diary. Among the properties belonging to the Admiral's Men mentioned in Henslowe's inventory of March, 1598, is "i chyme of belles." Here the fact that Munday wrote frequently for the Admiral's Men, taken in conjunction with the chime used in *John a Kent and John a Cumber*, seems to point to the company for which that play was written. But this is a digression. It is much more pertinent to point out that, properties being essentially movable and storable, the Admiral's Men's chime must have been some special sort of contrivance, and not a permanent theatrical fixture. What, then, could have been its nature? Well, all we know for certain is that it occupied a small compass and could be readily moved about. We have indication of this in that highly popular old play, *The Merry Devil of Edmonton*. In the induction we see Peter Fabel, the magician, asleep in his bed at midnight, safeguarded from evil spirits by the warning chime at his head. But he is suddenly awakened by the ringing of the chime, and beholds Coreb drawing near to bear him off to Hell. As the Prologue at the beginning had pulled aside the traverse to reveal the sleeping man, we know that the scene was acted on the rear stage, and, if Fabel lay with his feet outwards so that he might face the audience while speaking, the obvious position for the chime would be behind the bed, where a crouching man could have played upon it unseen.

In that very useful little book already referred to, John

Bate's *The Mysteries of Nature and Art*, I find an illustrated description of a curious hydraulic bell-playing machine, but I hesitate to believe that the Elizabethan players used anything so complicated. Possibly there may be some significance in the fact that Tyrwhitt, who was sub-dean of the Chapel Royal from 1569 to 1584, had invented an artificial chime which enjoyed some vogue. All that can be learned about it was that it consisted of three bells of varying sizes. Intelligence of this having reached the Queen, she ordered Tyrwhitt to make her one of these devices to play pavans and galliards.[1] She evidently intended to use it for dance purposes, much as some people now use a gramophone.

In our present state of ignorance regarding the precise nature of Tyrwhitt's invention, it would be impossible to say whether it could have been adapted for theatrical purposes. For aught we know to the contrary, the Elizabethan players may have utilised for bell-pealing purposes a simple device known a century earlier. Details of this are to be found in the *Theorica Musicae* of Gafurius, an erudite tome printed at Milan in 1492. This presents a rude composite engraving depicting certain musical feats, in the right-hand upper compartment of which one man is shown playing upon the musical glasses while another is accomplishing the task of a set of bell-ringers. Hanging close to a taut, strongly secured rope on a level with the latter man's head is a row of six numbered bells of varying sizes, on which he is playing with two metal bars. It seems to me that one has only to transfer these bells to a strong movable stand to become possessed of a serviceable theatre chime.

[1] Jusserand, *Literary History of the English People* (2d edition, 1926), ii, 240. See also a letter of Tyrwhitt to Burleigh in Lansdowne MSS, 108, ff. 100, 102.

All knowledge being contributory, I may perhaps be pardoned for recalling the interest excited forty years ago by a horse-trotting illusion made use of in William Gillette's five-act drama of the American Civil War, entitled *Held by the Enemy*. This device lent itself readily to effects of distance as well as of contiguity, and consisted of two mounted horse-shoes adroitly worked by hand on a marble slab. Now, the same illusion was procured in the Elizabethan theatre, but we are ignorant of the means. There it sprang into being owing to the prime necessity of conveying to the audience a keen sense of the nearness, almost the presence, of horses, at a time when it was inexpedient, if not impossible, to bring them on the stage. Though none is to be traced earlier than the Jacobean period, there were many junctures in the old drama when illusions of sounds conveying the galloping of horses and associated noises were imperative. The earliest known examples occur in *Macbeth*, III, 3, and IV, 1, the first being the scene in which the three murderers hear Banquo's approach, and the second the scene in which Macbeth abruptly asks Lennox, "I did hear the galloping of horse: who was't came by?" In neither of these instances do we get an elucidative stage direction, and it might be thought that the inference was mere guesswork, were it not for the circumstance that in *The Insatiate Countess*, II, 4, we read that "a trampling of horses [is] heard," signifying that the Countess of Suevia has taken horse and fled from her husband. So, too, in *The Elder Brother*, I, 2, Busac suddenly asks, "What tramplings that of horses?" and immediately Eustace and others enter as from horseback.[1] In *The Chances* great attention was paid to the illusion of sounds. In Act III, scene 4, we read of "a noise within like horses,"

[1] Cf. *The Queen of Corinth*, IV, 4, and *The Great Duke of Florence*, V, 1.

and in Act IV, scene 3, where the action passes in front of a house, first music and a song are heard, then the "clapping of a door," followed by "trampling above," the noises signifying disturbance and scurry.

In the old days, the difficulty of procuring any particular illusion of sounds formed no check to the attempting of it, a circumstance which testifies to the dominance of the realistic principle. At the opening of the fourth act of Massinger's *The Guardian*, just before Durazzo appears and cries, "Hell take the stumbling jade!" we get instructions for "a noise within, as of a horse falling." Not an easy impression to give, this, but it was no more difficult than an effect necessary in *The Life and Death of Captain Thomas Stukeley*, wherein we read of "a noise within of driving beasts."[1] This conveyed that, after defeating the Irish, Stukeley had seized their cattle. Few dramatists hesitated about setting the players posers of this order. In *The Elder Brother*, III, 3, Charles hears the rumble of wheels, and is told it is "the coach that brings the fair lady." And immediately the fair lady and her train enter. To become disabused of the idea that the rumbling was imagined, one has only to turn to *A New Way to Pay Old Debts*, III, 2, and note the direction, "Noise within, as of a coach."

If only a few more of the old prompt-books had been preserved, or if only the old printers had oftener exceeded their duties and set up many more of the prompter's marginal notes, we should not now be in our present state of ignorance regarding the *modus operandi* of divers old effects. Some of the notes of this sort in the Beaumont and Fletcher folios are remarkably illuminating. Thus, in the scene in *The Spanish Curate* where Bartolus proceeds to smash up things off the stage, we

---

[1] Line 1102 in Simpson's reprint.

are vouchsafed the prompter's marginal warning, "Pew-
ter ready for noyse."

If that dramatist is great who makes the best use of his
resources, then there can be no question of Fletcher's
greatness. Among his contemporaries none has relied
more, or to greater advantage, upon the imaginative aid
of illusions of sounds. Whether he excited his audience
by the unseen clashing of swords, as in *Rule a Wife and
Have a Wife*, V, 3, or aroused expectation by the shaking
of madmen's irons, as in *The Pilgrim*, IV, 3, he always
showed himself to be a master of theatrical art. In his
hands, faded effects received a rich, new colouring. Take
that illusion of sound which was also an illusion of distance, — a normal exemplification of which occurs in
Massinger, Middleton, and Rowley's *The Old Law*, IV, 2,
where the blasts of the horn gradually get nearer and
nearer, — and note how readily he puts his impress upon
it. I refer, of course, to the scene in the third act of
The Pilgrim where the outlaws, in their stronghold, hear
the beating of a slowly approaching drum. Their imag-
inations proceed to conjure up visions of an approaching
army, so much so that they become panic-stricken and
fly for their lives. Yet they had really nothing more to
fear than a boy engaged upon hunting squirrels in the
woods by moonlight.

Like all great peoples, the Elizabethans lived an open-
air life and delighted in the ardours of the chase. That is
why hunting scenes are so often audibly suggested (since
they could not be visualised) in early drama. Even Jonson, for all his avoidance of the theatrical *cliché*, resorts
to the effect in the second act of *Every Man out of his
Humour*. Rarely are we given indication of the full
method of procuring this happy illusion. In most cases,
as in *The Maid in the Mill*, II, 1, the direction simply

runs, "Hounds in full cry within," but occasionally, as in *The Shoemaker's Holiday*, II, 4 and 5, we read also of the holloaing of the hunters and the cheerful winding of horns. There was, no doubt, poetry of a sort for the spectators in these sounds: for many of them they spelled emotion recollected in tranquillity.

X

ELIZABETHAN STAGE REALISM

IN the old, open-roofed theatre, the only theatre of its time which catered for all classes, Elizabethan predilection showed itself to be for high romance expressed in terms of uncompromising realism. A simple-minded, imaginative, and credulous people with an almost childish curiosity, a people as eager for keen emotional experience as for tense adventure, the Elizabethans delighted in the strange and the new — the far-fetched, whether in conceits or story; but in hungering after the remote they desired to get in touch with it in a familiar way. They had no liking for that aloofness between character and spectator which the intervention of the vast picture-frame and of the fiddlers has so long fostered in the modern playhouse. The very physical conditions of their stage made for a peculiar intimacy: if ever there were a *théâtre intime*, it was theirs. Viewing these facts and the innate conservatism of the race, it is not surprising to find the Elizabethan dramatist sedulously preserving the spirit of the native mediaeval literature. In Chaucer's pages, romanticism and realism proved to be congenial bedfellows. Writing on this score, Maurice Francis Egan points out that

if the poetry of Chaucer is romantic in spirit, it is only in the sense that it was bound to no narrow treatment of subject or to no fixed models of imitation outside the poet's intellectual sense. The introduction to *The Canterbury Tales* is realistic. No modern novel could, in the best sense, be more so. *The Knight's Tale* is romantic, if you will, because it clothes the Greeks of the old legends with the panoply of the Middle Ages. Theseus, the Greek, becomes a Duke, and the apparatus of the story of Arcite is brought down to the point of view of the fourteenth century.[1]

The Elizabethan dramatist had no difficulty in preserving the Chaucer tradition: his difficulty was when he attempted to escape from it. Ben Jonson, we know, strove to portray the ancient Romans as they really were, and paid the price of his temerity. It would be futile to assume that Shakespeare was ignorant of the fact that Brutus and the conspirators went hatless or that the Danes of Hamlet's time had no gunpowder. The Elizabethan audience desired him to tell his story in a familiar way, and he bowed to that desire. Anachronisms never troubled him, for in the contemporary theatre the sense of anachronism did not exist. It is the noble army of superior-minded commentators who have blundered, not Shakespeare. They forget that he was not writing for us, much less for them.

It must not be thought, however, that because the Elizabethan playgoer liked to rub shoulders, as it were, with the characters, great and small, which figured in the dramatic pageant, even going so far as to tolerate and encourage occasional recognition of his own presence, he had no relish for poetic or rhetorical flights or for the delicate delineation of idiosyncrasy. It would be worse than foolish to underestimate the genius of the people who made Shakespeare vocal. It was an extraordinary, perhaps unparalleled, genius. Cruel as the grave, it was animal enough to wallow in ordure, and it was godlike enough to fly with the poet on ready wing into the empyrean. There are fashions in Shakespearean interpretation as in other things, and it is fashionable now to say

[1] See the essay on "The Ebb and Flow of Romance" in Egan's scholarly little book, *The Ghost in Hamlet and Other Essays*.

that Shakespeare in writing his plays propitiated the
mob by mixing in all the ingredients it liked, but added
poetry purely to please himself — as a salve to his artistic
conscience, as it were.[1] An artistic conscience of this dis-
turbing order would have been given short shrift by a
body of players employing an actor-dramatist to amuse
and augment its public. The playgoing world has never
been very tolerant of superfluities, and Shakespeare was
not the man to indulge in them. He who had marvellous
inventive powers, and yet saved time and trouble by taking his plots ready made, was hardly likely to drop into
poetry simply for his own satisfaction.

In keeping with this scheme of making the spectators
participants in the scene was the scrupulous attention
paid to realism in matters of minor detail. We must assume that this was deemed an essential factor, if only
because of the difficulties often encountered in procuring
it. Things were not then as they are now, when illusion
is aided by the remoteness of the stage and the jugglery
of artificial light. On a central, sunlit platform, deception
of the senses had to be brought cleanly off or not attempted. Sleight of hand became a necessary histrionic
accomplishment. The player had perforce to take a leaf
out of the book of the conjurors of his day, and we
know from Reginald Scot's *Discoverie of Witchcraft*[2] what
marvels the conjurors could perform even when surrounded by peering spectators.

At every turn in the study of the old drama we come
across denotements of this immense painstaking in minor
detail. Doubtless much of it was rendered imperative
by the crippling contiguity of the stool-holding gallant.

[1] *E. g.*, Jusserand, *The School for Ambassadors*, p. 304 ("What to Expect
of Shakespeare").

[2] London, 1584; Bk. XIII, chap. 33.

But for his presence on the stage one would be inclined to view some of the precautions taken as supererogatory. There is a scene in the third act of *The Spanish Tragedy* in which a letter flutters down from above and falls at Hieronimo's feet. It is a warning from the confined Bell' Imperia, written in her blood, and beginning, "For want of ink, receive this bloody writ." The prompter's note of "Red ink," which has contrived somehow to elude ordinary vigilance and slip into the margin of the quarto, indicates the care taken in such trifling matters. It is otherwise a helpful memorandum, since it serves to elucidate the direction in *Bussy D'Ambois*, V, 2: "Enter Montsurry, like a Friar, with a letter written in blood." Occasionally, however, one is puzzled to know whether it is always safe to take these notes literally. In Chapman's *May Day*, where Quintiliano takes out the "two brace of angels" and gives them to Innocentio, the accompanying memorandum is "a purse of twenty pound in gold." Here, unless we can assume the reference is to counters, realism attains its climax.

Recall how in *The Tempest*, at the close of the vivid shipwreck scene, it sufficed not for the mariners to rush in and cry that all was lost: they had to come in dripping wet. This realistic touch is often to be found recurring in Elizabethan drama, and it would look as if at such junctures the unfortunate players, before making their appearance, were drenched with a bucket of water. An earlier example occurs in *The Two Angry Women of Abington*,[1] where Coomes, on going off, immediately bellows out that he has fallen into a pond, and, on subsequently making his grumbling reappearance, evokes from Nich-

---

[1] The play is undivided, but see *Nero and Other Plays* in the Mermaid Series, pp. 173–175 (Act IV, scene 3).

olas the comment, "Looke, the water drops from you as fast as hops." [1]

Natural phenomena were, as far as possible, carefully imitated, though there were occasional drawbacks, as, for instance, when heavy thunder had perforce to come from a clear blue sky. Nor is it surprising to find that in the open theatre the procurement of sustained darkness baffled the players and that the surrounding gloom had to be imaginatively conveyed by iterative textual allusion and the bringing on of torches. But if in this the unenclosed nature of the house proved a drawback, it was certainly advantageous in scenes where choking fumes had to be emitted through a trap. One recalls how in the initial dumb show in that stirring Globe play, *The Divil's Charter*, a conjured-up devil ascends amidst "exhalations of lightning and sulphurous smoke," as the stage direction puts it. Such an effect, if practised in the small enclosed private theatres, would have proved highly objectionable to the stage stool-holders, and perhaps to the audience generally.

All manifestations of this order, however, were not stifling: a delicate and pleasing smoke effect was used in mist scenes. But it may be that here I beg the question; certainly I encounter a difficulty. A steady progressiveness was taking place in matters of stage effect, and one must be careful not to read into Elizabethan and Jacobean times all the effects procurable in the days of the first Charles. There are many scenes in the late sixteenth-century drama which positively clamour for visualisation of mist, yet in the complete absence of confirmatory stage directions one cannot say that visualisation occurred. There is the scene in *The Raigne of King*

---

[1] For other examples, see *Modern Language Notes*, vol. xl (November, 1925), T. S. Graves's article on "Allegory in *The Tempest*."

Edward the Third,[1] where Philip comments upon "this sodain fog"; the scene in the fourth act of Lyly's private-theatre play, *Love's Metamorphosis*, in which Proserpine sends "a thick mist," under cover of which the transformation of the three nymphs takes place; the fairy fog in *A Midsummer Night's Dream*; and the connective stage business between the second and third acts of *Histriomastix*, where Pride casts a mist round about, "wherein Mavortius and his company vanish off the stage, and Pride and her attendants remaine," a possible parody of some recent stage effect. If fogs and mists were imagined in the public playhouse in the period represented by these plays, it is somewhat remarkable that a prolonged mist should have been resorted to in the fourth act of *Arden of Feversham* to enable Arden once more to escape from his would-be assassins, more particularly as the mist is not mentioned in the account in Holinshed on which the dramatist based. At first in reading the play one comes across so many references to the abounding obscurity in two successive short scenes that the conviction steadily grows that the fog must have been realised; indeed, Black Will's reference to it as smoke seems to imply the very method of its procurement. After-reflection, however, brings its doubts; one recalls then that iterative references to any phenomenon generally mean that the effect was left to the imagination. All that can be said for certain is that, if the players desired to visualise the fog, they knew how to do it. In the Gray's Inn masque of January 3, 1594-95, there was an effect of "troubled smoke and dark vapour."[2]

I do not pretend to know exactly when the practice

[1] Act IV, scene 5.

[2] Lyly's *Works*, ed. Bond, i, 380, note; Chambers, *The Elizabethan Stage*, iv, 56.

had its origin, but there was in later Elizabethan days a device of censing, known as "a mist of delicate perfumes," much used for freshening ill-ventilated rooms and relieving the oppressiveness of the atmosphere in overcrowded assemblies. We find Sir Epicure Mammon, in *The Alchemist*,[1] saying (in a speech always wrongly punctuated):

> My mists
> Ile have, the perfume vapour'd 'bout the roome
> To lose ourselves in.

My impression is that this device, having been used at court at times of special festivity, came in time to be made an occasional feature of the court masque. We find evidence of its employment in this way in Ben Jonson's entertainment of *The Barriers*, as given at Whitehall on January 5, 1605–06, the night after *The Masque of Hymen* was performed.[2] According to Jonson's preliminary description of this, "there appeared at the lower end of the hall, a mist of delicate perfumes; out of which (a battle being sounded) did seem to break forth two ladies, the one representing Truth, the other Opinion." [3]

A few years earlier, however, censing effects illustrative of the social habits of the time were written into plays produced at both the public and the private theatres. One is to be found in *Every Man out of his Humour*, a Globe play of 1599, and another in the opening scene of *The Malcontent*, a Blackfriars play of 1603. It seems not improbable that the effect had already been used illusively in mist scenes, such as the scene of the

---

[1] Act II, scene I.

[2] Thorndike finds an effect of a mist of delicate perfumes in *The Masque of Hymen* which was in reality an effect of movable painted clouds. See his *Shakespeare's Theater*, p. 184, note 2.

[3] Henry Morley, *Masques and Entertainments of Ben Jonson* (Carisbrooke Library Series, 1890), p. 80.

fairy fog in *A Midsummer Night's Dream*, but we have
no clear trace of its use in this way until a later period,
and then for the most part in plays written or altered
for court performance. In Heywood's Part II of *If You
Know not Me, You Know Nobody*, an undivided play
registered in September, 1605, and printed in 1606,
we find at one juncture[1] a reference to the presence of
"a thick mist," but there is no direction to show that
the mist was manifested. Curiously enough, however,
in the playlet entitled *Jupiter & Io*, forming part of
Heywood's "Pleasant Dialogues" published in 1637, "a
great damp ariseth," being conjured up by the Thun-
derer to hide Io's blushes. In the belatedly printed first
quarto of *The Maid's Tragedy* there is, in Act I, scene 2,
what I take to be, from the elaborate nature of its mounting, a court-added masque; and in this we have the direction, "Night rises in mists," Night here being a personification. Wholly of the court order is the mysterious
Four Plays in One, belonging to the period 1619–25,[2] in
which, in *The Triumph of Honour*, there is an effect of
wizardry recalling Wagner's steam curtain, indicated in
the direction: "Solemn music, a mist ariseth, the rocks
remove." But, so far as the public theatre is concerned,
we do not stand on firm ground until we reach *The Prophetess*, a play licensed for the King's Men in May, 1622,
and presumably produced at the Globe. In this, at the
opening of the fourth act, one finds an elaborate dumb
show, at the end of which Delphia raises "a foggy mist"
for a purpose afterwards explained by the Chorus thus:

[1] Heywood's *Plays*, ed. Pearson, i, 302.
[2] The much earlier date for the production given by me in the article on
"The Date of *Four Plays in One*" in the *Times Literary Supplement* of December 11, 1919, is untenable. For some random guesses on this score, see
Chambers, *The Elizabethan Stage*, iii, 231.

> Then too weak
> Had been all opposition and resistance
> The Persians could have made against their fury,
> If Delphia by her cunning had not raised
> A foggy mist, which as a cloud conceal'd them,
> Deceiving their pursuers.

It is noteworthy that in Jonson's unfinished pastoral, *The Sad Shepherd*, which I take to have been designed for court performance, with scenery, in the late Caroline period, the intention was to press the fog effect into service at a certain juncture in the third act. In the argument prefixed to that uncompleted act, we read of the timely darkness conjured up by Maudlin the witch: "There ariseth a mist suddenly, which darkening all the place, Clarion loseth himself and the tree where Earine is inclosed, lamenting his misfortune," and so forth.

I have dwelt with some minuteness on the evidence for these fog effects because it illustrates the difficulties which beset the conscientious investigator, and the great necessity for the exercise of caution. After reviewing it, it seems impossible to arrive at any definite conclusion. There is little arguing against the actual manifestation of fog in the sixteenth-century theatre, and nothing beyond the recurrence of fog scenes in support of it. The facts seem to point to a steady progressiveness, in the Jacobean period, in matters of stage realism.

Storm effects were very popular in the Elizabethan theatre. Thunder, lightning, even the moaning of the wind, could be so well imitated that when seen and heard together there was practically no further need for any other exemplification of the disturbance of the elements. Yet more in that way came to be done: showers of rain eventually descended. It may be conceived that, in the public theatre, effects of this latter order must have possessed a very considerable illusion. Often drenched by the elements where they stood, the groundlings had an undesirable criterion of judgement which they would not have been slow in exercising.

Deep down is the genesis of the simulated rainstorm or hailstorm. It preceded the establishment of the modern theatre, not by decades but by centuries. It is related that when Henry VII visited York in 1486 and pageants were shown in his honour in various parts of the city, at one halting-place a shower of rosewater fell upon his august person, at another a hailstorm of comfits, and at a third a snowstorm of "waffrons." [1] We learn also, somewhat indefinitely, from Sidney W. Clarke's little book on *The Miracle Play in England*,[2] that an extant bill of costs for the provision of a storm and an earthquake in a miracle play called *The Day of Judgment* includes an item,

Payd for starche to make the storm . . . . vi*d*.

This needs no great speculation: evidently the starch was used to make pellets of hail.

So too, when George Peele — dramatist-to-be and then a university scholar — superintended the performances given at Oxford in June, 1583, in honour of Albertus Alasco, the Polish Prince Palatine's visit, one of the plays given was Gager's tragedy of *Dido*, in which there was a tempest, "wherein," according to Holinshed,[3] "it hailed small confects, rained rosewater, and snew an artificiall kind of snow, all strange, marvellous and abundant." Something of the sort had previously been seen at court in *The Masque of Janus*, in 1573, as the bill

<hr>

[1] J. Raine, in *English Miscellanies* (Surtees Society), lxxxv, 53, 56, 57.
[2] Page 74.
[3] Holinshed's *Chronicles* (ed. 1808), iv, 508.

of costs testifies.[1] But what is really surprising is to find
how long these somewhat puerile spectacles persisted
in the halls of the mighty. According to Menestrier's
anonymously issued book on ballets,[2] the French court
of a century later was still being entertained with showers of perfumed water, musk-flavoured hail, and snow-
storms of flowers.

There is a time and place, however, for everything,
and one has serious doubts whether the facetious George
Peele, once he had turned playwright, would have ven-
tured to regale the groundlings with conceits of this
order. As a matter of fact, only a very faint indication
exists to show that they were ever seen even in the early
and essentially select private theatres. In William Percy's
manuscript play, *The Aphrodysiall, or Sea Feast*, written
for the Children of Paul's at the close of the sixteenth
century but seemingly never acted, a direction is given
in the fifth scene of the first act for "a showre of Rosewater and confits, as was acted at Christ Church in
Oxford, in Dido and Æneas." [3] Curiously enough, the
same boys, *circa* 1599, brought out Lyly's *Love's Metamorphosis*, in which, late in the action, Proserpine first
created a mist to obscure the nymphs during their transformation, and Venus afterwards sent down what is
vaguely termed "a showre" to hide them again while
they resumed their original shape.

Chambers points out that in the Cornish miracle
play, *The Creation of the World*, which belongs to about
1599, the Flood began with a shower of rain, but we have
no clue to the *modus operandi*, as the direction simply

[1] Peter Cunningham, *Revels Accounts* (Shakespeare Society), p. 35.
[2] *Des Ballets anciens et modernes selon les règles du Théâtre*, Paris, 1682.
[3] *Modern Philology*, xii (1914), 126, note 2, G. F. Reynolds's article on
"William Percy and his Plays."

says, "let rayne appear." [1] Rain effects, however, seem to have been deemed superfluous in the public theatres of the sixteenth century. One bases here on the fact that all incidental references to rain showers, such as would have suggested or demanded their simulation, are sedulously avoided. Heywood's *If You Know not Me, You Know Nobody* can hardly be dated earlier than 1605, and it is not until we reach that play that we encounter a situation in any wise calling for such simulation. In this undivided piece we get a direction for "A Storme" (uncommon in this form), where Gresham says to Ramsie:

> Now Passion-a-me, Sir Thomas, a cruell storme,
> An we stay long we shall be wet to the skin.

Much depended on that sudden traditional wetting, for Gresham there and then expresses his intention of building the Exchange as a shelter for merchants. If ever excuse was afforded a poor investigator for jumping to a conclusion it is here; but happily my athletic days are past. I content myself by pointing out that in a slightly later Heywood play, *The Brazen Age*, a Red Bull attraction of 1611 or 1612, an actual shower was most certainly seen. Again, we have to deal with an undivided play, but in the detail of a certain dumb show [2] we read:

> Enter Busyris with his Guard and Priests to sacrifice; to them two strangers, Busyris takes them and kils them upon the altar, enter Hercules disguis'd . . . discovering himselfe beates the guard, kils Busyris and sacrificeth him vpon the altar; at which there fals a shower of raine.

Homer, the presenter of the show, explains that there had been a drought in Egypt, and that it had been prophesied that no rain would fall until a stranger was sacrificed. Hence the killing of all strangers.

[1] *The Mediaeval Stage*, ii, 392.
[2] Heywood's *Plays*, ed. Pearson, iii, 183.

Whether or not rainstorms had ever been imitated in the public theatre earlier, I should be inclined to say that about this period some ingenious method of procuring the illusion had been hit upon, seemingly by the Red Bull players, and that it was being exploited for all it was worth. A scheme of spectacular sensationalism, giving a foretaste of nineteenth-century melodrama, was then being followed at the popular Clerkenwell house, and of this it would appear to have formed a part. It was there, late in 1610, that was produced Dekker's play with the quaintly apposite title of *If it be not Good, the Devil is in it,* in the course of which a direction occurs for "Rayne, thunder, and lightning," the rain doubtless being mentioned first in order that it might not be overlooked.

The Tempest followed so hard on Dekker's play that one is prompted to ask whether the King's Players in producing it had not taken a leaf out of the Red Bull Men's book. It seems not at all unlikely that Shakespeare's play presented a rainstorm. Act II, scene 2, opens with "Enter Caliban with a burthen of wood (a noyse of thunder is heard)." No subsequent storm direction occurs throughout the scene, though a repetition is demanded by the ensuing action, and it would certainly seem as if a direction for rain had somehow dropped out. One recalls that Trinculo, before taking refuge under Caliban's gaberdine, had been perturbed by the menaces of a black cloud, dreading lest it should "shed his liquor." What he had feared had probably been shown to happen, as his last remark before seeking shelter is, "Alas! the storme is come againe; my best way is to creepe under his gaberdine."

Truly, rain was in the air for long at this period. Even the sheltered court did not escape its visitations. When Beaumont's masque, *The Marriage of the Thames and the*

Rhine, was given at Whitehall on February 20, 1612–13, in honour of the nuptials of the Prince Palatine and the Lady Elizabeth, a slight shower was seen to fall at that juncture where Iris prays to Flora for her benefactions.[1]

If you ask me how the thing was done, I should say that, in the theatre, it was by sending down a copious shower of dried peas from the tiring-house garret. The rattle of the peas on the tiled shadow covering the stage would have created a sufficient illusion. A hundred years, nay, a hundred and seventy years, later, no other or better method of imitating rain and hail was known of in the English theatres. Recall what Pope wrote in *The Dunciad* of John Rich, the celebrated harlequin:

> Immortal Rich! How calm he sits at ease,
> Mid snows of paper and fierce hail of pease;
> And, proud his mistress' orders to perform,
> Rides in the whirlwind and directs the storm.

We take a jump of nearly half a century and land at Covent Garden in 1774, just as a new play entitled *The Romance of an Hour* is about to be produced. We listen to the Prologue, and find the audience is being assured that it is not going to be frightened by ghostly apparitions or claps of thunder:

> Nor will the tempest, rushing through the trees,
> Once rouse your horror — with a storm of peas.

The Elizabethan attitude towards stage realism was rather one of temperament than of taste. Not all the efforts of Ben Jonson could succeed in establishing an aesthetic standard or a liking for neo-classic principles.

---

[1] No clue to this is to be found in the masque as printed in Francis Beaumont's *Poems* (London, 1652, 2d edition, enlarged); but the shower is referred to in Foscarini's description of the performance, for which see the *Calendar of State Papers, Venetian,* 1610–13, no. 775.

Precisely what that temperament dictated has been best seen by the old French critics. St. Amand found that even in late Caroline days the taste of the populace was for plays full of murders, battles, and bloodshed.[1] René Rapin, in his *Reflections on Aristotle's Poetry* (as translated by Rymer in 1694), says: "The English, our neighbours, love blood in their sports, by the quality of their temperament; these are *insulaires*, separated from the rest of men; we are more human." Yet he conceded that they had more genius for tragedy than the French, "as well by the spirit of the nation which delights in cruelty, as also by the character of their language, which is proper for good expressions." Later French opinion was not so dispassionate. Writing in English to Sir George Lyttelton, Voltaire wholly ignored the qualities of the British defects.

Yr nasion [he says] two hundred years since is us'd to a wild scene, to a croud of tumultuous events, to an emphatical poetry mix'd with loose and comical expressions; to murthers, to a lively representation of bloody deeds, to a kind of horrour which seems often barbarous and childish; all faults which never sully'd the greak, the roman, or the French stage. And give me leave to say that the taste of yr politest countrymen in point of tragedy differs not much from the taste of a mob at a Bear-garden.

One cannot get away from the facts: the Elizabethans *were* a bloodthirsty people — their attitude in the playhouse proves it. There was no element of effeminacy in the race that could relish the crude barbarities of *Titus Andronicus* or the blinding of Gloster, the race whose insatiate longings could urge the philosophic Chapman to sully his pages with the scene in which Cato plucks out his entrails. Horror was not only dwelt upon but intensified by every possible stage artifice; rarely was there any

[1] Cf. Jusserand, *Shakespeare in France*, pp. 124-129.

mitigation of the asperities. Torture scenes in which the rack, the strappado, and burning with hot irons figured were carried out with rigorous exactitude.[1] Nor was all this mere mob-catering. *Bussy D'Ambois*, which presented one of these scenes, was a private-theatre play, and in the private theatre the rule of the mob had no moral writ. Note what Gifford, writing with a characteristically English purblindness, says of *The Virgin Martir:*

> Certainly there is too much horror in this tragedy. The daughters of Theophilus are killed on the stage. Theophilus himself is racked, and Dorothea is dragged by the hair, kicked, tortured and beheaded. Its popularity must, therefore, in a considerable degree be attributed to the interest occasioned by the contrary agencies of the two spirits, to "the glorious vision" of the beatified Dorothea at the conclusion of the piece.

One would think from this that the manifold horrors of the play were sheer dead weights, which its spiritual qualities had to struggle hard to carry. This is blindly to ignore the curious complexity of the Elizabethan temperament, which so paradoxically united high spirituality with the rankest animalism. It was a case of extremes meeting.

Make-believe was never expected of the frequenters of the old public theatres save where the circumstances rendered it obligatory. In the many bloody scenes shown, real blood was always utilised. This might long ago have been surmised by our theatrical historians from the practice in the early miracle plays, but the fact seems for the most part to have escaped observation. Hence, some evidence on the point is necessary. It will be recalled that in Peele's *The Battle of Alcazar* there is an induction

---

[1] For examples, see *A Larum for London* (1602), *The Travailes of the Three English Brothers*, *Bussy D'Ambois*, V, 1, *The Double Marriage*, I, 2, and *The Virgin Martir*, V.

to the third act in which Sebastian, Stukely, and Mahamet are brought in one by one and butchered in horribly realistic fashion. In the corresponding part of the "plott" of this play [1] details of the properties required are given in the margin, namely, "3 violls of blood and a sheep's gather." Commenting on this, Dr. W. W. Greg writes: "Since a 'gather' consists of the liver, heart and lungs, we are presumably to infer that one of these organs was to be torn out of each of the unhappy trio in this gory performance." [2]

No doubt this spectacle was very horrible, but I am moved here to point out, by way of rejoinder to St. Amand and Voltaire, that bloody scenes were witnessed on the French stage early in the seventeenth century, and that there also real blood was pressed into service. Here are three items culled from Mahelot's inventory of scenic requisites for Hôtel de Bourgogne plays: [3]

(1) Blood, sponges, a little skin, to do the trick of the sacrificer's blow.[4]

(2) A trick breast-plate to bleed when pierced by a sword, and some blood.

(3) A severed head and a woman's headless body on a bier.

Whatever the custom in France, on the old English stage it was generally calves' blood or sheep's blood that was used in these scenes, blood that did not usually congeal. On both stages alike, however, the necessity to produce a sudden flow of blood led to the practice of some neat legerdemain. Thus, in Munday's *The Down-*

---

[1] Greg, *Henslowe Papers*, p. 138.

[2] *Two Elizabethan Stage Abridgements*, p. 56.

[3] Eugene Rigal, *Le Théâtre Français avant la période classique*, p. 257.

[4] The little skin was probably equivalent to the "leder bag for the blode," one of the provisions for the old Canterbury pageant of St. Thomas the Martyr, for which see Chambers, *The Mediaeval Stage*, ii, 164.

fall of Robert Earl of Huntington, II, 1, where Prince John strikes the Messenger in the face, we find the direction, "Smites him; he bleeds." A very simple and very effective trick this, based on the fact that the natural act of a struck person is to put the hand or hands on the injured spot. The Messenger had a small, blood-saturated sponge concealed in his palm, and had only to press it against his face to produce the necessary effect. This trick is still employed on the stage in similar situations, the only variation on the old method being that deeply coloured water is now used instead of blood.[1] But it is perhaps necessary to add that no contemporary stage direction reveals the *modus operandi*, and that I have been compelled to deduce it from directions given in two of Thomas Killigrew's plays, as published in the folio of 1664. In *The Princess*, IV, 10, we have in the margin, "Bragadine shoots, Virgil puts his hand to his eye, with a bloody spunge and the blood runs down," and so forth. Again, in the First Part of *Thomaso, or The Wanderer*, V, 9, a dark, bedroom scene, one finds the direction:

Edwardo strikes him and they cuff on the bed. Edwardo throws him down, then they cuff and struggle upon the floore, and are both bloody, occasion'd by little spunges ty'd of purpose to their middle fingers in the palmes of their hands.

One can readily surmise how realistic in its issue this simple device would prove in a scene of deadly combat. That the horrible fascination of such scenes lasted long after the days of the chronicle history is established by a stage direction in the fifth act of Dryden's *King Arthur*, a play belonging to the close of the century. This deals with the stirring encounter between Arthur and Osmond, and reads: "They fight with Sponges in their hands dipt

[1] Cf. W. B. Robertson on "Some Stage Effects," in *Cassell's Magazine* for December, 1899.

in Blood; after some equal Passes and closeing they appear both wounded."

But there were some gruesome Elizabethan effects of which I cannot pretend to know the secret. Take the situation near the end of *Arden of Feversham*, where Mrs. Arden is led to the body of her murdered husband. On reaching it, she moans out:

> Arden, sweet husband, what shall I say?
> The more I sound his name, the more he bleedes;
> This blood condemnes me, and in gushing foorth
> Speaks as it falles, and askes me why I did it.

This gushing forth was in keeping with an old superstition, and, viewing the phrasing of the speech in association with the Elizabethan predilection for bloody sights, I hardly think it was left to the imagination. The situation is paralleled in *The Insatiate Countess*, V, 1, where there was evidently a somewhat similar effusion of blood from the dead body of Count Massino. One sees no valid reason for the bringing on of the corpse save for the realisation of this uncanny effect, and it is obviously indicated in Don Sago's conjuration of the man he had murdered:

> O cease to weep in blood, or teach me too!
> The bubbling wounds do murmur for revenge.

Likewise, one finds in the first quarto of *Romeo and Juliet*, in Act V, scene 3,[1] an equally mysterious — and what a modern audience would deem wholly supererogatory — stage effect, an effect to which no attention has hitherto been drawn. Friar Lawrence comes into the churchyard immediately after Romeo's death, and, in the midst of his forebodings, according to the direction, "stoops and lookes on the blood and weapons." That is

---

[1] Hubbard's recension, Act V, scene 3, lines 94, 95.

to say, the blood of Paris, and the weapons with which he and Romeo had fought. At once he ejaculates:

> What blood is this that stains the entrance
> Of this marble stony monument?
> What means these masterless and gory weapons?

The stage direction, I think, shows that blood was somehow scattered about the place where Paris met his end.

Later on, in the Caroline period, we meet with another puzzling effect. It is to be found in Act V, scene 2, of Ford's *The Broken Heart*, a play written, be it noted, for the fastidious audience of the Blackfriars. Orgilius opens a vein in his arm, and has another opened by Bassanes in the other arm; he is seen to bleed slowly to death, falls, and is carried off. One is at a loss to know how this was done. Orgilius's arms were bared, tape was tied round his elbows, and he held sticks in his hands. So much we are told, but it seems impossible to deduce the rest.

If it was not to gratify the mob that this effect was introduced, neither was it for the mob that the varied horrors of Marston's Paul's play, *Antonio's Revenge*, were fashioned. On first thoughts, one would be inclined to believe that Hieronimo's biting out and throwing down of his tongue in *The Spanish Tragedy* [1] was a sop to the groundlings — even although the action was dramatically justifiable as a device to enable him to procure a knife, ostensibly to "mend his pen," though for murderous purposes; but the idea has to be surrendered when one finds the conspirators at the close of Marston's play gathering round Piero and plucking out his tongue. This, however, is a mere side reflection; why I referred to *Antonio's Revenge* was because it is peculiarly illustrative

[1] Act IV, scene 4.

of the universal desire for bloody sights. It actually opens with one: "Enter Piero, unbrac't, his armes bare, smeer'd in blood, a poniard in one hand bloodie, and a torche in the other." But there is no need to pillory Marston, when effects of this order are to be found in Shakespeare and Webster. Read the first act of *Coriolanus*, and note how, after Marcus has entered bleeding, Cominius refers to him as looking like a flayed man; note also how Marcus speaks later of

> this painting
> Wherein you see me smear'd.

As for Webster, observe how, in *Appius and Virginia*, IV, 2, Virginius enters, after the sacrifice of his daughter, "with his knife, that and his arms stripped up to the elbows, all bloody."

Of these gruesome spectacles one has not yet told more than half the story. Something remains to be said of hangings and beheadings. I remember reading somewhere an account of one of the old French *mystères* in which it was related how the Judas of the play nearly hanged himself in real earnest. Such was the apparent thoroughness of hanging scenes in Elizabethan times that one is apt to wonder if similar misadventures were not occasionally experienced. But the trick had been so often done at an early period that mayhap it had been quickly perfected. In Pickering's *Horestes*, which had been performed at court as early as 1567, Egistus is hanged from a ladder, and Orestes' mother — hardy woman! — comes in to view the spectacle. So, too, in *Sir Thomas More* a gibbet is brought in and set up, and Lincoln, after mounting up to it by means of a ladder, "leapes off." A similar leaping off was witnessed in the second act of *A Warning for Faire Women*. An illusion equally difficult to procure was Absalom's suspension by the hair to an oak tree in *David & Bethsabe*, though in this case, as in that of the hanging of Horatio in *The Spanish Tragedy*, the rear stage was undoubtedly used. Regarding this, one notes the record in October, 1602, in Henslowe's Diary:

pd. for poleyes and worckmanshipp to hange absolome . . . xiiij *d*.

But it would take a very ingenious mind to deduce the *modus operandi* from these scant details. At a later period we find Boutcher, in the last act of *Ram Alley*, hanging himself outside Will Smalshanke's door, but precisely where he hanged himself, with what, and how he was got down, are all equally unapparent. It is our misfortune that no helpful stage direction tells us how any of these hanging effects were performed.

Apart from the fact that beheading scenes were (for reasons presently to be given) not of so early a popularity as hanging scenes, there is a distinction between the two which has never been clearly recognised. Albright is wrong in stating that scaffolds were erected on the outer stage for both.[1] Scaffolds were not always erected, or thrust out, on the outer stage, and they were never used for hangings. The scaffold, with stairs, was reserved for beheading scenes and certain kinds of torture scenes, such as breaking on the wheel. Scholarship has yet something of importance to learn about the old beheading scenes, something I myself — though a lifelong student of stage effect — grasped only while preparing the Harvard lecture upon which the study is based. It is eloquent of the steady progressiveness of seventeenth-century stage realism. The one fact to be primarily noted is that, while beheading scenes (of a sort)

[1] *The Shaksperian Stage*, p. 136.

occur in late sixteenth-century drama, no attempt to procure the illusion of actual decapitation was made until Jacobean times.[1] A typical example of the earlier method is afforded us in *Sir Thomas More*. At the close of the play More ascends to the scaffold, prepares for his execution, says farewell to the world — and then walks quietly off. This is much how the thing would be done on the existing stage, but Elizabethan audiences were seldom content to be baulked in this way, and we have to ask ourselves why, in days when hangings were so commonly shown, — one of them is in this very play, — beheadings were as commonly shirked. Squeamishness had nothing to do with the matter: in neither public nor private theatre did it operate. It was simply that the players were wholly unable to procure the illusion. Let us look at other early examples. In *The Life and Death of Thomas, Lord Cromwell*, a Globe play of 1602, Cromwell goes off at the end to the block, and four lines later we get the direction, "Enter one with Cromwels head." In *Sir Thomas Wyatt*, a play of a little later date, Lady Jane Grey's execution is managed in precisely the same way. Half a loaf being better than no bread, the sight of the severed head gave some content to the audience; one wonders, indeed, why that sight was not vouchsafed them in *Sir Thomas More*. Dummy heads were not invented for decapitation scenes: from an early period they had been utilised for other purposes in the chronicle histories. With them a horrible realism also intrudes, since they had to be carefully modelled, painted, and wigged so as to correspond with the *persona*. There is a scene in *The Travailes of the Three English Brothers*

---

[1] For the method adopted in decapitation scenes in the French *mystères*, see Gustave Cohen, *Histoire de la Mise-en-Scène dans le Théâtre Religieux Français du Moyen Age*, p. 147.

which emphasises this. When the Sophy wishes to learn the exact truth regarding the intimacy between his niece and Robert Shirley, he induces her to believe that Shirley has been decapitated, with the hope that she will lose self-control and make confession. The direction says, "Enter an officer with a counterfeit head like Shirley's."

The new idea has generally to fight very hard for existence, and I do not anticipate that mine will prove an exception. Possibly, indeed, there may be some attempt to hoist me with mine own petard. I have claimed that the bringing in of scaffolds was reserved for beheading scenes and certain scenes of torture, and I can foresee the triumphant pointing to the fact that scaffolds were used in beheading scenes before the close of the century. The evidence is certainly undeniable, but it is not at all difficult to explain away. Let us look at two items in Henslowe's Rose Theatre inventory of March 10, 1598:

> Item. j whell and frame in the Sege of London.
> Item, j frame for the heading in Black Jone.

The first item really deals with a side issue, but I cannot refrain from discussing it here, because its import has been woefully misinterpreted by Sir Edmund Chambers.[1] The play mentioned in it is not extant, but to my mind the "frame" was a scaffold put up to bear the "whell" upon which some poor unfortunate was broken. The second item is much clearer in import, the "frame" again being a scaffold, but the presence of the scaffold no more proves the actual decapitation than does its presence in *Sir Thomas More*. It was simply an aid to the imagination, the players, in the circumstances, having anxiety to give all the illusion in their power.

Let us then feel our way carefully along the opening

[1] *The Elizabethan Stage*, iii, 97.

decade of the seventeenth century with the view of determining when a bloodthirsty audience was first regaled with the sight of a man having his head cut off. We have already seen how, in the Cromwell play of 1602 and in the Sir Thomas Wyatt play of about the same period, the issue was shirked; but even six years later there is evidence to show that as yet nobody knew how to do the trick. It is presented in Chapman's *Byron's Tragedy*, as acted at the Blackfriars. Byron, at the close of the play, ascends the scaffold, blindfolds himself, and finishes a long speech while kneeling at the block by bidding the executioner strike. But he does not strike; and just here the play ends without as much as an "exeunt" to mark the departure of the characters. I can only conclude that the scaffold was erected on the rear stage, and that the play ended with a tableau on which the curtains closed.

If it were possible to fix the date of that mysterious Whitefriars tragedy, *The Insatiate Countess*, one could, I think, make sound approximation to the period when decapitation scenes first came into vogue. As it is, the play — it was printed in 1613 — yields us the earliest known scene of the sort. The fifth act opens with the direction, "A scaffold laid out," the scene of action being the place of execution at Pavia. When the Countess comes to meet her end, we read: "Enter Isabella, with her hair hanging down, a chaplet of flowers on her head, a nosegay in her hand; Executioner before her, and with her a Cardinal." After a good deal of speechifying, she ascends the scaffold, and is asked to tie up her hair and blind her eyes. She complies, and a final direction says, "The executioner strikes off her head." Then the play ends almost immediately. Chambers's date [1] for the production is *circa* 1610, and with this I agree. It is more likely to have been

---

[1] *The Elizabethan Stage*, iii, 433, 434.

a little later than a little earlier. On this evidence it is
reasonably assured that decapitation scenes first came
into vogue sometime between 1610 and 1613. It is to
be noted that, although scenes occur in later plays in
which elaborate preparations are made for executions
which — owing to the necessities of the plot — never
take place,[1] no subsequent play was produced in which
the condemned person went off to be beheaded. Unless legitimately baulked, aroused expectations had to be
fulfilled. Look, for example, at the execution scene in
the last act of *Sir John van Olden Barnavelt*, a Globe play
of 1619. We have evidence in this that an actual blow
of the axe was struck. The Executioner asks if he had not
done well, and the First Lord replies that he had done
only too well, having struck his fingers too, meaning
that the blow had been aimed at Barnavelt's head while
his hands were still raised in supplication to Heaven.[2]

How, then, was the problem finally solved? I think
the secret is revealed to us in *The Imperial Tragedy*, an
anonymous blank-verse melodrama from the Latin, published in folio in 1669, and attributed by Langbaine to
Sir William Killigrew. In the fifth act of this piece there
is a scaffold at the back for the execution of Pelagius,
who is in no hurry to die but finally lays his head on the
block. Says the direction: "He puts up a false head,
which is cut off."

Not much of a clue this, but probably sufficient. Apparently the method pursued in decapitation scenes was
somewhat as follows. A scaffold was half thrust out from

[1] See *The Two Noble Kinsmen*, V, 4; *The Knight of Malta*, II, 5. An
earlier example is in *The Dumb Knight*, II, 1.
[2] For other decapitation scenes of this period see *The Virgin Martir*, IV, 3,
and Markham and Sampson's *Herod & Antipater*, V. Both were Red Bull
plays.

the rear stage, bearing the block at the back. By kneeling down behind it with his face towards the groundlings the victim could readily at the last moment make the necessary substitution. But what, then, was the nature of the dummy head? Heads, we know, have an ugly habit of bleeding when suddenly severed from the body, and to produce a good illusion the dummy head must have bled. Happily, we have a clue to this secondary secret. In 1649 there was published in duodecimo a curious anonymous play called *The Rebellion of Naples*, which was said to have been written by an eyewitness of the upheaval. In the last act the mob is shown thirsting for Masaniello's gore. They demand his head, and he tells them curtly to "take it." Then comes the direction: "He thrusts out his head, and they cut off a false head made of a bladder filled with blood. Exeunt with his body."

This, besides revealing how a certain ghastly illusion was obtained in decapitation scenes, serves another useful purpose. It throws light on a curious bit of stage business in the revised *Doctor Faustus*,[1] an interpolation to be found only in the quarto of 1616, and hardly dating more than five or six years earlier. I refer to the scene in which we get the direction, "Enter Faustus with a false head"—a head, be it noted, which Benvolio soon strikes off, both head and body falling to the ground together. Up to this, Faustus has remained silent, but he quickly arises and makes good use of his tongue.

My firm belief is that there is some close association between this trick and the decapitation trick performed in execution scenes; indeed, I have no hesitation in saying that the one suggested the other, the only question being which came first. There has been a good deal of con-

[1] Bullen's *Marlowe*, i, 307.

troversy over the date of this revised version of Marlowe's play, but I think the date may be soundly approximated. Professor Tucker Brooke has materially contributed towards that end by showing in a recent article [1] that the mordant prologue for a revival of *Every Man in his Humour*, first published in the Jonson folio of 1616, girds, not at Shakespeare's plays in general as has been foolishly supposed, but for the most part at the revised *Doctor Faustus*. I say "foolishly supposed" because a moment's reflection should convince any sensible person of the great unlikelihood that the King's Players would have lent themselves to an attack on their leading dramatist in the house of his many triumphs. That would have meant that some serious rupture had taken place, and we know that Shakespeare from first to last lived in complete harmony with his fellows. Disdainfully I sweep aside all the rubbish that has been written about this prologue, and approach the problem from a new angle. Besides the references to the revised *Faustus*, so clearly demonstrated by Professor Tucker Brooke, Jonson indulges in a sneer, not at Shakespeare's three *Henry VI* plays, as has been generally thought, but at their analogues, the Contention plays. It is to them that the jibe at "Yorke, and Lancasters long jarres" refers. One can approximate the date of Jonson's prologue if one can prove a Jacobean revival of at least one of the Contention plays, and that I hope now to do.

The analogue to *3 Henry VI* is the anonymous play entitled, *The True Tragedie of Richard Duke of Yorke, and the Death of good king Henrie the Sixt, with the whole contention betweene the two Houses Lancaster and Yorke*. Now, it is particularly noteworthy that in the Shake-

---

[1] "The Reputation of Christopher Marlowe," *Transactions of the Connecticut Academy of Arts and Sciences*, xxv, 347 ff.

spearean play there is nothing in any way corresponding to the direction in the other play, "Enter Clifford wounded, with an arrow in his necke." Yet there was authority in Holinshed for this, for we read in the *Chronicles:* "The lord Clifford, either for heat or paine, putting off his gorget suddenlie, with an arrow (as some saie) was stricken into the throte, and immediately rendered his spirit."

As it happens, this is a very vital differentiation between the two, because, as Steevens long ago pointed out, the arrow incident is ridiculed in *The Knight of the Burning Pestle*, in the scene where Ralph, the grocer's apprentice, comes on with a forked arrow through his head. This burlesque implies a recent revival of *The True Tragedie.* Consequently, to date *The Knight of the Burning Pestle* is to make fair approximation to the date of the revival of *The True Tragedie*, the date of Jonson's prologue, and the date of the revised *Doctor Faustus.* Here I have a difficult, though intensely fascinating, problem, and in attacking it I elect to rely upon my own personal research. Not to beat about the bush, I am of the opinion that Beaumont's famous burlesque and *The Alchemist* of Ben Jonson belong to the one period, since both indulge in the same transient topical allusions. In Act III, scene 2, of the former, and in Act V, scene 1, of the latter, reference is made to two recent shows, to "the boy of six year old with the great thing" and to the "motion" of Jonah and the Whale. *The Alchemist* was entered on the Stationers' Register in October, 1610, but remained unpublished until 1612. Internal evidence shows that it was written in 1610, but the exact date of production cannot be determined.[1] Accordingly, one

[1] Chambers, *The Elizabethan Stage*, iii, 371, 372; Herford and Simpson, *Ben Jonson*, ii, 87, 88.

cannot go very far wrong in assuming that *The Knight of the Burning Pestle* saw the light late in 1609 or early in 1610. This, then, would be the period of Jonson's prologue and of the performances at which it girds.

I have already shown, in discussing *The Insatiate Countess*, that decapitation in execution scenes came into vogue after 1608 and before 1613, most likely in 1610. The evidence to hand does not permit of a decision, but my opinion, offered for what it is worth, is that the *Faustus* trick was an entire novelty, and that it was afterwards pressed into service to give illusion to beheadings of a more serious order.

XI

CHARACTERISTICS OF PLATFORM–STAGE SPECTACLE

FOR those who labour under the erroneous impression that the Elizabethan theatre catered for no other taste than the dramatic, there is stern corrective in Hamlet's description of the players as "the abstract and brief chronicle of the times." It hints at a burning desire, not only for the episodic discussion of topicalities without rhyme or reason, but for an indulgence in keen personal satire far beyond the bounds of safety in the venturing. These were cravings born of the ebulliency of the times, and, in striving to allay them, the stage had forestalled some of the attributes of the newspaper. More insistent, and better responded to, was the demand for pageantry. The masses had a longing for colour and movement and melody which life itself could but rarely gratify, and to which it was in part the function of the playhouse to administer. So constant was the reaction, and so permeative were its manifestations, that what we call, for distinction's sake, the old platform stage might as readily be styled the pageant stage.

For the lack of the glamour and pictorial graces of painted scenery there were compensations. Colour and glitter were provided by rich costuming, the Elizabethan player's only extravagance, and movement brought the necessary kaleidoscopic variety. One recalls Longshank's suit of glass in Peele's *King Edward I*, the flamboyancy of the high-astounding Tamburlaine in his copper-laced cloak and red velvet breeches. It is scarcely an exaggeration to say, as has been said by Professor Wallace,[1] that the value of the costumes housed in an old Elizabethan theatre was equivalent to the value of the theatre itself. When one reckons that, in the late sixteenth century, money had something like ten times its present purchasing power, one can only marvel over the disbursement of as much as £19 on a fine cloak or fifteen shillings on a pair of silk stockings. Yet such prices are to be found noted in Henslowe's Diary. And not only was there splendour of dress but splendour of ornament. The Red Bull Theatre was the lowest-class house of its time, yet when Webster's *The White Divel* was produced there *circa* 1611 the ambassadors in the play were arrayed in elaborate jewelled collars of their various orders. This was apparently somewhat of an innovation, and it set a precedent that rival companies could not afford to ignore. Consequently, as we learn from a letter written in 1613 by Sir Henry Wotton to his nephew, when the King's Men came to produce *Henry VIII* at the Globe the play was

set forth with many extraordinary circumstances of pomp and majesty, even to the matting of the stage; the Knights of the Order with their Georges and garters, the Guards with their embroidered coats and the like: sufficient in truth within a while to make greatness very familiar, if not ridiculous.[2]

Nor was this all. Where the circumstances demanded it, fantasy was occasionally displayed in costume-designing. In Brome's *The Antipodes*, a late Caroline comedy, there is a scene in the fifth act where Discord comes on attended by Folly, Jealousy, Melancholy, and Madness. All were fantastically garbed, Jealousy particularly so:

[1] C. W. Wallace, *The Children of the Chapel at Blackfriars*, p. 178.
[2] Chambers, *The Elizabethan Stage*, ii, 419.

anti coincertaince ___

his was a composite black-and-yellow costume, half male, half female, with a horn on one side of his head and an ass's ear on the other.[1]

It was doubtless to this popular longing for pageantry that we owe the early chariot play, presumably a device of Marlowe's. Imitation being the sincerest form of flattery, one can deduce the delight taken in Tamburlaine's king-drawn chariot from sundry iterations of the effect. To find precisely the same bit of pageantry recurring in *The Contention between Liberality and Prodigality*, a children's play first published in 1602, is to arrive at certain conclusions concerning the period of that play, and to disagree with Chambers [2] in his dating of it. And to find an effect not identical, but similar, in *The Life and Death of Captaine Thomas Stukeley* [3] is to become seized of the suspicion that the date latterly assigned to it, namely, 1596, is seriously belated. But it must not be taken by this that I imply that the employment of stage chariots was entirely confined to the Marlowean period. Experience, however, shows that after a new theatrical device has been exploited *ad nauseam* it is generally laid aside until a new generation of playgoers springs up; and this is apparently what happened in this particular case. My impression is that after the Marlowean period no new play was written to utilise the chariot until the first James's reign had got well under way. A recurrence is to be noted in Heywood's *The Silver Age*, a Red Bull play of *circa* 1611, in the fifth act of which Pluto came on in a devil-drawn car.

[1] For the subsequent history of this hermaphroditic attire, see the mis-entitled article on "The First English Stage Costume Design" in *The Printseller* for July, 1903, p. 317.
[2] *The Elizabethan Stage*, iv, 26.
[3] Line 2305.

Such were the sops that had to be flung to Cerberus. To appease the many-headed beast so that he might gain patient hearing for his glowing imagery, abundant rhetoric, and deep philosophy, the dramatic poet had to make occasion for the introduction of ghosts, enthralling combats, descending gods and goddesses, nay, even fireworks. There were few serious plays in which one or other of these spectacles was not resorted to, and one can only marvel over the adroitness with which they were frequently made integrants of the whole.

Italy in the days of Shakespeare's boyhood had already brought pyrotechnics to a high pitch of perfection, but in England serious practice of the art began belatedly, with the result that the Elizabethans were revelling in a new wonder. When the Virgin Queen visited Warwick Castle in 1572 she was given as a special treat a display of fireworks, and again in 1575 on the occasion of her memorable visit to Kenilworth. A score of years later the London wayfarer was to gain a familiarity with squibs which, so far from evoking his contempt, only whetted his curiosity. Among the many things that the old drama reveals and emphasises is the fact, so little recognised, that the more human nature changes the more it remains static. A curious reference in *A Warning for Faire Women* shows that the end-of-the-century street urchin, like the latterday American boy on Independence Day, took great delight in letting off crackers. Not a great while passed, indeed, before fireworks were made an almost annual feature of the Lord Mayor's Show. London boasted an expert pyrotechnist in the person of Humphrey Nichols, a genius who covered himself with glory by his fireworks display in the Show of 1613.

Unquestionably, the Elizabethan players needed no

urging to press the new wonder into the service of the stage. Rivalry left them no option: they had no resource but to fight their opponents with their own weapons. As early as 1584, the capacious open amphitheatre known as the Bear Garden had begun to supplement the cruel sport of bear-baiting by other amusements, principally puppet shows and fireworks.[1] But it was not every sort of play that admitted of the introduction of squibs running on lines, and Catherine wheels. In sixteenth-century stage slang a piece with devils in it was known as an "infernal," and it was the infernal that lent itself most readily to the employment of an abundance of minor fireworks. One has a sad suspicion that it was the fascination of these puerilities, and not persistent admiration of the mighty line, which gave to *Doctor Faustus* its perennial vogue. This unholy thought is fostered by a passage in Melton's *Astrologaster, or The Figure Caster*, a pamphlet issued in 1620, wherein we learn that when Marlowe's old tragedy was acted at the Fortune it was usual for its shaggy-haired devils to run about the stage spitting fire and brimstone from the squibs in their mouths, while the lightning flashed and the thunder rumbled. One can give a shrewd guess at how long this had been the practice from an allusion in Dekker's *Worke for Armorours, or the Peace is Broken*, a racy tract of 1609, in which one reads that "wild-fire flew from one to another like squibs when Doctor Faustus goes to the devil."

Squibs had other effective theatrical uses. Their existence explains how it was that that fearsome monster

---

[1] See *The Cornhill Magazine* for September, 1922, p. 317, account of Lupold von Wedel's visit to London in 1584–85. Chambers (*The Elizabethan Stage*, ii, 455) mistakes this puppet show for a dance. Cf. Ordish's *Early London Theatres*, p. 139, extract from Nashe's *Strange Newes* (1592).

known as a firedrake, or what we should call a dragon, so often a feature of old dramatic romance and notably so in Greene's *Friar Bacon and Friar Bungay*, was able to keep spitting fire all the time it was on the stage. Moreover, when covered with orsedue or some other shining substance, and sent on their spluttering way down an almost perpendicular wire to an accompaniment of stage thunder, squibs answered remarkably well for those awe-inspiring thunderbolts which were obliging enough, on occasion, to kill off the villain of the piece. One recalls how the King in Henry Shirley's Cockpit play, *The Martyred Soldier*, met his end in this startling way.

There was good reason why the large open-air theatres affected by the multitude should have enjoyed a practical monopoly of the fireworks drama. In the small, select, enclosed theatres the consequent stench of gunpowder and smouldering brown paper would have been, in Dogberrian phrase, "most tolerable and not to be endured." To these choking after-effects quaint allusion is made in *Northward Ho*, an old Paul's Boys' play. One of the characters likens the riotous course of young prodigals, up in town fresh from the country, to a fireworks display. "Foh!" he says, "they, as soon as they come to their lands, get up to London, and like squibs that run upon lines, they keep a-spitting of fire and cracking till they ha' spent all; and when my squib is out . . . foh! he stinks." This unpleasant after-effect the Italian players of the period neatly avoided by perfuming their fireworks, but the secret had apparently not made its way to England.

Familiarly known as "blazing stars," comets, as portents, were part of the stock-in-trade of the Elizabethan dramatist, and their blazing was by no means left to the audience's imagination. In Peele's *The Battle of Alcazar*, which dates from about 1589, there is an inter-act dumb show in which Fame, in the garb of an angel, hangs sundry crowns upon a tree, after which a blazing star appears and the crowns fall down. So, too, in *The Life and Death of Captain Thomas Stukeley*, while the Chorus is interpreting a dumb show, a sudden thunder-clap is heard, "the sky is on fire and the blazing star appears." Not a whit perturbed by this awesome phenomenon, the Chorus calmly proceeds to interpret its significance.[1] Later examples of the effect are not uncommon. Blazing stars were seen in the last acts of two unascribed plays, *The Revenger's Tragedy* and *The Bloody Brother*. Even the academic drama was not wholly exempt from their visitations. Goffe introduced one into the fifth act of his *Courageous Turke* when that play was produced at Oxford in or about 1628.[2]

Little as he was given to reliance upon "those giltgauds men-children swarm to see," Shakespeare was not wholly averse from effects of this order. There is, for example, a scene in the second act of the Third Part of *Henry VI*, where Edward says, "Dazzle mine eyes, or do I see three suns?" and evokes from Richard the response:

[1] Greg has no doubt but that the blazing star in these two plays was none other than the comet which appeared in November, 1577, and was observed and described by Tycho Brahe.

[2] Early seventeenth-century methods of fireworks manufacture are revealed in John Bate's *The Mysteries of Nature and Art*, of which I have seen only the exemplar of the second edition (1635), preserved in the Bodleian. See Book II, pp. 115–118, for details regarding golden rain, rockets on lines, flying dragons, firedrakes, etc. At page 116 is an illustration showing the *modus operandi* of the blazing (or revolving) star. Another treatise dealing incidentally with the subject is William Leake's *Mathematical Recreations* (1635), pp. 269–272.

Three glorious suns each a perfect sun:
Not separated with the racking clouds,
But sever'd in a pale clear-shining sky.
See! See! They join, embrace and seem to kiss
As if they vow'd some league inviolable:
Now they are but one lamp, one light, one sun.
In this the heaven figures some event.

So far from giving a loose rein to mere poetic fancy, Shakespeare was here basing on Holinshed and preserving tradition,[1] but, as there is no accompanying stage direction, one is apt to jump to the conclusion that the audience did not see what Richard saw. That is a mistake. Not so very long ago, Mr. P. Alexander very ably demonstrated that the anonymous old play called *The True Tragedie of Richard Duke of Yorke*, published in 1595, is a surreptitiously abbreviated version of the Third Part of *Henry VI*, and not, as still too commonly supposed, the sketchy original on which Shakespeare based.[2] In the corrupt play, at the juncture corresponding with the episode just detailed, comes the stage direction, "three sunnes appear in the aire," which plainly shows that some attempt was made to realise the traditional phenomenon. I do not pretend to know how the thing was done, but it does not seem to me to have been a fireworks effect. Equally difficult to show must have been the vision in the last act of *The Troublesome Reign of King John*, Part I, an anonymous Queen's Men's play published in 1591, where five moons appear, a smaller one whirling round the other four. The Prophet of Pomfret interprets the portent, pointing out that the little moon is England and that the other moons represent Spain, Denmark, Ger-

---

[1] Cf. *Shakespeare's Library*, 2d edition, vi, p. 29.
[2] See his article on the subject in the *Times Literary Supplement* for November 13, 1924.

many, and France. Here we undoubtedly encounter some
sort of mechanical illuminant. Note that Shakespeare
avoids resort to this effect in *King John* by simply making reference to what had been seen:

> My lord, they say five moons were seen tonight,
> Four fixed, and the fifth did whirl about
> The other four in wondrous motion.[1]

Nothing of precisely the same nature as this mechanical
device is to be traced in the early Stuart masques, but
cognate effects were procured in Jonson's *Masque of
Hymen* in 1606, and in Daniel's *Tethys's Festival* four
years later. In the *Masque of Hymen*, the upper part of
the scene opened, and Juno was revealed; "above her,"
we are told, "the region of fire, with a continual motion,
was seen to whirl circularly." Much more elaborate was
the effect in *Tethys's Festival*. Here the description reads:

First at the opening of the heauens appeared 3 circles of lights and
glasses, one within another, and came downe in a straight motion
fiue foote, and then began to mooue circularly; which lights and
motion so occupied the eyes of the spectators, that the manner of
altering the Scene was scarcely discerned: for in a moment the whole
face of it was changed.

This leads by natural transition to the baffling problem of the moon. Obviously, if the Elizabethan players
were capable of visualising phenomena such as have been
discussed, they would not have experienced any great
difficulty in manifesting fair Luna. But there is absolutely no evidence, not so much as a solitary stage direction, to show that this was ever done. One takes it that
there was no alternative: either the moon was always
seen by the audience when it was referred to, or its
presence had always to be imagined. The weight of tex-

[1] Act IV, scene 2, lines 182–184.

tual evidence points to actual demonstration, but textual evidence on questions of this sort is apt to prove fallacious. If we are to take references literally, they must be carried to their logical issues: which means, for example, that if the moon was actually seen when Romeo said, "Lady, by yonder bright moon I swear," then the objects upon which he saw it shining must also have been seen. Another step, and we should have to postulate the use of painted scenery. Yet, despite all the difficulties with which the problem bristles, I am inclined to agree with the late Dr. Thornton Shirley Graves [1] that the moon was regularly simulated, though I am by no means fortified in my belief by his reliance on Serlio and the practice of the early Italian court theatres, or the usages of the Restoration picture-stage. Analogies of this kind are fallacious. It is not permissible for us to deduce from the stage direction in Tuke's *Adventures of Five Hours*, running, "The rising moon appears behind the scene," that the moon had previously risen or been seen at all on the earlier platform-stage. The Restoration stage carried on the principles of the court-masque stage, and we cannot be sure that any of the principles of the court-masque stage were ever followed in the contemporary public theatre. Therefore, it does not suffice to say that, because the moon was seen rising above the horizon in Jonson's masque of *Oberon* in 1611, and revealed the satyr by its shining, it must also have been commonly seen in the ordinary playhouses of the time. But there are sundry items of evidence advanced by plays strictly of this period, nay, almost of this very year, which point to the conclusion that common practice fell little short of court practice. Take the scene in Dekker's *If it be not Good, the Devil is in it,* an undivided Red Bull play to which the only

[1] "Notes on Elizabethan Theatres," *Studies in Philology*, ciii (1916), 116.

readily verifiable reference one can give is, *Dekker's Dramatic Works*, edition Pearson, volume iv, page 310. Here, although there has been no previous mention of the moon and a stage direction seems to be demanded, the Sub-Prior suddenly proceeds to apostrophise her in a speech beginning with "Blest Star of light." So too, in Act IV, scene 3, of *The Second Maiden's Tragedy*, a Globe play of 1611, the Tyrant, moralising in a cathedral, says:

> O, the moon rises! what reflection
> Is thrown upon this sanctified building,
> E'en in a twinkling! How the monuments glister
> As if death's palaces were all massy silver,
> And scorn'd the name of marble!

Here the description is so elaborate as to arouse the suspicion that the moonbeams were imaginary, and one would feel inclined to let it go at that, were it not for the fact that later in the scene a remarkable lighting effect is demanded. Note the direction: "On a sudden, in a kind of noise like a wind, the doors clattering, the tomb-stone flies open, and a great light appears in the midst of the tomb." This light is required to reveal the ghost which comes on immediately at the back. Let us now retrace our steps four years, and take a look at *The Revenger's Tragedy*, another Globe play. In the fifth act we find Supervacuo saying: "He shall not live: his hair shall not grow much longer. In this time of revels, tricks may be set afoot. See'st thou yon new moon? It shall outlive the new duke by much."

Of course, it is permissible for you to say that here the moon was imagined, just as Hamlet's cloud which was so "very like a whale" was imagined. But pause a moment. In the very next scene a blazing star appears, causing much perturbation. Lusurioso refers to it as "that ill-knotted fire, that blushing, flaring star." Surely in mat-

ters of staging there must have been consistency: we are
not at liberty to infer that the moon was imagined when
the comet was not.

King Lear belongs to much the same period as The
Revenger's Tragedy, as well as to the same theatre. In
Act II, scene 2, of the folio version, where Kent and the
Steward enter severally, we find Kent saying, "Draw,
you rogue, for though it be night yet the moon shines.
Ile make a sop o' th' moonshine of you." Afterwards,
when Kent is put into the stocks and left solitary, he says:

> Approach thou Beacon to this under-globe,
> That by thy comfortable beames I may
> Peruse this letter.

In some notes by my friend and sometime collaborator, the late William Archer, which came into my possession after his death, I found the above passages from
King Lear cited, together with the comment, "This looks
very much as though there were something to represent
the moon." Seeing that Archer was the last man in the
world to entertain hare-brained ideas, his opinion on this
point is worthy of consideration.

But if, on the strength of these references, we are to
assume that the moon when spoken of was always shown,
the difficulty is to know where to draw the line. What
conclusion are we to arrive at, for example, regarding
Achilles' observation in Troilus and Cressida, V, 8?

> Look, Hector, how the sun begins to set;
> How ugly night comes breathing at his heels:
> Even with the veil and darking of the sun,
> To close the day up, Hector's life is done.

Was this mere poetic imagery, or was some attempt
being made to take advantage of natural conditions?
Remember that we are in an open theatre, the Globe.
Assuming that the play was produced in the dead of

winter, the sun would be sinking just as the action drew to a close. This at first strikes one as a pretty neat solution, but an ugly afterthought obtrudes. In Elizabethan times new plays, when successful, were generally given about once a week for a period of six months or so, and there would certainly be occasions when the lines would not be in harmony with the natural conditions. Hence, it is very doubtful if dramatists, when in the throes of composition, were in any wise influenced by thoughts of the seasons.

In the representation of conflagrations, the Elizabethan theatre was at a great disadvantage compared with the theatre of to-day. To such a pitch has stage science now advanced that the illusion of fire can be given without any resort to it. In earlier days, save in the procuring of trivial effects by blowing rosin through a candle flame (the approved method of making stage lightning), this was impossible; consequently, there was always a certain amount of risk in realistic fire scenes. Yet realism of the sort was occasionally sought after. Marlowe had a curious predilection for fire effects of various kinds, but the tantalising thing is that one cannot always determine how these effects were procured. The First Part of *Tamburlaine*, III, 1, affords us the major puzzle. A direction says: "Enter Tamburlaine, with his three sons and Usumcasane; four attendants bearing the hearse of Zenocrate; the drums sounding a doleful march; the town burning." How was the conflagration indicated? No mere puff of smoke would have sufficed to convey the fearfulness of Tamburlaine's act or been in keeping with the rhodomontade he bellows in the scene. But alas! not in this or any subsequent play have we any slightest clue to the nature of the effect. All one can say with confidence on the point is that, if the theatre or inn-yard where this

Second Part was played escaped burning down, it was not
Marlowe's fault. He went so far as to introduce two other
fire effects later into the play. In Act III, scene 4, we have
a very curious scene, in which the Captain's Wife kills her
son immediately after her husband's death, and says:

> Whose body, with his father's, I have burnt
> Lest cruel Scythians should dismember him.

It may be noted in passing that the direction, "She
burns the bodies of her husband and son," does not occur
in the old editions. As a last request, the Captain's Wife
entreats Techelles to

> cast her body on the burning flame,
> That feeds upon her son's and husband's flesh.

But, so far from consenting, he carries her off. Here, as
I have no solution of the problem to offer, I resort once
more to William Archer's notes. "Is it possible," he asks,
"that her husband and son in dying, fell behind the
'wings' of the inner stage, and that she then burned two
dummies on an iron plate of some sort?"

We proceed along to the fifth act, and pause where we
find Tamburlaine saying:

> Now, Casane, where's the Turkish Alcoran,
> And all the heaps of superstitious books
> Found in the temple of that Mahomet
> Whom I have thought a god? They shall be burnt.

The books are immediatley presented to him, and he
orders a fire to be lit and the books flung upon it. No
stage direction occurs in the early editions to show what
was done, but evidently the books were openly burnt.
After this, one can hardly be blamed for tracing the hand
of Marlowe in the last scene of *Dido*. And here, too, we
encounter a puzzle. Dido commands Anna to order her

attendants to bring her fire. As soon as this is done, she says to Iarbus:

> Lay to thy hands, and help me make a fire
>
> . . . .
>
> So leave me now; let none approach this place
>
> . . . .
>
> Now, Dido, with these relics, burn thyself.

After she has consigned the relics to the flames, she takes farewell of life with

> Live false Aeneas! truest Dido dies;
> Sic, sic juvat ire sub umbras.

On which Anna cries out:

> O help Iarbus! Dido in these flames
> Hath burnt herself.

After all this, one is disappointed to find that the vision of Hell in the sixteenth scene of the *Faustus* quarto of 1616 is not Marlowe's work, so much is it in his vein. There is something Dantesque about this conception of "the vast perpetual torture-house," where Furies toss the damned on red-hot pitchforks and selfish epicureans are fed "with sops of flaming fire." Yet the emulation which this Fortune Theatre effect evoked was little short of ludicrous. Dekker, when he appended a spectacular epilogue of Hell to his oddly named play, *If it be not Good, the Devil is in it*, produced at the Red Bull in 1611, made the punishment fit the crime by placing Guy Fawkes in the midst of a number of flaming barrels. But his technical expertness must at least be accounted unto him for righteousness, since he availed of the presence of the rear-stage curtains to present a vision of Hell in two tableaux.[1]

[1] Cf. *The Brazen Age*, V, 3, where the princes break down the trees and make a fire in which Hercules burns his club and lion's skin, and is just about to throw himself into the flames when Jupiter kills him with a thunderbolt.

There was quite a remarkable spectacular outburst at the Red Bull at this period, and its influence can be traced to other theatres. I think there can be little doubt that Heywood's trilogy of *The Ages* had its origin in a desire to attract the public by feasting its eyes to the full. All the resources of contemporary stage mechanism were then brought into play, and familiar old effects were given new embellishment. It will be recalled that in the popular sixteenth-century play, *A Looking Glasse for London and England*, there was a scene in the fourth act where a hand from out a cloud threatened with a burning sword. Heywood went one better than this in the last act of *The Brazen Age*. Jupiter, in the heavens, was seen to strike Hercules with a thunderbolt, causing him to sink into the earth. Then, to the spot where he had disappeared, a cloud bearing a hand descended, and, on its return skywards, the hand was seen to be holding a star, which it eventually fixed in the firmament.[1] Moreover, in this play, as in its predecessor, *The Silver Age*, there was liberal employment of fireworks; and in both there were cloud effects and aerial flights rivalling anything of the sort already seen in the court masques. One also notes that attempts were now beginning to be made to give the illusion of fire without utilising it. In *The Silver Age* we have a direction, "Enter Pluto with a club of fire, a burning crowne, Proserpine, the Judges, the Fates and a guard of Devils, all with burning weapons." Here the necessary illusion was doubtless procured by a liberal use of red paint and crimson tinsel. Joey's red-hot poker in the pantomime had a very respectable ancestry. These demons with fiery clubs are to be found recurring in a much later Red Bull play, Kirke's *The Seven Champions of Christendome*. No doubt audiences in those days were

---

[1] The primitive effect is to be found recurring in *The Prophetess*, V, 3.

easily deluded, or, what amounts to the same thing, easily pleased. Even so late as in early Restoration days we find a piece of painted wood, virtually a scenic set-piece, doing duty for a bonfire in the last act of *The Rump*.[1] But we cannot safely make broad deductions from occasional makeshifts of this order. Such knowledge does not enable us to solve the problem set by the scene in the fourth act of *The Valiant Welshman* (a Prince's Men's play of *circa* 1613), in which a witch is flung into the flames of a burning castle.

There has been so much wild conjecturing regarding the probable influence of the court masque on public-theatre staging that the time is ripe for a rigidly scientific investigation of the subject. That I have made, but at present I find it inexpedient to do more than give a bald summary of my conclusions. The regular appearance of the Jacobean players at court as the speakers and anti-masquers in the Christmas and Shrovetide masques indicates a bridge between the masque stage and the public stage over which one would naturally expect to find something material being carried back. But all that it really brought about before the Caroline period was the intermittent transference of certain antimasque dances to the common stage.[2] Perhaps, however, in this — there is an "if" in the matter — there is a slight understatement. In process of time, from slavish copying the players proceeded to original production. At least, picturesque stage dances are on record of which one cannot trace court prototypes. In *The Mad Lover*, IV, 1, there is a Masque of Beasts and Trees in which a lion, a dog, an ape, a pied bird, and some trees danced. This play dates

[1] Cf. Lawrence, *The Elizabethan Playhouse and Other Studies*, ii, 21.
[2] Cf. *The Athenæum* for November 21, 1919, p. 1235, W. J. Lawrence on "The Date of *The Duchess of Malfi*."

from 1616, but it was first published in the Beaumont and Fletcher folio of 1647, and, for aught we know, the masque may date only from a belated revival. Equally noteworthy is the Dance of Frogs, given by four boys in *The Fair Maid of the Inn*,[1] a Blackfriars play of 1626.

With the increase in splendour in the court masque in the Caroline period came an aggrandizement of its influence upon the public stage. The intercalated theatre masque was now performed with greater luxury of detail. Look, for example, at the picture presented in the last act of Richards's tragedy of *Messalina*. One can revivify it simply by quoting an uncommonly elaborate stage direction:

> Cornets sound a Flourish, Enter Senate who placed by Sulpilius, cornets cease, and the Antique maske consisting of eight Bachinalians, enter guirt with vine leaves, and shap'd in the middle with Tunne Vessells, each bearing a Cup in their hands, who during the first straine of Musick playd foure times over, enter two at a time, at the tune's end, make stand; draw wine and carouse, then dance all: the antimasque gone off, and solemne musicke playing; Messallina and Silius gloriously crown'd in an Arch-glittering Cloud aloft, court each other.[2]

But it is noteworthy that, long before the court masque began to exert any consistent influence in the theatre, the steadily persisting convention of the visualised dream, so largely associated with dumb shows, gave intermittent opportunity for considerable spectacular display. One recalls the vision scenes in *Cymbeline* and *Henry VIII*,

---

[1] Eight years previously, long enough to be forgotten, a Frog Dance by twelve boys had been given in Jonson's masque, *Pleasure Reconciled to Virtue* (see *Jonson Allusion Book*, p. 105). *Quaere*, did the Revels Office indulge in periodical sales of old stock?

[2] In Jonson's masque, *Pleasure Reconciled to Virtue* (1618), dancers came in in tuns and wicker flasks (see *Jonson Allusion Book*, p. 105). But this occurred nearly a score of years earlier.

the former of which, with its descending god, was clearly inspired by the spectacular debauch at the Red Bull.[1] Other examples not so readily brought to mind by the scholar occur in *Wily Beguiled*, *The Atheist's Tragedie* (twice), *The Roman Actor*, V, *The Queen's Exchange*, III, *The Jewes Tragedy*, and *If You Know not Me, You Know Nobody*, Part I. It is interesting to note that this convention was given renewed life by the Restoration dramatist, and had exemplification in *The Indian Queen*, III, 1, in Otway's *Alcibiades*, V, and in Rochester's *Valentinian*, III.

There was another type of vision scene, one not so often accompanied by spectacular display, which I take the precaution to mention, not only with the view of preventing confusion, but also that I may take opportunity to point out that the principles which ruled its representation have been wholly misunderstood. Consider, by way of example, Chapman's *Bussy D'Ambois*, IV, 2. The Friar has invoked supernatural aid on behalf of D'Ambois and Tamyra. The lovers are anxious to gain possession of an incriminating document in Monsieur's custody, but to effect this is beyond Cartophylax's powers. That full knowledge of the situation may be gained, the Friar then demands of Behemoth that he show them the Guise, Monsieur, and Montsurry in whatsoever action they be conjunctively engaged. A vision follows in which Monsieur is seen presenting the desired document to Montsurry. The three characters in the vision speak to each other in order that the audience may thoroughly grasp the situation, but only their dumb show is patent to the anxious lovers. Yet we find Dr. F. S. Boas, in his redaction of the play,[2] saying:

---

[1] Compare with the scene already referred to in *The Brazen Age*.
[2] Belles Lettres Series, pp. 158, 159.

"The characters (as is evident from lines 102–104) are supposed to be far off, but rendered visible and audible to Tamyra and D'Ambois by Behemoth's power."

To predicate this dramatic audibility is to ignore the conventions which ruled over the magically conjured-up vision scene. Moreover, it is here a flagrant misreading of the text. Behemoth says:

> Behold
> They come here, and the Earl now holds the paper.
> *Bussy.* May we not heare them?
> *Friar.* No, be still and see.

An earlier example, in all respects analogous, is to be found in Greene's *Friar Bacon and Friar Bungay*, and at a much later period there is an interesting variant in Brome's *The Love-Sick Court*, III, 3. In the latter, Eudina, lulled by a song, falls asleep in the presence of two ladies, and has a dream which is shown to the audience in a dumb show. Meanwhile, the people on the stage are blissfully ignorant that a moving picture is in operation.

If I were asked for my opinion in brief on the vexed question of horses on the early stage, I should signify my hearty agreement with the humourist who once said that Richard III could very well afford to offer his kingdom for a horse, since he was fully aware that in the Elizabethan theatre there was no chance of anybody taking him at his word. I quote that unknown worthy because a witticism is often better calculated to establish the truth than the soberest marshalling of evidence. Most likely he had no other justification for his belief than the plea in the prologue to *Henry V*, but for the majority of sensible folk that plea will be justification enough:

> Think, when we talk of horses, that you see them
> Printing their proud hoofs i' the receiving earth;

For 't is your thoughts that now must deck our kings,
Carry them here and there.

There are those, however, who side with Sir Sidney
Lee in the view that the early seventeenth-century audience had really no imperfections of this kind to piece
out with their minds, and they generally pin their faith
to the following entry from Dr. Simon Forman's Diary:

In *Macbeth* at the Globe 1610, the 20 of Aprile Saturday there was
to be observed firste how Macbeth and Banko two noblemen of
Scotland ridinge thorow a wood, there stode before them three
women fairies or nimphs, and saluted Macbeth, saying three times
unto him, "Hail, Macbeth, king of Codor, for thou shalt be a king,
but shalt beget no Kings, &c."

One is not disposed to cavil over trifles, but when one
is asked to accept Forman as a scientific witness, there is
need at the outset to protest that April 20, 1610, so far
from falling on a Saturday, fell on a Friday. The main
thing, however, to recognise is that Forman was simply
recording the story of the play, and not minutely detailing the action. Apart from the difficulty of riding two
horses on to the stage, there was the question of risk to the
spectators who encumbered it. Every seasoned playgoer
knows how nervous a horse gets once he hears his hooves
rattle on hollow-sounding boards, how apt he is to grow
restive and launch out with his heels. But there is no
need to labour the point, since we have only to read farther in Forman to become convinced that his aim was
not to make scrupulously accurate report of what he saw.
Thus we find him writing:

Then was Macbeth crowned king, and then he, for fear of Banko,
his old companion, that he should beget kings, but be no king himself, he contrived the death of Banko, and caused him to be murdered on the way as he rode.

In a sense, this is accurate, and in another sense it is not. Strictly speaking, Banquo was not murdered "as he rode." It will be instructive to look at Act III, scene 3, of the play, because the very method of the murder shows how neatly the riding in on horseback was avoided:

Third Murderer.	Hark! I hear horses.
Banquo (within).	Give us a light there, ho!
Second Murderer.	Then 't is he; the rest that are within the note of expectation already are i' the court.
First Murderer.	His horses go about.
Third Murderer.	Almost a mile; but he does usually, so all men do, from hence to the palace gate make it their walk.
Second Murderer.	A light, a light!

(Enter Banquo and Fleance with a torch.

What curious kink is there in the modern mind which so stubbornly dictates a literal interpretation of Forman's narrative? Halliwell-Phillipps, not being able to convince himself that real horses were used, fell back on the absurd alternative that Macbeth and Banquo rode in on hobby-horses.[1] Nor did the aberration end with him: other brilliant scholars have fallen into line. Here is Barrett Wendell's endorsement:

As to the riding, Macbeth and Banquo probably made their first entry with wicker-work hobby horses about their waists, with false human legs, of half the natural length, dangling from the saddles, and with sweeping skirts to hide the actors' feet. Monstrous as such a proceeding seems, it might still occur in serious tragedy on the Chinese stage, and the Chinese stage is very like the Elizabethan.[2]

Superficially, that is so; but the Chinese character is not very like the English character. It is all a question whether the Elizabethan had no sense of the ludicrous; if he had not, it is difficult to know how Shakespeare ever

---

[1] *Outlines*, 3d edition, p. 348.

[2] Wendell, *William Shakespeare*, 1902, p. 308.

came to write his burlesque of Pyramus and Thisbe. But the truth is that some of the funniest things outside *Punch* have been written by the literalists in the course of this prolonged controversy. In his own opinion, Mr. R. Crompton Rhodes has said the last word upon the matter. This is how he proceeds to silence all opposition:

> It is certain, however, that horses were used on the stage by the Lord Chamberlain's Men, as in *A Larum for London, or The Seige of Antwerp*, where the Duke of Alva, who is pretending to be dead, is carried "upon a horse covered with blacke." There is no reason to suppose, therefore, that Forman was wrong about the men riding through a wood, and indeed woodland settings played a large part in this play.[1]

This is neither argument nor evidence: it is simply an amazing error. Published in quarto in 1600, the anonymous play referred to has been reprinted by Farmer in his *Tudor Facsimiles*. On turning to Signature B verso, one finds that, owing to a misprint, the Duke is represented as being carried in "upon a horse covered with black," but the blunder becomes apparent on reading farther on. On B 2 recto, a stage direction indicates that Alva is "in the hearse," and from it he says, "What are those villaines gone that rayl'd vpon me?" In his next speech, he bids his bearers "set downe and let me light," after which we have the direction, "He comes from under the hearse." [2] From which details the obvious deduction is that what Mr. Crompton Rhodes has found is not so much a horse as a mare's nest.

Perhaps, on careful examination, other Elizabethan stage horses might turn out to be hearses. I suspect some blunder of the sort in connexion with Legge's Cambridge

---

[1] See his paper on "The First Folio and the Elizabethan Stage" in *Studies in the First Folio* (1924), p. 119.

[2] Compare the hearses in *The Two Noble Kinsmen*, I, 5.

University tragedy, *Richardus Tertius*, as acted at St. John's College *circa* 1579. Here is part of a stage direction which occurs at the end of the last act: "After this let Henerye, Earl of Richmond come tryumphing, haveing ye body of K. Richard dead on a horse; Catesby and Ratcliffe and others bound." [1]

Even if we had proof positive that a horse was actually used in this play, it would have little bearing on the question, since it cannot be pretended that what was done on the university stage of 1579 and thereabouts had any influence on playhouse habitude. The only textual reference I know of that seems to point to the bringing of a horse on public boards occurs in Peele's *The Battle of Alcazar*, V, 1, and it, at a pinch, might be explained away. Here Mahamet, while flying from his enemies, encounters a boy, and cries out in desperation for a horse. The boy replies:

> Here is a horse my lord,
> As swiftly pac'd as Pegasus,
> Mount thee thereon, and save thy selfe by flight.

Proof, I think, that horses were rarely, if ever, employed on the old platform-stage lies in the very considerable number of situations where their use would have been natural and yet was avoided. A typical example occurs in *The History of King Leir and his Three Daughters*, I, 5, where the King of Cornwall and the King of Cambria come on booted and spurred and carrying riding wands. Realism here demanded that they should appear on horseback, if the use of horses was at all convenient, seeing that they are represented as travelling in the hottest of haste. The pretence in most of these cases was that the riders had reached a hill, and had dis-

[1] Printed in *Shakespeare's Library*, ed. Hazlitt, vol. i, part 3. Cf. G. C. Moore Smith, *College Plays*, p. 93.

mounted to breathe their horses while ascending. Examples are to be found in *Look About You*, I, 1; *The Revenge of Bussy D'Ambois*, IV, 3; and *The Witch of Edmonton*, III, 1. Other scenes where realism pleaded for the employment of horses, and deaf ears were turned to the appeal, are *Doctor Faustus*, scene 11;[1] *A Knack to Know an Honest Man*, I, 1; *Arden of Feversham*, III, 6, and IV, 1, 2; *Cymbeline*, IV, 1; *The Fair Maid of the Exchange*, I, 1; and *A New Way to Pay Old Debts*, II, 3, and III, 1.

Even on the court stage in the Caroline period the bringing on of horses was sedulously avoided. In Shirley's Whitehall masque, *The Triumph of Peace*, given in 1634, there is a dramatic episode in which a merchant travelling on horseback is waylaid and robbed by two highwaymen. One is apt to think that here realism demanded the use of an actual quadruped, but the protest of the Property Man's Wife near the close of the masque shows that the merchant was mounted on a hobby-horse.[2] Possibly there may be those who will deem this sound corroboration of Halliwell-Phillipps's contention regarding *Macbeth*, but it should be unnecessary to point out that what was fitting in a court fantasy was not always fitting in a tragedy.

Two years earlier Shirley had written, for the Queen's Men at the Cockpit, *Hyde Park*, the first racing play on record. His fourth act presented most of the excitements of a foot race and a horse race in a realistic way, even to the confused noise of the gamblers; but there was one noteworthy omission. For, whereas in the foot race the competitors crossed the stage twice, not a glimpse of the thoroughbreds was vouchsafed throughout. The horse race was conveyed imaginatively by illusive sounds and

[1] Marlowe's *Plays*, Mermaid Series, p. 215.
[2] Shirley's *Works*, Mermaid Series, pp. 454, 462.

shouts without. Perhaps one could not better illustrate the essential difference between platform-stage principles and picture-stage principles than by the fact that when *Hyde Park* came to be revived at the Theatre Royal in 1668 it was deemed requisite to bring in real horses.[1] Now that the public had become habituated to the use of scenery, the imagination could no longer be trusted to do its work.

[1] The first real horse seen on the French stage appeared in 1650 in the *Andromède* of Corneille. Cf. Corneille's *Works* (1862), v, 256.

XII

THE RISE AND PROGRESS OF THE COMPLEX–DISGUISE PLAY

IT would be with difficulty and only after much seeking that one could light upon a period in the history of European drama, whether ancient or modern, when disguise as a constructional expedient was wholly eschewed. Simple credibility, allied with the familiarity with certain postulates which theatrical conventions impose, makes improbabilities probable, but an age of scepticism, such as the present, finds itself indisposed in the playhouse either to take anything as granted or to surrender its intelligence into the keeping of the dramatist. One by one the old conventions have gone by the board, and to-day stage disguise is practically a creed outworn. Time out of mind there has been a fashion in plays as in other mundane things, but the great change which has come over the spirit of the drama in this respect is not so much a matter of progressive technique as of the orientation of mass psychology. Before we can realise how and why disguise came to play so prominent and permeative a part in the expansile scheme of Elizabethan dramaturgy we must recapture the Elizabethan mind. A difficult, perhaps dangerous, thing, to do this, since it involves the sloughing of one's modern skin. You will see at once the barriers which exist between past and present, if you recall your early wrestlings with Shakespeare—how, for example, he outraged your credibility by his resort, mild as it was for his period, to disguise. Yet Shakespeare knew well where to draw the line; there were other and not inconsiderable dramatists of his day who called for, not the exercise of greater powers of imagination, but a completer surrender of the intelligence. In resorting to the supremest artifice — for that in truth the complex-disguise play was — they demanded of the adult the child's capacity for make-believe. It was the possession of that childish quality, the dominance of simple faith, belief in what one is told, that distinguished the Elizabethan audience from all later audiences.

Though given exemplification well within living memory, as I as a lifelong playgoer can personally testify, the principle of the complex-disguise play would now take some swallowing. It involves the concession that for the furtherance of the plot a principal character may assume a variety of disguises and masquerade as several people. Essentially of the stage stagey, the scheme is one that has always had fascination for the accomplished showy actor with gifts of versatility, the Elliston type, and so long as the times bred him, just so long the complex-disguise play held its place in the theatre. Reduced to the proportions of a sketch and relegated to the houses of vaudeville, it has now become the prerogative of the quick-change artist. But we owe one play of note, Jonson's *Every Man in his Humour*, to its pristine vogue, and it is essential for a proper understanding of Elizabethan dramaturgy that we should make investigation of the circumstances of its rise and progress.

Fertile in ideas as were the Elizabethans, the complex-disguise play was not of English origin. Born of a Plautine convention, it came from Italy. Some traces of it are to be found in the *commedia erudita* of the late sixteenth century, but its existence is more readily detected in the buffooneries of the *commedia dell'arte*. No Elizabethan theatre play points directly to the source, but there is other evidence on which it can be predicated. Let us consider for a moment the characteristics of an anonymous Latin comedy called *Machiavellus*, which was based on some unknown Italian original and was performed at St. John's College, Cambridge, on December 9, 1597.[1] The scene in this is Florence, and the action passes in the open. Machiavellus and one Jacuppus, a Jew, are rivals in love, and plot and counterplot for the hand of Orlanda, the daughter of Andronicus. Orlanda is the betrothed of Philautus, who has betaken himself to the wars and is thought by his friends to have been killed; but he returns unexpectedly at the close, after the other two have exhausted the possibilities of every conceivable artifice to outwit each other, and claims his bride. As soon as the contest begins, Machiavellus appears to Andronicus as Philautus's ghost and warns him not to give his daughter to the Jew. Andronicus is so terrified by the visitation that, when Jacuppus and his man Grillio come to his house, they experience difficulty in gaining access. But at the opening of the second act Grillio learns from Gullio, Machiavellus's servant, of the ghostly trick, and the Jew, on being told of the matter, determines to retaliate. Disguised as a "trapezita," he serenades the dawn under Andronicus's window, and is surprised to see Machiavellus and him coming forth from the house at so early an hour. Perplexity, however, merges into glee when he learns that Machiavellus's suit has been rejected. In Act III, scene 2, Machiavellus assumes a fresh disguise as an Egyptian fortune-teller, pretends to reveal to Andronicus his future, and carries off the girl

---

[1] For the play, see Douse MSS, 234, f. 40 v (in the Bodleian). Cf. Boas, *University Drama in the Tudor Age*, pp. 393–401; *Cambridge History of English Literature*, vi, 305.

asleep in a chest. In Act IV, scene 1, Jacuppus, to prevent the marriage of Machiavellus and Orlanda, gets himself up as a blind musician, and sings beneath Machiavellus's windows. Obtaining access to the house, he drugs Orlanda's cup with an opiate, and Machiavellus, finding her, as he thinks, dead, bears her off in the chest for burial. Shortly afterwards the lost Philautus returns and has little difficulty in routing both intriguers. From this account it will be noted that two of the characters assume two disguises each, making intermediate resumption of their personal identity. Contrasted with what was shown in London on the public stage within a year or two, this was trick-and-shuffleboard of a very elementary order.

Whatever the motor that started the English complex-disguise play on its long journey, it was certainly not *Machiavellus;* already at the Rose Theatre the Admiral's Men had appeared with acceptance in one or two plays of this type. In all probability the vogue of the complex-disguise scheme began there with the production, on October 2, 1595, of the lost play of *The Disguises.*[1] At any rate, whether that was so or not, the Admiral's Men had won popularity for the new type before *Machiavellus* saw the light. A tolerably quick revival of a play can be taken as a sound indication of the play's initial success, and it is to be noted that Chapman's *The Blind Beggar of Alexandria*, originally produced at the Rose on February 12, 1596, was revived at the Fortune five years later. Meanwhile, in 1598, a much abbreviated version of the play had been published, a version no doubt made surreptitiously for a band of strollers, and from which it is difficult to deduce a fair estimate of the original. Remark that it has a descriptive title, indicating, as I like to be-

[1] Chambers, *The Elizabethan Stage*, ii, 144.

lieve, what were the prime qualities of its original appeal: "The blinde begger of Alexandria, most pleasantly discoursing his variable humours in disguised shapes full of conceite and pleasure."

In the play as we have it, Cleanthes (who is not seen *in propria persona* till near the close) figures as three other people: Irus, the blind prophet–hermit, Count Hermes, the mad-brained, and Leon, the old quasi-Semitic usurer. As in those days programmes had not been provided to explain who was who, Cleanthes, to prevent things from getting into a tangle, is compelled to hurl sundry soliloquies directly at the audience in order to keep it posted regarding his disguises and his motives in assuming them. The necessary changes of attire and of make-up gave the actor no great difficulty, as it was only at one juncture (about the beginning of the second act: the text is undivided) that he was called upon for any rapid work in that way. When Antistenes appears before the King with the hope of having his wrongs righted, Leon goes out, and, a poor four lines later, returns as the Count. Subsequently the Count departs, and six lines later Irus is discovered in his cave.[1] But, in connection with these quick changes, it must be borne in mind that the Elizabethan player had as many ready resources as the player of to-day. Red, white, and umber face-paint, false beards and noses, periwigs,[2] eye-patches, the facile expedient of the double cloak, all were at his command. Probably Irus was principally distinguished by his flowing white beard, from time immemorial the sign-manual

[1] The direction says "Enter Irus," but discoveries were not infrequently thus indicated.

[2] To reveal his disguise, the actor had often no more to do than doff his periwig. This is Lodovico's method in the Second Part of *The Honest Whore*, II, 3. Cf. Creizenach, *English Drama in the Age of Shakespeare*, p. 221; V. O. Freeburg, *Disguise Plots in Elizabethan Drama*, p. 121.

of the stage hermit. Leon, the usurer, shared one thing in common with the Marlowean Barabas, an immense red nose. Here the old disguise-assuming actor had an advantage over the actor of to-day, for his false nose, being a thing of painted iron, could be readily put on and readily taken off. The false nose of the present hour is a slowly acquired appendage made up of cotton wool, grease paint, and liquid glue. But, of all the disguises assumed by Cleanthes, we are best acquainted with that donned for his impersonation of the hare-brained Count. Winter or summer, on foot or on horseback, his invariable garb was a velvet gown with a ready pistol in his belt. And as he had lost an eye, he wore a velvet patch over the place of darkness. The face-patch of one kind or another formed perhaps the handiest resource of the old disguise-assuming actor. Mirabel in *The Wild Goose Chase*, III, 1, on finding that he has been tricked by the masquerading De Gard, ejaculates:

> What a purblind was I! Now I remember him;
> All the whole cast's on's face, though it were umber'd,
> And mask'd with patches.

It is noteworthy that the patch was still reckoned an efficacious mode of disguise, on the stage or off it, in post-Restoration days. Congreve makes Bellmour resort to it in the fourth act of *The Old Bachelor*.

Before parting from *The Blind Beggar of Alexandria*, it needs to be said that the cutting of Chapman's text has been fairly well done. Only once is the adapter seriously at fault. Owing to the unguarded elimination of a whole scene in the last act, Cleanthes is shown entering before Leon takes his departure, a somewhat difficult feat for even the quickest of quick-change actors to accomplish. As yet, only Sir Boyle Roche's bird has had the useful faculty of being in two places at once.

Whether it was a matter of cause and effect or simply the outcome of a blind convention, the fact remains that, for the next few years, disguise, both simple and complex, was rampant in Elizabethan drama. It is difficult to find a dramatist who makes no resort to it: even Shakespeare himself was in the vortex. The Admiral's Men, having succeeded in winning acceptance for the complex-disguise play — possibly through the presence in their ranks of one or two players of uncommon versatility — lost no time in making the most of its popularity. There is much chopping and changing of identity in Munday's *The Downfall of Robert Earl of Huntington*, a Robin Hood play produced at the Rose *circa* April, 1598, registered in 1600, and published in 1601. In November, 1598, Chettle was engaged in the composition of a play for the Admiral's Men bearing the title, *'Tis no Deceit to Deceive the Deceiver*, which, judging from its name, apparently dealt with a story of plot and counterplot and called for much masquerading. But no further trace can be found of this piece, and it either remained unfinished or else (what I deem more likely) figures later in Henslowe's Diary under another title.

An equal mystery attaches itself to *Look About You*, an anonymous Admiral's Men's play, published in 1600 and unmentioned by Henslowe, though it is not improbable that the one solution would answer for both problems. There is pressing need to read the riddle set by *Look About You*, seeing that it is, beyond question, the best complex-disguise play of its period. Though called "a pleasant Commodie," it is in reality a chronicle history humorously told, and the telling, one suspects, was by two collaborators. The puzzle is to know under what title it conceals itself in Henslowe's Diary. At first one is disposed to think it might be identifiable with *The*

Disguises of 1595,[1] but, though not so well constructed as *The Blind Beggar of Alexandria*, it is cleverer in its stage business, and was evidently the later of the two. Nearly half its characters figure at one time or another as somebody else. It somehow recalls, without at all resembling, *The Comedy of Errors*, doubtless because the characters often disguise themselves as, and are frequently mistaken for, other characters in the play.

Fleay thinks *Look About You* was written by Anthony Wadeson, and identifies it as *Bear a Brain*, a play written for the Admiral's Men in 1599, but this cannot be taken as anything more than guesswork, viewing the fact that Henslowe's only recorded payment for the play was made to Dekker.[2] It is nothing in favour of his supposition, that the proverbial expression, "bear a brain," occurs once in the play, since it is to be found in others of its own and a much later period. The Nurse in *Romeo and Juliet* uses it, and it crops up occasionally in Marston's plays. On the other hand, "look about you," as a catch phrase, occurs again and again in the latter half of the piece. Still, it is quite possible that neither saying afforded its original title. Mr. H. Dugdale Sykes attributes the play, on various counts, to Henry Chettle and a possible collaborator, hypothetically Munday.[3] Taking the text as divided in Dodsley, he considers that scenes 1, 2, 10, 15, 19, and 33 are entirely Chettle's, and he finds traces of Chettle's hand in eleven other scenes out of the whole thirty-three. In view of the nature of his after-work, Chettle has as good a claim as any, but if the play be mostly his it can be identified, if identified at all, only

[1] It is possible that *The Disguises* may have been Munday's *John a Kent and John a Cumber*.

[2] Fleay, *Biographical Chronicle of the English Drama*, ii, 267.

[3] *Notes and Queries*, 12th series, xii (1923), 324–327.

with *Tis no Deceit to Deceive the Deceiver*. This much, at least, can be said in support of that identification, that the title is in keeping with the action in *Look About You*. Chettle was certainly an adept in complex-disguise play-writing. The play called *The First Part of Thomas Strowde*, written for the Admiral's Men in 1600, and in which he collaborated with Day, is known to us now only as *The Blind Beggar of Bednal Green*, a belatedly published alteration. But in the play as it has come down to us the character of Momford indulges in complex disguising, added to which a good deal of elementary disguising occurs in the course of the action. More striking still is the evidence afforded by Chettle's *Hoffman*, a Fortune play of about 1603, and that despite the fact that the text is very corrupt. One gets so accustomed, as historical investigator, to associate complex disguising with drollery that it comes with a shock of surprise to find it interpenetrating a play of unrelieved gloom. In this grim revenge tragedy Hoffman, after murdering Prince Otho of Lunenburg, passes himself off in his place, besides figuring on occasion as Roderick the hermit and Lorrique the French doctor. Nor is this all. In the course of the action Lodowick, son of the Duke of Saxony, disguises himself as a Greek and is killed while so disguised.

On the whole, therefore, it would appear that Mr. Sykes's solution, when carried to its logical issue, is about the best that has been or is likely to be proffered. But, just by way of demonstrating the difficulties that hedge in puzzles of this order, I may say that, before coming across Mr. Sykes's analysis of *Look About You*, I was disposed on the strength of certain evidence, which may or may not be illusive, to identify the play as *The Mad Man's Morris*, a lost piece, written by Robert Wilson, Michael Drayton, and Thomas Dekker, and produced by the Admiral's Men at the Rose, *circa* August, 1598. It seemed to me that Gloucester was the madman who morris-danced it through the play, since the text abounds in references to his madness. I quote these references precisely as I found them in Hazlitt's *Dodsley*, volume vii:

P. 391, direction: ". . . Being set, enters fantastical Robert of Gloucester in a gown girt."

P. 420: "'Tis such a h-h-humorous earl . . ."
Gloster [of himself]: "Have a care of th-this madcap."
John: "Mad gloster mute, all mirth turn'd to despair?"

P. 422: "So near, mad Robin?"

P. 423: "Now, madcap, thou winn'st all: where art thou Robin?"

P. 441, *John,* referring to Gloucester's blood: "whose wanton current his mad humour fed."

P. 447, *Skink* to Gloucester: "But thou'st the maddest lord that e'er I met."

P. 453: "Would mad earl Robin saw these humourists."

P. 487, *Skink* to Gloucester: "whose mad tricks have made me love thee."

P. 495, *Henry* to Gloucester: "Madman, I give no ear to thy loose words."

The unfortunate thing was that, when I came to ponder over the possibilities of this identification, I found that Skink, and not Gloucester, was the real mainspring of the action. As the poisoner of Fair Rosamond, Skink has disguised himself at the opening of the play as a hermit, with long hair and a flowing white beard. Once young Robin Hood has interviewed him and gone his way, he throws off his "hermit's weed," and soliloquises as Skink. In the third scene he comes to court to seek pardon for his act of poisoning, and a general quarrel ensues, due to young Henry's having bestowed upon him some of the mad Earl of Gloucester's lands. So he flies for his life. In scene 6, by a subterfuge, he exchanges garments with the unsuspecting Redcap, a stammering messenger, giving him a cloak and hat and receiving in return a cap and jerkin. This proves unlucky, for in scene 7 the watch, bent on arresting somebody, lets the sprucely attired messenger pass, and carry off the stammering Skink (who takes care to personate Redcap) to the Fleet. Just as Skink is about to be released by his captors he encounters Gloucester, who, fearing ill from Prince Henry and Prince John and wanting a disguise, pulls off Skink's jerkin, but, on recognising him, gives him his gown and bids him imitate his gait. Prince John and the Porter come on — the latter is Redcap's father — and Gloucester escapes from gaol by masquerading as the stammerer. The Prince proposes a game of bowls to Skink-Gloucester, and takes off his hat and cloak, but Skink deems it impolitic to doff any of Gloucester's garments. A sudden message calls the Prince momentarily away in the midst of the game, and during his absence Skink disrobes and attires himself in the Prince's cloak, hat, and sword, and, calling for the porter, gains his freedom. John returns and, finding the supposed madcap gone, puts on his gown and goes after him. On coming back thus garbed, he is mistaken by the real Redcap for Gloucester, but reveals himself. Gloucester, being pursued, flies to the house of his sister, Lady Fauconbridge, who furnishes him with a grey beard and wig and a suit like her husband's, said suit having been formerly worn thither by Prince Richard in a masquerade. Thus disguised, Gloucester makes his escape just as the constables come on the scene.

Then, Skink, as Prince John, encounters the real Sir Richard Fauconbridge, and gets possession of his gold chain, on the pretext of wanting the pattern. No sooner, however, has Fauconbridge departed, than Gloucester, as his double, appears, much to Skink's amazement, and, learning about the chain, contrives to get a portion of it,

Skink breaking it in two for the purpose. Then Skink goes off in a fret, and John, Richard, and the Sheriff enter to Gloucester–Fauconbridge, who, by a trick, obtains the loan of John's sword, and departs. Immediately afterwards the real Fauconbridge appears and demands his chain from John, much to the Prince's indignation and puzzlement.

And so the merry game goes on. Gloucester–Fauconbridge tricks a pursuivant out of his box and warrant by doping his drink in a tavern, and makes off. Skink comes to the tavern as Prince John, learns that Fauconbridge is thereabouts, and orders a saucer of blood from a newly slaughtered pig to be brought to him. Just as he has besmeared his face with the blood, and exchanged his cloak and hat for the Drawer's apron, the sheriffs and their train arrive in hot pursuit of the sham Prince John, but he puts them on a wrong scent by telling them that the Prince has cracked his crown and gone upstairs. Up they go after him, and away flies Skink.

Later on, young Robin Hood disguises himself as Lady Fauconbridge, and speaks in her character out of a window. Skink resumes the beard, beads, and breviary of the hermit, and is visited by Lady Fauconbridge, disguised as a merchant's wife. Then he escapes from his cave in the guise of a falconer, with patch on face and falconer's lure in hand, and robs Fauconbridge and Prince John, after they have fallen into a pit, audaciously revealing himself to them as he departs. And so on, and so on.

I have gone to the trouble to recapitulate the greater part of the clever stage business in this remarkable complex-disguise play that you might the better appreciate the ingenuity with which the whole is contrived. But what I want you to note most particularly is that the actor of Skink had no fewer than seven characters to impersonate, and that the actor of Gloucester came in a good second in sustaining five. The cogency of an argument presently to be advanced depends to some extent on a grasp of these facts.

Harking back a little, I may say that if ever the scholarly world comes to see eye to eye with Fleay in the contention that *The Disguises* of 1595 is identical with Chapman's *May Day*, my theory that *The Disguises* was the *fons et origo* of the complex-disguise play will then fall to the ground. For *May Day* has no claim to be placed in that category. True, it presents a good deal of disguising, but there is no quick changing, and no character assumes more than one disguise. Whatever its period, it does not strike me as an innovative, mode-establishing play. An old magnifico disguises himself as a chimney sweep, a woman disguises herself as a man, and a man as a woman — that is all. But scholarship is never likely to agree with Fleay on this point. Professor T. M. Parrott, the acknowledged Chapman authority, cannot date *May Day* earlier than 1602, and Chambers is disposed to date it even later.[1] One item of internal evidence, not yet advanced, indicates that it was, beyond doubt, an early seventeenth-century play. In Act II, scene 4, Lorenzo offers to disguise himself as a friar for a certain purpose, and Angelo replies, in protest:

Out upon 't, that disguise is worn threadbare upon every stage, and so much villainy committed under that habit that 't is grown as suspicious as the vilest. If you will hearken to any, take such a transformation as you may be sure will keep you from discovery: for though it be the stale refuge of miserable poets, by change of a hat or cloak, to alter the whole state of a comedy, so as the father must not know his own child forsooth, nor the wife her husband, yet

---

[1] Chambers, *The Elizabethan Stage*, iii, 256.

you must not think they do it earnest to carry it away so; for say you were stuffed into a motley coat, crowded in the case of a base viol, or buttoned up in a cloak-bag, even to your chin, yet if I see your face, I am able to say, this is Lorenzo, and therefore unless your disguise be such that your face may bear as great a part in it as the rest, the rest is nothing.

This could certainly not have been written in 1595, for all the artifices of stage disguise had not then been staled, and it is doubtful even if all the references would have had pertinency six or seven years later. It does not seem at all likely that, after Chapman's sneer at the "friar" disguise as "worn threadbare upon every stage," Shakespeare would have resorted to it in *Measure for Measure*. On the other hand, Chambers's date for *May Day* — circa 1609 — is seriously belated.[1] I think that, on due reflection, it will be found that Chapman was indulging in personalities and dealing topically with concrete examples in the passage cited. Both Shakespeare and Dekker appear to have been vituperated. We have only to assign the play to the close of 1604 to see the possibility that Chapman had *Measure for Measure* and the two parts of *The Honest Whore* in his mind's eye when he made his attack on the absurdities of stage disguise. Dekker seems to have been his especial target. In the First Part of *The Honest Whore*, V, 2, Hippolito, Matheo, and Infelice disguise themselves as friars. It is true that neither in this nor its pendant do we get an example of the father not recognising his child, but we do get in the Second Part an example of the exact reverse. When, in Act IV, scene 1, Orlando Friscobaldo enters *in propria persona*, his daughter Bellafront recognises him before he speaks, but when he returns a little later, in the disguise of a serving-man, she has no suspicion of his identity.

[1] Chambers, *The Elizabethan Stage*, iii, 256.

It is curious how scholars have failed to note the steady influence exercised on the trend of English dramaturgy by the keen rivalry that existed between the Admiral's Men and the Chamberlain's Men from about 1594 until Shakespeare's closing years. Possibly the rivalry and its impulsions have remained unsuspected because it was not one of propinquity, the two companies having pursued their activities on different sides of the river. When the Chamberlain's Men deserted Shoreditch and came close to their rivals on opening the Globe, the Admiral's Men set about building the Fortune, and lost no time in departing to the side of the Thames the others had forsaken. But this scholarly oversight amazes, since there are many denotements of this rivalry and its influence. Both sides showed themselves masters of theatrical carte and tierce; a new idea, once its utility had been demonstrated, was bandied between them like a tennis-ball. Not only that, but there was emulation in trivial things. There is a curious parallelism between the prologue of *Old Fortunatus* and the prologue of *Henry V*, both so much of a period that it is difficult to say which company was the thief. And long after the Admiral's Men had become the Prince's Men, and the Chamberlain's Men had been given the King's livery, the old rivalry continued. When *Henry VIII* was produced at the Globe in 1613, the King's Men failed to resist the temptation to indulge, in the prologue, in an undignified attack upon *If You Know not Me, You Know Nobody*, a popular old Fortune play dealing with the same reign, which had recently been revived.

If we confine our consideration of the rivalry of the two companies to the last lustrum of the sixteenth century, we shall find that the Admiral's Men were distinctively the innovators, and the Chamberlain's Men the improvers. History repeats itself: there is only one way to-day of stealing a man's patent, and that is by perfecting it. The Admiral's Men had quite a number of capable playwrights in their employment, authors of varying ability but most of them fecund in ideas: Jonson, Chapman, Dekker, Drayton, Chettle, Munday, and others. On the other hand, the Chamberlain's Men had nobody in particular to rely upon except Shakespeare, but, as it happened, in skill and judgement Shakespeare was a host in himself. Steadily pursuing a policy of innovation, seeking to attract the public by sheer novelty, the Admiral's Men found, to their vexation, that they were only establishing new dramatic forms for their rivals best to exemplify. When one chooses one's own weapons, one does not expect to be ignominiously defeated. In devising the nocturnal, the Admiral's Men succeeded in evoking *A Midsummer Night's Dream* and *The Merry Devil of Edmonton*. Chapman, at their instance, created the comedy of humours in writing *A Humorous Day's Mirth*, produced at the Rose early in May, 1597, and in good time their rivals set their seal upon it by bringing out *Every Man in his Humour*. Once again the laurels went to the Chamberlain's Men and remained for long unfaded; there are ripe scholars to-day who even believe that Jonson originated the comedy of humours.

But what of the complex-disguise play? I take leave to think that in nothing was Shakespeare's judgement better shown than in his avoidance of this new mould, an avoidance not wholly to be expected, since his was the policy of giving the public what it wanted when it wanted it. At best, the type is theatrically effective, never dramatically convincing. So it was a case with Shakespeare of thus far and no farther. In the years when the complex disguise flourished abundantly, he constantly re-

verted to disguise as an expedient, but he used it spar-
ingly. This much he conceded to the vitiated popular
taste. It is curious to note, moreover, that we owe one
of the best-known set speeches in the whole Shakespearean canon to the great poet's ruminations over the
very type of play he had weighed in the balance and
found wanting. The metaphor on which Jaques's address on the Seven Ages is based has wholly escaped
modern scholarship because the circumstances which
inspired the address have never been divined. The poet
was not enlarging, as has been commonly inferred, upon
the old, old metaphor he had pressed into service in *The
Merchant of Venice* a few years earlier. Antonio says:

> I hold the world but as the world, Gratiano;
> A stage where every man must play a part,
>   And mine a sad one.

Contrast this with

> All the world's a stage
> And all the men and women merely players:
> They have their exits and their entrances;
> And one man in his time plays many parts,
> His acts being seven ages.

Over this rather simple figure of speech everybody has
stumbled. The fact that reference is here made to one
man playing many parts in the one play at the one time
has been obscured because nobody has failed to fall into
the trap set by the innocent word "acts." Most indubitably, Shakespeare, when he set it down, was not
thinking of the acts of a play; if he had been, he would
not have spoiled the similitude by exceeding the Hora-
tian number. We should have been given only five
ages. He is using the word in the sense of deeds or actions, a sense in which he and Jonson and others of his
contemporaries commonly used it. Let us look at a few
examples.

In *Richard III*, II, 2, 39, we have:

> What means this scene of rude impatience?

and the answer:

> To make an act of tragic violence.

Something similar to this occurs in *The Chronicle History of King Leir and his Three Daughters:*

> When will this scene of sadness have an end,
> And pleasant acts ensue, to move delight?

Clearer still is the example in *Macbeth*, II, 4:

> Thou seest, the Heavens as troubled with man's act,
> Threaten his bloody stage.

Ben Jonson's most interesting use of the word "act" in this sense occurs in *The Hue and Cry after Cupid:* "The device and act of the scene Master Inigo Jones's, with addition of the trophies."

That Shakespeare was not dividing his hypothetical play of Life into seven acts, as commonly supposed, is shown by the fact that he makes no further employment of the word "act," and is careful, in dealing with transitions, to make Jaques refer to "scenes." Nor can it be taken that by "one man in his time plays many parts" he was referring to the recognised Elizabethan practice of doubling. No actor of his time ever doubled seven parts; the maximum number was four. Clearly we must look elsewhere for the source of the similitude. Are we not justified in find it in the complex-disguise play? Recall that not long before *As You Like It* was written the exponent of Skink in *Look About You* had been delighting the town by impersonating seven characters in the play. It was surely this feat that inspired "his acts being seven ages."

But to say that Shakespeare never condescended to

write a complex-disguise play is not to say that the Chamberlain's Men failed to produce one. That would have been bad policy on their part. What they did do was to give Ben Jonson a commission to write a play which should neatly embody two new ideas recently lit upon and exemplified by their rivals, the scheme of the humour comedy and the scheme of the complex-disguise play. The result was *Every Man in his Humour*, brought out at the Curtain in September, 1598. It is probable that Jonson had no compunctions about indulging profusely in stage disguise: he had ancient precept for the practice, and that would have salved his quasi-classic conscience. One notes that later on there will be much disguising and shifting about of clothes in *The Alchemist*. But it seems not unlikely that it was the blatant artificiality of the complex-disguise scheme which induced him to lay the scene of *Every Man in his Humour* in Italy, that land of romance and intrigue, where, in popular opinion, nothing was impossible and anything might happen. By so doing he certainly gave his far-fetched plot the necessary aloofness; not otherwise could the vagaries of the masquerading Brainworm have attained plausibility. Some years afterwards, when he revised the play for a revival, Jonson made the mistake of transferring the action from Florence to London. It is this revised form in which the play is now best known and by which its merits are judged. Few scholars will ever share the whole-souled enthusiasm of Jonson's latest editors for the comedy. Beyond doubt, it is a mosaic of brilliant characterisation, but brilliant characterisation alone cannot make great drama. Plot and action are important factors. Inasmuch as the action of *Every Man in his Humour* is not consistently credible, it cannot be reckoned in the category of great plays.

There is a vast difference between a fine theatre piece and a great drama, and in the last analysis *Every Man in his Humour* proves no more than a fine theatre piece. There is a considerable spice of truth in what an anonymous critic wrote some few years ago in the *Times Literary Supplement:* "It is impossible to believe in Brainworm; it is impossible to believe in an audience believing in Brainworm."

Here there is lack of understanding of mass psychology: crowds are credible, and audiences may be juggled into believing anything. But if for the word "audience" we substitute "discriminating reader" the pronouncement may stand. It serves to place *Every Man in his Humour* in its true category, for the despised Brainworm, though not the be-all and end-all of the play, is the mainspring of its action. Exactly why Jonson's comedy fails to satisfy the critical mind while always succeeding on the stage has been best revealed by William Hazlitt in a review of its revival at Drury Lane, published in *The Examiner* in June, 1816:

Brainworm is a particularly dry and abstruse character. We neither know his business nor his motives; his plots are as intricate as they are useless, and as the ignorance of those he imposes upon is wonderful. This is the impression in reading it. Yet from the bustle and activity of this character on the stage, the variety of affected tones and gipsy jargon, and the limping distorted gestures, it is a very amusing exhibition, as Mr. Munden plays it. Bobadil is the only actual striking character in the play, or which tells equally well in the closet and the theatre. The rest, Master Matthew, Master Stephen, Cob and Cob's Wife, were living in the sixteenth century. But from the very oddity of their appearance and behaviour, they have a droll and even picturesque effect when acted. It seems a revival of the dead. We believe in their existence when we see them. As an example of the power of the stage in giving reality and interest to what otherwise would be without it, we might mention the scene in which Brainworm praises Master Stephen's leg. The folly here is insipid, from its seeming carried to excess, — till we see it; and then we laugh the more at it, the more incredible we thought it before.[1]

The private-theatre audience was not so fastidious as to taboo public-theatre innovations, and the private-theatre dramatist was not above taking a leaf out of the public-theatre dramatist's book. Examples of at least two of the new dramatic formulas are to be traced at Paul's and the Blackfriars. One of the earliest, perhaps the first, of private-theatre complex-disguise plays was Marston's *The Dutch Courtezan*, a Blackfriars play of *circa* 1604. In this lively piece, Cocledemoy disguises himself as a barber, a French pedlar, a bellman, and a sergeant.

Some revival of interest in the mould took place in Caroline days. In Richard Brome's *The City Wit; or The Woman Wears the Breeches*, a Cockpit play of *circa* 1629, a young citizen masquerades as a lame soldier, a doctor, a court messenger, and a dancer. So, too, in Massinger's *A Very Woman*, produced at the Globe in June, 1634, one finds in the fourth act a scene in which the player of Paulo is called upon for a good deal of quick changing, having to appear in swift succession as a friar, a soldier, and a philosopher, and then make final return to his own character.

A long period of silence followed, but early in the eighteenth century interest in the complex-disguise play was renewed with the production of Mrs. Centlivre's longevous comedy, *A Bold Stroke for a Wife*, at the Lincoln's Inn Fields Theatre in 1718. Later on, Bannister and the eccentric Elliston were successively to gain much popularity by their multiple character acting as the

[1] *Dramatic Essays of William Hazlitt*, ed. William Archer and Robert W. Lowe, p. 100.

three brothers Single in Prince Hoare's unprinted musical play, *The Three and the Deuce*. It was of this piece that Boaden wrote in 1825, "It will always be the vehicle of the theatrical Atalls; who, like Bottom, are for acting Pyramus and Thisbe, and the Lion also." [1] But it is now utterly forgotten, save by the theatrical antiquary.

With the dawn of the nineteenth century came the reign of the melodrama, a new and colourful genre whose accrescent popularity gave renewed life to individual complex disguising. How effective the old scheme could be made under wholly new conditions becomes apparent on perusal of Monk Lewis's melodrama, *Rugantino, or the Bravo of Venice*, a stirring piece which still held the stage a quarter of a century after its production at Covent Garden in 1805. But whether associated with the romantic and picturesque or with the farcical, the complex-disguise scheme long had its fascinations for the latterday untutored mind. The veteran playgoer of to-day, despite his interest in Shaw, Tchechov, and Pirandello, must needs recall the curiously absorbing interest it had for him in times when he had no scruples about the quality of his dramatic fare. I myself have a hazy recollection of a complex-disguise play of the lighter order, Alfred Maltby's ephemeral farce, *Bounce*, popularised by Charles Collette in the country forty-seven years ago, and of the delight it brought to a boy's unjudging mind. Ah, the youthful imagination! It is a mockery, a delusion, and a snare, but would that we all could preserve it to the end!

---

[1] *Memoirs of John Philip Kemble*, ii, 147.

XIII

ELIZABETHAN STAGE PROPERTIES

IN Shakespeare's day and for a quarter of a century afterwards the absence of painted scenery in the English theatre was largely compensated for by the use of properties. But, before we can adequately conceive how this came about, it needs to recall that the term "properties" had a wider significance then than it has now. In its present acceptation, the term signifies all the portable articles necessary for a performance, whether placed on the stage beforehand or brought on in the course of the action, the component parts of the scenery excepted. But in Elizabethan times this nice distinction could not be made, with the result that sundry things that would now be called set pieces were reckoned in among properties. Henslowe is to be found applying the term to such adjuncts as rocks, tombs, trees, moss banks, and scaffolds. Once we grasp that the old properties were often of the nature of fragmentary scenery, it can be readily seen that, in outlining a background, they afforded localisation. Scientific consideration of their use is therefore a matter of paramount importance, more especially as several erroneous concepts hold the field.

It is provoking that, although Brodmeier's once-popular alternation theory [1] has long since gone by the board, some ugly relics of the contingent theory concerning the employment of properties still remain. Owing to subse-

[1] For which see *The Quarterly Review*, no. 415 (1908), pp. 448–455, William Archer on "The Elizabethan Stage"; also *Shakespeare's England*, ii, 300.

quent bolstering, the fallacy of Albright's contentions on the point has not yet become fully apparent. Albright writes:

Another means of keeping the action in progress during the act was the alternation of inner and outer — propertied and unpropertied — scenes. One scene took place on the outer stage without properties and another on the two stages combined with the regular setting on the inner; and in both cases the action was mainly before the line of the curtain.[1]

We are asked to believe here that, despite the fact that stationary properties were used for illusive and localising purposes, the players lost no time in getting as far away from them as possible. This is hardly common sense. Subsequently, after Reynolds [2] and others had revealed the weakness of Albright's position, Thorndike, without arming himself for the fray, hastened to his old pupil's rescue. In his chapter on "Stage Presentation" in *Shakespeare's Theater*, published seven years after Albright's book, we are told that "when there was a succession of scenes requiring properties, the curtains closed before the end of a scene to permit a shift, or there may have been a pause between the scenes." [3]

Here the wheel came full circle. The undue confining of properties to the rear stage had finally resulted in the complete abandonment of the alternation theory, though, by an irony of circumstance, it had been the alternation theory which had primarily demanded the confinement.

Meanwhile, — to make the confusion the more confounded, — Darrell Figgis, in his *Shakespeare: A Study*,[4]

[1] *The Shaksperian Stage*, 1909, p. 116.
[2] *Modern Philology*, ix (1911), 74, G. F. Reynolds on "What We Know of the Elizabethan Stage."
[3] Page 107.
[4] Page 97.

had formulated a corollary on Albright's thesis, to the effect that all inner scenes were located scenes, and all outer scenes unlocated. The inner scenes, we are told, were localised either by tapestries, furniture, or painted back scenes.[1] Since stationary properties always spelled localisation of a sort, one has only to advance proof of the frequent placing of properties on the front stage in full view of the audience to show the absurdity of this assumption. Here I need hardly have said, "on the front stage," because the utility of the rear stage was that properties could be set there in advance, and cleared away again without delaying the action. Therein lay the special serviceableness of the traverses. The truth is that, so far as position was concerned, there was little restriction of properties. For the reason, however, that those of a heavier order were stored on ground-floor level, no great employment of them was made on the upper stage.

The list of scenes in which properties were brought on and carried off in sight of the audience is so extensive that I shall have to confine myself to a few noteworthy examples. The system was of early origin. In R. B.'s tragical comedy, *Apius and Virginia*, a possible inn-yard play registered in 1568 and published later, one finds in the last scene that "Doctrina and Memorie and Virginius bring in a tomb." This, of course, would have been more fittingly discovered, and nothing but the persistence of an early practice could justify the bringing on of properties of this order. A curious example occurs in *King Lear*, II, 2, where we have the direction, "stocks brought

[1] The punishment for those who have postulated the use of painted back scenes should be "something with boiling oil in it." Schelling and Baker are the principal culprits. Cf. Reynolds on "What We Know of the Elizabethan Stage," in *Modern Philology*, ix, 78.

out." But the properties most commonly carried on were tables and stools, and, in a good many cases, a demand on the part of the characters rationalised the action. The demand indicates the procedure even where stage directions are missing. An example of this is to be found in Wilkins's *The Miseries of Inforst Marriage*, towards the end of the last act, where, on the butler announcing Dr. Baxter, William Scarborow orders "a table, candles, stools, and all things fit." So too, in Part I of *The Fair Maid of the West*, IV, 2, Bess calls for a table and stools. But there were many occasions when properties of this kind were brought in without any order. In *Henry VIII*, I, 4, we have the direction:

> Hoboies. A small Table is under a State for the cardinall, a longer Table for the Guests. Then enter Anne Bullen and divers other Ladies and Gentlemen as Guests at one doore; at an other doore enter Sir Henry Guildford.

The word "then" here has considerable significance. It indicates that the two tables, together with the implied stools, had just been brought on in sight of the audience. Note that when the King is suddenly announced a direction says, "All rise and Tables remov'd." We get a clue to the expeditious manner in which furniture was brought in and placed in position in *The Iron Age*. At the opening of the fifth act a direction runs, "Enter Thersites with Souldiers, bringing in a table, with chayres and stooles plac'd above it." A curious example of stage setting in the midst of a dramatic situation occurs in *Bussy D'Ambois*, V, 1, where we read, at the opening, of "Montsurry bare, unbrac't, pulling Tamyra in by the haire; Frier; one bearing light, a standish, and paper, which sets a table."

It must not be taken, however, that there is anything very distinguishing about the bringing on and carrying off of tables and chairs. The practice persisted at the

Restoration and lasted until well within living memory. I quote the following from *The Belfast Newsletter* of December 24, 1813:

We cannot forbear noticing and commending an improvement in one particular hitherto unknown to the Belfast Theatre; two boys in livery are in constant attendance to bring on and remove chairs, tables and other articles necessary in a change of scene. They are a genteel appendage seen in the London and Dublin theatres, and since there must be persons to execute the office (for we know of no other means than the hands of servants) it is pleasing to see these well dressed boys, in lieu of perhaps a ragged little being without shoes or stockings, whom we formerly have seen obtrude himself for the purpose.

One sight, however, was occasionally seen on the Elizabethan stage which remained unparalleled in later times. Now and again, the actual dramatis personae brought on or pushed off sundry heavy properties. In the First Part of *Hieronimo*, I, 3, at the beginning of the dictation scene, Hieronimo enters while saying to Horatio, "Come, pull the table this way; so 'tis well." Wherever the table was situated, whether behind the curtains or in a doorway, it is plain to be seen that Horatio brought it forward. So too, in the middle of Act IV of *The Golden Age*, we have, "Enter the four old Beldams drawing out Danae's bed, she in it," and at the close of the scene they draw the bed in again.

Concerning bed scenes I shall have something of importance to say later, but it may be pointed out now that the handling of beds and the handling of scaffolds were much the same, both being generally thrust out when required. In *Volpone*, II, 1, the mountebank's stage is fitted up in sight under a tiring-house window. In *The Dumb Knight*, III, 1, we read, "Enter Chip, Shaving and a third with a scaffold." In execution scenes, separate stairs to go up were generally brought on with the scaffold. In the latter-mentioned play, Mariana's speech in ascending shows that they consisted of four steps, thus yielding some indication of the height of the scaffold. She says:

> This first step lower
> Mounts to this next; this thus and thus hath brought
> My body's frame unto its highest throne.

After the illusion of actual decapitation came into vogue,[1] that is, from about 1612, scaffolds for executions ceased to be brought on, their use being confined to the rear stage.[2]

Certain old stage directions, or prompter's notes, relative to the bringing in or setting up of properties are of ambiguous phrasing and call for some consideration. It would seem as if different people put different interpretations upon the same terms, a laxity which necessitates every example being scrutinised independently, without thought of any particular rule. To begin with, the term "set out" is painfully deceptive. It does not always imply, as one would be disposed to think, "placed in position on the front stage." In Dekker's undivided play, *If it be not Good, the Devil is in it*,[3] we have the direction: "A table is set out with a candle burning, a death's head, a cloke and a crosse; Subprior sits reading . . ."

Obviously, this was a discovery. To my mind, where we have "set out" in a direction at the beginning of an act

---

[1] For fuller details, see my chapter on "Elizabethan Stage Realism."

[2] Representations of those indoor tournaments called "barriers" (as in *Solyman and Perseda* and *The White Devil*) must have taken place on the front stage, and necessitated the setting up of some accessories. Cf. Jacques Callot's series of plates, "Combat à la Barriere faict en cour de Lorraine le 14 Febvrier en l'anne presente, 1627" (British Museum press mark, "564 c 30"). Racks were also brought in and set up in torture scenes. See *The Double Marriage*, I, 2.

[3] *Dekker's Dramatic Works*, ed. Pearson, iv, 331.

or scene, it means "place in position on the rear stage." This would apply to *The Taming of the Shrew*, V, 2, and to *Satiromastix*, IV, 1,[1] though in both cases the setting out of a banquet is mentioned first and the entrance of the characters afterwards. In the First Part of *The Fair Maid of the West*, IV, 2, we have the direction, "Enter Besse, Mayor, Aldermen, Clem, a table set out, and stooles." This means no more than "have the tables and stools ready," most probably behind the curtains. Had they been placed on the front stage, Bess would not have called for them on entering. There could be no clearer proof of a propertied front scene.

In Massinger's *The City Madam*, which was undoubtedly printed from the theatre prompt-book, we have in Act I, scene 2, the marginal warning, "Set out the Table, Count-book, standish, chaire and stool." This signifies that they were to be placed in good time on the rear stage, ready for the rear-stage counting-house scene which immediately follows.[2] In *The Two Noble Kinsmen*, which was also printed from a prompt-book, we read in Act III, scene 5, at line 73, "Chaire and stooles out," a warning 41 lines ahead. Here the procedure is uncertain. The properties might have been placed directly on the front stage as soon as the warning was acted upon, or they might have been placed ready behind the curtains. Most likely the former method was adopted. A better method of prompt-book marking, since it steers clear of ambiguity, is exemplified in *The Maid in the Mill*, at the end of Act I, where we have the warning for Act II, scene 2, "six

---

[1] In Penniman's recension in the Belles Lettres Series.

[2] Cf. *The Welsh Ambassador* (Malone Society), V, lines 1934, 1935, where the marginal "sett out a table" refers to V, 2, a rear-stage scene with the Clown sitting writing. In *The Spanish Curate*, III, 2, we have, "The Bar and Book ready on Table," followed in III, 3 (marginally at the opening), by "A Bar, Table book, standard set out." Here "set out" means in front.

chaires placed at the Arras," meaning, of course, on the rear stage.

Hence, though exceptions are to be noted, "set out," as Albright asserts,[1] commonly implies "have ready on the rear stage." But it is fallacious to argue, as he goes on to argue, without demonstration, that

very similar to "set out" for tables, chairs, etc., are the phrases, "thrust out," "put forth," "thrust forth," used in connection with beds. It is therefore probable that these directions, also, occasionally signified nothing more than the particular position of the bed on the inner stage or the placing of it there while the curtains were closed.

But, before proceeding to consider the methods employed in bed scenes, — for, as it happens, there was more than one method, — it might be as well for us to consider some examples of the use of that variant of "set out," "set forth." The first, in a direction in Massinger's *The Guardian*, III, 4, needs no elucidation. The whole reads: "Draws the curtain, and discovers Iolante seated, with a rich banquet, and tapers, set forth." In Brome's *The City Wit*, at the beginning of the play, "set forth" evidently means, "have handy on the rear stage," as, when the scene opens, the table is ordered to be brought in. Years earlier, however, the phrase had been used at least once in an entirely different sense. In *Westward Ho*, IV, 2, we read, "Whilst the song is heard, the Earl draws a curtain, and sets forth a banquet &c." This does not mean that he simply disclosed a banquet; he must have brought the banquet forward. An examination of the scene shows that the curtains must have closed again immediately, to admit of Justiniano's subsequent exposure of his wife's pretended corpse. In a much later play, *The Faithful Friends*, the phrase is used in exactly

[1] *The Shaksperian Stage*, p. 143.

the same way. In Act IV, scene 3, of this we have the direction:

Soft music. A Banquet being brought forth, enter Titus and Philadelphia, who sit down at each end of one Table; then at another Side-table sit down Marcellanus and other Senators, and old Tullius; then Rufinus, Learchus, and Leontius, who wait on the King.

It cannot be pretended that so full and elaborate a scene was acted on the rear stage. The same argument applies to Massinger's *The Unnatural Combat*, III, 2, for the very good reason that, in this scene, forms [1] were provided instead of the usual stools. First we have the direction, "Servants setting forth a banquet," after which the chief attendant, on being told to make haste, replies:

We are ready, when you please. Sweet forms, your pardon
It has been such a busy time I could not
Render that ceremonious respect
Which you deserve; but now the great work ended,
I will attend the less, and with all care
Observe and serve you.

But the phrase is just as frequently used in connexion with discovered scenes as with scenes acted in front. Thus, in Webster's *The Devil's Law Case*, III, 2, the opening direction reads: "A table set forth with two tapers, a death's head, a book. Jolenta in mourning: Romelo sits by her."

The conclusion is that, although old stage directions had certain definite meanings, they were not always used with scientific precision. Hence, to generalise from any specific acceptation is to fall into error. Generalisation, indeed, in connexion with most matters of Elizabethan

[1] A form is brought in for the ladies in the induction to *The Staple of News*.

stage procedure is fraught with danger. We have no better illustration of this than in the erroneous inferences
drawn in regard to bed scenes by three such scholars as
Albright, Thorndike, and Rhodes,[1] all of whom would
have us believe that beds were never really thrust forth
on the front stage, as many directions imply, but were
invariably disclosed by the withdrawal of the rear-stage
curtains. Their mistake has been in endeavouring to
reconcile contradictory stage directions. What we have
to recognise is that there were two methods of staging
bed scenes, a distinction necessitated partly by the difference in size between the public-theatre stage and the
private-theatre stage, and partly by the circumstances of
the case. The reason why, in the majority of instances,
beds had to be brought well to the front will be best
illustrated by two items of Restoration evidence. In the
Dryden–Shadwell version of *The Tempest*, at the opening
of Act V, scene 2, the direction reads, "Hippolito discovered on a couch, Dorinda by him." When asked how
he feels, Hippolito replies:

> I'm somewhat cold;
> Can you not draw me nearer to the sun,
> I am too weak to walk?

Then a direction says of Dorinda, "She draws the
chair nearer the audience." Hippolito's confession and
request were nothing more than mere theatrical subterfuge. In his recumbent position, it was necessary for him
to be drawn nearer to the audience that he might be fully
heard. That this is the proper deduction is apparent from
the stage direction in Dryden's *Love Triumphant*, II, 1,
reading, "The Scene is a Bedchamber, a couch prepar'd,
and set so near the Pit that the audience may hear." We

---

[1] *The Shaksperian Stage*, p. 144; *Shakespeare's Theater*, pp. 81, 82; *Studies in the First Folio*, p. 112.

must remember that the Restoration stage had a deep "apron" or *avant-scène*, corresponding with the open platform of the Elizabethan theatre.

Accordingly, in most scenes where its occupant had to say anything more than a few monosyllables, the bed was thrust out. Where the occupant was dead or sleeping, the mere discovery of the bed sufficed; and it also sufficed now and then on the smaller private-theatre stages, where the audience was less remote, and that, too, even when the occupant took considerable part in the dialogue. Although the stage directions are occasionally ambiguous, — as in *A Woman Killed with Kindness*, where we have, "Enter Mrs. Frankfort in her bed," — many of them are clear enough to enable us to distinguish the different methods.

The thrusting out of beds can be readily demonstrated. I have already cited a Jacobean example from Heywood's Red Bull play, *The Golden Age*, in the fourth act of which the four beldams draw out Danae's bed, and, at the close of the scene, draw it in again. Two later examples may now be given. In *The City Wit*, III, 1, the scene opens with: "Enter (in bed) the Tryman, attended by Isabell, Jone, Crasy, with an Urinall."

The action here is made clear by the direction at the close, "They put in the Bed, and withdraw all. Exeunt." Compare *A Mad Couple Well Match'd*, IV, 3, where Bellamy asks Saleware to go "into the next chamber," and both depart. Then, "the Bed put forth, Alicia in it. Enter Bellamy, Saleware, with light." Finally, at the close of the act comes the direction, referring to Saleware, "Puts in the bed. Exit." [1] In these instances it is the

---

[1] Cf. *A Tricke to Cheat the Divell*, V, direction, "The Bed pull'd in"; Cokain's *The Obstinate Lady*, III, 1, "Enter Cleanthe and Servants putting forth a bed, with Carionel upon it"; *The Lost Lady*, V, 1, "Exeunt. Draw in the Bed."

putting in of the bed that is the real proof of the thrusting out, because in the absence of instructions for the putting in, "Bed thrust out" might be construed to mean thrust out on the rear stage.

It is important to note that it was this frequent thrusting out and the necessity for it that confined bed scenes unillusively to the lower stage. Generally speaking, in Shakespearean times, admitting that sometimes in small country houses ground-floor parlours were converted at night into bedrooms, people slept on an upper story.[1]

Only one other point with regard to stage beds remains to be demonstrated. In proof of my assertion that beds in which the occupant remained silent were simply discovered, and never thrust out, I commend your attention to the following examples:

The Maid's Tragedy, V; *Cymbeline*, II, 2; *Amends for Ladies*, IV, 2; *The Devil's Law Case*, III, 2; *All's Lost by Lust*, V, 2; *Love's Sacrifice*, II, 4; *The Platonick Lovers*, II, 1; *Love's Maistresse*, III, 1; and *Brennoralt*, III.

Excepting the stage bed, no Elizabethan property has given rise to more speculation than the stage throne. Three theories concerning the method of its employment have been advanced. First, Creizenach, supported by Schelling, maintains that it "remained permanently on the stage — probably against the back wall — or at any rate that in the pieces where it was required it stood on the stage from the beginning to the end." [2] Secondly, Reynolds began by expressing the opinion that the throne was one of the properties which "usually, though not always, stood on the front stage," [3] but saw fit in the

[1] *Shakespeare's England*, ii, 63, J. Alfred Gotch on "Architecture."
[2] *English Drama in the Age of Shakespeare*, p. 381.
[3] *Modern Philology*, xii (1914), 118, article on "William Percy and his Plays."

course of a few years to modify and extend his view. Dealing with the subject of recurring properties in a paper contributed to *The Manly Anniversary Studies in Language and Literature*,[1] he was then disposed to believe that it was customary to lower the throne from the heavens to the front stage, when it was required, and to leave it there until the end of the play. Chambers[2] agrees with the lowering of the throne from the heavens, but refuses to concede the presence of incongruous properties on the stage, maintaining that, once the throne had served its immediate purpose, it had to return whence it came. Evidently he gave no consideration to the amount of raising and lowering and delay that this course would have occasioned in several of the chronicle histories. The third theory — really the second in order, as it succeeded Creizenach's — is my own. First advanced in a preliminary study of the subject published in *The Texas Review* for January, 1918, it maintains that the throne was confined to the rear stage, and placed there as required.

In pondering any question of the permanency or quasi-permanency of the throne, we must first take into consideration the nature of the throne. On a stage whose spaciousness was already somewhat reduced by the lateral presence of spectators, nothing seriously obstructive to the action or the general view could have been permitted; and, no matter where placed beyond the limits of the tiring-house, the throne must have proved obstructive to one or other, or both. Some investigators seem to be labouring under the delusion that it was nothing better than a slightly glorified armchair. Stage directions prove something far otherwise. They permit the deduction that the throne, or "state," as it was more commonly called, was a capacious chair, capable of accommodating two or

[1] Pages 76, 77.   [2] *The Elizabethan Stage*, iii, 77, 89.

three people, elevated on a daïs and surmounted by a canopy. It was the canopy that caused it to be called "the state," the term arising, as Cotgrave indicates,[1] from "the cloth of estate, canopie or Heaven" which stood over royal thrones.[2]

Concerning the seating capacity of the throne we get evidence in more than one play. In Marlowe's *Edward II*, line 301, at a juncture when the nobles are already on the stage, there is a misleading direction reading, "Enter the King and Gaveston." So far from really entering, they were simply discovered sitting side by side on the throne. The proof of this is that the King at once says:

> What? Are you mov'd that Gaveston sits heere?
> It is our pleasure, we will have it so.

Lancaster's reply shows that Gaveston is seated by the King's side, not below him. The whole situation, it may likewise be noted, is early evidence for the placing of the throne on the rear stage.

In another play of about the same period, *Solyman and Perseda*,[3] sitting accommodation for three people on the throne proper is also indicated. Moreover, considerably over a quarter of a century later we have trace of a similar amplitude. In Massinger's *The Great Duke of Florence*, V, 3, Cozimo conducts the two ladies, as his deputies, to the state. They refuse to pronounce judgement on their lovers, and, according to the direction, "descend from the state," Florinda having said to the Duke,

> We do resign
> This chair, as only proper to your self.

---

[1] Cotgrave's *Dictionarie of the French & English Tongues*, 1611, under "Dais."

[2] For reference to the canopy in throne scenes, see *3 Henry VI*, I, 1; *Satiromastix*, V, 2; *Henry VIII*, I, 2, and V, 3; *The Gentleman Usher*, II, 1; *The Bondman*, I, 3; *The Knight of Malta*, I, 3; *The Noble Gentleman*, IV, 4.

[3] Act IV, in Hazlitt's *Dodsley*.

Proof that the throne stood on a daïs is to hand, not only in certain throne scenes where several people are seated at the King's feet, but in scenes where the King and others are represented as ascending or descending. We have an example of the first kind at the opening of Peele's *King Edward I*, where the direction says: "The Queen Mother being set on one side, and Queen Elinor on the other, the King sits in the midst, mounted highest, and at his feet the ensign underneath him."

Another is to be found in Chettle's *Hoffman*, a direction in the second act reading:

Enter Ferdinand leading Clois Hoffman; Mathias and Lodowick leading Lucibella; Lorrique, with other lords attending; comming neere the chayre of state Ferdinand ascends, places Hoffman at his feete, sets a Coronet on his head, a Herald proclaimes.[1]

As for references to characters ascending to and descending from the state, they are legion. A few examples may be cited:

Richard III (Q. 3), IV, 2; *The Downfall of Robert Earl of Huntington*, I, 1, and IV, 1; *3 Henry VI*, I, 1, and III, 3; *The Valiant Welshman*, II, 3, and IV, 1; *The Maid of Honour*, I, 1, and IV, 4; *The Picture*, I, 2, and II, 2; *The Bondman*, I, 1, and IV, 4.

The state, then, as I have said, was a capacious chair, affording accommodation for two or three people, situated on a daïs and overhung by a canopy. I am inclined to believe that this frequently used property was constructed in at least two parts, with chair and daïs separate, to admit of speedy removal; but, even if it were a solid structure, I cannot conceive such an elaborate and cumbrous piece of furniture being lowered from the heavens. The truth is that the idea of its having been

[1] Cf. *Look About You* (Hazlitt's *Dodsley*, vii, last scene), where six people are seated on the throne and its steps.

so lowered has arisen from a rank misconception. Unfortunately, the fact has not yet dawned on any scholar that, although in common Elizabethan–Stuart parlance, "throne" and "state" were synonymous terms, they were far from being so as theatrical technicalities. Among players, the term "throne" was almost wholly confined to the car in which a divinity descended; when they wanted to signify an earthly throne, they used the term "state." And the dramatists fell into line.

First, let me review the evidence conveying the theatrical meaning of the term "throne." In June, 1595, Henslowe records a payment of £7.2.0, "for carpenters worke & mackinge the throne in the heuenes" at the Rose Theatre,[1] an item which might be taken as establishing a *prima facie* case for the lowering of the normal royal throne from above, if only in the whole body of the Elizabethan drama we could find one solitary direction to show that such a course was ever adopted. That we cannot do. Every specific lowering of a throne can be otherwise accounted for. Let me cite a few examples in chronological order:

1594. *A Looking Glasse for London and England*, I: "Enters, brought in by an Angel, Oseas the Prophet, and let down over the stage in a throne."

Q. 1616. *Doctor Faustus*, V: for the descent of the Good Angel we have, "Musicke while the throne descends"; and again, later on, "Exit, the throne ascends."

1622. *The Prophetess*, II, 3: "Enter on a cloud, Delphia and Drusilla in a throne, drawn by Dragons." Later on comes the terse direction, "Ascends throne." Here we have the fullest proof of the technicality, the word "throne" being applied to what was really a chariot.[2]

---

[1] *Henslowe's Diary*, ed. Greg, i, 4.

[2] Cf. *A Wife for a Month* (masque), II, direction, "Cupid and the Graces ascend in the Chariot."

1641. *The Antiquary*, IV: Petrucio, on being told by the Cook that a banquet of twelve dishes had been provided, symbolising the signs of the Zodiac, says, "So then will I add one invention more of my own; for I will have all these descend from the top of my roof in a throne, as you see Cupid or Mercury in a play."

1649. *The Varietie*, IV, near end: "Musicke. Throne descends."

1649. Lovelace's epilogue to his lost play, *The Scholars*, was published this year with his poems (*Lucasta*). The play itself had been produced at Salisbury Court *circa* 1636. I cite the following from the epilogue:

> His *Schollars* school'd, sayd if he had been wise
> He should have wove in one two comedies.
> The first for th' gallery, in which the throne
> To their amazement should descend alone,
> The rosin-lightning flash and monster spire
> Squibs, and words hotter than his fire.
> Th' other for the gentlemen o' th' pit
> Like to themselves all spirit, fancy, wit.

These verses, I think, should have given Sir Edmund Chambers and Professor Reynolds pause. Why should the occupants of the gallery be amazed to see the throne descending unoccupied, if regal thrones commonly descended from above? The reference is surely to the surprise that would be felt on seeing the car come down without the usual god or goddess, since we have good reason to believe that the frequenters of the gallery took great delight in the *deus ex machina*. Recall what Jonson wrote in his famous epilogue for the revival of *Every Man out of his Humour*, circa 1612:

> Where neither Chorus wafts you ore the seas;
> Nor creaking throne comes downe, the boyes to please
> Nor nimble squibbe is seene, to make afeard
> The gentlewomen.

Ben's "creaking throne" has been largely relied upon by Reynolds and Chambers to establish their thesis, though it should have been evident to them that anything which came down to please the boys must have been a stage effect, something part and parcel of the play, and not a mere matter of property conveyance. The assumption is about on a par with the abounding fallacy, that Jonson in his epilogue was sneering throughout at Shakespeare. In reality his shafts were directed against the players of the Fortune and Red Bull, who had recently been endeavouring to fill their houses by outbursts of spectacular display and sensationalism. At the Fortune, a new version of Marlowe's *Faustus* had just been produced, a version whose prime features are embalmed in the quarto of 1616. In it, Chorus wafted the audience twice over the seas, the creaking throne came down carrying the Good Angel, and the Devils were profuse in their scattering of squibs. Moreover, in Dekker's *If it be not Good, the Devil is in it* at the Red Bull, there had been a bounteous fireworks display and a rousing supply of thunder, not to speak of the numerous spectacular excesses witnessed at the same house in Heywood's *The Golden Age*. Is it feasible to suppose that the King's Men would have lent themselves ignobly to an attack on their own great dramatist, when so much good material for ridicule was being presented by their rivals?

The fact that the technical term for the royal throne was "the state" is established by a host of stage directions and textual references. The term is really an abbreviation of "chair of estate," one reason why the royal throne is occasionally referred to as "the chair." Thus, in *1 Tamburlaine*, III, 3, we find Tamburlaine requesting his wife to "sit here upon this royal chair of state"; and in Act IV, scene 2, we have the direction, "Tamburlaine get upon him to his chair." [1] Now and again textual ref-

[1] For "chair of state" see also *The Knight of Malta*, I, 3; *Hoffman*, II; Davenport's *King John and Mathilda* (Bullen's *Davenport*, iii, 29).

erence to "the throne" crops up, but personally I know
of only two instances where the term is used in a stage
direction in the sense of royal seat. One is in *Richard III*
(Q. 3), IV, 2, where we have, "Here he ascendeth throne";
the other, presently to be discussed, occurs in *Histriomastix*. Opposite these may be placed the following eighteen instances in which the throne is called the state. Except where otherwise specified, the reference occurs in a
stage direction:

1 Henry IV, II, 4, 412, text; *Macbeth*, III, 4, 5, text; *Coriolanus*, V, 4, 20, text; *Satiromastix*, V, 2, 16, 17, text and direction;
The Poor Man's Comfort, III, senate scene; *The Noble Gentleman*, V,
2; *The Great Duke of Florence*, V, 3; *Henry VIII*, I, 2, and V, 3; *The
Picture*, II, 2; *The Staple of News*, II, 5; *The Coronation*, II, 3; *Aglaura*, V, 1; *Hoffman*, II; *The Knight of Malta*, I, 3; *Thierry and Theodoret*, III, 1, text; *The Fawne*, V, 1; *Four Plays in One*, induction, text.

We come now to consider the normal position of the
throne. I am compelled to admit that we have a few
indications that thrones were sometimes placed on the
outer stage, but the circumstances, I think, were altogether exceptional. One thing is certain: the weight of
evidence is wholly adverse to the throne occupying, in
council scenes, an outward position. Some of the apparent front-stage thrones prove on close examination
to have been otherwise. A curious example is to be
found in *Histriomastix*, a mysterious play first printed in
1610, when it was at least twelve years old. At the opening of the second act we have the direction, "Enter
Plenty in Majesty upon a Throne; heapes of gold; Plutus,
Ceres, and Bacchus doing homage." This is really only
one of the many instances in which a discovery is spoken
of as an entrance. A typical example is that in *George a
Greene*, IV, 3, "Enter a Shoemaker sitting upon the stage
at worke, Jenkin to him." An analogous situation in *The*

Staple of News, II, 5, shows that the throne in *Histrio-mastix* was discovered. Speaking of the expected Pecunia, Pennyboy Canter says:

> Here she comes at last, and like a galley,
> Gilt i' the prow.

But she does not come. The ensuing direction says, "The Study is open'd, where she sits in state." "The Study," as I have elsewhere pointed out, was the technical term for the curtained rear stage.[1]

If I mistake not, the known examples where a throne occupied the front stage are not more than three in number, and these three are certainly of an exceptional order. It would appear that the state brought on in *Satiromastix*, V, 2,[2] was placed somewhere in front, but we have no clue to the position.[3] In Marston's *The Fawne*, V, 1, the Duke is seated on one state and Cupid on another, and both can hardly have been on the rear stage. In *Thierry and Theodoret*, III, 1, two thrones are called for, one for the King and the other for his brother, the "business" of the scene requiring that they should be seated apart.

Nothing can be deduced from scenes of this exceptional order. The vast majority of throne scenes were scenes in council, and it is only by dissecting these that one can arrive at the normal position of the state. At the beginning of council scenes there was, as a general rule, a processional entry of the characters, but explicit directions on this point are so rare that it is vital to quote

---

[1] See *The Physical Conditions of the Elizabethan Public Playhouse*, pp. 54 ff.

[2] According to Penniman's division.

[3] This scene has a curious resemblance to Chapman's *The Gentleman Usher*, II, 1, where the throne must have already been in position.

in extenso a direction from Davenport's *King John and Mathilda:* [1]

A Chaire of state discover'd, Tables and Chaires responcible, a Guard making a lane; Enter between them, King John, Pandulph, the Pope's Legate, Chester, Oxford, and all the King's Party; after them Fitzwater, Leister, and Bruce. The King (holding the Crown) kneeling on the left side of the Chaire, Pandulph possessing it.

To my mind, this one direction alone establishes the rear stage as the normal position for the state, but to allay all doubt I hasten to append corroborative evidence. It must first of all be noted that the principle of making a lane in such scenes for the approaching king or duke was essentially fundamental. We find it exemplified in the First Part of *Antonio and Mellida*, II, 1, 643:

Enter Piero, Antonio, Mellida, Rosaline, Galeatro, Matzagente, Alberto, and Flavia. As they enter, Feliche, & Castilio make a ranke for the Duke to passe through. Forobosco ushers the Duke to his state. . . .

Other examples, not so clearly indicated, are to be found in *The Birth of Merlin*, I, 2; *If it be not Good, the Devil is in it*, I, 1; *The Downfall of Robert Earl of Huntington*, IV, 1; *Cymbeline*, III, 1; *King Henry V*, I, 2; and *Look About You*, scene xxxii and last. Occasionally, I think, an alternative method was adopted, the courtiers coming on in the usual processional way, but not the king, he being discovered afterwards seated on his throne. Clear examples of this practice are rare, but I can speak positively of two. The first occurs in Marlowe's *Edward II*, line 301, where the King and Gaveston are revealed side by side on the throne, and the second in Shirley's *The Coronation*, II, 3. Other possible examples are to be found in *King John*, IV, 2, and *The Prophetess*, IV, 4.

[1] The play is undivided, but see Bullen's *Davenport*, iii, 29.

Apart from scenes of this order, some other scenes may be cited in which the state had an indisputable rear-stage position. At a certain juncture in Munday's undivided play, *The Death of Robert Earl of Huntington*,[1] the curtains at the back are opened, and a dumb show, expounded by the Friar, is presented on the rear stage. While the King "sits sleeping," the Queen ascends the daïs, and, on finding him motionless, "descendeth wringing her hands and departeth." In Marston's *Antonio's Revenge*, V, 5, one of the many unspecified state scenes to be found in the old drama, Piero, while seated on his throne, is murdered by the masked conspirators, and the curtains are drawn at the close (to obviate the necessity of carrying off the body). Here we are bound to accept one of two conclusions, either that the curtains drawn were the curtains of the rear stage, or that the throne, as Neuendorff has postulated, had curtains of its own. All I need say is that to accept Neuendorff's hypothesis would be to make an elaborate, cumbrous property still more unwieldy.

Another example occurs in *The Divil's Charter*, a Globe play of 1606. At the close of the last act, the dying pope drags himself towards the concealed seat of St. Peter, and, on tearing the curtains aside, is horrified to find Satan ensconced there in full papal pomp. Here, in my view, the conventional position of the state suggested the startling *jeu de théâtre*. My final example is taken from *The Dumb Knight*, a Whitefriars play of 1608. Act I, scene 2, is a list scene. Four combatants are in front, and the Queen is seated, as I take it, on a throne at the back. No other position is available, because when Philoclea overcomes Epire we learn that "The Queen descends," and she could not have descended from the upper stage

[1] Hazlitt's *Dodsley*, viii, 252.

in time to save the Duke's life. Moreover, she is not likely to have been there, since Prate and Lollia were seated above.

In dealing with Elizabethan problems, my system for a score of years past has been, not to start with a preconceived theory and seek for its substantiation, but to assemble all the evidence on a moot point, and let the evidence tell its own story. Few workers on preconceived theories have been able to withstand for long the temptation to burke unreconcilable data. Approach the problem with an open mind and you are more likely to arrive at the truth. That is the spirit in which I have pursued the present investigation, and I confidently await the verdict.

I cannot conclude without saying a few words on the pressing problem of recurring properties, a subject on which Dr. G. F. Reynolds has contributed a thoughtful, but to my mind not wholly convincing, paper to *The Manly Anniversary Studies in Language and Literature*.

There can be little doubt that the necessity for the expeditious staging and removal of heavy properties, imposed by the aim of preserving unbroken the traffic of the scene between act and act, was the main urge which led (in pre-theatrical times) to the creation of the rear stage. About the earliest trace we have of the rear stage is in *Godly Queene Hester*, *circa* 1561, where, following upon the delivery of the prologue, a curtain is drawn and King Ahasuerus revealed sitting in state and addressing his council. Assuming that from this period the rear stage was the normal place for most heavy properties, it is conceivable that in plays where such properties were required in more than one scene there would be a tendency, especially in the inn-yards, to leave them in position, once they had been placed. This in time would

develop into a crude principle and have a modicum of
influence on dramatic construction. Not otherwise than
by some such hypothesis can we account for the clumsy
iterations occasionally to be found in old plays. Thus,
in *The Spanish Tragedy*, I, 1 and 2, we have two throne
scenes in swift succession, though laid in different countries; and, more remarkable still, in the First Part of *The
Contention of the Two Famous Houses of Yorke and Lancaster* we find, early in the play, not only two successive
bed scenes, but two throne scenes with but a single outer-
stage scene intervening. One might proffer the excuse
that dramaturgy was then in its infancy, were it not for
the striking circumstance that an exact analogue of the
clumsy arrangement in Kyd's play is to be found in
Pericles. Here, in Act I, scenes 2 and 3, we are again
confronted by two successive throne scenes laid in different countries. Mark, it is only by assuming a rear-
stage position for the state that one can divine how the
change of locality was indicated. It is to be noted that
towards the close of scene 2 Pericles descends from the
throne of Tyre and departs, leaving the others to finish
the scene. This means that with his exit the curtains
of the rear stage were closed, and that sufficient indication of the subsequent change to Tharsus was given by
the reopening of the curtains at the beginning of scene 3,
just as a new set of characters entered.

This grouping of rear-stage scenes of identical setting
was undoubtedly resorted to to avoid the constant handling of unwieldy properties, but the system became restricted by the monotony of the effect. Other difficulties
also operated; convenience or no convenience, the dramatist had to get on with his story. Thus it was that even
a rear-stage setting which recurred at irregular intervals
throughout the play could not always be permitted to

remain permanently *in situ*. In the study already referred to, Dr. Reynolds argues that the shop in the First Part of *The Honest Whore*, after being staged for Act I, scene 5, remained in position until its final use in Act IV, scene 3, maintaining with slight inaccuracy that all intervening propertied scenes were front-stage scenes. He should have seen, however, that, despite the clumsy phrasing of its opening direction, Act III, scene 3, cannot be adjudged a front scene. The direction reads, "Enter Bellafront with lute, pen ink and paper being placed before her." This, Ernest Rhys in the Mermaid edition of Dekker very properly takes to be a discovery. Bellafront is seated at a table, writing, and, with the opening of the scene, sings as she writes.

The truth is that the playwright was not to be restricted by theatrical necessity. At all costs the plot had to make natural progression. So little were authors stayed by consideration of the tiremen's convenience that they even went the length, on occasion, of placing two differently propertied rear-stage scenes contiguously. No doubt there were attempts at mutual compromise, but the dice were permanently loaded against the tiremen. There was no rigid system, and each problem had to receive its own solution. There were plays like *Nobody and Somebody*, where the throne, once set, was allowed to remain in position until the end; and there were other plays where the throne had occasionally to be shifted. No doubt, recurring heavily propertied rear-stage scenes were left intact in all cases where convenience permitted; but even if we could stretch a point and concede that the desire was elevated into a principle — that examples were as common as Dr. Reynolds avers — we should still be compelled by sheer sway of common sense to dispute the validity of his analogous inference that outer-

324 PRE-RESTORATION STAGE STUDIES

stage recurring properties were allowed to remain. Such
a system would have created the direst confusion. Before long all sense of localisation would have been lost.
Labour would have been saved at the expense of lucidity.
Hence, we are forced inevitably to conclude that, once
having served their primary purpose, no properties could
have been allowed to remain *in situ* save those which
could be obscured. On the whole, Chambers expresses
himself very sensibly on this subject in that chapter of
his great work dealing with "Staging in the Theatres," [1]
but with him, too, one must break a lance. He says, "It
is chiefly the state and the trees which have caused the
trouble," and, by way of solving half the problem, prof-
fers the suggestion that trees came up and went down
traps. I think that the bogey of the state has at last been
laid, and that we need not despair of a complete solution.
But it will not be furthered, I fear, by Chambers's hypothetical trapwork. My opinion is that all recurring properties which were allowed to remain *in situ* occupied the rear
stage. This is, in part, borne out by the evidence presented by *Alphonsus, King of Arragon.* Though the scene
in Greene's *Comicall Historie* shifts, several trees, typifying a grove, stood on the stage throughout. In the opening scene of the fourth act occurs the instruction, "Let
there be a brazen Head set in the middle of the place behind the Stage, out of which cast flames of fire. . . ."
Since the text plainly indicates at this juncture that Ma-
homet's brazen head speaks from a grove, the inference is
that the trees were placed on the rear stage, where they
could be, from time to time, obscured.

[1] *The Elizabethan Stage*, iii, 88, 89.

XIV

THE ORIGIN OF THE SUBSTANTIVE
THEATRE MASQUE

LIKE travellers in the desert, historico-literary investigators are apt to be deluded, on occasion, by mirage.
Those among Elizabethan scholars to whom the end of
the long and toilsome journey already appears in sight,
and who yet somehow dread the cessation of labours
which physic pain, may take heart of grace. Much as has
been written about the early drama and stage, a good deal
remains unsaid; apart from the possibilities of full-armed
research, the most has not been made of available data.
In proof of this assertion I proffer now a new chapter in
early theatrical history. My aim is to demonstrate how
the Lenten embargo regularly laid upon the early seventeenth-century players led to the establishment of, not
exactly a new dramatic genre, but a new kind of theatrical entertainment — what I may venture to style the substantive theatre masque. Though obviously derivative,
this had a certain distinctiveness. Much more full-bodied
than the intercalary lopped masque of drama, it was likewise distinguished from the highly ornate court masque
which had inspired it, not only by the simplicity of its
mounting but by its closer approach to dramatic form.

Mutually hostile as were the Protestants and Catholics
of Elizabethan times, they united in their strict observance of Lent. To one and all, flesh meats and common
amusements were equally taboo. It had come to be recognised as a period of double penance for the player. "To
think, my lord," says Rosencrantz to Hamlet, "if you

delight not in man, what lenten entertainment the players shall receive from you." As far back as March 13, 1578–79, we find the Privy Council sending an order to the Lord Mayor of London and the Middlesex magistrates, forbidding acting during either the ensuing or any coming Lent.[1] Afterwards, however, some lenity was now and again shown to the players. During the Lent of 1592, Strange's Men were allowed to act at the Rose on all days save Good Friday. In 1595 and 1596 the Admiral's Men, who were then occupying that house, remained silent throughout the Lenten period, but in 1598 they began there a system of playing three days a week in the weeks just before Easter. But with the dawn of the new century a period of severity set in. In 1600 all acting at the common theatres during Lent was forbidden; and in March, 1601, the Privy Council, in renewing the order, made it applicable to Blackfriars and Paul's, though it is doubtful if either was strictly under jurisdiction, both being places of private acting, and not theatres in the common acceptation of the term.[2]

With the accession of King James, prohibition continued. But, unless I greatly mistake, Malone, in discussing the matter, arrived at an erroneous conclusion, and set a trap into which later historians have fallen. Here is the offending passage:

Plays in the time of King James the First (and probably afterwards) appear to have been performed every day at each theatre during the winter season, except in the time of Lent, when they were not permitted on the sermon days, as they were called, that is, on Wednesday and Friday; nor on the other days of the week, except by special license: which however was obtained by a fee paid to the Master of the Revels.[3]

---

[1] Collier, *History of English Dramatic Poetry*, i (1831), 310, note.

[2] Chalmers, *Apology*, p. 310.

[3] *Variorum Shakespeare*, iii (1821), 151. Summarised and tacitly endorsed by Collier, *op. cit.*, i, 394.

While I distrust and deprecate all generalisations of this order, I do not intend criticising Malone's statement in detail, my immediate concern being with his painful misreading of the authority on which he based his concluding assertion. It is little less than absurd to infer from the evidence available that the Master of the Revels had the power to give Lenten dispensations for the acting of plays. Dispensations were certainly given by Sir John Astley and Sir Henry Herbert, but, as I shall show later, these simply permitted the playhouses to be used otherwise than for their normal purposes during the period of abstinence.

Concerning the accuracy of Malone's general statement one begins to harbour doubts, on stumbling across sundry allusions in the Jacobean period indicating that, for the player, Lent still remained a period of privation. There is, in the first case, that significant metaphor in Middleton's *A Mad World, My Masters*, I, 1, "'T is Lent in your cheeks: the flag is down." When the flag failed to fly, the theatre was closed. A little less than a decade later, or in 1615, Cocke is to be found writing in his "Character" of "A Common Player":

Hence it proceeds, that in the prosperous fortune of a play frequented, he proves immoderate, and falles into a Drunkards paradise, till it be *last* no longer. Otherwise when adversities come, they come together: For Lent and Shrove-tuesday be not farre asunder, then he is dejected daily and weekely.[1]

The theatrical records of a year later go to show that the Master of the Revels had no power to give Lenten dispensations for acting, otherwise the players would hardly have gone the length of taking the law into their own hands. Though the Lord Chamberlain had given them due notification, through the Revels Office, that

[1] Chambers, *The Elizabethan Stage*, iv, 256.

playing in the penitential period would not be permitted, the four London companies, evidently by common agreement, had kept their theatres open. The result was that the leaders of each of the companies were summoned late in March to appear before the Privy Council and answer for their offence.[1] What punishment, if any, was inflicted upon them is not recorded; but it would seem that, not long after, some compromise was arrived at. In the following year we find Sir George Buc, the Master of the Revels, entering in his Office Book: "[Received] Of the King's players for a lenten dispensation, the other companys promising to doe as muche, 44s. March 23, 1616."[2]

It has been generally assumed that all the Lenten dispensations from this date were for the continuance of acting,[3] although none of the entries says as much, but I hope to convince scholars of the unreasonableness of that conclusion. Let us, in the first case, give careful consideration to the following records, extracted by Malone[4] from the Master of the Revels's Office Books for 1622–26:

1622. 21 Martii. For a prise at the Red-Bull, for the howse; the fencers would give nothing. 10s.

From Mr. Gunnel, in the name of the dancers of the ropes, this 15 March, 1624. £1.0.0.

From Mr. Gunnel, to allowe of a Masque for the dancers of the ropes, this 19 March, 1624. £2.0.0.

---

[1] Collier, *op. cit.*, i, 394, 395.

[2] J. Q. Adams, *Dramatic Records of Sir Henry Herbert*, p. 48. Adams (as also Chambers, *The Elizabethan Stage*, i, 316, note 2) includes among Lenten dispensations Buc's entry "Of John Hemminges, in the name of the four companys, for toleration in the holy-dayes, 44s. January 29, 1618"; but, judging by the date, this appears to refer to the recent Christmas holy days. Lenten payments were never made so far in advance.

[3] *E. g.*, Chambers, *op. cit.*, i, 316.

[4] *Variorum Shakespeare*, iii, 65, 66.

From Mr. Blagrave, in the name of the Cockpit company, for this Lent, this 30th March, 1624. £2.0.0.

1626. March 20. From Mr. Hemminges, for this Lent allowanse, £2.0.0.

It must first be noted that we have no reason to believe these entries are exhaustive for the Lenten periods comprised between 1622 and 1626. Although Malone made a transcript of all the records in Herbert's Office Books, he never published them in their entirety, and all the documents are now lost.[1] But these later Lenten entries, as we have them, show that, from at least 1623, the theatre owners were letting their houses for the holy days to fencers and ropedancers. As the profits in this way cannot have averaged as satisfactorily as the profits from playing, the inference is that playing had long been rigorously prohibited during the period of abstinence, but that a loophole of escape from an intolerable position had been found. Finding that exhibitions of fencing and acrobatics gave little offence in the close time, the Master of the Revels availed of the circumstance to extract an extra fee and make things a trifle less stringent for the players. Though the proceeds of Lenten letting were the prerogative of the theatre owners, they doubtless shared them, by arrangement, with the players.

Particular attention must now be drawn to one of these later Lenten entries, one referring by implication to the Fortune Theatre, where Richard Gunnel was manager: "From Mr. Gunnel, to allowe of a Masque for the dancers of the ropes this 19 March, 1624. £2.0.0."

Herbert, a fortnight previously, had been paid £1 for licensing the ropedancers at the Fortune, and he now received another £2 — or as much as he charged for the

---

[1] See my article on "New Facts from Sir Henry Herbert's Office Book" in the *Times Literary Supplement* for November 29, 1923.

allowing of a new play — for licensing their masque.
Clearly, from the fee charged, this masque could have
been no triviality: it was doubtless of the order of what
I have styled substantive theatre masque, though certainly not the first of that order. But I fancy I hear
someone ask how a mere troupe of ropedancers could
have performed a masque of any pretentiousness, and
to that very pertinent, if imaginary, question I reply by
citing once more from Sir Henry Herbert's invaluable
Office Books:

> 1630, Feb 18, warrant to Francis Nicolini, an Italian and his
> company, to dance on the ropes, to use Interludes and masques, and
> to sell his powders and balsams.
> To John Puncteus, a Frenchman, professing Physick, with ten in
> his Company, to exercise the quality of playing, for a year, and to
> sell his drugs. [1]

The secret is out. After acting in Lent had been
regularly prohibited for some years in James's time, the
players got out of their difficulty by letting their theatres
during Lent to foreign mountebanks. It is a well-known
circumstance that, on the Continent, these perambulating
quacks were in the habit of employing buffoons and acrobats to draw the crowd.[2] They made so much money
out of the sale of their nostrums that the chances are
that, when they held forth in the London playhouses,
they either admitted the public free or made but a trifling
charge for admission.

It is noteworthy that the John Puncteus to whom
one of the two licenses was granted is to be traced in
England and Scotland many years later. In 1642 he had in
his employment a ropedancer named Knowles, who was

---

[1] Adams, *Dramatic Records of Sir Henry Herbert*, p. 47.
[2] Cf. Karl Mantzius, *History of Theatrical Art*, iv, 8, 9; Eugène Rigal,
Le Théâtre Français avant la Période Classique, p. 19, note 2.

arrested in that year for robbery.[1] A score of years later, he was mountebanking in Edinburgh.[2] Both he and Nicolini had their own performers, but it seems not unlikely that when they held forth in London they supplemented their forces by engaging some of the players belonging to the theatre they had hired. Otherwise, it would be difficult to account for the performance, under their auspices, of masques in English.

We have seen that Lenten dispensations for some unspecified purpose were given to the players at least as early as 1617, and I am disposed to think that by that period mountebanks had already begun to rent the theatres in the Lenten season, and were responsible for the emergence of the substantive theatre masque. This would explain whence some unknown author drew the idea for *The Mountebank's Masque*, performed at Gray's Inn by Inns-of-Court gentlemen on February 2, 1617–18, and shortly afterwards at court.[3] This masque was not at all of the ordinary type, and it may be that in burlesquing the methods of the mountebanks the author adopted the style of masque they had introduced.[4]

[1] *Studies in Philology*, xviii, 273, Hyder E. Rollins on "A Contribution to the History of the English Commonwealth Drama."

[2] J. C. Dibdin, *Annals of the Edinburgh Stage*, p. 26. Cf. *Evelyn's Diary*, under "August 9, 1661."

[3] First printed in Nichols's *Progresses of Queen Elizabeth*, afterwards by Collier in *Inigo Jones* (Shakespeare Society, 1848), pp. 111 ff. A copy of the masque is also to be found in Additional MSS, 5956. In this the "Paradoxes" are given at the end, and a note says they were "read at Gray's Inn but left out at Court to avoid tediousness." No authority exists for ascribing the masque to Marston.

[4] Similarly, if we could assume that some of these foreign quacks had introduced characters from the *commedia dell'arte* into their Lenten entertainments, we should have a clue to the source of inspiration of the Mountebank, Zany and Harlequin, in the fourth entry of Davenant's court masque, *Britannia Triumphans* (1638).

Some bolstering can be given to this conjecture. If Buc's dispensation of 1617 to the King's Players permitted them to continue acting plays throughout Lent, it is curious that the same mode of escape was not followed in subsequent seasons. That in 1619 Lent was still for them a truly penitential period is shown by some lines on Burbage, the tragedian, addressed to his fellows at the time of his death in the Lent of that year:

> And you his said companions, to whom Lent,
> Becomes more Lenten in the accident,
> Henceforth your wavering flag no more hang out
> Play now no more at all.[1]

It seems unlikely, however, that at any Lenten period there could have been enough mountebanks to occupy all the theatres, but this shortage, if shortage there were, was apparently soon obviated. Some little evidence exists to show that in the later Jacobean period an occasional theatre was kept open during Lent by its own players with some sort of non-dramatic entertainment. On March 3, 1623–24, a period of the year when plays were seldom, if ever, licensed, Herbert records the licensing "For the Cockpit Company; *The Sun's Darling;* in the nature of a masque by Deker, and Forde." [2]

This memorable masque, of which I shall have something to say later, was clearly intended for Lenten performance. It would hardly have been written had the Cockpit players had the power to give plays in Lent, and I think, therefore, that the entry of its licensing elucidates that other entry: "From Mr. Blagrave, in the name of the Cockpit company, for this Lent, this 30th March, 1624, £2."

Note also that a fortnight after *The Sun's Darling* was

---

[1] Sloane MSS, 1786.
[2] Adams, *Dramatic Records of Sir Henry Herbert*, p. 27.

allowed, that is, on March 16, 1623–24, Herbert records the licensing "For the King's company. *Shankes Ordinary*, written by Shankes himself, this 16 March, 1623, £1.0.0." [1]

A lineal descendant, artistically speaking, of Dick Tarlton, John Shanks was not only a comedian of some popularity, but a character vocalist and a monologue entertainer. He was the author and interpreter of "The Irish Beggar," a pathetic character song first published in *Wit Restored* in 1658.[2] That *Shankes Ordinary* was not of the nature of a play is shown by the fee charged for licensing it, just half the sum exacted for the allowing of a new play. The inference would be that Shanks had written some sort of entertainment — probably a monologue — for Lenten performance at the Globe.

Some slight evidence exists to show that, in 1629, plays were still tabooed in Lent, and that, whatever the fare then proffered in the theatres, gallants did not patronise it. In Francis Lenton's *The Young Gallants Whirligig; or Youths Reakes*, published in that year, we read:

> Your Theatres hee daily doth frequent,
> (Except the intermitted time of Lent),
> Treasuring up within his memory,
> The amorous toyes of every comedy.

There is some reason to believe, however, that within a year or two the old embargo on Lenten acting had been

[1] Adams, *op. cit.*, p. 27.

[2] Variants exist under the titles, "Shanks's Song" and "The Irish Footman's Ochone." For the former, see Collier, *History of English Dramatic Poetry*, iii (1879), 484. This is a debased version from Ashmolean MSS, 83, f. 114, no. 131. The latter is given in *Westminster Drollery*, Part II (1672). A MS. copy, without title, is to be found in Rawlinson MSS Poet. 142, f. 125, otherwise a common-place book of the period of 1630–35. For the whole subject, see my article in *The Lady of the House* (Dublin) for Christmas, 1923, on "The Irish Exile's Ochone."

removed.[1] Writing in 1633 in his *Histriomastix*,[2] Prynne says:

> There are none so addicted to stage-playes, but when they go unto places where they cannot have them, or whenas they are suppressed by publicke authority, (as in times of pestilence, and in Lent, till now of late) can well subsist without them.

But it is doubtful how long this release lasted. In the pen-picture of a player given in 1638 in the seventh edition of Earle's *Characters*, we read that "Shrove-tuesday, hee feares as much as the bawdes, and Lent is more dangerous to him than the butchers."

There may be in this, however, a particular application. On February 23, 1637, the theatres reopened after a long spell of plague, only, however, to be closed again on the second of March. But with the abatement of the fell visitation, in the first week in Lent, the players once more set up their bills. Forthwith the Archbishop of Canterbury complained to the Privy Council of their conduct, acting in the time of Lent being, in his eyes, doubly unfitting when sickness was rife. Evidently the players had full authority for their act, for the Earl of Pembroke and Montgomery, then Lord Chamberlain, openly resented this interference with his office; but the King sided with the Archbishop and ordered the players to be silenced.[3]

Having now postulated the probable origin of the substantive theatre masque, I may proceed to consider the few examples of the type which have come down to us. In 1620 there was issued in quarto, with an illustrative engraved title-page, *A Courtly Masque: The Deuice*

---

[1] No particular significance can be attached, I think, to Herbert's licensing, on March 11, 1630–31, of Massinger's *The Emperor of the East*, unless we can assume with Malone that the players took the risk of learning their parts beforehand, and that plays were produced as soon as licensed. To this I cannot agree.

[2] Page 784. [3] Thorndike, *Shakespeare's Theater*, p. 242.

called, The World tost at Tennis. As it hath beene diuers times Presented to the Contentment of many Noble and Worthy Spectators: By the Prince his Seruants. Inuented and set downe by Tho: Middleton & William Rowley, Gent. Deceived by this long-tailed title, Fleay assumed that the masque had been given at court, but the positive evidence of its induction and the negative evidence of its registration show this to be untenable. The entry made on the Stationers' Books on July 4, 1620, simply reads: "A Courtly Masque or The World Tossed at Tennis acted at the Princes Armes by the Prince his hyghnes seruantes."

At this period the Prince's Men had no theatre of their own, and were acting in the yard of the Prince's Arms Inn in Leadenhall Street. My belief is that *The World Tost at Tennis* had been produced by them there in the previous Lent. It was not originally intended for public performance, and how it came to be given publicly is an interesting story. In 1618 Middleton had written for Christmas performance at the Inner Temple, by the Prince's Men, his *Masque of Heroes;* and it would appear that its success had emboldened the company to give him and his old collaborator, Will Rowley, a commission to write a masque for performance at court, the result being *The World Tost at Tennis.* As may be deduced in part from the later induction, the intention was to give this before the King at Denmark House, the Prince of Wales's new residence, in the Shrovetide of 1620; but during the Whitehall festivities of the previous Christmas the Prince's Men were unlucky enough to act a play there before the King which gave him mortal offence, and he refused to allow them to appear before him again.[1]

[1] For fuller details, see my article, "Early Substantive Theatre Masques," in the *Times Literary Supplement* for December 8, 1921.

With the masque thus left upon their hands, they decided to produce it publicly; and the statement on its title-page that it had been performed "to the contentment of many noble and worthy spectators" would go to show that divers of the courtiers who had been baulked of their entertainment by the King's fiat made their way to the King's Arms to see the masque.

Much as I am at a loss to date the genesis of the substantive theatre masque, that event can hardly have taken place more than two or three years before the production of *The World Tost at Tennis*, since, judged by later examples of the type, Middleton and Rowley's masque was of a primitive order. Though its stage directions savour more of the common theatre than the court, its form (as was to be expected from the circumstances of its origin) is essentially court-like. Moreover, unlike the maturer substantive theatre masque, which is distinguished by its division into acts, it runs on continuously. Both unite, however, in giving song, satire, and anti-masque dancing, and both are differentiated from the contemporary court masque in their avoidance of scenery and of the three orthodox terminal dances. On the other hand, most of them had, what the court masque had not, prologues and epilogues. The tone of the epilogue to *The World Tost at Tennis* might at a pinch be taken to substantiate the belief that the substantive theatre masque was then a comparative novelty, hardly an established Lenten institution; but we must take care not to apply references to court entertainments to the public theatres. "Gentlemen," it began:

> We must confesse that we have vented ware
> Not always vendible: masques are more rare
> Than Playes are common; at most, but twice a year
> In their most glorious shapes doe they appeare.

Which, if you please accept, wee'le keep in store
Our debted loves, and thus content you more.
Insert the Proverbe now, and suffer not,
That which is seldom seene, be soone forgot.

Masques that appeared in their most glorious shapes
but twice a year were, of course, not theatre masques but
court masques, which were given only at Christmas and
Shrovetide. But *The World Tost at Tennis* was not soon
forgot. Some slender evidence exists to show that it bore
revival at the Cockpit years later. In a list of Cockpit
plays furnished by William Beeston to the Lord Chamberlain in 1639, the plays are enumerated in groups according to their authors, and Middleton and Rowley's
pieces are given thus: "The Changeling, A Fayre Quarrell, The Spanish Gypsie, The World." [1]

As no play of the period is known called *The World*,
it is reasonable to conclude that the title represents *The
World Tost at Tennis*. It cannot be objected that masques
would not be included in the list, though the list pretends
to be one of plays only, seeing that it comprises also *The
Sun's Darling*.

In the absence of definite data we cannot, of course, be
sure that *The World Tost at Tennis* was a Lenten production, but no such uncertainty exists about the next and
best of extant substantive theatre masques. Dekker and
Ford's *The Sun's Darling* was licensed for the Cockpit
company on March 3, 1623-24.[2] Written in five acts like
an ordinary play, it is chiefly remarkable in its existing
form for its dainty, care-free song. Remaining unpublished until 1656, it has come down to us in altered guise,

---

[1] Malone, *Variorum Shakespeare*, iii, 159. The position here of *The Spanish
Gypsy* runs counter to H. Dugdale Sykes's attribution of that play to Ford
(*Sidelights on Elizabethan Drama*, p. 183).

[2] Adams, *Dramatic Records of Sir Henry Herbert*, p. 27.

having been tinkered and topicalised for a revival early in 1639.[1] It was given then by Beeston's Boys, otherwise the King's and Queen's Young Servants, not only at the Cockpit but several times at court. There is absolutely no warrant for the belief that it was originally a court masque, a belief that I formerly shared. That impression arose through a misreading of its title-page. The title-page says that it had first been acted by Beeston's Boys at Whitehall and afterwards at the Cockpit, true enough as far as it goes, but the licensing entry shows that it had been publicly acted years before the King's and Queen's Young Servants was organised. Note also that the title-page describes the masque as "a moral masque," a description never given to a pure court masque but one commonly applied to the later substantive theatre masques. This seems to imply that with the view of propitiating the Puritans — if such a thing were possible — care was taken to emphasise the morality of Lenten masques.

Next in order comes the *Microcosmus* of Thomas Nabbes, "a moral masque" in five acts, entered on the Stationers' Register on August 6, 1636, and published in the following year. Beyond these details, no clue to the period of production has come down to us. All that can be gleaned concerning the masque is yielded by its title-page, which informs us that it was "presented with generall liking at the private house in Salisbury Court, and heere set down according to the intentions of the Authour." It is obvious from this that the masque was not performed exactly as it was written and contrived, and that consequently it would be perilous to make deductions from either its text or its stage directions. The

[1] For fuller details, see my article, "The Problem of Lyly's Songs," in the *Times Literary Supplement* for December 20, 1923.

best we can do is to indulge in idle speculation as to the nature of the indicated alterations, whether they consisted of textual abridgements or — what is much more probable — some simplification of the scenic effects. All that I can permit myself to say on that score is that I cannot agree with Professor Thorndike that there is no internal evidence of the intended use of movable scenery, any more than I can agree with him that Nabbes's masque and *The World Tost at Tennis* had been performed at court.[1] The quarto enables us to determine that, however it came to be presented, Nabbes had designed the masque for performance behind an elaborate frontispiece — itself an indication of the employment of movable scenery — and with no fewer than five sets of scenes. But, possibly because of the small stage of Salisbury Court, the court system of visual, quasi-magical scene-changing could not be followed, and Nabbes had to arrange for the changes to be effected behind a constantly dropping pictorial curtain. Such is the method indicated in the book, but the misfortune is, we cannot be sure that in the actual performance scenery was used at all. If we could assume that the original intention was carried out, — a supposition running counter to the implications of the title-page, — there would be some grounds for characterising the performance as epoch-marking.

[1] *Shakespeare's Theater*, p. 192.

XV

EARLY DRAMATIC COLLABORATION
A THEORY

SOMETHING more than the inductive qualities of a well-trained modern mind is required of the investigator who shall essay to pierce the mysteries which still enshroud the great Elizabethan dramatic era. Vital as is strategic approach, the spear of science will splinter in his hands unless he brings also to the attack the antiquary's capacity to live in the atmosphere and think the thoughts of the period he is studying. If it be retorted that this is a truism, I can only reply that progress is being stayed by failure to act upon it. Scholarship has not wholly ceased its mischievous habit of reading into the theatrical customs of Shakespeare's day the customs of our own. In this respect nothing, to my mind, has proved more harmful than the widespread and firmly rooted belief in the complete correspondence between the broad methods of dramatic collaboration pursued universally during the past century and the methods which ruled in the pre-Restoration epoch. We conceive of collaboration to-day as the marriage of complementary minds, a state in which each writer is at once creator and critic, not only contributing his allotted portion of the work, but reviewing and revising his co-worker's portion. In affording a measure of self-criticism more searching and ruthless than one-man authorship is capable of, this system has its advantages, but it needs to be recalled that it spells slow progress. For reasons presently to be advanced, I am firmly of the opinion that, generally speaking, this was not the system pursued in either the last decade of the sixteenth century or the first half of the seventeenth. The truth on this score has become sadly distorted through the sturdy persistence of the Beaumont and Fletcher legend, which, like all legends when placed under the microscope, proves to have incrustations of falsity.

What we have clearly to bear in mind is that playwriting in Shakespeare's day was simply a trade, that plays were written wholly and solely to order, and that they were never ordered until they were wanted. Facility of composition was the great desideratum: the goods had to be delivered within a limited period or not at all. This was the secret of the railing at Jonson's tardiness, his incapacity to bring forth much more than a play a year; lacking rapidity of workmanship, he was not deemed to have learned his trade.[1] That attitude curiously persisted, and it is not improbable that Milton was thinking of Jonson when, in praising Shakespeare for his copiousness, in the lines contributed anonymously to the Second Folio of 1632, he wrote:

> For whilst to th' shame of slow-endeavouring art
> Thy easie numbers flow.

Elizabethan dramatic collaboration was matter of necessity, not choice. It implied an urgent demand for the goods. So far from the playwright seeking a complementary mind to aid him in his work, the choice was seldom, if ever, his. The association of collaborators was mostly mere matter of chance, an arbitrary arrangement on the part of the intermediary who commissioned the play.

---

[1] See *Satiromastix*, V, 2, 218, "you and your itchy poetry breake out like Christmas, but once a yeare." Jonson replied to his detractors on this score in the "Apologeticall Dialogue," appended to *Poetaster* in the quarto of 1602.

The more pressing the necessity for a new piece, the greater the number of collaborators engaged to write it. Sometimes there were as many as five. In the late sixteenth century, when the remuneration for play writing was by lump sum,[1] collaboration could not have been viewed as anything better than a necessary evil: the splitting of a fee into three or four parts was abomination. Not but that, now and again, it had secretly to be indulged in. There were occasions when an odd playwright, in working single-handed on a play required to be finished by a certain date, found his progress so slow that he had perforce to enlist the services of some budding, cheaply secured author to help him out with his task. This, however, was not collaboration as collaboration was then understood; no journeyman of this type was ever credited on a title-page with the honours of part-authorship. The Elizabethan literary hack bore the same relationship to the dramatist for whom he worked as the eighteenth-century art pupil bore to the fashionable portrait painter whose backgrounds he filled in. It is indeed only at rare intervals that we have any glimpses of him. Possibly because he had been so often sneered at for his slowness of composition — he had taken fifteen weeks to write *Poetaster* — Jonson was so proud of the fact that from the drafting of *Volpone* until the production of the play but two months had elapsed, that he could not refrain from boasting of it in his prologue:

> Five weeks fully penned it,
> From his own hand, without a coadjutor,
> Novice, journeyman, or tutor.

Grades of collaborators are here indicated, but except for the coadjutor all the rest were mere leather and prunella.

[1] Thaler, *Shakspere to Sheridan*, pp. 22–25.

A little later, one conscientious dramatist — he afterwards took holy orders — made honest confession. In 1613 Daborne had received a commission from Henslowe to furnish him with a new play, but, finding time running short, was compelled to call in Tourneur to write one of the acts. When Henslowe remonstrated over the delay, Daborne, by way of showing that he had not neglected his interests, wrote him an apologetic letter revealing what he had done.[1]

A score of years later, in Caroline times, the journeyman was still to the fore. One recalls how, in the third act of Randolph's *The Jealous Lovers*, Asotus, after crowning Charylus and Bomolochus poets laureate, warns them:

> I will not have you henceforth sneak to taverns,
> And peep like fiddlers into gentleman's rooms,
> To shark for wine and radishes; nor lie sentinel
> At ordinaries, nor take up at plays
> Some novice for a supper. You shall deal
> No more in ballads, to bewail an execution
> In lamentable rhythm; nor beg in elegies;
> Nor counterfeit a sickness to draw in
> A contribution; nor work journeywork
> Under some playhouse poet, that deals in
> Wit by retail.

The playhouse poet of Randolph's day was precisely the man who was not expected to collaborate, as he was engaged under articles for a considerable term, and was paid a weekly salary by the players on the understanding that they were to have a monopoly of his services and that he was to write for them three plays a year.[2] But one can well conceive that there were occasions when, to fulfil his contract, he found it necessary to employ a "ghost." Moreover, the dilettante dramatists

---

[1] Greg, *Henslowe Papers*, p. 72.
[2] Thaler, *Shakspere to Sheridan*, pp. 29, 30.

who buzzed about the Caroline court, and sought to gain favour in the Queen's eyes by writing plays dealing with platonic love, were not above employing a professional hand to polish up their work, much in the subterranean way that the Duke of Newcastle employed Shirley. It was at this lordly crew that Falkland tilted when in 1638, in his "Eclogue on the death of Ben Jonson," he made Meloboeus say of the lamented one:

> Who, (not like those who with small praise had writ,
> Had they not call'd in judgment to their wit)
> Us'd not a tutoring hand his to direct,
> But was sole workman and sole architect.

Assuredly, no investigator of early methods of dramatic collaboration can afford wholly to ignore the journeyman — this collaborator who was no collaborator; but now that we have duly noted his trail, we may dismiss him from consideration.

It is a curious fact that the earliest printed plays known to have been written in collaboration were amateur plays, plays all written for performance at the Inns of Court or by their members. Early as these were in date, it would probably be hazardous to see in them an inspirational precedent for the professional playwright, but there is good reason to believe that amateur collaboration arose from the same necessity as professional collaboration, namely, shortage of time and a need for haste. Inns-of-Court plays were mostly given at the Grand Christmases, as the term went; and it would appear that the arrangements for these extraordinary Christmas entertainments were not made more than a couple of months in advance. But the reason for the collaboration is immaterial; what is important for us to note is that in connexion with these plays it is possible to determine how the division of labour was made. No more than five authors have ever combined to write a play, but, taking that as the maximum, no matter what the number, the quickest method of collaboration is allotment by acts; and that was precisely the method adopted by the Inns-of-Court authors. It is on record that that epoch-marking tragedy, *Ferrex and Porrex* (otherwise *Gorboduc*), was first performed at the Inner Temple at the Grand Christmas of 1561–62, and repeated shortly afterwards before the Queen at Westminster. The title-page of the first quarto reads, in part, *the Tragedie of Gorboduc, Where of three Actes were wrytten by Thomas Nortone, and the two laste by Thomas Sackuyle*, and the entry on the Stationers' Register makes practically the same assignment. What is chiefly remarkable about this, the primordial blank-verse play, is that the style throughout is so uniform that, failing the information yielded by the title-page, we should be wholly at a loss to attribute to each author his due portion of the work. This has the tendency to fortify one's doubts concerning the scientific accuracy of the conclusions arrived at by latterday analysts of old collaborated plays, whose habit it is to base on stylistic analogies, iterations of phrase, and what not.

A year or two later — the exact date is uncertain — the Inner Temple produced *The Tragedie of Gismond of Salerne*, a play better known now by the title given it on the belated quarto of 1591, when a revision of the text was printed as *Tancred and Gismund*. Two manuscripts of the original, now preserved in the British Museum,[1] show that the tragedy had at least four authors, and probably five. The fifth act is unassigned, but we learn that each of the first four acts had a different author. Such a division, to my mind, would have been made only under

[1] Lansdowne MSS, 786, f. 1; Hargrave MSS, 205, f. 9. Cf. Chambers, *The Elizabethan Stage*, iii, 514.

conditions of haste; the only reward was gratification, and no author could have been much gratified by it.

Gray's Inn soon fell into line. In 1566 was produced there the tragedy of *Jocasta*, pretended to be from Euripides, but in reality a blank-verse translation from the Italian. We learn from the quarto that the first and fourth acts were "done by F. Kinwelmarshe," and the remainder by George Gascoigne. It is noteworthy that even a score of years later, at a time when the Honourable Society of Gray's Inn had progressed in its playwriting to one-man authorship, the old principle of a division of labour was still in some measure followed; for, although, when the tragedy of *The Misfortunes of Arthur* was arranged for, Thomas Hughes wrote the whole of the play proper, no fewer than six other authors were called in to write the induction and choruses and devise the dumb shows. And as it was with Inns-of-Court plays, so too was it with Inns-of-Court masques, despite the fact that elsewhere, and more especially at court, masque writing was essentially a one-man job. In 1595, at a time when the masque was in its transitional stage and devoid of complexity, we find Francis Davison and Thomas Campion combining at Gray's Inn in the composition of *The Masque of Proteus*.

The earliest known collaborated play by professional authors is the *Dido, Queen of Carthage* of Marlowe and Nashe, published in 1594 as "played by the Children of her Maiesties Chappell." Since no clue exists to the period of production, it is idle, of course, to guess at the circumstances which occasioned the collaboration; but I take leave for the moment to doff my gravely scientific attitude and to indulge in this idleness. *Dido, Queen of Carthage* was undoubtedly written for performance on a stage provided with multiple scenery, otherwise a simultaneous setting,[1] and therefore might very well have been designed for performance at court. Possibly it was the outcome of a hasty commission for the Queen's Christmas festivities, inspired much as Peele's *Arraignment of Paris* was inspired. But the problem here is no greater or more baffling than the problem of individual authorship. On that score there is remarkable diversity of opinion. Almost a century ago a writer in *The Retrospective Review*[2] expressed the belief that

Nash wrote the greater portion, indeed nearly the whole of this play. The only part which we can decidedly ascribe to Marlowe's hand is the greater part of the first scene of the third act, and the conclusion of the second act; although we can trace him in several places where he appears to have added a few touches, but of no great extent.

This dissection bears a family resemblance to many later ones, but to those who conceive that collaboration meant haste and was seldom undertaken under other conditions, it and its congeners must prove unconvincing. My main aim in quoting it is to show how early the modern mind began reading itself and its surroundings into alien times. Fleay,[3] in discussing the play, adopts what is to me the maddening method of assigning certain scenes only in certain acts, as well as a fragment of the opening scene, to Nashe. So far as this can imply any system, it is a system that would have defeated its own ends. Moreover, it puts collaboration on the plane of choice, not necessity. Chambers is hardly less irritating when he says that "whether Nashe's own share in the work was as collaborator, continuator, or merely editor,

---

[1] For which see Lawrence, *The Elizabethan Playhouse and Other Studies*, 1st series, pp. 239–243; Gustave Cohen, *Histoire de la Mise en Scène dans le Théâtre Religieux Français du Moyen Age*, pp. 85–89.

[2] Vol. ii (1828), pp. 11–13.

[3] *Biographical Chronicle of the English Drama*, ii, 147.

remains uncertain." [1] To my mind there is no ground for uncertainty in cases where an author's name is given as part-author on the title-page of a sixteenth-century or early seventeenth-century play. Even when publication was belated and the play had been revised — perhaps more than once — by other hands, the names on the title-page had no other significance than that their bearers had collaborated on the original play. To-day, when a play has come down to us wholly in sophisticated form, and we are able to determine (or deceive ourselves into the belief that we are able to determine) the identity of its reviser, we very properly reckon the reviser as part-author. But that was not the seventeenth-century custom. The reviser, *qua* reviser, was a negligible quantity. Even the continuator, to adopt Chambers's phrase, did not count. Here is the proof. In 1633 Herbert records the payment of the usual licensing fee for a new play: "for a play of Fletcher's corrected by Sherley, called *The Night Walkers*." [2] In this case Fletcher had left an uncompleted manuscript and Shirley had finished it. He was virtually entitled to claim part-authorship, but when the play was published in 1640 it was attributed to Fletcher alone.

Title-pages, on the whole, are not good evidence. Even when they tell the truth they do not always tell the whole truth. Occasionally the name of a collaborator is omitted. Henslowe's Diary reveals that Middleton was part-author of *The Honest Whore*, Part I, but when the play came to be printed it was credited solely to Dekker. So, too, there is good reason to believe that at least one other name besides Shakespeare's should have appeared on the title-page of *Pericles*, but this I shall speak of later.

[1] *The Elizabethan Stage*, iii, 426.
[2] Adams, *Dramatic Records of Sir Henry Herbert*, p. 34.

Henslowe's Diary, in recording the productions of the Admiral's Men at the Rose and the Fortune from 1597 to 1603, throws a flood of light on contemporary collaboration. During this period the company averaged twenty new plays a year and gave employment to half-a-dozen dramatists, who sometimes wrote singly and sometimes in collaboration, but always at high speed. Had the much later system of strictly sequential performance known as "a run" then been in vogue, fewer productions and less haste in the writing would have been demanded; but it was not even usual throughout Shakespeare's time to give any play two consecutive performances, and the custom with a virgin piece was to act it once a week until the end of the season, and perhaps revive it for a time in the season following. This, of course, was provided it escaped disaster on its trial trip.

How far one would be safe in drawing broad analogies from the system pursued by the Admiral's Men it would be difficult to say. But it would certainly appear that in the late sixteenth century there was a constant need for new plays and that production was fairly frequent.[1] Later on, as repertories increased, the dramatic output diminished, but the custom in and about this period, of laying a successful new play aside for a stretch of some five years after its initial vogue, made constant production imperative. Apart from this, however, the safest plan in consider-

---

[1] Under "Vulgi expectatio" Jonson writes, in his *Discoveries:* "Expectation of the vulgar is more drawn and held with newness than goodness; we see it in fencers, in players, in poets, in preachers, in all where fame promiseth any thing; so it be new, though never so naught and depraved, they run to it and are taken. Which shews, that the only decay, or hurt of the best man's reputation with the people is, their wits have out-lived the people's palates. They have been too much or too long a feast." Here we have the reason why (1) the players always charged double prices on the first day of a new play, and (2) why good new plays were periodically laid aside.

ing the records of the Admiral's Men is to look upon their habitude as purely individual. It may not have been, but one cannot say. Of the 128 new plays produced by them between 1597 and 1603, I find that three were the work of five collaborators, fourteen of four, fifteen of three, and thirty-eight of two; but it is to be noted that no fewer than fifty-eight, or almost fifty per cent of the total output, fell to the lot of a single author. From this it can be safely deduced that one-man authorship was preferred by players and playwrights alike, and that nothing but pressure of circumstances kept collaboration alive.

Henslowe's evidence regarding plays written in parts is curiously informative. It is germane to our subject. Plays written in parts were of two kinds, what I shall venture to style the legitimate and the illegitimate. The legitimate kind was of the chronicle-history order, where the matter was too diffuse for compression into a single play. Frequently in plays of this type a second part was promised in the epilogue to the first. The illegitimate kind is indicated where advantage was taken of the popularity of a self-contained new play to provide it with an unexpected sequel. I think this was the case with *The Honest Whore*, the First Part of which was published in 1604, not as a first part, but as an entity, though its belatedly issued sequel was described as the Second Part. On the other hand, some romantic plays in parts, such as, if evidence were lacking, one would be disposed to put into the illegitimate category, are in reality legitimate. Thus Marston, in the induction to *Antonio and Mellida*, promises a second part, "if this obtaine gratious acceptance."

What is noteworthy concerning the plays in parts recorded in Henslowe is that, although as a rule the authors of the first part are generally the authors of the other parts, exceptions occur. Thus Munday is credited with the whole of the First Part of *Robin Hood*, though in working on the Second Part he certainly had Chettle as collaborator.[1] So, too, though Chettle, Dekker, Drayton, and Wilson collaborated on the First Part of *Black Bateman of the North*, only Chettle and Wilson worked on the Second Part. Evidently circumstances dictated systems. On the three parts of *The Civil Wars of France* Dekker and Drayton alone collaborated.

It is to be noted also that we are provided by Henslowe with some faint clues to the initial procedure in matters of collaboration. The *sine qua non*, the one thing the players were particular about and had to be assured of, was a striking plot. The plot had to be ratified by them before the labour of composition began, but that once done, the rest was left to the discretion of the author or authors. In the Elizabethan theatrical world the scenario writer was quite as important an individual as the scenario writer in the moving-picture world of to-day. Reputations were gained in this way. Nashe, when accused by Gabriel Harvey of imitating Greene, repudiated the charge in his *Have with You at Saffron Walden*, in which he wrote of Greene (with whom he had formerly collaborated) as "subscribing to mee in anything but plotting Plaies, wherein he was his craft's master." One recalls that Francis Meres, writing in his *Palladis Tamia* in 1598, characterised Anthony Munday as "our best plotter," a description into which it might be read that Munday was then chief scenario-writer to the Admiral's Men. There can be little doubt that the old scenario was

[1] The reason why traces of Chettle are to be found in the First Part is that he was called in to "mend" the play shortly after its production. See H. Dugdale Sykes, *Sidelights on the Elizabethan Drama*, pp. 222, 223.

divided into acts, and a copy of it given to each collaborator. Whether the play was to be the work of one author or many, a synopsis of the plot was drawn up, as much for the author's guidance as for the players' approval. We know that Jonson, in designing his unfinished pastoral, *The Sad Shepherd*, for Caroline court performance, made an act-by-act scenario of the piece.

The fact that under circumstances of extreme pressure as many as five writers could be employed on a play, and that the maximum was five in correspondence with the regulation number of acts, would go to show that the division of labour was by acts, certainly the quickest possible method for a duality or multiplicity of authors habituated to working apart after preliminary consultation. But there were grades of authorship, and it must not be rashly assumed that where there were five collaborators each received equal payment for his work. Note that for *The Fair Constance of Rome* the sum of £6 was paid to the quintet of authors in unequal proportions, Wilson's share amounting to no more than 11 shillings.[1] My firm belief in the allotment by acts forces me to the conclusion that there was a hierarchy of the pen and that Wilson was at the foot of the ladder. I should also be inclined to say that, when four authors wrote unitedly, the plotter supplied the first and last acts, and the others an act apiece. That the act unit was in force at the close of the sixteenth century is established by the following entry in Henslowe: "Lent unto Robert Shawe, & Jewbey, the 23 of octob. 1598, to lend unto Mr. Chapman, one his playe boocke, & ij actes of a tragedie of Bengemen's plott, the some of iiij lb."

There can be little doubt that, next to one-man authorship, dual collaboration was, of all possible arrangements,

[1] Greg, *Henslowe Papers*, p. 55.

the most approved of by authors and players alike. When contracts of this order were undertaken, one writer supplied the first three acts, and the other the remainder. Dual collaboration, proving much less scrappy and disconnected than any other, produced the happiest results. No great play was ever due to the union of three or more writers. To this larger practice are to be attributed some of the blemishes apparent in the great bulk of the Elizabethan drama. It made for melodrama, a groping about for striking situations at any cost. Disjointedness, inability to attend to the nexus, awkward handling of lapses of time, static and imperfectly psychologised characterisation — all these defects arose from multiplex collaboration and became conventionalised and ineradicable.

I come now to the question of the double plot. Now and again one finds it argued that the double plot was fostered by early collaboration, that it readily lent itself to composite authorship. Another theory, too, has been proffered in explanation of its vogue. Writing of Shakespearean times, and expressing hypothesis somewhat audaciously in terms of hard fact, Mr. William Poel says:

A dramatic representation was a continuous performance given without pause from beginning to end, and the dramatists, in compliance with the custom, used the double story, so often to be found in plays of the time, in order that the movement should be continued uninterruptedly. The characters in each story appeared on the stage in alternate scenes, with every now and then a full scene in which the characters appeared together.[1]

Since the double plot could hardly have lent itself satisfactorily to collaboration unless the two themes were kept rigidly apart, the two theories are incompatible. But I see no good reason why we should pin our faith to either. Both beg the question. We are almost asked to

[1] *Shakespeare in the Theatre*, p. 14.

believe that the Elizabethan dramatists had invented the double plot to serve some immediate purpose; yet the device was as old as Terence, and its resurgence was due to Italy's adoption of a neo-Terentian dramaturgic scheme. As for the theory of continuous performance now so widely entertained, I have no hesitation in characterising it a popular fallacy.[1] "Q. E. D." has never been written, and never will be written, to the problem. Save as an expedient of dual authorship, the nice conduct of a double plot by collaboration seems to me a task of sufficient intricacy to defeat the collaborators' ends, always assuming that the ends were the saving of time. Whether the plots were kept apart or not, it would have meant a scene-by-scene, not act-by-act, division of labour, a system devoid of convenience for more than a couple of collaborators, and demanding even from them close communion and slow progression. What Beaumont and Fletcher could do was one thing, and what a more or less accidental combination of authors could do, another.

Let us not forget, however, that our knowledge of the relations of Francis Beaumont and John Fletcher is almost wholly derived from traditional sources. Aubrey, basing on information given by Sir James Hales and others, tells us that they "lived together on the Banke-Side, not far from the Play-house, both bachelors; lay together; had one wench in the house between them, which they did so admire; the same cloathes and cloake, &c., betweene them." But this would only have been for five years at the most, or from 1608 until Beaumont's marriage and retirement in 1613. Such also was the

[1] Cf. my article on "The Shakespearean Fallacy of the Hour" in *The New Statesman* for September 20, 1924; also Sir Mark Hunter on "Act- and Scene-Division in the Plays of Shakespeare," in *The Review of English Studies*, ii, 295 ff.

period of their collaboration, a collaboration memorable enough in its way, but one over which the world, long deluded into the belief that all the plays in the so-called Beaumont and Fletcher folio were its fruitage, has unduly marvelled. We cannot be sure that more than seven plays were due to this association, though it certainly would have been notable enough, had it produced nothing more than *Philaster* and *The Maid's Tragedy*. Here, beyond question, was a marriage of true minds, but to lay stress on the fact that Beaumont and Fletcher's gifts were complementary would be to postulate deficiencies which did not exist. Independently considered, both were dramatists of more than common capability, and Fletcher gave colour after Beaumont's death to the ever-glowing Beaumont-and-Fletcher tradition by the copiousness and variety of his work. One of Fletcher's latest plays, *Rule a Wife and Have a Wife*, held the stage to within living memory.

Let me attempt to realise the situation. So much emphasis has been laid on the fact that Beaumont and Fletcher were gentlemen authors, that an impression has sprung up that they wrote merely for pleasure, oblivious of all economic considerations. This is erroneous. Theirs was a position of genteel poverty, and they extricated themselves from its embarrassments by uniting forces and writing plays. Whatever means they had were insufficient for their subsistence. No doubt they had immense relish for their work; no good work has ever been done without it. But assuredly there was some other urge, beyond the itch of writing, which kept Fletcher's nose to the grindstone year in and year out for a considerable period after Beaumont's retirement. The main question is, how long could the artistic-minded professional dramatist have afforded to linger over the composition of a play? We know that, owing to his slow, laborious method of working, Jonson was never able to make a living with his pen and underwent humiliation in having intermittently to depend on the bounty of his noble friends. But there is no reason for believing that Beaumont and Fletcher lacked the normal facility of their times. Their average output during their period of collaboration cannot be scientifically determined, but, between what they wrote separately and what they wrote in conjunction, it must have exceeded two plays a year. This approximation does not indicate either hasty or laborious work. Later on, when writing alone, Fletcher steadily turned out his three plays a year.

Impressions not very complimentary to Beaumont were once rife regarding his relationship with his distinguished ally. Aubrey, in his usual gossiping irresponsible way, averred that "Master Beaumont's main business was to correct the overflowings of Mr. Fletcher's wit," but I make bold to say that, had Beaumont's share of the partnership involved no more serious labour, his name would never have stood side by side with Fletcher's on a title-page. In Elizabethan–Stuart days, tutors and revisers were not given collaborative rank. Yet I shall doubtless be told that Aubrey had authority for his statement. I can fancy someone pointing out in protest that in some lines by William Cartwright, "Upon the report of the printing of the Dramaticall Poems of Master John Fletcher," prefixed to the Beaumont and Fletcher folio of 1647, we have the necessary confirmation:

> Though when all Fletcher writ, and the entire
> Man was indulged unto that sacred fire,
> His thoughts, and his thoughts dresse, appeared both such,
> That 'twas his happy fault to do too much;
> Who therefore wisely did submit each birth
> To knowing Beaumont e'er it did come forth,

Working againe, untill he said 'twas fit,
And made him the sobriety of his wit;
Though thus he call'd his judge into his fame,
And for that aid allow'd him halfe the name,
'Tis knowne, that sometimes he did stand alone,
That both the Spunge and Pencill were his owne;
That himself judged himselfe, could singly do,
And was at last Beaumont and Fletcher too.

This is a very confident statement to be made by a man who was a baby in arms when Francis Beaumont died. Let those swallow it who can; I am no believer in its truth. Double writing of this order is a slow and tedious business, and, so far from our having evidence of its pursuit by Fletcher when associated with Beaumont, what evidence exists is to the contrary. Burre's dedicatory epistle to Keysar, prefixed to the unassigned first quarto of *The Knight of the Burning Pestle*, reveals that the play was written in the short space of eight days. Opinions differ as to whether it was the work of both authors or of Beaumont alone, but, let the truth on that point be what it may, the speed with which the play was written shows that it was the outcome of a hasty commission, and that leisurely revision, if practised by the two, was not always possible. If criticism constituted the entire stock in trade brought by Beaumont to the partnership, and Fletcher was so convinced of its efficacy as to give him the open honours of collaboration purely on that score, the marvel is that Fletcher ever gained self-confidence enough to write unaided. As a matter of fact, it has been argued by Professor Joseph Quincy Adams that after Beaumont's secession he did not readily gain self-confidence, and that that was the secret of his mysterious association with Shakespeare. On that point I shall have something to say later, but meanwhile it is essential to say that some months before December,

1614, or within a twelvemonth of his partner's retirement, Fletcher had written both *Valentinian* and *Bonduca*. There may have been more than one reason for his occasional post-Beaumont collaborations, but it hardly seems likely that lack of self-confidence operated among them. His association with two other dramatists in the writing of a play points, not to any need of a curber of his exuberance, but to a commission demanding great rapidity of execution. In 1654 there was entered on the Stationers' Register, as the work of Fletcher, Field, and Massinger (from what we know, a most likely combination), a play belonging to the period of 1617 or thereabouts, entitled, *The Jeweller of Amsterdam, or The Hague*. So, too, because of its intense, sensational topicality, *The Tragedy of Sir John van Olden Barnavelt*, which was produced a bare two months after the death of its eponymous hero, cannot be considered anything better than a brilliant piece of theatrical journalism. Fletcher and Massinger were undoubtedly part-authors of this play, but one finds traces of a third hand, possibly Field's. So far, however, from any revising hand being detectable in the text, it bristles with inconsistencies. Fletcher was a courtier, a believer in the divine right of kings; Massinger, on the other hand, was, as Coleridge styled him, "a decided Whig," a hater of oppression and fearlessly independent. The result is that there are two Barnavelts in the play, the one a hero and the other a villain. To Massinger he was a lion, to Fletcher a fox. Hybrids of this order were only too often produced by old-time collaboration.

It is impossible to reconcile the Cartwright–Aubrey tradition with the findings of latterday investigators. Sir Edmund Chambers [1] tells us, of *A King and No King*, that critics are practically unanimous in dividing the

---

[1] *The Elizabethan Stage*, iii, 225.

play thus: to Beaumont, all of Acts I, II, and III, Act IV, scene 4, and Act V, scenes 2 and 4; to Fletcher, Act IV, scenes 1, 2, and 3, and Act V, scenes 1 and 3. One does not require to pin one's faith to the traditionalists to be moved here to remonstrance. No sort of system is here indicated. Surely, while Beaumont was completing three acts, Fletcher, the facile, could have written two. We must bear in mind that the play was not published for eight years, and that there is a possibility of subsequent revision — even by a third hand.

Though, in the last analysis, there is not a sufficiency of scientific evidence to prove conclusively that Beaumont and Fletcher, as collaborators, followed a rigorous system of leisurely progression, it would probably be safe to assume that tradition had some basis for promulgating the story that Beaumont sat in judgement on Fletcher's work (besides doing — what it ignored — his own share), and that the haste of normal collaboration was not characteristic of theirs.[1]

Of a less meticulous order, seemingly, were the collaborative methods of Gervase Markham and Lewis Machin, whose Whitefriars comedy, *The Dumb Knight*, was entered on the Stationers' Register in October, 1608, and doubtless performed some months earlier. The clumsy handling of a double plot in this play goes to

[1] How little we really know of Beaumont and Fletcher's methods is shown by the remarkable diversity of opinion which exists on the subject. Cf. Professor E. N. S. Thompson on "Elizabethan Dramatic Collaboration," in *Englische Studien*, xl, 30; Miss O. L. Hatcher on "Fletcher's Habits of Dramatic Collaboration," in *Anglia*, xxxiii, 219; and Louis Wann on "The Collaboration of Beaumont, Fletcher and Massinger," in *Shakespeare Studies by Members of the Department of English of the University of Wisconsin* (Madison, 1916), p. 147. Professor Thompson concludes that the division was one of structure, *i. e.*, by acts and scenes; Miss Hatcher fails to find sufficient data to warrant any decision; and Mr. Wann, basing on unstable premises, plumps for allocation by subject-matter.

demonstrate the truth of my contention that collaboration on a complex theme was incompatible with rapid work. In such conditions it could only be done badly. In an interesting article on *Every Woman in her Humour* and *The Dumb Knight*, contributed some years ago to *Modern Philology*,[1] Professor Joseph clearly shows that *The Dumb Knight* was not the product of two men working together in the traditional Beaumont and Fletcher way, since internal evidence of mutual criticism is sadly to seek. Markham evidently undertook the serious main plot and Machin the comic underplot, the former confining himself to blank verse and the latter mostly to prose. Whatever their particular method, its defects are glaring. The two plots are separate and complete units dealing each with virtually an independent set of characters, since where the characters are common to both they act so inconsistently as to lose their homogeneity. All sorts of discrepancies arise through inadequate and inartistic dovetailing, and between the two plots there is a grave conflict of time.

I have dwelt so much on urgency as the inspiring cause of the great bulk of early collaborated work that I can conceive of some doubting Thomas becoming so far exasperated by the iteration as to ask bluntly, if collaborated work was mostly rapid work, how came it that Ben Jonson, a notoriously slow writer as one-man author in his meridian, was now and again engaged to do collaborative work? My answer to that would be that Jonson never really suffered from a constipated mind, that his slowness was matter of principle, not of temperament. It was due to his growing sense of self-importance. Once he came into his own he preferred carving from the solid, enduring marble, though cares of pence compelled him

[1] Vol. x, p. 413.

on occasion to model rapidly in clay. That he was not reckoned an incorrigibly slow worker in his earlier day is shown by the fact that he was entrusted with quick commissions. Recall the entry in Henslowe's Diary:

> Lent unto Bengemen Johnsone, the 3 of desember, 1597, upon a booke which he was to writte for us before crymas next after the date hereof, which he showed the plotte unto the company: I saye, lent in redy mony unto hime the some of xxˢ.

In all, so far as our knowledge goes, Jonson entered into collaboration six times. In 1598, at a time when Francis Meres spoke of him as one of the leading dramatic poets, he united with Henry Porter and Henry Chettle in writing the lost *Hot Anger Soon Cold* for the Admiral's Men. For them also, in 1599, he collaborated on two other lost plays, *Page of Plymouth*, written in association with Dekker, and *Robert II*, otherwise *The Scot's Tragedy*, of which the other authors were Chettle, Dekker, and Marston. Afterwards, though thirty years of activity remained to him, he entered into collaboration only three times, once on *Sejanus his Fall*, once on *Eastward Ho*, and once on *The Widow*. The circumstances under which a second hand came to be associated with *Sejanus* seem to me clear, though they have never been fully grasped. When the play was issued in quarto, it had an "Epistle to the Readers," in which Jonson made the following notification:

> I would inform you, that this Booke, in all numbers, is not the same with that which was acted on the publike Stage, wherein a second pen had good share; in place of which I had rather chosen, to put weaker (and no doubt less pleasing) of mine own, then to defraud so happy a *Genius* of his right, by my lothed usurpation.

To my mind, much as we are apt to look upon Jonson as candour personified, he was not here wholly sincere. In avoiding the usual practice of publishing collaborated work as collaborated work, he had done the very thing he pretended to steer clear of, and defrauded the happy genius of his right. It is difficult to see why the play was not published, if published at all, in its original form. One cannot understand this attitude if Jonson had entered willingly into collaboration in the beginning, and one is forced to conclude that at some later stage collaboration had been forced upon him. That could have come about in only one way. If we assume that Jonson had contracted to deliver a new tragedy to the King's Men by a certain date, and that, owing to his slowness of work, the time had expired before the play was much more than half finished, then it can be readily comprehended that the players might have insisted upon the calling in of another poet to help complete the work. Possibly the unknown collaborator wrote the last act or the last two acts. Jonson's mortification over this insistence would have been renewed and intensified by the failure of the play, and, if it should have chanced that the reflections which evoked "the people's beastly rage" were the work of the other man, what more natural than that he should carry out his original intention and strive to redeem himself from obloquy by finishing the play in his own way? To-day a consensus of scholarly opinion elects to see in Chapman the happy genius whose work Jonson so scurvily flouted, but on this score I find myself in a minority of one. To me it hardly seems likely that a collaborator on a play would have addressed a long, commendatory poem to his coadjutor, designed for publication, and acknowledging this coadjutor's sole authorship. Yet such a poem, the work of Chapman, is prefixed to the Jonsonian quarto. One can understand Jonson's unwonted insincerity only by assuming that the happy genius was some person of authority whom he deemed it impolitic to offend. The only person to whom that could possibly apply was William Shakespeare.

Whether enforced or voluntary, Jonson's seventeenth-century collaboration brought him little but vexation. In 1605, the audacious personalities of *Eastward Ho* landed him and Chapman in jail, whither Marston, who completed the offending triad, would have accompanied them, had he not made good his escape. And just here let me say that I find it both anomalous and puzzling that the editors of the new *Ben Jonson* should have devoted considerable space in their second volume to a discussion of *Eastward Ho* and at the same time wholly ignored *The Widow*. Even if they believe the attribution to Jonson of a part-authorship of *The Widow* to be unfounded, they should have at least said so. For such belief I fail to see any solid grounds. Seemingly a Blackfriars play of *circa* 1607, *The Widow* was published in quarto in 1652, as by Jonson, Fletcher, and Middleton, and from "the original copy." Whether or not from the original, the play was certainly printed from a prompt-book, but the attribution has to be taken on trust. In looking, however, for traces of Jonson in collaborated plays, we must bear in mind that his work on these plays was essentially of a sketchier order, and therefore unlikely to bear many of the hall-marks of his slowly composed and carefully finished single-handed work. To ignore this is not to find Jonson at all, even where Jonson lurks. That is precisely what has happened in the case of *Eastward Ho*. One's belief in the accuracy of scholarly analyses of collaborated plays falls below zero when one becomes fully conversant with the diversity of opinion which exists regarding the share taken by each particular author in the writing of this comedy. That the multitude of counsellors is just as apt to bring confusion as wisdom will become apparent to those who look at Chambers's summary of the findings on this subject,[1] and compare it with the pronouncement of the editors of the new *Ben Jonson*.[2] After making feeble attempt to resolve the play, Herford and Simpson arrive at a conclusion which, if it has any potency, practically shows the worthlessness of all such dissections.

In other words, *Eastward Ho* must be regarded as one of the most remarkable among the known examples of successful collaboration. For not merely is the fact of collaboration to an extraordinary degree successfully concealed, but the alliance appears to have elicited a result superior in some features to the independent work, single-handed, of any of the three.

The possibility of revision before publication is not here taken into account. Jonson's single-handed work apart, this was not the practice, but in this instance offending passages had to be excised and the gaps neatly closed. Revision by an expert unifying hand would tend to the smoothing out of asperities. Were it not for this possibility, one should be disposed to take Herford and Simpson's laudation of the play as exaggerated. We are told that

notwithstanding the multiple authorship, the play presents an appearance of singular wholeness and unity. It is in fact one of the best made of Elizabethan comedies. Its clear-cut strength and simplicity of structure was rarely, if ever, approached by any of the three authors elsewhere. Of the disparities of technique so rarely absent from work by several hands in common, it has less than many a piece entirely shaped by one; and the attempt to distribute the play among the three reported authors has not hitherto advanced beyond the plausible assignment to one or other of them here and there, of a scene, a passage of dialogue, or a speech.[3]

---

[1] *The Elizabethan Stage*, iii, 255, 256.

[2] Herford and Simpson, *Ben Jonson*, ii, 29-46.

[3] The scene containing the line, "A boat . . . a boat . . . a full hundred marks for a boat," was undoubtedly written by Marston, since he was ob-

So far as they indicate any sort of collaborative system, all the analysts of the play agree that there was a scene-by-scene, not act-by-act, division of labour, but Herford and Simpson, taking a leaf out of Bullen's book, go farther, and on two occasions find traces of the hands of two writers in the same scene. They point to a juncture in Act III, scene 2, "where," we are told, "there is an abrupt change from compact and matter of fact prose to expansive verse," and they think that there Chapman suddenly took up the work. This appears to me more the result of revision than of collaboration. In collaboration there was only one possible way in which it could have been done, and I very much doubt if that way were ever taken. The work would have had to be continuous, done in the one place and in shifts. It is difficult to conceive of the exigency which would have demanded such an expedient.

As historical investigator I have made some blunders in my time, and I may be blundering again; but nothing has been able to uproot from my mind the deep-seated conviction that evidence of two or more hands in the one

sessed by the famous cry in *Richard III*, and had already parodied it in *The Scourge of Villainy*, *What You Will*, and *The Fawne*.

Bullen (Marston's *Works*, vol. I, p. xli) finds in the opening scene unmistakable traces of Marston, but thinks that Jonson's hand is to be detected in the same scene. This could be accounted for only on the supposition that Jonson had revised the play for publication. Bullen adds:

"Jonson and Marston worked on the first scene together; and it seems to me that throughout the first two acts we have the mixed work of these two writers. In the second scene of the third act, as Mr. Swinburne notices, Chapman's hand is clearly seen in the quaint allusion to 'The ship of famous Draco.' Quicksilver's moralising in IV. I, after he has scrambled ashore at Wapping on the night of the drunken shipwreck, is again in Chapman's manner; but his elaborate devices for blanching copper and sweating angels (later in the same scene) must, without the shadow of a doubt, be ascribed to the invention of the author of *The Alchemist*."

scene is not evidence of collaboration, but proof of later revision. Even a dramatist's "ghost" is not likely to have been allowed to finish or in any way tamper with a particular scene on which he was engaged. Scholars have only to become convinced of the truth of this to have a useful new test at their command. In the generality of cases, it will enable them to determine whether a belatedly published unique text is in its original state or has suffered sophistication. Where sophistication has taken place, it is an aid towards the discovery of how many times the play has been revised. But what we have first to bear in mind is that the names of the authors on the title-page are, in accord with custom, the names of the original authors, and not the names of the author and his subsequent revisers — this, of course, apart from the possibility that the attributions may be wholly or partly false or of an incomplete accuracy. To ignore this premiss is to fall grievously into error. For example, that is why there has been little but blundering over *The Old Law, or A New Way to Please Ye*, a play which, when printed in 1656, was assigned to Massinger, Middleton, and Will Rowley. Fleay set the ball a-rolling by dating it from 1599, when Massinger and Rowley were boys. Misled no doubt by Fleay's fumbling, Edgar Cort Morris, in the course of his minute dissection of the play,[1] maintains that it was not collaborated work, that Middleton was the original author, and that it was subsequently twice revised, once by Rowley and once by Massinger. But, apart from the fact that the published attribution admits of no such gloss, internal evidence effectually counters this theory. The play discusses an

[1] Fleay, *Biographical Chronicle of the English Drama*, ii, 100, 101; Morris on "The Date and Composition of *The Old Law*," in *Publications of the Modern Language Association*, xvii, 1–70.

extravagant postulate from three different standpoints, each standpoint being illustrated by a separate set of characters; and we may agree with Dr. C. W. Stork [1] that "roughly these three treatments may represent respectively Massinger, Middleton and Rowley." The logical deduction is that there was a scene-by-scene division of labour.

This leads me by natural transition to a necessarily brief consideration of Shakespeare as collaborator, since reasoning equally fallacious with that which has been applied by Morris to *The Old Law* has been indulged in in Shakespeare's case. In his *Sidelights on the Elizabethan Drama* Mr. H. Dugdale Sykes, in discussing *Timon of Athens*, argues that Shakespeare was nothing more than reviser of an old play written by Middleton and Day. If that were so, it is surprising that *Timon* should have been included in the Folio and *Pericles* not, apart from the fact that it was wholly unprecedented to give a mere reviser any of the honours — and least of all the sole honour — of authorship. To my mind, Mr. Sykes completely gives his case away when, in analysing the play, he finds on three occasions in as many scenes distinct traces of three several hands. From his standpoint and from mine this is an impossibility. The normal conditions of collaboration would have precluded the delay indicated in two authors working on the one scene or revising each other's work. [2] To conceive that Shakespeare revised *Timon* would be to write him down the clumsiest of play-patchers, for the play has many loose ends. But assuredly he did *not* revise *Timon*. All that Mr. Sykes

---

[1] *William Rowley*, pp. 48, 49.

[2] Cf. Ernest Rhys's introduction in the Mermaid edition of Dekker, pp. xli, xlii, where a similar statement is made regarding *The Witch of Edmonton*. This play, originally acted in 1621, was not published until 1658, and was

has proved, so far as he has proved anything, is that the play was twice revised (and that uncouthly), leaving us to speculate whether Day and Middleton were the revisers. It is as well to bear in mind in this connexion that revivals, usually with revisal, took place about every five years. If Shakespeare wrote *Timon*, say, in 1607, it would have been quite in keeping for Middleton to have tinkered the play in or about 1612, and Day again in 1617, or some years before its first publication. Belonging to the category of the shorter Shakespearean plays, *Timon*, it is to be noted, is exactly of the same length as *Macbeth* and *The Tempest*, both of which bear indications of having been revised by an alien hand.

Credit, however, must be given where credit is due. If Mr. Sykes misses the target in discussing *Timon*, he scores a bull's-eye in his investigation of *Pericles*.[1] He is surely right in maintaining that the play was a dramatisation of the novel, not the novel a transliteration of the play. The one was common practice, the other unprecedented. A *Pericles*, whether the novel or the play, was entered on the Stationers' Register on May 20, 1608, but the play itself was not published until 1609, when Henry Gosson, in issuing the first quarto, attributed it to William Shakespeare, as it had "been divers and sundry times acted by his Majesty's Servants at the Globe on the Bankside." In the matter of the genesis of the piece there is parallelism, I think, between it and *Sejanus*. The theory would be that the vogue of the

most likely revised in the interim, since it presents a prologue and epilogue for its revival *circa* 1636–38. So, too, E. F. Pierce (*The Collaboration of Webster and Dekker*, 1909, p. 159), in dealing with *Sir Thomas Wyatt*, argues that some of the scenes written by Dekker were retouched by Webster, and thinks that all of them may have been. Such statements imply dubiety and only serve to reflect on the judgement of their utterers.

[1] Sykes, *Sidelights on Shakespeare*, p. 143.

novel suggested its dramatisation to the King's Men, and that Wilkins, its author, was given the commission. But he progressed so slowly and unsatisfactorily that when he had completed two acts the players took the thing out of his hands, paying him for his work as far as it had gone, and asked Shakespeare and Rowley to finish it. This hypothesis receives some bolstering from the fact that three distinct styles are traceable in the play, but only two of them in the last three acts. Shakespeare, it is generally believed, confined himself to the treatment of the Marina story in its cleaner aspects, leaving the offensive scenes in the fourth act to Rowley's uncompromising hand. The two remained faithful to Wilkins's scenario, rounding off the play in the vein in which it was begun, the stodgy, antiquated, lumbering vein of *The Travailes of the Three English Brothers*, a recent Red Bull play, in the writing of which Wilkins had been concerned. Were it not for the fact that the problem is rendered complicated by the corruptness of the text, one would be disposed to ask with some confidence for full acceptance of this theory. It may be that the corruption was due to an attempt to correct Wilkins's botching. After reviewing all the probabilities, one at last begins to understand why the play was omitted from the Folio. Not only was it not Shakespeare's originally, but it had little of Shakespeare in it.

As to the circumstances of Shakespeare's brief association with Fletcher, they are so mysterious that one despairs of ever being able to read the riddle. Some consideration, however, must be given to Professor Adams's interesting speculations on the subject. Writing in his *Life of William Shakespeare*,[1] he says:

[1] Page 432.

Accordingly, when Beaumont withdrew from the stage in 1612-3, Fletcher stood in need of some experienced hand to guide his pen; and although the Globe Company soon engaged Phillip Massinger to take Beaumont's place, we find Shakespeare temporarily setting himself to the task. In the year 1613 he helped Fletcher with *Henry VIII*, probably with *The Two Noble Kinsmen*, and possibly, though we cannot be sure, with the non-existent *Cardenio*.

There is no hint here as to the circumstances of their actual collaboration, a subject into which no one has made inquiry; but it seems not improbable that Fletcher, having become habituated to close communion with a coadjutor, had not yet gained sufficient self-confidence to work alone, and that, under the persuasions of the King's Men, Shakespeare had obligingly stepped into the gap. But this would mean that the collaboration between the two was not of the normal order, not undertaken under conditions of pressing haste, for Shakespeare had retired to Stratford and Fletcher would have had to repair thither. In the circumstances, the alliance was fated to be brief; although still emitting flashes of his old compelling genius, Shakespeare was suffering from exhaustion and lacked his pristine staying power.

Meagre as is the evidence upon the point, we are forced to ask ourselves, why was *Henry VIII* selected for publication in the First Folio, and *The Two Noble Kinsmen* and *Cardenio* thrown aside? In searching for an answer, the first thing to be noted is that the three plays were all produced, and doubtless all written, within a period of twelve months. That of itself would go to establish Fletcher's extended sojourn in Stratford. *Cardenio* belongs to the early spring of 1613, *Henry VIII* to the ensuing June, and *Cardenio* to the succeeding winter. Now, there are reasonable grounds for the belief that Fletcher collaborated for a time with Shakespeare, but proof with regard to any particular play is lacking. That

he was part-author of the original text of *Henry VIII*
might be opposed on the plea that the Folio does not give
the original text.[1] *Cardenio*, though never published, was
entered on the Stationers' Register by Humphrey Moseley in 1653 as by "Mr. Fletcher and Shakespeare," some
slight evidence of authorship. *The Two Noble Kinsmen*
was registered on April 8, 1634, as the work of John
Fletcher and William Shakespeare, and attributed to the
same authors on its publication from a late prompt-copy [2]
in the same year. If these two plays were quite as much
Fletcher's as Shakespeare's, if Fletcher was responsible
in both cases for about half the work, one can understand
why they were omitted from the Folio. But that omission
would have been wholly inconsistent had Fletcher collaborated with Shakespeare on *Henry VIII*. Perhaps,
however, it would be idle to look for consistency from
Heminge and Condell. It is to be noted that, much as
they disagree in other respects, Spedding, Fleay, Boyle,
Oliphant—in fact, all the analysts of *Henry VIII*—unite
in the belief not only that two hands are to be detected
throughout, but that traces of two hands are to be found
more than once in the one scene. This admits of but
one conclusion: either that the play was written by two
authors in very close communion, or that it was originally
the work of a single author and afterwards drastically
revised. As I am little of a believer in dual work on the
one scene, I am inclined to justify *Henry VIII*'s inclusion
in the Folio on the ground that Shakespeare was its sole
original author. On the other hand, it is quite possible
that Fletcher was part-author, and that subsequently, say,

[1] Cf. my article, "A New Shakespearean Test," in *The Criterion* for October, 1923, pp. 88–94.
[2] Cf. article on "New Light on *The Two Noble Kinsmen*," in the *Times
Literary Supplement* for July 14, 1921.

after Shakespeare's death, he made revision of the play. This would best account for the traces of two hands in the same scenes. It seems unlikely that, after they had collaborated on *Cardenio*, Shakespeare would have proceeded to write *Henry VIII* single-handed, and then associated himself again with Fletcher in the composition of *The Two Noble Kinsmen*. Whatever the solution, I feel assured that, as we have it, the text of *Henry VIII* is not the original text of the play.

With the rise of the dilettante dramatist in Caroline times, play writing ceased to be wholly a trade, and collaboration dwindled. Never again was it to be resorted to with anything like the old frequency, though once in a while in Restoration days the old conditions ruled. Under the compulsions of haste, Dryden united with Lee in writing *Oedipus*, himself providing the first and third acts, besides drafting the scenario. This working against time was indeed the secret of the divers defects to be found in the seventeenth-century collaborated drama. In this connexion it is curious to note that it was a necessity of this kind which operated on the only occasion on which Molière joined forces with other writers. In order to keep faith with the King, who had commanded him to write a *tragédie-ballet* by a certain date, he was compelled, in undertaking *Psyché*, to call in old Pierre Corneille to help him out with the tragic part, and Quinault to supply the lyrics.

XVI

EARLY PROMPT–BOOKS AND WHAT THEY REVEAL

IT is remarkable that, although Elizabethan investigators have been giving their attention for some time past to questions of early stage routine, the important subject of prompting and prompt-book making has been almost wholly neglected. Nobody has detailed for us the distinguishing characteristics of a primitive prompt-book, and scholarship is in the dark concerning the degree of progress made in scientific prompt-book marking in the first half of the seventeenth century. Yet, if we desire fully to grasp the theatrical conditions of the times, to savour the playhouse aroma of the Shakespearean hour, this knowledge is essential. Nor is it in one direction alone that progress has been stayed by lack of careful investigation of this subject. So long as the desiderata indicated remain unknown, just so long will all examination of early playhouse manuscripts be superficial. Half their message to us will continue unconveyed. No doubt the difficulties of the quest are serious, but it is time that a beginning should be made. If, in this study, I fail to fill the gap, it will not be through lack of labour. To change the metaphor, I can at least claim that after a long and toilsome journey over rough roads I have reached the half-way house; and my hope is that, inspired by my experiences, younger and stronger legs may trudge on to the goal.

Since one cannot estimate the rudimentary without full knowledge of the complete, it is requisite that we should begin our inquiry by determining what were the principles of the perfected prompt-book, as practised, say, early in the nineteenth century. Apart from the preliminary work of play-book marking and the necessity for alertness during the performance so as to give the player the word when his memory lapsed, the prompter of that period had manifold duties. On the wall by his stand were a number of bell-pulls for the warning of divers people in divers places, and round his neck hung a boatswain's whistle wherewith, when the occasion demanded, he gave the scene-shifters their cue. It was his preliminary duty to ring in the fiddlers and ring them out again before giving the signal for the raising of the curtain; and his subsequent duty, to warn all the players a stated time before they were required, to raise and lower the lights, to see that all the properties required during the action were brought on, to attend to all incidental noises, such as those of thunder, the pattering of rain, or the breaking of glass, to ring to the under-stage trapmen when the ghost had to be sent up, and to make sure that the scenery was shifted and the curtain lowered at the proper time. All these acts had marginal indications in the prompt-book. The duration of the actor's warning varied. At Covent Garden he was called three "lengths" (or 120 lines) ahead, equivalent to about five minutes, but elsewhere only half that time was allowed.[1] Each advance warning was numbered in the prompt-book separately, act by act, and a corresponding list of numbers for each act, with key-names, was given to the call-boy. In some theatres these key-names were the names of the players, in others, the names of the characters they sustained; and the call-boy, on being given a number,

---

[1] George Vandenhoff, *An Actor's Note-Book, or the Green Room and Stage*, chap. 4.

looked at his list, tripped off to the green-room, or maybe to a dressing-room, and called out the name of the player or of his character. There was a certain advantage in calling by the character rather than by the actor, because a book so marked remained available for future use, at a time when the cast was, in whole or in part, changed.

Circumstances conspired to render the Elizabethan prompter's duties much less complex. His was not a peep-show stage, and consequently he had no front curtain to raise or lower, no scenery to shift, no centrally controlled system of lighting to attend to. Added to this, there was in vogue in his day a supplement to the prompt-book, known as "the plot," which materially lightened his labours. The purpose of this device was for long misconceived by scholars,[1] and is not yet fully understood. Its use was ultimately superseded by the maturer prompt-book, but it is difficult to say when. It is to be doubted whether there is any significance in the fact that none of the seven plots that have come down to us can be dated later than the first lustrum of the seventeenth century.[2] Only accident leads to the preservation of ephemeralities of the kind. Personally, I am of the belief that a plot was provided for every theatre play until the advent of the picture-stage. Arranged in two columns, it was legibly written on paper mounted on cardboard, and was provided with a hole at the top for hanging for inspection on a nail in the tiring-house. Though varying somewhat in detail, some having mar-

[1] For the old opinion, only just controverted, see Collier, *History of English Dramatic Poetry* (1831), iii, 398.

[2] Cf. Greg, *Henslowe Papers*, p. 127; Chambers, *The Elizabethan Stage*, iv, 404. For facsimile reproductions, see Halliwell-Phillipps, *The Theatre Plots of Three Old English Dramas* (1860) and *The Shakespeare Homage Book*, p. 208.

ginal or running instructions for music, thunder, and properties, and some being devoid of these particulars, all the extant plots have a common factor, a factor indicating their main utility. This I may call the action-sequence. The entrance of the characters, whether in groups or singly, accompanied in most cases by the names or nicknames of the players, is noted, and a careful division into scenes (though not always into acts) observed.

The deduction to be made, and properly made, from the plots is that, in Elizabethan and Jacobean times, it was not the business of the prompter to summon the players, although, as I shall have occasion to point out, it was deemed necessary now and then for him to warn one or two of the hard-working minor players. In this we have an explanation of the striking sparsity of actors' calls in the early prompt-books. What, however, I find it difficult to determine is, whether the player was individually responsible for his timely appearance on the stage and had to keep consulting the plot, or whether the plot was solely for the use of some functionary — say, the stage keeper [1] (the name is suggestive), whose business it was to warn the players and assemble the properties. From the fact that the Elizabethan players had no common rallying place, the institution of the green-room dating from the Restoration, it may be assumed that they were accustomed to lurk about the passages of the tiring-house when absent from the stage. Accordingly, they might have been expected to keep an eye on the plot, to be ready for their next entry. But, while giving

[1] For whom see the induction to *Bartholomew Fair*. Occasionally one finds the term improperly applied, mostly to the tiremen, who were the stage keeper's underlings. The stage keeper of *The Return from Parnassus* (Part I, induction) should rather have been called the prompter or bookholder.

expression to the probability, I have no belief in it. The practice would have led to grave confusion: it would not always have been an easy matter for the player to find his place in the plot. Hence, one is safe perhaps in concluding that the plot was designed for the use of one man, a man who stuck by it throughout and is most likely to be identified with the stage keeper. That it was in part, at least, intended for the stage keeper's service is shown by the fact that the majority of the extant plots have marginal instructions for music, thunder, and properties. But just here we have to pause and ask ourselves, what were the stage keeper's precise duties with regard to these marginal instructions? When we note warnings for music, noises, and properties, not in contemporary prompt-books — of which there are practically none — but in the prompt-books of a score of years later, the suspicion is apt to arise that the notifications in the plot signified "Get ready," not "See the thing done." It must always be borne in mind that in pre-Caroline days there were absolutely no runs, that it was not even usual to give two consecutive performances of any play, no matter how popular, and that consequently neither player nor attendant had an opportunity to get thoroughly familiarised with the action. Constant vigilance on the part of the prompter and stage keeper was essential. Because of this ill acquaintance with the action of the play, I doubt if the marginal instructions in the plot would have sufficed, without secondary cue, to enable the stage keeper to have the trumpets sounded or the thunder rattled at the proper moment. Things would not have come off pat. Let me give you an illustration: it is from a Caroline play, but an earlier analogue could doubtless be found. In Brome's *The Antipodes*, IV, By-play says, amidst certain accompaniments:

A voyce that dothe informe me of the tydings
Spread through your kingdome of your great arrivall,
And of the generall joy your people bring
To celebrate the welcome of their king. — *Showts within* —
Hearke how the countrey shouts with joyfull votes
Rending the ayre with musick of their throats. — *Drums & Trum-
pets* —
Hearke how the souldier with his martiall noise
Threatens your foes, to fill your crowne with joyes, — *Haugh-
boyes* —
Hearke how the city, with loud harmony,
Chaunts a free welcome to your majesty. — *Soft musick* —
Hark how the Court prepares your grace to meet
With solemne musick, state and beauty sweet.

A rapid series of varied musical interruptions such as we have here could not be provided by a stage keeper working from a plot and unfamiliar with the action. But he could warn the musicians to be ready, and the prompter would do the rest. The question is, what pressure of circumstances could have brought about this divided duty? And why should it not have fallen to the lot of the early prompter to warn all the players, instead of merely a few, the practice followed in the English theatre from the dawn of the eighteenth century, if not before? Can it be that, owing to the constant change of bill, the players' memories proved so treacherous that the prompter was compelled to stand openly on the stage so as to be able constantly to give them the word? After all, the position was not wholly impossible; it had already been assumed on the University stage. There is in existence an anonymous account of Queen Elizabeth's visit to Cambridge in August, 1564, in which we are told, of the performance of Edward Haliwell's *Dido* on the second night, that

while Dido was a-handling, the Lo. Robert [Dudley] steward to the universitie, and mr. secretarie Cecil, chancellor, to signifye their good wille, and that things might be orderlye done, vouchsafed to hold both books on the scaffold themselves, and provided also that sylence might be kept with quietness.[1]

Dido was acted on a wide stage reaching across a large hall, and it would appear that two prompt-books were provided for the distinguished prompters, and held by them in full sight of the audience at the two extremities, the idea being that the forgetful player might not have far to travel for the word when his memory lapsed. But academic acting was a thing apart, and, even if it could be assumed that this was the method of prompting regularly employed at the Universities, we should not be justified in jumping to the conclusion that a similar openness was adopted in the public theatre. What was tolerated in the amateur was not always conceded to the professional. Relative to the sixteenth-century Guary miracle play, as performed in the open, Carew, writing in 1602 in his *Survey of Cornwall*, says:

The players conne not their parts without booke, but are prompted by one called the ordinary, who followeth at their back with the book in his hand, and telleth them softly what they must pronounce aloud.[2]

Town and country were not on a par, and all contemporary amateur acting was not of a similar incompetence, yet in play and masque the prompter was, to some extent, similarly kept busy. This is partly borne out by the reference in *Romeo and Juliet*, I, 4, 4:

We'll have no . . .
. . . without-book prologue faintly spoke
After the prompter, for our entrance.

---

[1] Boas, *University Drama in the Tudor Age*, p. 93. The reference to the books is here misinterpreted.

[2] Quoted from Ordish's *Early London Theatres*, pp. 21, 22, where an amusing connective anecdote is related.

The reference here is purely to masque-custom, and occasionally in the bye-masques given in old plays we find realistic presentment of this constant or intermittent method of prompting. Examples occur in Middleton's *No Wit, No Help Like a Woman's*, IV, 2, and Davenport's *The City Night Cap*, IV.

A faint clue to the position and the methods of the playhouse prompter is given in contemporary metaphorical uses of the term "cue." Bottom says, "When my cue comes, call me and I will answer," [1] and Othello indulges in the rebuke,

> Were it my cue to fight, I should have known it
> Without a prompter. [2]

More important still is it to find Caesar in *The Roman Actor* [3] employing the term literally, in saying, "When my cue's to enter, prompt me."

To-day, the prompter — where there is a prompter — does not give the actor his cue. He gives him preliminary warning and expects him to take up his own cue. The actor was supposed to know his cues even in Shakespeare's day, but the examples of the use of the term I have just cited imply that the prompter notified the player just when he was to enter, an impossible act unless the prompter stood well within the tiring-house. It would appear also that, in ordering the player to go on, he gave him the first few words of his speech. In *The Return from Parnassus*, Part I, the Stage Keeper prompts the Prologue in this way. So, too, in Shirley's *Hyde Park*, III, 2, we have the metaphorical gibe:

> Have you no prompter to insinuate
> The first word of your studied oration?
> He's out on 's part.

---

[1] *A Midsummer Night's Dream*, IV, 1.
[2] *Othello*, I, 2. [3] Act IV, scene 1.

Chapman vouchsafes us a momentary glimpse of old-time stage routine in *The Gentleman Usher*, a Blackfriars play of *circa* 1604. In Act II, scene 1, an interlude is given by the Duke in Margaret's honour, and Bassiolo, the usher, acts as a sort of stage-manager-*cum*-prompter. Before the Duke's arrival we find him calling out, "Sound, music," and afterwards, just as the performance is about to begin, he gives the command, "Sound concert; warn the Pedant to be ready." Here "warn" and "be ready" are orthodox prompt terms. Sarpego, the pedant, had been deputed to deliver the prologue.

Nothing in all this argues of the unseen presence of the prompter, but other evidence does. In the induction to *Cynthia's Revels*, while the three boys are squabbling as to which shall speak the prologue, a voice within — surely that of the prompter — is heard calling, "Why, children! are you not ashamed? Come in there." So, too, in a much later induction of Jonson's, the one prefixed to *The Staple of News* in 1625, the bookholder calls out from within, "Mend your lights, gentlemen. Master Prologue, begin." And then the tiremen enter to snuff the candles. In *The Maid in the Mill*, II, 2, a bye-masque is being acted, and the business of the scene is interrupted by Gerasto's abduction of Florimel. On hearing a cry for help from within, Bustapha says:

> they are out of their parts sure,
> It may be 't is the book-holder's fault; I'll go see.   *Exit.*

Again, in Brome's *The Antipodes*, III, 9, there is a bye-play in the course of which the prompter—as he is there called—gives the word from within. We have a still further, and perhaps better, clue to the prompter's position in the highly mysterious play of *Lady Alimony*, which belongs to a period much earlier than the date of its publication.[1] In Act I, scene 2, Timon, the foolish author, says to Siparius, the bookholder:

> Be sure that you hold not your book at too much distance. The actors, poor lapwings, are but penfeathered; and once out, out for ever. We had a time, indeed — and it was a golden time for a pregnant fancy — when the actor could embellish his author, and return a paean to his pen in every accent; but our great disaster at Cannae, than which none ever more tragical to our theatre, made a speedy dispatch of our rarest Rosciuses.

I think it may be taken that Siparius derived his name from *siparium*, the light inner curtain of the old Roman theatre, especially as a passage in the play indicates that one of his duties was to draw the traverses. Though this did not always hold good regarding the genus prompter, since we occasionally find players and attendants fulfilling the duty, it warrants us in assuming that the normal position of the prompter was behind the rear-stage curtains. It was the best position for giving the word, and the entering player, as he came on by one of the doors on either side, could be whispered to as he passed. And we know that the Elizabethan prompter did speak in a penetrative whisper. Overbury, in his character of "An Excellent Actor," first printed in 1615,[2] says that his voice is "not lower than the prompter, nor lowder than the Foile and Target." A little earlier, Cotgrave, in his French–English *Dictionarie*, had luminously equated the term prompter with the French *souffleur par derrière*, otherwise, the "whisperer from behind." One or two scholars have already given expression to their belief that the prompter occupied an unseen position, but, so far as I am aware, only Creizenach has suggested that he stood behind the hangings. In that position, one can quite well

[1] 1659.
[2] The authorship is doubtful. See Chambers, *The Elizabethan Stage*, iv, 257.

imagine him drawing the curtains at the beginning of a rear-stage scene. To whom, if not to him, is the instruction in the fourth act of Day's *Law Tricks*, "Discover Polymetes in his study"?

But if Creizenach scored heavily here, he shot wide of the mark in taking the terms "bookholder" and "bookkeeper" to be synonymous. They appertained to entirely different offices, though the two offices were sometimes held by the one individual. In all probability, the confusion of terms is due to a wrong use of the term bookkeeper in the anonymous early Jacobean comedy, *Every Woman in her Humour*, wherein it is said of a certain person that "he would swear like an elephant and stamp and stare (God bless us!), like a playhouse book-keeper, when the actors miss their entrance." The man who so expressed himself evidently had in his mind's eye some bookholder who was also bookkeeper to his company. But he misled Collier,[1] and Collier probably misled Creizenach. The best proof that the terms stood for two separate offices is to be found in the *Roscius Anglicanus* of John Downes. Downes tells us in his "Address to the Reader" that he was "bookkeeper and prompter" at the Duke's Theatre in 1662, and there or elsewhere fulfilled both offices until his book was published in 1706.[2] He also states that he wrote out all the parts, attended all the rehearsals, and prompted at the performances — all, I should say, in his capacity as prompter. It is noteworthy that Higgins, in his *Junius Nomenclator* published in 1588, defines "bookholder" as "he that telleth the players their part when they are out and have forgotten. The

---

[1] *History of English Dramatic Poetry* (1831), iii, 445.

[2] The version of *Wit Without Money* issued in quarto, without date, in 1707 has an unsigned facetious dedication "to Thomas Newman, Servant to her Majesty, one of the Gentlemen of the Great Room. Book Keeper and Prompter to her Majesty's Company of Comedians at the Haymarket."

prompter or Bookholder." The bookkeeper was a much more responsible individual, even if the bookholder was sometimes deemed trustworthy enough to hold the post. He was the librarian of the theatre, and had to answer for the safe custody of the manuscripts. Sir Henry Herbert, in his Revels Account Books, speaks twice in 1632–33 of one Knight [1] as bookkeeper of the King's Men, but as Knight may also have been their bookholder it is difficult to know in which capacity he waited on Herbert. This is unfortunate, as the Revels Account Books reveal that it was Knight's business to wait upon Herbert with plays for licensing, to pay the necessary fees on getting return of the books, and to see that all of Herbert's reformations were strictly observed.

I fear I have been a mighty long time in coming to Hecuba, but all these details are germane to our subject. Even now, before we can enter upon a chronological consideration of the few extant early prompt-books, it is necessary that we should first obtain a clear idea of the characteristics of an author's fair copy before the marking of the play for performance. The fair copy was usually written on folio sheets, and, to get the requisite broad margins, the practice was first to double the sheet lengthwise and then to double it again, the second doubling yielding the margins.[2] If we examine the facsimile of Munday's manuscript of *John a Kent and John a Cumber* issued by Farmer in the *Tudor Facsimile Texts* in 1912, we shall see how the experienced Elizabethan dramatist finally wrote out his play. As the left-hand margin was practically the prompter's prerogative, the author

---

[1] Adams, *Dramatic Records of Sir Henry Herbert*, pp. 21, 34.

[2] This practice was of long continuance. There are one or two manuscript Restoration plays in the Bodleian which still retain the creases made in the doubling.

trenched upon it as little as possible. Speech allocation
was, however, made there, and there also is to be found
an occasional addition to, or correction of, the text. On
the other hand, the margin on the right was wholly at the
service of the author, and it was there that he marked all
the exits of the characters and noted down the incidental
"business" of the scene. Munday's right-hand margins
present such sidelights on his text as "aside," "he offers
to depart," and "John a Cumber stamps about." To
grasp these facts is to read an otherwise perplexing riddle.
When the old playhouse copies were sent to the press,
it was customary for the compositor to ignore all the
marginalia, with the result that vital things were often
omitted. Hence the puzzlement of a long line of unknow-
ing commentators.

It is noteworthy that no early prompt-book has come
down to us in which the text proper is in more than one
hand. Where the play was the work of more than one
author, it was customary for the bookkeeper or bookholder to make a fair copy from the "foul sheets," which,
for some reason, were apparently preserved for some time
afterwards.[1]

Once the fair copy was made, whether by author or
bookkeeper, it was sent to the Revels Office for licensing,
and, save on the rare occasions when license was refused,
came back with indications in writing, or by cancellation,
of what objectionable passages of a political, profane, or
personal nature were to be omitted. Although it has been
somewhat foolishly argued to the contrary in connexion
with the manuscript of *Sir Thomas More*, plays were
never submitted for licensing in loose sheets. The sheets

---

[1] For the preservation of the foul sheets of *Bonduca*, see Greg's article on
"Prompt Copies, Private Transcripts, and the Playhouse Scrivener," in *The
Library* for September, 1925.

had to be sent in in stitched form, and, most probably, in a parchment cover. This practice was so invariable that all official licensing records of plays refer to the play as "the book."

When the book was returned by the Master of the Revels it bore his license on the last page.[1] For the reason that this license had always to be available for inspection by the authorities while the play held the boards, in case complaint was made of some particular offensiveness, the licensed copy was almost invariably converted into the prompt-copy. It was open, of course, to the players, if they desired to hasten production, to make a transcript on receipt of the author's fair copy, and from this to write out the parts and proceed with the rehearsals, pending receipt of the license. In such cases the transcript would become the prompt-copy, since prompt-copies were made just before or during rehearsal. This course, however, was rarely pursued, being fraught with serious danger. Little time would be saved in the event of the licenser making drastic alterations, as these would necessitate some revision of the text and of the parts, not to speak of further rehearsing. But, unless Malone blundered in transcribing Herbert's records, there is evidence to show that this hazardous course was occasionally taken in Caroline days. Shirley's *The Ball* was apparently licensed for the Queen's players on November 16, 1632, and two days later we find Herbert noting down that complaints had been made of personalities in the play.[2] But I am

---

[1] A. W. Pollard, *Shakespeare's Fight with the Pirates, and the Problem of the Transmission of his Text*, p. 59. For facsimiles of old licenses, see Adams, *Dramatic Records of Sir Henry Herbert*, p. 48, and his *Life of William Shakespeare*, p. 502.

[2] Adams, *Dramatic Records of Sir Henry Herbert*, pp. 19, 34. Note also that Massinger's *Cleander* was licensed for the King's Men on May 7, 1634, and that six days afterwards the Queen saw the play at the Blackfriars

inclined to believe that in earlier times such deviations from the normal were rare.

Knowledge of the methods pursued in early prompt-book making is derivable from two sources: first and foremost, from the few actual prompt-books of the pre-Restoration era that have come down to us, about a dozen in all; and secondly, from a good many printed plays of the period in which sundry prompt warnings have been accidentally preserved. Unfortunately, however, one cannot speak with any certainty regarding the system of prompting or prompt-book marking pursued in the late sixteenth century, since only two manuscript plays of the time bearing any indication of the prompter's hand, and that the meagrest, have survived. These are Munday's *John a Kent and John a Cumber*, and the much-discussed *Sir Thomas More*.

Generally speaking, where, in an old play, a considerable quantity of left-hand marginalia written in a hand differing from the hand in the body of the manuscript is to be found, it is safe to take the play to be a prompt-copy. But, unless we can assume that in the late sixteenth century the art of prompt-book marking was in a very rudimentary state, there is risk in applying the test to the two manuscripts mentioned. If I choose to enter upon a consideration of *Sir Thomas More* first, it is that I may hasten to recant the opinion I expressed in my article on the play in the *Times Literary Supplement* of July 1, 1920, to the effect that the manuscript as we have it, plus the missing sheets, was originally used as a prompt-copy. That was a woeful exaggeration. All that I deem

(Collier, *History of English Dramatic Poetry* [1831], ii, 64). This was pretty rapid work, if the parts had to be written out and the play rehearsed after licensing. Moreover, it is by no means certain that the Queen was present on the first day.

388 PRE-RESTORATION STAGE STUDIES

it safe to say now is that one sheet has an unmistakable prompt warning, and that on a few others there are possible warnings. Contrary to accepted opinion, my belief is that the play was certainly acted; and I pin my faith to that one unmistakable (though disputed) prompt warning. According to my view, *Sir Thomas More*, while it held the stage, must have been more than once revived, and the extant manuscript, which, it must be borne in mind, consists of a number of sheets of irregular sizes in various hands, represents discarded matter after the final revision had been made. It is contrary to the evidence to assume, as has been assumed in this connexion, that an Elizabethan play, whether produced or unproduced, could have as many as three or four revisers at the one time. Henslowe's Diary bearing witness, the practice in revision was to give the work to a single person. That the manuscript is made up of discarded sheets another circumstance goes to show. There is not a solitary act or scene division throughout. Very curious this, considering that many of the sheets are in Anthony Munday's handwriting and that Munday has been surmised by Dr. Greg and his coadjutors to be the original author of the play. Yet one finds on examining the MS. of *John a Kent and John a Cumber* and the printed plays attributed to Munday — particularly *Fedele and Fortunio, or The Two Italian Gentlemen* — that he was accustomed to make latinised act and scene divisions in his plays. Moreover, in *John a Kent and John a Cumber* Munday is careful to draw dividing lines between the speeches, whereas in the alleged Munday parts of the *More* manuscript, lines are lacking. The inference would be that Munday, so far from being the original author of the play, was not even a reviser: he was simply a transcriber, and mechanical at that.

What, then, is this unmistakable prompt warning upon which I have laid such stress? Well, on folio 23 of the *More* manuscript a portion of the text is pasted over at the bottom, and on this pasted part, in the left-hand margin, one notes, written longitudinally and followed by a line or two of text, the direction, "Enter a messenger to moore," opposite which, encircled, is the warning, "Mess. T. Goodal." The remarkable thing is that this is the only specific mention of a player in the manuscript. But to my mind it is no more remarkable than Dr. Greg's contention — first made in his useful redaction of the play published by the Malone Society — that the occurrence of Goodal's name merely indicates that the play had reached the rehearsal stage, that it had been cast, not that it had been acted. He firmly believed then, and believes still, that production never took place. What I want to know is, if this is a symptom of casting, how comes it that it is the only symptom? Why note down the representative of a trivial character, a mere messenger, and ignore the exponents of the leading dramatis personae? Such an argument will not serve. The jotting is undoubtedly a prompt warning, but it does not occur in a homogeneous manuscript, else, where other messengers and such minor fry come on, we should find similar memoranda.

Since the provision of a plot precluded the prompter from the necessity of calling the players, we are urged by this Goodal memorandum to ask ourselves why, right up to the Civil War, he should have frequently deemed it requisite to jot down the names of the players of messengers and servants while almost wholly ignoring the players of important parts. But before we can answer that, it is vital to observe that in the great majority of cases these notings of players' names occur, not marginally, but in the body of the book, and are usually additions to, or emendations of, the author's stage directions. Unlike marginal warnings, these internal reminders were not calculated readily to catch the eye: they could have been encountered only when the player or players mentioned were already, or at least should have been, on the stage. Let us look at a few examples. In *The Two Noble Kinsmen*, IV, 2, 74, we have, "Enter Messenger. (Curtis)," a reference to Curtis Greville; and in Act V, scene 3, the opening direction reads, "Enter Theseus, Hipolita, Emilia, Perithous: and some Attendants. (T. Tucke: Curtis)." Thomas Tuckfeild and Curtis Greville are the only players mentioned in the book, though it has a considerable number of prompt notes. So, too, in *Much Ado About Nothing*, where, in Act II, scene 2, the Quarto has "Enter Don Pedro, Leonato, Claudio and a musician," the Folio substitutes "Jack Wilson" for "a musician." Again in *The Chances*, III, 2, we get, "Enter Rowl. with wine." Here the bookholder evidently crossed out some such word as "servant" and wrote the contraction "Rowl." above it. Fleay, in his *Biographical Chronicle of the English Drama*, castigates Dyce for expanding "Rowl." into Rowland, maintaining that the actor referred to was Will Rowley, but Dyce was right, though the actor's full name was Rowland Dowle. We find his name cropping up again in two other plays. In *The Coxcomb*,[1] V, 3, is to be found the direction, "Enter Mother, Alexander Andrugio and Rowland"; and in *Love's Pilgrimage*,[2] II, 1, we have, "Enter two Servants, Row: Ashton."[3] All these players were of the inferior, or

---

[1] Note that the folio text gives the revised version of *circa* 1636, in November of which year the play was acted at court.

[2] Folio 1647, as re-licensed on September 16, 1635.

[3] Note also *King and No King* (Q. 2, 1625), V, 3, "Enter Servant, Will Adkinson"; *The Late Lancashire Witches* (Q. 1634), "Enter an invisible Spirit F. Adson with a brace of greyhounds."

"hireling," order: only once have I encountered the name of a sharer in a stage direction. In Fletcher's *The Wild Goose Chase*,[1] III, 1, there is a direction reading, "Enter Leverduce, Des Lugier, Mr. Illiard." This requires some elucidation. Only one character really came on, Des Lugier, of whom Hilliard Swanston was the representative. Swanston's speeches are here assigned, puzzlingly enough, to "Lev," for no better reason than that Lugier comes on disguised as Leverduce, a merchant occasionally spoken of throughout the play but never really seen. I do not pretend to know exactly what was the prompter's intention at this juncture, but it looks as if he was desirous of emphasising, as a personal reminder, that Swanston was to come on in disguise and speak out of character. Happily, no such puzzlement arises in connexion with the frequent naming of minor players in textual stage directions. It was customary for the smaller fry to double several trifling parts in the play, and, what with a lack of thorough familiarity with the action, due to inadequate rehearsal and the infrequency of the play's performance, there was a risk that the hireling might overlook one of his characters. In that case, to minimise a stage wait it was vital that the bookholder should at once be able to recall the name of the absentee, in order that he might forthwith be summoned.

To return to *Sir Thomas More*. What we have to determine in examining this mysterious manuscript is whether any of the left-hand marginalia other than the Goodal warning are prompter's notes, and, if so, what they signify. That the manuscript was not prepared as a prompt-book (though it has, as I have shown, at least one relic of such a book) is revealed by the fact that the first

[1] First printed in quarto in 1652, probably from a revised prompt-book of *circa* 1632.

five folios are practically devoid of prompt marginalia. Afterwards, marginalia which may or may not have been for the bookholder's use sporadically occur. Authors' directions for a grouped entry of characters are sometimes repeated exactly opposite, now in the left margin and now in the right, but no apparent rule is followed, and the warnings, if warnings, are never anticipative. A few of these marginal repetitions have lines drawn round them, as if for distinction. A direction for the playing of the waits is repeated exactly opposite to where it occurs. There are no separate warnings for properties or noises, but the properties borne by the characters are mentioned in the directions for entry: for example, "Enter Moore, with attendants with Purse and Mace," and again, "Ent. Gough and Catesbie with a paper." Of these, the first, encircled, occurs in the right margin, and the second, which is unenclosed, in the left. Not the sharpest bookholder could have kept an eye on both margins during the performance, and only the contents of the right-hand margin of the manuscript could have proved of any service to a bookholder of the time. Where the trumpet sounds for the bye-play to begin we get a stage direction, but no prompt warning. My conclusion is that if, in this heterogeneous manuscript, we have any leaves from a prompt-book, the sixteenth-century prompter must have had little to do beyond giving the actor the word and calling for those who had missed their entrance. In all probability that is a fair estimate of his duties during the time of action: to assign him more work would be to deprive the "plot" of its *raison d'être*.

It is relevant here to draw attention to the fact that only one Elizabethan actor's part has come down to us, Edward Alleyn's in *Orlando Furioso*.[1] Following con-

---

[1] For a reproduction, see Greg, *Henslowe Papers*, p. 155. The significance of the part in its relationship to the quarto of *Orlando Furioso* is

temporary custom, it is written on slips of paper six
inches wide and pasted together, the whole forming
originally a long scroll. I refer to it now because it has
value for us in demonstrating that the author's marginal
notes relative to the "business" of the scene were written
into the actor's part, and were solely for his guidance.

When we turn to the manuscript of *John a Kent and
John a Cumber*, we find that its arrangement is very much
the same as that of *Sir Thomas More*. Miss St. Clare
Byrne, who has made a special study of Munday's work,
has given it as her opinion that the left-hand marginalia
in his play were written with a view to the play's publication, but it is difficult to see what service notes of this
kind could have had for the reader.[1] To confirm this idea
would be to concede that *Sir Thomas More* was also prepared for the press, so great is the family resemblance
between the marginalia in both. Collier, on the other
hand, in his redaction of *John a Kent* states that some
of the marginal notes are anticipative, and assumes the
manuscript to have been a prompt-copy. Personally, I
can trace only one anticipative note; it occurs at the bottom of folio 15, where we get, on the left hand, "Enter
Shrimp, manet John," a duplication of the stage direction
at the top of the next folio. A few of the other notes
might be taken, however, as designed for the prompter's
service. On folio 4 the word "Enter" is written on the
left, to indicate exactly where John a Kent comes on, in
the middle of a speech. A stage direction for his entrance
afterwards occurs in the body of the text. There are also
one or two apparent music cues, but as they are not an-

fully discussed in the same scholar's *Two Elizabethan Stage Abridgements*,
pp. 135 ff.
[1] See her letter on "The Date of *Sir Thomas More*" in the *Times Literary
Supplement* for August 19, 1920.

ticipative, I cannot see their utility. On folio 12, opposite the line, "Silence! methinkes I hear sweet melodie,"
Munday has written, on the right, "Musique whyle he
opens the door"; and on the right, in a different hand
and fainter ink, one finds the word "Musique." Similarly, the word is repeated on folio 14, opposite the line,
"Sound musique while I shewe to John a Kent." This
is practically all the evidence. On reviewing it, I can only
repeat what I said about the *More* manuscript, namely,
that if this is a prompt-copy, the duties of the sixteenth-
century prompter during the performance were neither
complex nor onerous.

The Munday manuscript is dated 1596, and we are
now compelled to take a long jump to 1611, the date of
the next-earliest playhouse manuscript. Here, at last,
we find our feet on firm ground. The manuscript of *The
Second Maiden's Tragedy*,[1] whose characteristics, by the
way, are admirably reproduced in the Malone Society
reprint, is at once the licensed copy and the prompt-
copy. It bears Sir George Buc's allowance at the end.
Some progress towards a thoroughly scientific prompt-
book had now been made, though the advance is not very
material. Warnings were not yet anticipative, and the
principle of the plot must still have been followed. The
sinister marginalia are in two hands, the one identical
with the handwriting of the text, presumably the author's,[2] and the other the prompter's. The author's notes
were seemingly made to save the prompter labour, since

[1] Lansdowne MSS, 807.
[2] Boas, *Shakespeare at the Universities*, p. 10, states that the text of this
play is in the hand of a professional scribe. This implies that it was the work
of collaboration, but no one has found reason to suspect more than one
author. It is generally attributed to Tourneur. Cf. Chambers, *The Elizabethan Stage*, iv, 45; also *Studies in Philology*, xxiii (1926), 158, 159, E. H. C.
Oliphant on "The Authorship of *The Revenger's Tragedy*."

they simply indicate the entrance of the characters, together with the properties — such as pistols — that they carried. The prompter also jots down entrances of characters, sometimes of specific players, besides recording the trumpet flourishes, knocks, music, and so forth. Two players only are mentioned, each on one occasion only, but if these are special warnings, as they would seem to be, it is curious that they are not anticipative. Opposite line 1723 is written, "Enter Mr. Goughe," and opposite line 1927 (where the ghost comes on), "Enter Ladye Rich. Robinson."

It remains for us now to determine, or at least approximate, the period when prompt warnings became anticipative; but before proceeding on that interesting quest I cry a halt, that we may consider certain peculiarities of the Shakespearean texts which are deemed to have some connexion with our main subject. Occasionally, in these texts as well as elsewhere, we find the players' names substituted in speech headings for the names of the characters. In the Folio *Taming of the Shrew*, once in the induction, where we should read, "First Player," Sincklo's name occurs instead. In the 1600 Quarto of *2 Henry IV*, Act V, but not in the Folio, is the direction, "Enter Sincklo and three or foure officers," and the Beadle's speeches are assigned to Sincklo. In the Folio *3 Henry VI*, I, 3, for "Enter a Messenger" we have, "Enter Gabriel," doubtless a player's name, and the character speaks as Gabriel throughout. Later on, in Act III, scene 1, for the "Enter two Keepers, with crossbows in their hands" of the Quarto, we have, "Enter Sincklo and Humphrey," and it is as Sincklo and Humphrey that they are represented as speaking. Then again, in Act IV, scene 2, of both the Quarto and the Folio *Much Ado* occur some sixteen speeches, before which the names of Kempe and

Cowley are substituted for Dogberry and Verges. Some more curious prefixes still are to be found in *All's Well that Ends Well*, as first printed, belatedly, in the Folio. In Act I, scene 2, certain speeches are allotted to the "1 Lo. G." and the "2 Lo. E." In Act III, scene 1, two French lords enter with others at the opening, and their speeches are headed "French E." and "French G." In Act III, scene 6, and Act IV, scene 3, this protean pair of "lettered" hirelings figure again in similar fashion as two captains. There has been a good deal of idle speculation as to the significance throughout of "E." and "G.," but the student who has made a careful examination of early prompt-books will have no difficulty in determining that the letters stood for the names — more probably the Christian names — of two hard-working minor players.

Of a somewhat different order is the "Enter Will Kemp" of Act IV, scene 5, of the second and third Quartos of *Romeo and Juliet*, since Kempe's ensuing speeches are assigned to Peter, and not to Kempe. Excepting that Kempe was a player of prime importance, and not the inferior type of player whose name is usually associated with stage directions, this is on a par with the Folio direction in *A Midsummer Night's Dream*, V, 1, 134. As already explained, one can understand the necessity for adding a minor player's name to a stage direction, but what one cannot readily understand is why, in some cases, after this had been done, the player's name should also have been placed before his speeches. The further course seems a work of supererogation.

What is particularly noteworthy about these occasional substitutions of the actor's name for the name of the character is that the aberration was peculiar neither to Shakespeare nor to his company. Though as an occasional expedient it seems to have become obsolete in the late

Jacobean period, it had been resorted to earlier by various bodies of players. In the anonymous *Taming of a Shrew*, printed in 1594, the abbreviation "San" occurs before the First Player's speeches, and the name of the clownish servant in the play is Sanders. It has been conjectured, with some plausibility, that the one actor played both parts, and that he was the "Saunder" mentioned, *circa* 1592, in *The Plott of the Seven Deadly Sins*, otherwise, according to Greg, Alexander Cooke. Here, however, is a much clearer example. Dekker's *The Honest Whore*, Part I, was produced by the Prince's (formerly the Admiral's) Men at the Fortune early in 1604, and printed in the same year. The play is undivided, but in scene 15 we read, "Enter Towne like a sweeper" — a remarkable variant of the usual type of direction in which a player is mentioned; and all the Sweeper's speeches are assigned to Towne. This Thomas Towne had been associated with the producing company since 1594. So far from bearing marks of prompt-book interpolation, the stage direction here reads as if written by the author, and it may be that Dekker had Towne in mind when he conceived the character. Plays in Dekker's earlier day were written wholly to order, and the average dramatist was well acquainted with the company for which he wrote, and sought to make the most of the idiosyncrasies and physical attributes of its members. It is certain, for example, that Shakespeare had a sort of living skeleton among his fellows and wrote him a variety of parts so that fun might be poked at his thinness. But in this particular case there would have been no need for the great actor-dramatist to jot down on his manuscript the name of the player for whom the part was intended. Even if the fact were not obvious, he had abundant opportunity to convey his wishes by word of mouth. Still, there is something to be said for the theory that the substitution of the player's name for the name of his character in speech headings was the work of the author, and Professor Allison Gaw has well said it.[1] What the theory, however, does not explain is why the author should have been so solicitous over the casting of purely minor characters; for it is a fact that in the vast majority of cases the substitution is made in connexion with trifling, colourless rôles. Mr. C. J. Sisson's alternative hypothesis has the merit of clearing up this mystery.[2] It bases on the circumstance that, in the manuscript of *Believe as You List*, Massinger occasionally omits the speech headings, especially in places where he is copying his first draft, and that the prompter takes care to repair the omission. It is quite possible, if the corrections were made when the parts were being written out, that now and again the prompter would be moved to insert the name of the player instead of the name of the character, the manuscript being primarily for stage use, and not necessarily for publication. It is noteworthy that some of the speech headings for minor characters in the alleged Shakespearean additions to *Sir Thomas More* were at first omitted, though the defect was subsequently corrected. Curiously enough, when I ask myself to which theory I should give my allegiance, I seem to have no option and am compelled to vote for both. In other words, it appears to me that these abnormalities were sometimes due, positively, to the author, and sometimes to the prompter.

Having now exhausted the possibilities of *The Second*

[1] See his article, "Actors' Names in Shakespearean Texts," in the *Journal of the Modern Language Association* for September, 1925, and likewise the paper on "John Sincklo as one of Shakespeare's Actors" in *Anglia*, xlix (1916), 289 ff.

[2] "Some Stuart Dramatic Manuscripts," in *Review of English Studies* for October, 1925, p. 429.

Maiden's Tragedy, I look some eight years ahead, and take up the manuscript of Fletcher and Massinger's *Sir John van Olden Barnavelt,*[1] a topical tragedy brought out at the Blackfriars by the King's Men in 1619. In this we have, both marginally and in stage directions,— though mostly in abbreviated, and sometimes cryptic, form,— abundant noting of the players' names, but never anything, I think, of the nature of a genuine warning. What is important to note, however, is that properties have now come to be jotted down separately among the prompter's marginalia. His duties were increasing. I select from the manuscript a few of the most important markings:

Act I, 2, direction: "Enter 2 Captains." Opposite this in right-hand margin: "Jo: R; migh." (= John Rice; Michael).

I, 3, opening, in margin opposite entry: "Mr. Rob."

II, 2, direction: "Enter Leidemberge, Mr. Gough." In the same scene, opposite the Messenger's speech: "R. T."

II, 5, in margin opposite "Enter Holderus," is "T. P."(= Thomas Pollard).

III, 2, memorandum: "Table: Bell." The bell was evidently a table-bell to summon the officer, but there is no direction for its ringing, though the officer comes in without being called, and asks what is wanted.

III, 6, opening, marginal note: "Taper, pen & inke; table."

IV, 2, opposite Bredero's first speech, is "Tho: Po," showing that Pollard doubled the parts of Holderus and Bredero.

Concerning the acting of the play, one thing can be deduced from this prompt-book. There was considerable doubling of small characters, and the prompter had to keep a wary eye on the doublers. To give only one example, "R. T.," whoever he may have been, had to sustain no fewer than five characters.

Our next prompt-book was made a little over five years

[1] British Museum Additional MSS, 18,653.

later, and belonged to the same company. It is a transcript of *The Honest Man's Fortune*, a play originally acted by Lady Elizabeth's Men in 1613, and bears Herbert's reallowance to the King's Men, under date of February 8, 1624–25.[1] In this case, the prompter was undoubtedly the scribe. The manuscript is in the same hand as the prompt notes in *Believe as You List* and the text of the British Museum manuscript of *Bonduca*.[2] The entrances are for the most part written marginally, and in a bold hand. The prompt indications are few. There are no property warnings, and nothing whatever of an anticipative nature. Three abbreviated memoranda occur referring to the entrance of minor players, two marginally and one above a stage direction. There are some erasures and some passages lined laterally for omission. Opposite a lined passage at the end the word "stet" has been written three times. Transcription is proved at folio 25 recto, where a short speech of Charlotte's was overlooked and written afterwards transversely in the margin.

I come now to a number of prompt-books whose dates can be only roughly approximated, and whose evidence, therefore, must be cautiously handled. The earliest of these is, apparently, *The Welsh Ambassador*, now reposing in the Cardiff Free Library. It has been recently printed by the Malone Society under the scientific editorship of Professor H. Littledale and Dr. Greg. Internal evidence shows that the play dates from 1622, but the manuscript is a transcript, both text and prompter's warnings being all in the one hand, and was seemingly made for country use a few years later.[3] The marginal

---

[1] Dyce MS. 9/25, f. 9.

[2] See Greg, "Prompt Copies, Private Transcripts, and the Playhouse Scrivener," in *The Library* for September, 1925.

[3] According to Greg (article on "Massinger's Autographs" in *The Library* for December, 1923), the manuscripts of *The Welsh Ambassador* and *The Par-*

notes are of two kinds, but all are on the left-hand side. A few are ordinary short stage directions, but the directions mostly start in the margin and run across the page. An exception is made at act-openings, where they start from the centre. No player's name occurs throughout, all the players being called by their characters—a peculiarity which suggests that the play was not cast until considerably after the transcript was made. What is otherwise important for us to note is that the warnings for players are clearly anticipative. The formula adopted was, "Be ready, so and so," marked down from 24 to 30 lines ahead; but, to make assurance doubly sure, opposite the place in the text where the character enters the entrance is noted in the margin. There are no warnings for the openings of acts, plain proof that performances were not then continuous, and that beginners were warned in the intervals. Music and property warnings are also given, but it is noteworthy that the flourishes for the King's entrances and exits are marked only two lines ahead, and that in Act III, scene 2, the warning for "Hoboyes" occurs exactly opposite the direction to which it applies. On page 37 of the printed copy we have, "Bee ready Carintha at a Table," proof that the subsequent scene opened with a discovery, although the direction has the ambiguous phrasing, "Enter Carintha at a Table reading." At page 60 (Act V, scene 2, lines 1934, 1935) the margin has "sett out a table," a use of the common technicality which illustrates its meaning. It was a warning to see the table placed ready on the rear stage. The subsequent scene opens with "Enter Clowne, in his study writing: one knocks within."

liament of Love (Dyce MS. 39) are in the one hand, and were probably kept together, as both have suffered equally from damp. Massinger's play was licensed for the Cockpit players on November 3, 1624. Both manuscripts are undoubtedly transcripts, and of a later date.

In No. 1994 of the Egerton Manuscripts in the British Museum there are several prompt-copies of pre-Restoration plays, but, despite the fact that nearly all present faint clues to their period in including actors' names, very few of them can be approximately dated. For the reason that we have no records of the licensing or performance of *Charlemagne* (otherwise *The Distracted Emperor*), *Thomas of Woodstock* (generally miscalled *Richard II*),[1] and *Edmond Ironsides*, I leave them out of the calculation. It is true that a possible reference to *Thomas of Woodstock* in *The Devil is an Ass*[2] seemingly dates the play earlier than 1616, but the prompt-book undoubtedly belongs to a later period. It has anticipative property warnings, made some twenty lines in advance, and cannot therefore have been marked before early Caroline days. I find myself on somewhat safer ground in dealing with another play in the same group, Heywood's *The Captives*, licensed for the Queen of Bohemia's Men at the Cockpit on September 3, 1624. But in the absence of a licensing endorsement we have no reason to believe that this was the original prompt-copy, and it would rather appear, from the recurrence of obscure players' names in it and in one or two other plays of the group, that it was a later transcript made for country acting. The period would be *circa* 1625–28. The book presents some anticipative warnings, but not all players were called. In Act III, scene 2, we have marginally, "Fellowes ready, Scribonia, with Godfrey, Mildew, Sarley," about twenty lines ahead. Here, again, we get a warning for characters, not for specific players. Other warnings synchronise with the stage direction to which they apply — a puzzling disparity. There are separate notes for properties and

---

[1] Cf. Chambers, *The Elizabethan Stage*, iv, 42, 43.
[2] Act II, scene 1.

noises, all of an irregular prematurity. Thus, while in Act II, scene 1, the warning, "Bell rings," occurs only two lines ahead, in Act III, scene 1, we meet with the jotting, "Ink: paper ready," sixteen lines before they are required.[1]

But the problem of the genesis of actor calling, as part of the prompter's duties, can be attacked in another way. Some years ago, in an article published in the *Times Literary Supplement*,[2] I advanced evidence to show that the first quarto of *The Two Noble Kinsmen*, issued in 1634, was printed from a prompt-copy representing a revision made *circa* 1626–28. Probably only a few of the prompt warnings have been preserved, and those accidentally, but in Act I, scene 3, line 68, we have, "2 Hearses ready with Palamon: and Arcite: the 3 Queenes. Theseus: and his Lordes ready." This is a warning 40 lines ahead, for the opening of the next scene. On the strength of this, and of previously detailed evidence, I should be inclined to say that reliance upon the plot began to wane in late Jacobean days, and that *circa* 1626 the prompter was beginning to call the players.

Undoubtedly, the most valuable and illuminative of all early prompt-books is that of Massinger's *Believe as You List*, now in the British Museum. Licensed for the King's Men on May 6, 1631, it neatly indicates the normal progression of the play of one-man authorship, from author's copy to the allowed copy and thence to the prompt-copy. Happily, its details are readily accessible to the student through the excellent facsimile issued by

[1] Note also that, for the first time in a prompt-book, we have marginally, at the end of Act III, "Clere" (*i. e.*, "clear the stage"). But in Q. 2 (1625) of *A King and No King*, at the end of the first scene of the fifth act, is the direction, "Exeunt clear." At this juncture Q. 1 (1619) has simply "exeunt."

[2] "New Light on *The Two Noble Kinsmen*," in the issue for July 14, 1921.

Farmer. No very clear principle of prompt-book making emerges. Evidently because his labours were increasing in other respects, the prompter was still doing his best to evade the responsibilities of wholesale calling. One notes that the Caroline Globe prompter had a trick of crossing out the author's stage directions (which were mostly written in the right margin) and of rewriting them boldly in the left, sometimes appending the players' names to the characters mentioned, and sometimes not. These redirections are seldom, if ever, anticipative; two of them — one on folio 6 and one on folio 9 — are slightly so. If a play thus marked had been sent not long afterwards to the printer's, the published copy would have been so devoid of act and scene divisions and stage directions that, on encountering it, some of the harebrained commentators of to-day would have unhesitatingly maintained that it had been made up from assembled parts. But that is a digression. These redirections, since they frequently comprised players' names, must have been of some service in prompting, but it is difficult to say what. It is not apparent how they enabled the prompter to make calls; they simply told him who should come on. But on special occasions he gave a long call to one of the principals. Thus in Act II (folio 11) he noted, quite a whole page ahead, "Mr. Hobs. called up." Again, in Act IV (folio 33) we have, "Harry Wilson & Boy ready for the Song at ye Arras," [1] the space of seven speeches ahead. Once, near the close of the play, this distinction is vouchsafed to a couple of minor players. On folio 46 is noted, thirteen speeches ahead, "Be ready: ye 2 Marchants: Wm. Pen: Curtis: & Garde."

It was the Caroline prompter's business to mind the

---

[1] A warning strangely misinterpreted by R. Crompton Rhodes, *Shakespeare's First Folio*, pp. 56, 57.

traps. In Act IV, on folio 30, is the warning, "Gascoine: Hubert below ready to open the trap doore for Mr. Taylor." A little later on, Taylor himself was called. On folio 31 we have, "Antiochus ready: under the stage," and Taylor was the Antiochus. On folio 32, where Taylor has to speak through the trap, comes the final memorandum, "Antiochus below." Evidently great care was taken to prevent a hitch at important junctures. Flourishes had double noting, the first slightly anticipative, and the second where the general entrance occurred which the flourish heralded. It was the business also of the Caroline prompter to keep a careful eye on the properties. On folio 11 comes the warning, a whole page ahead, "Table ready: and 6 chairs to sett out." On folio 17 Massinger himself takes the precaution to enter, in the margin, "The great booke of accompte ready"; but it is not until the end of folio 19 that we come across simultaneously the sinister and dexter reminders, — duplicated doubtless for surety's sake, — "Ent. Rowland wth the booke of the records," and "Ent. Rowland wth the Records." Similarly, on folio 39 comes the circled warning, "All the swords ready," but it is not until folio 45 that the swords are brought in.

Other peculiarities remain to be noted. Though Massinger made act divisions, there are no blank spaces between the acts. But, purely for his own service, the prompter scores out all the author's act divisions and rewrites them in the left-hand margin. When this practice began I cannot say, but if it should happen to have dated from thirty years earlier, one can quite understand how the printers got into the habit of printing plays without act or scene divisions. On folio 10 the prompter has cancelled Massinger's "Actus secunda, scena prima," and written in the margin, in two lines, "Act 2. | Long."

Where Act IV is similarly transferred, we again get the word "long." Here we have proof that the intervals varied in length according to the necessities. In this connexion it is noteworthy that in *The Fair Maid of the West*, Part I, a Cockpit play of the same period, we have, at the end of the fourth act, "act long," and, between the second and third scenes of that act, "Hautboys long." [1]

On folio 48 comes the epilogue, and on folio 49, not a comprehensive list of properties, as might have been expected if anything of the sort were compiled, but merely a list of the letters and papers required for the play. The main reason for this provision is that letters and other documents used in the traffic of the stage were not memorized by the players, and had to be written out in full. Nay, more: letters supposed to be written in blood —as in *The Spanish Tragedy*, III, 2, and *Bussy D'Ambois*, V, 3 — were realistically indited in red ink. Because of this system, not a few letters and other documents have disappeared from old plays. In Marlowe's *Edward II*, line 1678, the King is desirous of hearing the list of executions and asks Spencer to read it. A direction says, "Spencer reads their names." But no speech of his comprises the names, and it is plain that they must have been written on the paper presented by Arundell.

We have now pretty well exhausted all the material evidence afforded by the early prompt-books, and the labour of marshalling the details has, I think, been distinctly worth while. One conclusion of importance clearly emerges, namely, that so far as the prompter was concerned, the system of advance calls for players, musicians, and properties first came into vogue somewhere in the period of 1625–31. There is, however, another source of information, and this it is politic to tap with the view of

[1] Cf. *Bussy D'Ambois* (1607), I, 2, direction, "Flourish short."

confirming or confuting our primary inferences. We have about a score of early seventeenth-century printed plays in which marginal prompt warnings of one kind or another have been accidentally preserved. Eight of these are plays which were first published in the Beaumont and Fletcher folio of 1647: *The Fair Maid of the Inn*, *The Spanish Curate*, *The Maid in the Mill*, *The Mad Lover*, *The Little French Lawyer*, *The Chances*, *The Custom of the Country*, and *Love's Pilgrimage*. What we have to bear in mind in examining these is that in no case can the evidence yielded be applied to the date of the play's production, even when the date is known. When publication took place after a considerable stretch of years, it was mostly the practice to print from the latest revised copy; and practically all these eight plays had borne revival and revision — some of them, indeed, more than once. Consequently, their evidence applies only to the period conterminous with, or subsequent to, the period in which, according to the evidence of the prompt-books, advance prompter's calls of various kinds first came into vogue.

In *The Fair Maid of the Inn*, III, 1, we have marginally, "See they enter," a warning relative to the subsequent appearance of the Tailor, Dancer, and others in a group. Dyce, not understanding this, actually dovetailed the warning into one of the speeches. This play, it should be noted, was licensed in January, 1626, and bore at least two revivals. The probability that it was twice revised mitigates Mr. H. Dugdale Sykes's offence in finding so much of Webster and of Massinger, and nothing at all of Fletcher, in the play.[1]

The Maid in the Mill was licensed in August, 1623, and revived in 1628 and doubtless later. At the end of Act I, one notes the memorandum, "Six chaires placed at the

[1] *Sidelights on the Elizabethan Drama*, p. 140.

Arras," a warning a long way ahead, as the chairs were not required until the middle of the second scene of the next act. *The Spanish Curate* was licensed in October, 1622, and, since it bears signs of revisal, certainly was revived later. It presents more marginalia, I think, than any other early printed play, with the possible exception of *The City Madam*, but I quote only the more important items. In Act III, scene 2, we have, "The Bar and Book ready on table," and at the opening of Act III, scene 3, where the properties were required, comes the reminder, "A Bar, Table-book, standard set out." This was a front-stage scene, not a discovery. Later on in the same scene is the note, "Chess-board and men set ready," a warning of 117 lines, since the board was not wanted until the middle of the next scene.

The Mad Lover dates from 1616, but was not published until some thirty years later, facts which (knowing as we do the early seventeenth-century craze for revisal) warrant us in believing that it is not in its original state. The date of the text may be conjectured from the circumstance that in Act II, scene 2, mention is made of Edward Horton, a boy player, the direction speaking of him as a boy. Horton was cast for a female character in Carlell's *The Deserving Favourite*, a Blackfriars play, published in 1629, not long after its production. Coupled with Horton's name in the direction in *The Mad Lover* is the name of R. Baxter, and Baxter figured in the cast of *Believe as You List* at the same theatre in 1631. On this showing, the date of the extant text would be *circa* 1630. In Act V, scene 1, we have, 36 lines ahead, a warning, reading, "The Hearses ready, Polydor, Eumenes and Captains."

The Little French Lawyer was originally produced in 1619 or thereabouts, but we have no record of its performance. In Act III, scene 3, we have marginally the word "Recorders"; subsequently there is a direction for music. *The Chances* dates from *circa* 1627, and was played at Court by the King's Men in November, 1638. Rowland Dowle, whose name is mentioned in a stage direction in Act III, scene 2, was a minor member of the company from 1628 to 1636, and it must have been somewhere between those dates that the prompt-book used by the printers was made. In Act IV, scene 2, we have, 60 lines ahead, "Bawd ready above." *The Custom of the Country* dates from 1623, and was revived in May, 1628, as well as later. In Act I, scene 1, is a warning for the song and dance in the next scene, "Boy ready for the songs." *Love's Pilgrimage* saw the light as early as 1614, but it was re-licensed in September, 1635, and exists only in its revised form. In Act IV, scene 1, one finds the marginal warning, 50 lines ahead, "Rod. above."

A few plays of Fletcher fell from the press before the appearance of the first folio, and of these, *Monsieur Thomas* was published in quarto, from a revised manuscript, in 1639, about twenty-three years after its first production. In Act III, scene 1, at line 257 of the quarto, is the marginal note, "Physicians and Servants within," a warning which conveys what we should otherwise remain in ignorance of: namely, that the direction, "Enter three Physicians, apothecary and Barber," which comes seven lines later, refers, not to an entrance but to a discovery. Warnings of irregular duration, some long, some short, are characteristic of the late Caroline period, but it would appear that when the prompter first began to give them they were comparatively brief. Thus, in *The Virgin Martir*, a play licensed in October, 1620, and published in 1622, the marginal entry in Act V, "Rise Consort," occurs only eight lines before the direction for "musick."

Not only that, but in the same act, warnings for a "Book," "Flowers," and "a crosse of flowers" come exactly at the places where they are required.

Three Blackfriars plays, all licensed after 1626, present prompt warnings typical of their period. These are Davenant's *The Cruel Brother* and *The Unfortunate Lovers*, and Massinger's *The City Madam*. *The Cruel Brother* was licensed in January, 1627, and published in 1630. Warnings for properties occur in Act III, scene 2, and Act V, scene 1, and at the latter reference there is also a warning for music. The progress made since the days of *The Virgin Martir* is illustrated by the fact that in Act III, scene 1, we have, considerably in advance, "Chair at the Arras," meaning, "place the chair on the rear stage," it being wanted in the ensuing scene. *The Unfortunate Lovers* was licensed in April, 1638, and printed in 1643. In Act II, scene 1, comes the warning, "Call guard," a matter of eleven lines ahead. As for *The City Madam*, I regret very much that the time is not at my disposal to deal as fully with its features as its importance merits. It is worthy of special study, not only for its marginalia, but for the prompt indications it otherwise presents. Besides actor calls, it has both music and property warnings. It practically says the last word in pre-Restoration prompt-book making. To illustrate the method employed, a couple of examples will suffice. As early as Act V, scene 1, comes the warning, "The Banquet ready. One chair and Wine," though it is not until two scenes later that the properties are required. With players it was much the same as with properties; in Act V, scene 3, the prompter takes care to note, "Plenty and Lacy ready behind." Massinger's play, let it be recalled, was licensed in May, 1632, though not published until 1659.

After what has just been advanced, I think I may safely

say that nothing to be found in the plays printed from prompt-copies seriously contravenes the deductions I have made from actual prompt-copies. It seems to me fairly well established by the evidence that actor calling by prompters dates from the beginning of the Caroline period. But to those who contemplate making further investigation of the subject a word of caution is necessary. In advancing marginalia or stage directions as evidence, one must be careful to state in what particular edition of a play they occur, and, if it is a late edition, to determine whether or not they are peculiar to that edition. Some recent Elizabethan investigators have obscured the issue through not taking this precaution. Dr. Albright is a prime offender. In his book on *The Shaksperian Stage*[1] one finds him stating, without reference to any particular quarto, that in *Bussy D'Ambois*, I, 1, 153, some 69 lines ahead, occurs the warning, "Table, Chesbord, & Tapers behind the Aarras," leaving us to draw the inference, since the play was first printed in 1608, that such warnings were *à la mode* at the beginning of the century. But the truth is that the warning first appears in the third quarto, issued in 1641, and affords proof — if proof were needed — that the play bore late revival. It is not needed, because Herbert records a performance of *Bussy D'Ambois* at court on April 7, 1634, and another on March 27, 1638.[2]

Another example occurs in Albright's book.[3] From *The Rape of Lucrece*, V, 3, he quotes from the middle of the scene a warning for the next scene, reading, "A Table and Lights in the Tent," but again mentions no particular quarto, once more leaving us to assume that the citation was from the original prompt-book of 1607 or there-

[1] Page 107.
[2] Adams, *Dramatic Records of Sir Henry Herbert*, pp. 55, 76.
[3] Page 108.

abouts, the play having been printed for the first time in 1608. But there had been four reissues of the text and several revivals of the piece before 1638,[1] and, although I have been unable to examine all the quartos, I feel certain that the warning was peculiar to a Caroline prompt-book, and must therefore have been quoted from the fourth or fifth impression.

Once we are armed with full knowledge, these old prompt warnings enable us to approximate the date of the prompt-book from which they were printed, and thus, in some cases, to determine whether we are in possession of a late or early text. An important matter this, since late texts generally connote sophistication. Here is an interesting example. Day's *The Blind Beggar of Bednal Green* was produced in 1600 by the Admiral's Men, but not printed until 1659. The title-page bears the intimation, "as it was divers times publickly acted by the Prince's Servants," and Chambers thinks that the players referred to were the later Prince Charles's Men of 1631–41.[2] In that he is pretty near the mark, though my own belief is that the company was the first Prince Charles's Men. At line 2177 of the play comes the stage direction, "Enter old Playnsey, old Strowd, and Captain Westford, Sill. Clark," a direction which has proved mystifying to the erudite author of *The Elizabethan Stage*, since he has been unable to find any trace of this Sill Clark. And for very good reason: the name is a printer's misreading of the contraction, "Will Carp," which stood for William Carpenter, the name of a minor member of the first Prince Charles's company from 1619 to 1625, when it was dissolved. It is possible, of course, that Carpenter may have been connected with the later company, but on that score we have no evidence.

[1] Chambers, *The Elizabethan Stage*, iii, 343, 344.   [2] *Ibid.*, 285.

Other proofs can be advanced to show that the prompt-book from which the play was printed cannot have been made earlier than the late Jacobean period. In Act IV, at line 1992, comes the marginal warning, "Ready Swash," just eleven lines ahead — a type of warning not to be traced before that time. Again, both cornets and trumpets were employed in the theatre at the time this particular version was played,[1] and, as I have fully demonstrated elsewhere,[2] cornets and trumpets were not used together, or in the same theatre, until after 1620.

One may apply our new-found test to *Appius and Virginia*, that much-discussed play published in 1654 as Webster's. Mr. H. Dugdale Sykes's recent contention, that the play cannot have been written much before 1630,[3] receives some support from the fact that in Act V, scene 2, it presents, some ten speeches ahead, a marginal warning for wine. This at least assigns to the Caroline period the prompt-book from which it was printed.

[1] End of Act IV, "Exeunt. Musick, Cornet"; in Act V, scene 1, direction for the heralding of the King's entry, "Sound Trumpet."

[2] See "A New Shakespearean Test" in *The Criterion* for October, 1923 (vol. ii, no. 5, pp. 77–94).

[3] *Sidelights on the Elizabethan Drama*, p. 112.

Index

Index

Acts, division into. See Breaks.

"Acts," meaning of, in Jaques's speech in *As You Like It*, and elsewhere, 293, 294; and in Jonson, 294.

Adams, Joseph Q., *Shakespearean Playhouses*, 13 n.; *Life of Shakespeare*, 45, 369 f.; 357.

Admiral's Men, in inn-yards, 39 ff.; and Chamberlain's Men, influence of rivalry of, on trend of English dramaturgy, 129, 292; playwrights in employ of, 292; 134, 135, 136, 183, 215, 280, 283, 284, 286, 326, 349 f., 361.

Albertus Alasco, Polish Prince, 230.

Albright, *The Shakespearean Stage*, 145, 146, 147, 242, 300, 306, 308, 411.

Alexander, P., 258.

All's Lost by Lust, 310.

Alleyn, Edward, 75, 392.

Anachronisms, in Shakespeare's plays, 222.

Andreini, Giambattista, *La Centaure*, 177.

Antiquary, The, 315.

Archer, William, 262, 264.

Arden of Feversham, 128, 156, 226, 239, 275.

Armour, imitation, use of, 108, 109.

Astley, Sir John, 327.

Atheist's Tragedie, The, 269.

Attewell, George, 89.

Aubrey, 354, 356.

Audience, the, and the dramatist, 222, 223.

Ayrer, Jacob, "Der Münch im Kesskarb" (jig), 85.

B., R., *Apius and Virginia*, 301.

Bacon, Francis, Lord, "On Masques and Triumphs," 80; *Sylva Sylvarum*, 203, 204.

Baker, George P., *Development of Shakespeare as a Dramatist*, 16, 17, 22.

Bale, John, *Kynge Johan*, 52; *Three Laws*, 52.

Bang, 184.

Banks de Theatre, 1.

Bannister, John, 297, 298.

Barclay, Sir W., *The Lost Lady*, 309 n.

Barker, Henry Granville, 3.

"Barriers," 304 n.

Barry, Lodowick, *Ram Alley*, 242.

Bate, John, *The Mysteries of Nature and Art*, 201, 206, 207, 216, 257 n.

Baugh, Albert C., 135.

Baxter, Richard, 77, 408.

Beaconsfield, Lord. See Disraeli.

Bear a Brain, 284.

Bear Garden, The, 255.

Beaumont, Francis, *The Marriage of the Thames and the Rhine*, 233, 234 and n.; 354 ff.

Beaumont, Francis, and Fletcher, John.

Bonduca, 23, 211, 212, 358, 400.

The Chances, 217, 218, 390, 407, 409.

The Custom of the Country, 407, 409.

The Fair Maid of the Inn, 268, 407.

Four Plays in One, 162, 182, 183, 186 ff., 228, 317.

A King and No King, 358 ff.

The Knight of the Burning Pestle, 249, 250, 357.

Love's Pilgrimage, 390, 407, 409.

The Mad Lover, 267, 268, 407, 408.

The Maid in the Mill, 219, 220, 305, 381, 407.

The Maid's Tragedy, 220, 310.

The Spanish Curate, 218, 219, 407, 408.

"Bed scenes," 306, 308–310, 322.

Beech's Tragedy, 185.

Beeston, W., 337.

Beeston's Boys, 338.

Beheading scenes, 242 ff.; method pursued in, 246, 247.

Belfast Newsletter, The, 303.

Bell Inn, 7.

Belle Sauvage Inn, 7.

Bells, on the stage, simulation of sound of, 214–216.

Bird song, references to, accompanied by warbling, 200 ff.

Birth of Merlin, The, 55, 319.

Black Bull Inn, 7.

"Black Man, The" (jig), 99.

Blackfriars Theatre, 20, 63, 64, 77, 130, 141, 155, 166, 203, 214, 227, 240, 268, 297, 326.

"Blazing stars," 256 ff.

Blood, of calves or sheep, use of, 237; simulation of effusion of, from a dead body, 239, 240; from wounds, 240.

Blood-and-thunder drama, 208.

Bloody Brother, The, 257.

Bloody scenes, real blood used in, 236 ff.; in France, 237; the universal desire for, 241.

Boaden, James, *Life of John Philip Kemble*, 109, 119, 120, 298.

Boar's Head, The, 33, 42.

Boas, F. S., 269, 270.

Boccaccio, Giovanni, *The Decameron*, 85, 187.

Bookholders, 383 f.

Bookkeepers, 383 f.

Boys and female characters, 43.

Brandl, 72.

Brayne, John, 12, 26.

Breaks between acts, 38, 39, 69, 345, 352, 359, 405.

Brodmeier, and stage traps, 145; "alternation theory," 299, 300.

Brome, Richard.

The Antipodes, 252, 253 and n., 378 f., 381.

The City Wit, 297, 306, 309.

Covent Garden Weeded, 16.

The Jovial Crew, 207.

The Love-Sick Court, 270.

A Mad Couple Well Match'd, 130, 309.

The New Academy, 97.

The Northern Lasse, 7.

The Queen and Concubine, 208, 269.

The Queen's Exchange, 214, 269.

Brooke, C. F. Tucker, 186, 209, 248.

Buc, Sir George, 394.

Bullen, A. H., 20, 83, 365 n.

Burbage, Richard, 27, 332.

Burre, 357.

Byrne, St. Clare, 393.

Call-boys, 374.
Calverley, Walter, 186.
Calvert, Louis, *An Actor's Hamlet*, 107.
Campbell, Lily B., 172 and n.
Campion, Thomas, *Masque in Honour of Lord Hay's Marriage*, 171, 172. And see Davison.
Campra, Andrá, *L'Europe galante*, 196.
Careless Shepherd, The, 98.
Carew, Richard, *Survey of Cornwall*, 379.
Carlell, Lodowick, *The Deserving Favourite*, 408.
Carleton, 49.
Carow, John, 109.
Carpenter, W., 312.
Carriers, use of inn-yards by, 6 ff.
Cart, John, "The Cunning Age," 98.
Cartwright, W., "Dramaticall Poems of Master John Fletcher," 356.
Catherine de Medicis, 201.
Caus, Salomon de, *Les Raisons des Forces Mouvantes*, 201.
Censing effects, 227 ff.
Centlivre, Susannah, *A Bold Stroke for a Wife*, 297.
Chamberlain's Men, and Admiral's Men, rivalry between, 291, 292; Shakespeare their only reliance, 292; 134, 135, 136, 295.
"Chambers," 212, 213.
Chambers, Edmund K., *The Elizabethan Stage*, 3, 12, 45, 48, 52, 95, 182, 186, 187, 231, 244, 245, 253, 289, 290, 311, 315, 324, 347, 358, 412.
Chapman, George, 64, 191, 192, 292.
The Blind Beggar of Alexandria, a complex-disguise play, 60, 134, 280–282, 284.

Bussy D'Ambois, 224, 236, 269, 270, 302, 406, 411.
Byron's Tragedy, 245.
Caesar and Pompey, 131, 235.
The Gentleman Usher, 312 n., 318, 381.
A Humorous Day's Mirth, 292.
May Day, 224, 289, 290.
The Revenge of Bussy D'Ambois, 275.
The Widdowes Tears, 63.
Characters, lists of, 74.
Charges for admission, early methods of "gathering," 24; fixed, evolution of, 25.
Charlemagne, 402.
Charles, Prince (Charles I), 190.
Chaucer, Geoffrey, romanticism and realism in his works, 221.
Cheaters Cheated, The, 100.
Chettle, Henry, perhaps the author of *Look About You*, 284, 285; an adept in complex-disguise plays, 285, 292, 361.
The First Part of Thomas Strowde (The Blind Beggar of Bednal Green), 285.
Hoffman, 285, 313, 316, 317 n.
Kind Heartes Dreame, 84.
Tis no Deceit to Deceive the Deceiver, 283, 285.
Chettle, Henry, and Wilson, Robert, *Black Bateman of the North*, 351.
Chimes. See Bells.
Chinese stage, horses on, 272.
Choir-boy players, 62.
Chronicle histories, 30, 31.
Chronicle History of King Leir and his Three Daughters, The, 274, 294.
Chronicle plays, 64.
Clark, Andrew, 89.

Clarke, Sidney W., *The Miracle Play in England*, 230.

Classification of Elizabethan plays, method of, 28 ff.

"Cloudings," 191.

Clown, the, 31.

Cobler's Prophesie, The, 35.

Cocke, "A Common Player," 327.

Cockpit Theatre, 22, 78, 131, 207, 256, 332, 337, 338.

Cokain, Sir A., *The Obstinate Lady*, 309 n.

Coleridge, S. T., 358.

Collaboration, defects of, 353; modern, 340.

Collette, Charles, 298.

Collier, J. Payne, *Annals of the Stage*, 55, 83, 150, 179, 383, 393.

Comets. See "Blazing stars."

Common Conditions, 202.

Common Council of London, Act of 1574 and inn-yard playing places, 12, 15, 25 and n.

Complex-disguise play, 60, 134. And see Chapter XII.

Conflagrations on the stage, 263 ff.

Conflict of Conscience, The, 46, 53, 57.

Congreve, William, *The Old Bachelor*, 282.

Contention between Liberality and Prodigality, The, 253.

Contention of the Two Famous Houses of York and Lancaster, The, 17, 322.

Contention plays, 248.

Continuators, 348.

Cooke, A., 397.

Corneille, P., 372.

Corneille, T. See Montfleury.

Cotgrave, Randle, *Dictionarie*, 312, 382.

Counterweighting in stage traps, 170, 172.

Court masque, influence of, on public-theatre staging, 267 ff.

Courtier plays, 29.

Covent Garden Theatre, 191, 197, 234, 298.

Cox, Robert, *The Wits, or Sport upon Sport*, 90, 99, 100.

Coxcomb, The, 390.

Coxeter, 136.

Creede, Thomas, 86.

Creizenach, *The English Drama in the Age of Shakespeare*, 20, 130, 310, 382 f.

Croker, Crofton, 61.

Cross Keys Inn, 7.

Cruikshank, George, 169.

Cumber, John, 98.

Cunliffe, J. W., 151, 152.

Cure for a Cuckold, A, 77 n.

Curtain, The, 80, 136, 231, 295.

Daborne, Robert, 343.

Dance, "jig" originally a certain type of, 79.

Dance tunes, 81.

Daniel, Samuel, *Hymen's Triumph*, 138; *Tethys's Festival*, 259.

Darkness on the stage, how managed, 128, 129 and n., 130 ff.

Davenant, Sir W.

 Antony and Cleopatra, 194.
 Britannia Triumphans, 331 n.
 The City Night-Cap, 380.
 The Cruel Brother, 410.
 A Playhouse to be Let, a composite play, 193, 194.
 The Unfortunate Lovers, 410.
 The Wits, 96.

Davenport, Robert, *King John and Mathilda*, 316 n., 319.

Davey, Henry, 72.

Davison, F., and Campion, T., *The Masque of Proteus*, 346.

Day, John, *The Isle of Gulls*, 214; *The Blind Beggar of Bednal Green* (see Chettle), 285, 367 f.; *Law Tricks*, 383, 412, 413.

Day of Judgment, The, 230.

Dekker, Thomas, 132, 133, 136, 201, 284, 292, 361. And see Rowley.

    The Honest Whore, 290, 323, 348, 350, 397.

    If it be not Good, the Devil is in it, 92, 174, 233, 260, 261, 265, 304, 316, 319.

    News from Hell, 168.

    Northward Ho, 256.

    Satiromastix, 305, 312 n., 317, 318.

    The Seven Deadly Sinnes of London, 124, 125, 126.

    The Shoemaker's Holiday, 59, 73, 220.

    A Strange Horse Race, 91, 92.

    Westward Ho, 306.

    The Whore of Babylon, 162, 173.

    Worke for Armourers, 125, 141 and n., 255.

Dekker, Thomas, and Drayton, Michael, *The Civil Wars of France*, 351.

Dekker, Thomas, and Ford, John, *The Sun's Darling*, 207, 332, 337.

Dekker, Thomas, and Webster, John, *Sir Thomas Wyatt*, 243, 245.

Dialogue of Dives, The, 123 n.

"Discoveries," 304.

Disguise, new practice relating to, in Shakespeare's day, 59, 60; in Shakespeare, 277, 278; face-patch as, 282; rampant in Elizabethan drama, 283.

Disguises, The, probably the first complex-disguise play given in England, 280, 284, 289.

Disraeli, Benjamin, Earl of Beaconsfield, 71.

Distance, illusion of, 219.

Distracted Emperor, The. See *Charlemagne*.

Divel and Dives, The, 123 and n., 124.

Divil's Charter, The, 160, 225, 320.

Dodsley's Old Plays, 286.

Donne, John, "A Nocturnal," etc., 143.

"Doublers" and "disguisers," 59, 60.

"Doubling," first trace of, 48.

Dowden, Edward, 139, 141.

Dowle, Rowland, 77, 390, 409.

Downes, J., *Roscius Anglicanus*, 383.

Drama. See Plays.

Drayton, Michael, 136, 292. And see Dekker, Wilson.

Dreams, visualised, 268, 269.

Drebbel, Cornelius, 143, 144.

Drury Lane Theatre, 119, 296.

Dryden, John, *Mac Flecknoe*, 90; *King Arthur*, 238, 239; *Love Triumphant*, 308.

Dryden, John, and Lee, Nathaniel, *Oedipus*, 111, 169, 372.

Dryden–Shadwell revision of *The Tempest*, 308.

Duffet, *Psyche Debauch'd*, 191.

Duke's Theatre, 194.

Dumas d'Aiquebert, *Les Trois Spectacles*, a composite play, 197.

Dumb Knight, The, 22, 303, 304, 320.

Dumb shows, 320.

Durand, 14.

Dyce, Alexander, 390, 407.

Earle, Characters, 334.

Edmond Ironsides, 402.

Egan, Maurice F., 221.

Elizabeth, Princess, 234.

Elizabeth, Queen, 177, 254, 378.

Elizabethan drama, a jumble of opposites, 175. And see Plays, Elizabethan.

Elizabethan plays. See Plays, Elizabethan.

Ellis, Havelock, 135.

Elliston, Robert W., 297, 298.

Eltham, Sir John, 60.

"Enter" in stage directions, 170.

Every Woman in her Humour, 205, 383.

Examiner, The, 296, 297.

Face-patch, as disguise, 282.

Fair Constance of Rome, 352.

"Fair copy" (author's), 384–386.

Faithful Friends, The, 306 f.

Falcon Inn, 11.

Falkland, Viscount, "Eclogue on the Death of Ben Jonson," 344.

Famous Victories of Henry V, The, 35, 39.

Farrant, 64.

Female characters played by boys, 43; leading, never doubled, 72, 73.

Ferrex and Porrex. See Norton and Sackville, *Gorboduc*.

Field, *Amends for Ladies*, 88, 310; 358.

Fielding, Henry, *Pasquin*, 118, 119; *Tom Jones*, 119, 120.

Figgis, D., *Shakespeare, A Study*, 300 f.

Fights, by sea or land, simulation of noise of, 211–213.

Filmer, A. E., *The Unnatural Brother*, 196; 159.

Finlay, John, 120.

Fireworks, 254 ff.

Five Plays in One, 184.

Fleay, F. G., *Biographical Chronicle of the English Drama*, 136, 180, 181, 182 and n., 183, 184, 284, 289, 335, 347, 366, 390.

Flecknoe, Richard, *A Short Discourse of the English Stage*, 13, 14.

Fletcher, John, and the illusion of sound, 219; 354. And see Beaumont and Fletcher, Shakespeare and Fletcher.

　The Elder Brother, 217, 218.

　The Faithful Shepherdess, 141, 142.

　The Island Princess, 212.

　Monsieur Thomas, 409.

　The Pilgrim, 204, 219.

　Rule a Wife and Have a Wife, 219, 355.

　The Two Noble Kinsman, 96, 212 n., 305, 370 ff., 390, 403.

　Valentinian, 358.

　A Wife for a Month, 188, 314 n.

　The Wild Goose Chase, 282, 391.

Fletcher, John, and Massinger, Philip.

　The Double Marriage, 304 n.

　The Jeweller of Amsterdam, or The Hague, 358.

　The Prophetess, 228, 229, 314, 319.

　The Sea Voyage, 23.

　Thierry and Theodoret, 317, 318.

　The Tragedy of Sir John van Olden Barnevelt, 358, 399.

Fletcher, John, and Shirley, James, *The Night Walker*, 214, 215, 348.

Fog, simulation of. See Mist.

Ford, John, 132. See Rowley.

　The Broken Heart, 240.

The Fancies Chaste and Noble, 127, 128.

Love's Sacrifice, 310.

The Lovers Melancholy, 21.

"Fori," 13.

Forman, Simon, 271, 272.

"Forms," 307.

Fortnightly Review, 131, 138.

Fortune players, 316.

Fortune Theatre, 19, 20, 92, 93, 95, 165, 173, 209, 285, 291, 329.

Four Elements, The, 81.

France, composite plays in, 192, 193, 194 ff.; scenes of blood on the stage in, 237; first real horse seen on stage in, 276.

Fratricide Punished (German version of *Hamlet*), 113 and n.

Frederick and Basilea, 58.

Gafurius, *Theorica Musical*, 216.

Gager, *Dido*, 230.

Galleries in inn-yards, 10, 13, 14, 15.

Gammer Gurton's Needle, 123.

"Garlic jigs," 92, 93.

Garrick, David, 118.

Gascoigne, George and Kinwelmershe F., *Jocasta*, 108, 151, 152, 213, 346.

Gateways, arched, in inn-yards, 10, 11, 12.

"Gathering" (method of collecting charges for admission), 24, 25, 26, 27.

Gaw, Allison, 398.

Gay, John, *The Beggar's Opera*, 82.

George a Greene, 106, 317.

Ghost trap, construction and working of, 169, 170.

Gifford, W., 236.

Gillet, J. E., *Molière en Angleterre*, 194.

Gillette, William, *Held by the Enemy*, 217.

Gismond of Salerne. See *Tancred and Gismunda*.

Globe Theatre, 22, 23, 25, 77, 80, 105, 155, 165, 227, 243, 246, 261, 262, 291, 297.

Gloucester, the New Inn at, 5 and n., 9, 10.

Goad, Christopher, 78.

Godfrey, Walter H., 5, 9, 10.

Godly Queene Hester, 321.

Goffe, Thomas, *The Courageous Turke*, 257.

Goldsmith, Oliver, 175.

Goodal, T., 389.

Gosson, H., 368.

Gosson, Stephen, *Playes Confuted in Five Actions*, 79 n.

Grave traps, 152 ff.

Graves, T. S., *Notes on Elizabethan Theatres*, 18 n.; *The Court and the London Theatres during the Reign of Elizabeth*, 8, 14; 94, 260.

Gray's Inn, 331, 346.

Greene, Robert, 123, 351. And see Lodge and Greene.

Alphonsus, King of Arragon, 35, 37, 38, 104, 167, 324.

Comicall Historie, 324.

Friar Bacon and Friar Bungay, 35, 37, 38, 256, 270.

Orlando Furioso, 163, 392.

Scottish Historie, of James IV, 35, 87.

Greg, W. W., *Pastoral Poetry and and Pastoral Drama*, 141; 61, 74, 182, 184, 237, 257 n., 389, 397, 400.

Greville, C., 390.

"Ground-stands," 14, 15, 26.

Guary miracle play, 379.
Gunnel, R., 329.

H., J., *This World's Folly*, etc., 92, 93.
Hack-writers, 342 ff.
Hail. See Rain.
Hales, Sir J., 354.
Haliwell, Edward, *Dido*, 378, 379.
Halliwell-Phillips, J. O., 272, 275.
Hanging scenes, 241, 242.
Harper, Charles G., *The Holy Head Rood*, 10 n.
Harvey, Gabriel, *Two Other . . . Letters*, 178; *Four Letters*, 179; 351.
Haughton, William, *Englishmen for My Money*, etc., 18 and n., 135; *Grim the Collier of Croydon*, 156, 157.
Haymarket Theatre, 119.
Hazlitt, William, 286, 296, 297.
Hazlitt, W. Carew, 157.
Heads, dummy, used in beheading scenes, 243, 247.
Hell-fire, how the effect was procured, 174, 175.
Heminge, William, *The Fatal Contract*, 115; *The Jewes Tragedy*, 269.
Henderson, John, 120.
Henri II, 201.
Henrietta Maria, Queen of Charles I, 190.
Henry VI, 179.
Henry VII, 44, 230.
Henry VIII, 44, 45.
Henslowe, Philip, his Diary, 88, 91, 183, 215, 242, 252, 283, 284, 348 ff., 361, 388; 165, 244, 343.
Herbert, Sir Henry, Revels Account Books, 180, 183, 384, 386; Office Books, 188, 329, 330, 332, 333; 192, 327, 348.

Herford, and Simpson, *Ben Jonson*, 363 ff.
Herold, Louis J. F., 210.
Heywood, John, *Interlude of the Wether*, 49, 75.
Heywood, Thomas, composite plays by, 184; 136.
  The Ages, 266.
  The Brazen Age, 173, 174, 184, 232, 265 n.
  The Golden Age, 303, 309.
  The Silver Age, 76, 173, 184, 253, 266.
  The Captives, 22, 211, 402 f.
  The Fair Maid of the Exchange "doubling" in, 74, 75, 275.
  The Fair Maid of the West, 78, 302, 305, 406.
  If You Know not Me, You Know Nobody, 228, 232, 269, 291.
  The Iron Age, 129, 130, 302.
  Jupiter & Io, 228.
  Love's Maistresse, 211, 310.
  The Rape of Lucrece, 411.
  A Woman Killed with Kindness, 309.
Hickscorner, 52.
Hieronimo, 303.
Higgins, *Nomenclator*, 13; *Junius Nomenclator*, 383.
"Hirelings," in theatre plays, 57, 58, 64.
Histriomastix, or the Player Whipt, 123, 226, 317, 318.
Hoare, Prince, *The Three and the Deuce*, 298.
Holinshed, R., 230, 249, 258.
Honest Man's Fortune, The, 400.
Hope Theatre, 8, 9, 164, 166.
Horses, illusion of sounds made by, 217, 218, 270 ff.

Horton, E., 408.
How a Man May Choose a Good Wife from a Bad, 41, 42.
Howard, Edward, *The Woman's Conquest*, 101.
Hughes, Thomas, *The Misfortune of Arthur*, 153, 346.
Hunter, Sir Mark, 38 n.
Hunting, scenes in early drama, 219, 220.

Impacient Poverty, 53.
Imperial Tragedy, The, 246.
Indian Queen, The, 269.
"Inferno," an, 123, 124, 255.
Innkeepers and playing places, 25, 26.
Innovation, dramatic, in late 16th century, 133 ff.
Inns-of-Court plays, 28, 29, 30, 344 f.
Inn-yard playhouses, significance of first establishment of, 30, 31; companies that acted in, 34 ff.
Inn-yard plays, confused with public-theatre type, 30; means of distinguishing them, 31 ff.
Inn-yards, salient characteristics of, 19 f.; influence of playing places in, on physical characteristic of first regular theatres, 23 ff.
Interlude of Welth and Helth, The, 47, 48.
Interlude of Youth, The, 52.
Interludes, doubling of parts in, 44 ff.; importance of solution of problem of, 46.
"Irish Beggar, The," 333.
Irving, Sir Henry, and the two portraits in *Hamlet*, 112, 113.
Italian comedians in England, 177, 178.
Italy, type of composite play originated in, 176; fireworks on stage in, 254, 265; complex-disguise play originated in, 278 ff.

Jacob, Sir H., *A Nest of Plays*, the last composite play, 197.
James I, 143, 326, 334, 335.
Jeffes, Humphrey, 74.
Jig, three meanings of, closely interlinked, 79 ff.; the precursor of 18th-century ballad opera, 82; purely a public-theatre feature, 91; attempted suppression of, 93, 94; independent, 95 ff.; under the Commonwealth, 98, 99; under the Restoration, 100, 101.
"Jig of the Slippers, The," 86, 87.
"Jigge of Rowland's Godsonne, The," 84, 85.
Jones, Inigo, 171 and n., 191.
Jonson, Ben, 64, 209, 210, 221, 234, 293, 341, 356, 360 ff., 381.
The Alchemist, 95, 227, 249, 295.
The Barrier, 140, 227.
Bartholemew Fair, 95, 100.
Catiline, 105, 130.
Cynthia's Revels, 162, 166, 381.
The Devil is an Ass, 21, 56, 402.
Discoveries, 95, 349 n.
Eastward Ho, 361, 363 ff.
Every Man in his Humour, 134, 208, 209, 248, 250, 278, 292, 295, 296, 297.
Every Man out of his Humour, 91, 123, 219, 227, 315 ff.
The Fortunate Isles, 190.
The Hue and Cry after Cupid, 294
"Lines to Mr. John Fletcher," 142, 143.
The Masque of Hymen, 227, 259.
The Masque of Oberon, 207, 260.

Neptune's Triumph, 190.
Pleasure Reconciled to Virtue, 268 n.
The Poetaster, 63, 111, 163, 167, 168.
The Sad Shepherd, 229, 352.
Sejanus his Fall, 361, 367, 368.
The Staple of News, 140, 307, 317, 381.
Volpone, 303, 342.
The Widow, 313, 361.
Jonson, Ben, and Chettle, Henry, *Hot Anger Grown Cold*, 361; *The Scots Tragedy*, 361.
Jonson, Ben, and Dekker, Thomas, *The Page of Plymouth*, 261.
Jordan, Thomas, "The Cheaters Cheated," 100; *A Rosary of Rarities*, 100.
Joseph, Professor, 360.
Juby, Dick, 58. And see Rowley and Juby.

Kean, Edmund, 120, 121.
Kemble, John Philip, 120.
Kempe, 86, 89.
"Kempe's New Jigge," etc., 90.
Killigrew, Thomas, *The Princess*, 238; *Thomaso, or the Wanderer*, 238.
Killigrew, Sir W., 246.
King and No King, A, 403.
King Daryus, 56.
King's Company, The, 77.
King's Men, 186, 188, 193, 209, 248, 252, 267, 291, 316.
King's Old Players, The, 45.
Kinwelmershe, F. See Gascoigne.
Kirke, John, *The Seven Champions of Christendome*, 131, 266.
Knack to Know an Honest Man, A, 275.

Knacke to Know A Knave, A, 106, 170.
Knight, 384.
Knight of Malta, The, 312 n., 316 n., 317.
Knoblock, Edward, *My Ladies Dress*, 197, 198.
Kyd, Thomas, *The Spanish Tragedy*, 204, 224, 240, 242, 322, 406.
Kynaston, Sir Francis, *Corona Minervae*, 207.

Lady Alimony, 14, 381, 382.
Lambarde, *Perambulation of Kent*, 13.
Langbaine, 246.
Larum for London, A, 273.
Laud, William, Archibishop of Canterbury, 334.
Laumann, E. M., *La Machinerie au Theatre*, 169.
Lawrence, W. J., *The Elizabethan Playhouse and Other Studies*, 24 and n.; "New Light on the Elizabethan Theatre," 131; "A Plummet for Bottom's Dream," 138; *Bells on the Elizabethan Stage*, 213, 214 and n.
Le Bas des Isles, *L'Air Enjoué*, a composite play, 192, 193.
Lee, Nathaniel. See Dryden and Lee.
Lee, Sir Sidney, 271.
Legge, Thomas, *Richardus Tertius*, 274.
Lent, status of 17th-century players in, 325, 338.
Lenton, F., *The Young Gallants Whirligig*, 333.
Lewis, Monk, *Rugantino, or the Bravo of Venice*, 298.
Lidgate, 179.
Life and Death of Captain Thomas Stukeley, The, 218, 253, 257.

Life and Death of Thomas, Lord Cromwell, 243, 245.

Like Will to Like, 48, 56.

L'Impromptu de Versailles, 194.

Lincoln's Inn Fields Theatre, 297.

Littledale, H., 400.

Lloyd, Robert, "The Actor," 118 and n.

Locrine, 159.

Lodge, Thomas, *The Wounds of Civil War*, 41, 170, 171.

Lodge, Thomas, and Greene, Robert, *A Looking Glasse for London and England*, 160, 161, 266, 314.

London, inn-yards of, 4, 5, 6, 10.

London *Times Literary Supplement*, 187, 295.

Long Meg of Westminster, 88.

Look About You, a complex-disguise play, 18, 134, 157, 158, 275, 283, 284, 285, 294, 313 n., 319.

"Loth to Depart," 85.

Lovelace, poems (*Lucasta*), 315; *The Scholars*, 315.

Lowe, Robert W., 113.

Lupton, Donald, *London and the Country Carbonadoed*, 97; *All for Money*, 149, 150.

Lusty Juventus, 47.

Lyly, John, *Love's Metamorphosis*, 226, 231.

Lyrical farce, short, a "jig," 79 ff.; the genesis of English opera, 81.

Lyttelton, Sir G., 235.

M., T., *The Black Book*, 136.

Machiavellus, 279, 280.

Machin, L. See Markham.

Mahelot, 237 and n.

Maid of Honour, The, 313.

Malone, Edmund, *Variorum Shake-speare*, 11, 125, 179, 326, 327, 328.

Maltby, Alfred, *Bounce*, 298.

Mankind, 24.

Manly, *Specimens of the Pre-Shakespearean Drama*, 48.

Manuscript. See "Fair copy," Marginalia.

Marbeck, Thomas, 58.

Marginalia, 384–387, 392, 393–395, 399, 400 ff., 408, 409.

Maria, Infanta, 190.

Markham, G., and Machin, L., *The Dumb Knight*, 359, 360.

Marlowe, Christopher, as writer of "jigs," 83.

  Dido, Queen of Carthage, 264, 265, 346 f.

  Doctor Faustus, 208, 209, 255, 275, 314, 316; (revised), 247, 248, 249, 250, 265.

  Edward II, "doubling" in, 68–70; 312, 319, 406.

  The Jew of Malta, 147.

  Tamburlaine, "doubling" in, 67, 68; 39, 41, 126, 251, 253, 263, 264, 316.

Marmion, Shackerley, *Holland's Leaguer*, 77.

Marriage of Wit and Wisdom, The, 43, 55, 56.

Marston, John, 64, 361, 363, 365 n.

  Antonio and Mellida, 63, 213, 319, 350.

  Antonio's Revenge, 116, 161, 166, 240, 241, 320.

  The Dutch Courtezan, 63, 141, 203, 297.

  The Fawne, 317, 318.

  The Insatiate Countess, 217, 239, 245, 250.

INDEX

Jack Drum's Entertainment, 91.
The Malcontent, 227.
What You Will, 123, 140.
The Wonder of Women, or Sophonisba, 17 n., 63, 124, 155, 203.
Martinelli, Drusiano, 178.
Masked marriage, the, 56.
Masque of Janus, The, 230.
Masques, of the Stuart times, influence of, 171; first employment of under-machinery in, 171; court, 337; 138.
Massinger, Philip, 132. And see Fletcher and Massinger.
  Believe as You List, 61, 77, 161, 398, 400, 403–405, 408.
  The Bondman, 312 n., 313.
  The City Madam, 97, 305, 410.
  The Great Duke of Florence, 312, 317.
  The Guardian, 218, 306.
  A New Way to Pay Old Debts, 218, 375.
  The Roman Actor, 76, 77, 380.
  The Second Maiden's Tragedy, 22, 37, 211, 261, 394.
  The Unnatural Combat, 307.
  A Very Woman, 297.
  The Virgin Martir, 111, 168, 236, 409, 410.
Massinger, Philip, with Middleton and Rowley, *The Old Law, or A New Way to Please Ye*, 219, 366 f.
Melodrama, and complex disguising, 298.
Melton, John, *Astrologaster, or the Figure Caster*, 209 and n., 210, 255.
Menestrier, 231.
Meres, F., *Palladis Tamia*, 351; 361.
Merry Devil of Edmonton, The, 130, 136, 140, 143, 215, 292.

Meymott, 11.
Michel, Jean, *Le Mistere de la Resurrection de Nostre Seigneur*, 148.
Middleton, Thomas, 348, 363, 366, 368. And see Massinger, Rowley.
  Blurt, Master Constable, etc., 140, 203.
  The Family of Love, 19, 20.
  A Mad World, My Masters, 87, 162, 327.
  The Masque of Heroes, 335.
  No Wit, No Help like a Woman's, 300.
  The Phoenix, 141.
Middleton, Thomas, and Rowley, William, *The Changeling*, 337; *A Fayre Quarrell*, 337; *The World Tost at Tennis*, 335–337, 339.
Mill-hopper, the, 210 and n.
Milton, John, 341.
Mind, Will, and Understanding, 55.
Miracle plays, English, derived from France, 149.
Mist, simulation of, 225 ff.
"Mr. Attowel's Jigge," 89.
Mönkemeyer, 201, 202, 204, 205.
Molière (J. B. Poquelin), *Psyche*, 372.
Montfleury, A. J., *L'Ambigu Comique*, a composite play, 194, 195.
Montfleury, A. J., and Corneille, T., *Le Comédien Poète*, a composite play, 195.
Moon, on the stage, baffling problem of, 259 ff.
Morality play, burden of players in, 52–54; alternation of characters in, 53; differentation of characters in, by dress, 54, 55, 56. And see Interludes.
Morgan, Appleton, 12 n.
Morris, E. C., 366 f.

Moseley, H., 371.

Motteux, Peter A., and Oldmixon, *The Novelty*, a composite play, 196.

Mountebank's Masque, The, 331.

Mountebanks, 330–332.

Mucedorus, 51, 58, 74.

Munday, Anthony, Robin Hood plays, 60; 292.

    The Death of Robert Earl of Huntington, 320.

    The Downfall of Robert Earl of Huntington, 237, 283, 313, 319.

    Fedele and Fortunio, 388.

    John a Kent and John a Cumber, 166, 214, 215, 384, 385, 387, 388, 393.

    The Weakest Goeth to the Wall, 33, 159, 160.

Munday, Anthony, and Chettle, Henry, *Robin Hood*, 351.

Murray, J. Tucker, 181 and n.

Mysteries, early French, stage traps in, 148, 149.

Nabbes, Thomas, *Hannibal and Scipio*, 78; an innovative dramatist, 78; *Microcosmus*, 338, 339; 207.

Nashe, Thomas, *Pierce Penilesse*, 83, 179; *Summer's Last Will and Testament*, 84; *Strange News*, 179; *Have with You at Saffron Walden*, 351.

Natural Phenomena, imitation of, 225. And see Storms, Thunder.

Neuendorff, 320.

Newe Custom, 51.

Nichols, Humphrey, 254.

Nicolini, F., 330, 331.

Nightingale, simulation of song of, 202, 203, 204.

Nineteenth Century, The, 112.

Noble Gentlemen, The, 312 n., 317.

Nobody and Somebody, 323.

"Nocturnal," the, characteristics of, 124 ff.; what it was, 133; first trace of in the private theatre, 140, 141; 292.

Norton, T., and Sackville, T., *Gorboduc*, 151, 345.

Offenbach, Jacques, *Tales of Hoffman*, 196.

Old Fortunatus, 291.

Oldmixon, John. See Motteux.

Oliphant, E. H. C., 138.

Opera, English, the lyric farce or "jig" the genesis of, 71.

Ordish, T. F., *Early London Theatres*, 11.

Orphan's Tragedy, The, 185.

Otway, Thomas, *Alcibiades*, 269.

Overbury, 382.

Oxford's Men, 33, 42.

Pageantry on the stage, public demand for, 251 ff.

Pallant, R., 73.

Parr, William, 58.

Parrott, T. M., 289.

Parsons, Thomas, 58.

Patrick, William, 77.

Paul's Boys, 123, 256.

Paul's Theatre, 63, 166, 168, 213, 297, 326.

Pavier, 185.

Peele, George, 230, 231.

    The Arraignment of Paris, 152, 202, 347.

    The Battle of Alcazar, 41, 58, 61, 236, 237, 257, 274.

    King Edward the First, 104, 105, 167, 251, 313.

The Life and Death of Jack Straw, 35, 37.

The Love of King David and Fair Bethsabe, 35, 36, 37, 242.

The Old Wives Tale, 108, 156.

The Troublesome Raigne of King John, 35, 238, 239.

Wily Beguiled, 269.

Pembroke and Montgomery, Earl of, 334.

Penn, W., 77.

Percy, William, *The Aphrodysiall or Sea Feast*, 168, 212, 213, 231.

Performances, frequency of, 349.

Perfumed mists. See Mists.

Philaster, 21.

Phillips, Augustine, *Pacient Grissel*, 56; 86, 88.

Pickering, *Horestes*, 56, 241.

Picture, The, 313, 317.

Pictures on the stage, 113 ff.

Platonick Lovers, The, 310.

Platter, Thomas, 80.

Plautus, *Mostellaria*, 195.

Play Boys, The, 213.

Play of the Sacrament, The, 48.

Players, compensation of, 24 ff.; number of, in More's time, 43, 44; number of, in 16th-century plays, 50, 51, 56, 57.

"Players of the King's Chapell," 44.

"Players of the King's Interludes," 44.

Plays, Elizabethan, methods of classifying, 28; opulence of characterisation, a distinguishing quality of, 64; construction of considered, 66 ff.; influence of doubling on, 67. And see Staging.

Plays, licensing of, 385 f.

Plots, 58, 375-377, 403.

Plots, double, 353 f.

Plott of the Seven Deadly Sins, The, 397.

Poel, W., *Shakespeare in the Theatre*, 353.

Pollard, T., 77.

Poole, John, *Hamlet Travestie*, 120.

Poor Man's Comfort, The, 317.

Pope, Alexander, *The Dunciad*, 234.

Porter, Henry, *Two Angry Women of Abington, The*, 135, 234; 361.

Preston, Thomas, *Cambyses, King of Persia*, 56, 57.

Prince Charles's Men, 412.

Prince's Men, 209, 291, 335.

Printseller, The, 253 n.

Private-theatre plays, the source of modern musical comedies, 29.

Private theatres, and refreshment rooms, 26; "doubling" at, 62 ff.; first trace of nocturnals in, 140, 141; realism in, 236; complex-disguise plays in, 297.

Privy Council, 326, 328, 334.

Programmes, absence of, 54.

Prompter, duties of, 374, 375, 378-382, 389, 392, 394, 398, 403-405.

Prynne, William, *Histriomastix*, 334.

Public-theatre dramatists, problem of, and its solution, 64 ff.

Public-theatre plays, and inn-yard plays, 30 ff.; 38.

Public theatres, and charges for admission, 25, 26; realism in, 236 ff.; influence of court masque on staging in, 267 ff.

Punch, 205.

Puncteus, J., 330.

Queen's Men, in inn-yards, 34, 35; 78, 180, 182, 258.

Quinault, T., *La Comedie sans Comedie*, a composite play, 192; influence on Restoration drama, 193; 372.

Raigne of King Edward the Third, The, 225, 226.

Rain, simulation of, 229, 230.

Raleigh, Sir Walter, *Shakespeare*, 65; 129.

Randolph, *Amyntas*, 206; *The Jealous Lovers*, 343.

Rapin, René, *Reflections on Aristotle's Poetry*, 235.

Rare Triumphs of Love and Fortune, The, 153.

Ravenscroft, Edward, *Dame Dobson*, 162.

Rawlins, Thomas, *The Rebellion*, 106, 162.

Raymond, George, *Life of Elliston*.

Realism, in minor details, 223 ff.; on the stage, attitude of Elizabethan England toward, 234 ff.

Rear stage, uses of, 301, 304 ff., 321–324.

Rebellion of Naples, The, 247.

Red Bull players, 316.

Red Bull Theatre, 99, 131, 168, 173, 174, 232, 233, 252, 253, 265, 266.

Red Lion Inn, "scaffolds" in yard of, 12.

Retrospective Review, The, 347.

Return from Parnassus, The, 29, 380.

Revels, Master of, 327–329.

"Reversible cloak, the," 56.

Review of English Studies, The, 3.

Revisers, 348, 366 ff.

Reyher, *Les Masques Anglais*, 189, 190.

Reynolds, G. F., 300, 310 f., 315, 321, 323.

Rhodes, F. Crompton, *Studies in the First Folio*, 182, 273, 308.

Rhys, Ernest, 323.

Rich, John, 234.

Richards, Nathaniel, *Messalina*, 268.

Robert II. See Jonson and Chettle, *The Scots Tragedy*.

Rochester, *Valentinian*, 269.

Rollins, Hyder E., 82, 89, 98.

Romance, in terms of realism, 221 ff.

Romance of an Hour, The, 234.

Ropedancers, 329.

Rose Theatre, 18, 60, 135, 165, 166, 183, 244, 280, 283, 292, 326.

Rousseau, J. J., 175.

Rowe, *Shakespeare*, 113, 114, 116.

Rowley, William, 366, 369. And see Massinger.

Rowley, William, with Dekker and Ford, *The Witch of Edmonton*, 162, 275.

Rowley, William, and Juby, Dick, *Samson*, 19, 20.

Rump, The, 267.

Russell, Anne, wedding of, 129.

Sabbattini, 151, 174, 210.

Sackville, Thomas. See Norton.

St. Amand, 235, 237.

"Scaffolds," in inn-yards, 12 ff.; in beheading scenes, 244; 304.

Scala, F., *L'Alvida*, 176, 177.

Scenery, absence of in early days, 102; movable, first seen at Oxford in 1605, 150, 151.

Schelling, Felix, *Elizabethan Drama*, 32, 78, 310.

Scot, Reginald, *Discoveries of Witchcraft*, 223.

Seating, special, in inn-yards, 12 ff.
Second Maiden's Tragedy, The, 261.
Sganarelle ou le Cocu Imaginaire, 194.
Shadwell. See Dryden–Shadwell.
Shakespeare, William, and posterity, 66; changes in the method of producing his plays, 102 ff.; fragment of composite play attributed to, 185, 186; and Jonson, 208; and his audience, 222, 223; the only reliance of the Chamberlain's Men, but a host in himself, 292; did not resort to the complex-disguise play, 293, 294; as collaborator, 357, 367 ff.; and Fletcher, 357, 370 ff.; 134, 175, 213, 248, 315, 341, 363, 397 f.
  All's Well That Ends Well, 396.
  As You Like It, "doubling" in, 72; Jaques's Seven Ages speech in, 293; 65 n.
  A Comedy of Errors, 284.
  Coriolanus, 241, 317.
  Cymbeline, 108, 127, 268, 269, 275, 310, 319.
  Hamlet, "doubling" in, 70 ff.; the Ghost, 104 ff., 116 ff.; the two portraits, 112 ff.; the last of his plays to suffer sophistication, 117, 118; topical allusiveness in, 122 and n.; the grave scene, 153, 154; 169, 200, 206, 251, 261, 325.
  Henry IV, 317, 395.
  Henry V, 211, 213, 270, 271, 291, 319.
  2 Henry VI, 67.
  3 Henry VI, 248, 257, 258, 312 n., 313, 395.
  Henry VIII, 252, 268, 291, 302, 312, 317.
  Julius Caesar, "doubling" in, 72; 17, 80, 127, 129.
  King John, 35, 259, 319.
  King Lear, 66, 72, 208, 262, 301.
  Love's Labour's Lost, 139.
  Macbeth, 96, 139, 160, 162, 163, 217, 271, 294, 317, 368.
  Measure for Measure, 290.
  The Merchant of Venice, 293.
  A Midsummer Night's Dream, a nocturnal, 136–140; 205, 226, 228, 292.
  Pericles, 322, 367, 368.
  Richard III, 127, 294, 313, 317.
  Romeo and Juliet, 127, 155, 239, 240, 260, 284.
  The Taming of the Shrew, 204, 305, 395.
  The Tempest, 96, 211, 224, 233, 368; Dryden–Shadwell revision, 308.
  Timon of Athens, 367, 368.
  Titus Andronicus, 156, 235.
  Troilus and Cressida, 115, 262.
  Twelfth Night, 114.
  Venus and Adonis, 127.
  A Winter's Tale, 62, 65, 66, 96.
Shakespeare Apocrypha, The, 186.
Shakespeare Journal, The, 59.
Shakespeare Society Papers, The, 73.
Shank, J., *Shankes Ordinary*, 333.
"Sharers," in theatre plays, 57; disguise limited to, 60; in *Hamlet*, 72; 77 and n.
Sheridan, Richard B., *The Critic*, 118.
Shirburn Ballads, The, 84, 86, 89.
Shirley, Henry, *The Martyred Soldier*, 256.
Shirley, James. See Fletcher and Shirley.
  The Ball, 97, 386.

The Changes, 97.

The Coronation, 317, 319.

Hyde Park, 97, 207, 275, 276, 380.

The Triumph of Peace, 206, 275.

The Wedding, 78.

Shoreditch Theatre, 11.

Shutters. See Windows.

"Singing Simpkin," 90, 91.

Singspiel, German imitations of jigs, 85.

Sir Thomas More, 43, 241, 243, 244, 385, 387, 391, 393, 398.

Sisson, C. J., 61, 398.

Skelton, John, 60.

Slip, The, 87, 88.

Solyman and Perseda, 304 n., 312.

Somersett, George, 58.

Sounds, never imagined but always heard in Elizabethan drama, 200 ff.

Spanish Gypsy, The, 337.

Spectators on the stage, 223, 225.

Spenser, Edmund, "The Teares of the Muses," 2, 83, 84; did he write the first English composite play? 178; 137.

Squibs. See Fireworks.

Stage, removable or permanent, in inn-yards, 8 ff.; permanent, first appearance of, in England, 150; impermanent, 150; removable, problem of, 164 ff.

Stage archaeology, how far should it be carried? 102 ff.

Stage directions, 304 ff.

Stage keepers, 376, 377.

Staging Elizabethan plays, how to arrive at correct methods of, 103 ff.

Staircases in inn-yards, 10 and n.

Stapylton, Sir R., *The Stepmother*, 193.

"State," the, 312–314, 316, 319 f., 324.

Stationer's books, 335.

Steevens, George, 248.

Stock, C. W., *William Rowley*, 367.

Stockwood, John, 6.

Stoolholders. See Spectators.

Storms, sound of, how simulated, 208 ff.; 229.

Strange's Men, 182, 183, 326.

Street ballsds, known as "jigs," 82.

"Substitution," 61, 62.

Suckling, Sir John, *Brennoralt*, 21, 22, 310; *The Sad One*, 76; *Aglaura*, 317.

Swan Inn, The, 15.

Swan Theatre, 26, 165, 166.

Swanson, H., 391.

Sykes, H. Dugdale, *Sidelights on the Elizabethan Drama*, 187, 188, 284, 351, 367, 407, 413.

Sylvester, William, 12, 26.

Tamar Cam, 58.

Taming of a Shrew, 397.

Tancred and Gismunda, 151, 152, 348.

Taphouses, and the first theatres, 25.

Tarlton, Richard, the creator of the dramatic jig, 82; *The Seven Deadly Sins*, a composite play, 82, 178 ff.; 39, 86, 89.

Tarlton's Jests, 39.

Tarlton's Newes out of Purgatorie, 82.

Taylor, John, *The Carrier's Cosmography*, 6, 7.

Theatre plays, regulation of "doubling" in, 57.

Theatre Royal, The, 193, 276.

Theatres, origin of shape of, 15; regular, influence of inn-yard playing places on physical characteristics of, 23 ff.; in London, public and private, distinction between, 125, 126. And see Private theatres, Public theatres.

Thomas of Woodstock, 402.

Thorndike, Ashley H., *Shakespeare's Theater*, 146 and n., 227 n., 300, 308, 339.

"Throne," the, 310–320, 322.

Thunder, simulation of, 209 ff., 229.

Tieck, Ludwig, 121.

Tolman, Albert H., *Falstaff and Other Shakespearean Topics*, 65 n.

Tooley, Nick, 73.

Tourneur, Cyril, *The Atheist's Trag-edie*, 131, 132, 158, 159, 269; 343; *The Revenger's Tragedy*, 257, 261.

Towne, T., 397.

Tradition, unreliability of, 103.

Tragedy of the Plantation of Virginia, A, 192.

Traps (stage), 8, 9, 145–175.

Trapwork, use of, in ghost scenes, especially in *Hamlet*, 104 ff.; among the oldest of stage sciences, 148.

Triall of Treasure, The, 48, 56.

Tricke to Cheat the Divell, A, 309 n.

True Tragedie of Richard Duke of York, The, etc., 35, 38, 248, 249, 258.

Tu Quoque, 20.

Tuckfield, T., 390.

Tuke, *Adventures of Five Hours*, 260.

Two Maids of More-Clack, 153, 154.

Two Merry Milkmaids, The, 98.

Two Murders in One, 16, 17, 22.

Two Noble Ladies, The, or the Con-verted Conjuror, 174.

Tyrwhitt, 216.

Underwood, actor, 73.

University plays, 28, 29, 30.

Valiant Scot, The, 49.

Valiant Welshman, The, 156, 267, 313.

Varietie, The, 315.

Vecchi, Orazio, *L'Amfiparnaso*, 82.

Vie de Saint Martin, 148.

Vizard, The, 55, 56.

Voltaire, Arouet de, 235, 237.

Wadeson, Anthony, 284.

Wager, W., *The Longer Thou Livest*, etc., 51, 53; *Enough is as Good as a Feast*, 56.

Wallace, C. W., *Evolution of the Eng-lish Drama*, 44, 45; *The Children of the Chapel at Blackfriars*, 252.

Wapfull, George, *Tyde Taryeth for No Man*, 47, 51.

Warning for Faire Women, A, 109, 241, 254.

Webster, John, 132.
    Appius and Virginia, 241, 413.
    The Devil's Law Case, 307, 310.
    The Duchess of Malfi, 96, 173, 176.
    The White Devil, 115, 252, 304 n.

Webster, John, and Dekker, Thomas, *Sir Thomas Wyatt*, 243, 245.

Welsh Ambassador, The, 400, 401.

Welsh characterisation, 134.

Wendell, Barrett, 272.

Whitefriars Theatre, 22, 245.

Whitehall, 234.

Whitelock, Sir Bulstrode, *Memorials*, 206.

Wilkins, George, *The Miseries of In-forst Marriage*, 302.

Wilkins, George, with Rowley and Day, *The Travailes of the Three English Brothers*, 213, 243, 244, 369.

Wilson, Robert, 352. And see Chet-tle and Wilson.

Wilson, Robert, with Drayton and

Dekker, *The Mad Man's Morris*, a complex-disguise play, 285–289.

"Window," significance of in Elizabethan times, 126, 127.

Winds, simulation of sound of, 229.

Wit Restored, 333.

Worcester's Men, 33, 41, 42.

Wotton, Sir Henry, 252.

Yarrington, R., *Two Tragedies in One*, 182, 184, 185.

Yorkshire Tragedy, A., 185, 186.